I0820346

Conflict and Controversy
in the Confederate High Command

Davis, Johnston, Hood
and the Atlanta Campaign of 1864

Dennis B. Conklin II

Savas Beatie
California

First edition, first printing

Library of Congress Cataloging-in-Publication Data

Names: Conklin, Dennis B., II, 1972- author.
Title: Conflict and Controversy in the Confederate High Command: Johnston, Davis, Hood, and the Atlanta Campaign of 1864 / by Dennis. B Conklin II.
Other titles: Johnston, Davis, Hood, and the Atlanta Campaign of 1864
Description: El Dorado Hills, CA : Savas Beatie, [2025] | Includes bibliographical references. | Summary: "The Atlanta Campaign of 1864 was critical in determining the outcome of the American Civil War and helped reelect Abraham Lincoln that November, assuring eventual victory. Conklin's account, which originally appeared as a Ph.D. dissertation, offers a look at the dysfunctional relationships that permeated upper echelon leadership and helped lead to the defeat of the Army of Tennessee and the loss of the important logistical rail city. This is a fascinating fast-paced study on the politics of command, human nature, and the stress of war, and how it all combined to influence the outcome of the Civil War's most important campaign"-- Provided by publisher.
Identifiers: LCCN 2024061105 | ISBN 9781611217339 (hardcover) | ISBN 9781954547667 (ebook)
Subjects: LCSH: Atlanta Campaign, 1864. | Davis, Jefferson, 1808-1889--Military leadership. | Johnston, Joseph E. (Joseph Eggleston), 1807-1891--Military leadership. | Hood, John Bell, 1831-1879--Military leadership. | Confederate States of America. Army of Tennessee. | United States--History--Civil War, 1861-1865--Regimental histories.
Classification: LCC E476.7 .C75 2025 | DDC 973.7/371--dc23/eng/20250226
LC record available at https://lccn.loc.gov/2024061105

SB

Savas Beatie
989 Governor Drive, Suite 101
El Dorado Hills, CA 95762
916-941-6896 / sales@savasbeatie.com / www.savasbeatie.com

All of our titles are available at special discount rates for bulk purchases in the United States. Contact us for information.

Printed and bound in the United Kingdom

To my mother and father

TABLE OF CONTENTS

LIST OF MAPS

Photos have been placed throughout the text for the convenience of the reader.

Acknowledgments

Some years ago, this book began as my dissertation. As is generally the case, the process was long and arduous, and I am forever indebted to faculty and fellow graduate students at the University of Southern Mississippi for helping me navigate through it all. In particular, I would like to thank Dr. Susannah J. Ural for her insightful commentary and her ability to help me look at the project from a broader perspective. Without her guidance the project would have been too myopic to have warranted publication as a monograph. Susannah's door was always open, and she never hesitated to provide guidance and support. Her insistence that I stay focused on the big picture was instrumental in shaping a polished, finished product. Her mentorship has made me a better scholar, and I am forever in her debt.

I would also like to thank the late Dr. William K. Scarborough for his support, advice, and consummate attention to detail. Additionally, Dr. Kyle Zelner and Dr. Phyllis Jestice both had a profound influence on me during my time at USM. They always challenged me to consider different perspectives and were always willing to act as a sounding board. Further, I am indebted to historian Richard McMurry; I consider him to be the Dean of Atlanta campaign studies, and though our conclusions conflict at times, his work has been invaluable to my own.

I am also truly grateful to Ted Savas and his Savas Beatie team for publishing my work. It has been a pleasure to work with all of those involved with seeing the manuscript through to its final form. My editor David Snyder helped to produce a more readable and accessible narrative. Ian Hughes designed an impressive cover, while Derrick Lindow provided indexing, and Sarah Keeney supplied exceptional marketing for the monograph. Finally, Veronica Kane has worked tirelessly and has been indispensable in transforming the manuscript into a polished final product.

Being associated with the Savas Beatie team has been a real joy. Each of them has demonstrated dedication and professionalism, and I could not have chosen a better troupe to work with.

My mother and father, both of whom have passed away, always encouraged me to pursue my dreams. My father introduced me to what has become a life-long fascination with history and the American Civil War in particular, during a family vacation to Gettysburg when I was a young boy. My passion for the subject has only intensified since. My mother instilled a love of reading and saw to it that I had every Civil War title that a boy or a young man could want. I miss you both. Finally, I could not have done it without my wife, Claudia. Not only did you endure my long absences on research trips and while I locked myself away in my office for hours and days on end, but your assistance in editing the manuscript was invaluable. You are my best friend and the love of my life.

Introduction

In 1864, even after three long years of fighting, neither side seemed closer to victory in the American Civil War. Despite the imbalance in manpower and industrial productivity that favored the North, the Confederacy still fielded strong and capable armies in both major theaters of operation: Virginia and northern Georgia. With the presidential election looming in November, Southerners understood that if they could repel Federal advances into Virginia and Georgia, inflicting significant casualties in the process, they might achieve independence if the Democrats prevailed in the Northern presidential campaign. The mid-term elections in 1862 had demonstrated that support for the Union war effort faded when battlefield results favored the Confederates. While Abraham Lincoln's defeat at the ballot box would not guarantee a Southern triumph, the prospects for a negotiated peace and Southern independence remained a distinct possibility in 1864. In Virginia, Robert E. Lee faced Ulysses S. Grant and thwarted his opponent as Grant attempted to seize Lee's communications in a series of flank marches. By the middle of June, the two eastern armies had settled into a siege at Petersburg which lasted until March 25, 1865. In the process, Lee kept Richmond safe and his army inflicted 60,000 casualties on the Union host during the first six weeks of the campaign.[1] Lee's success during the spring and summer meant that Lincoln's best hope for reelection hinged on the capture of Atlanta in the West.

At the beginning of September, William Tecumseh Sherman delivered Atlanta into Federal hands, thereby securing Lincoln's victory in the November elections. Sherman accomplished the task without achieving any significant battlefield

1 Albert Castel, *Decision in the West: The Atlanta Campaign of 1864* (Lawrence, KS, 1992), 26–27; David Herbert Donald, *Lincoln* (New York, 1995), 382–383; William F. Fox, *Regimental Losses in the American Civil War* (1898; repr., Dayton, OH, 1985), 541.

triumphs until the engagements at Peachtree Creek, Bald Hill, and Ezra Church at the end of July. Even those victories proved inconclusive and the Confederates held Atlanta for over a month until Sherman captured Jonesboro, thereby depriving the Confederates of their last supply line. Furthermore, in each of these battles the Federals acted on the defensive, which meant that Sherman never used his superior manpower to affect a decisive victory on the battlefield. As a result, it is reasonable to suggest that something other than a disparity in troop strength and manufacturing played a primary role in determining the outcome in the Western theater in 1864. The present study therefore seeks to identify the principal reasons for Confederate failure in the decisive campaign for Atlanta.

Among the several factors that contributed to defeat, the dysfunctional nature of the Confederate high command in the West stands out as the most significant. In particular, the campaign for Atlanta exposed Jefferson Davis's primary shortcomings as commander-in-chief. Davis had not learned three important lessons prior to the campaign season in 1864.

First, the president failed to appreciate the benefit of a centralized command system, opting instead for a departmental structure that often left authority in the hands of departmental commanders who did not always coordinate their activities.[2] The decentralized Confederate command system hampered the ability of Joseph E. Johnston, in charge of the Army of Tennessee, to secure assistance from outside of his own department, particularly in the form of a cavalry raid against Sherman's communications.

Second, the president's tendency to allow his personal feelings to affect his decisions regarding strategy and his handling of officers proved disastrous to Confederate chances in the West. Davis's friendship with Braxton Bragg resulted in Bragg's appointment as the president's chief military advisor despite his deplorable record in the field. Davis should never have accepted Bragg's advice concerning his former army, considering his many feuds with officers still serving under Johnston. The president's antagonistic attitude toward Georgia governor Joseph E. Brown deprived Johnston of adequate militia during the opening stages of the campaign. Their absence likely resulted in Johnston's withdrawal from a strong defensive position at Dalton. Additionally, Davis's long-standing dispute with Johnston compromised his relationship with the general and made him more inclined to relieve Johnston when his close associate Bragg recommended the action.

Finally, Davis accepted and even solicited correspondence that violated accepted military protocols requiring that communications from subordinate officers be

2 Thomas Connelly and Archer Jones, *The Politics of Command: Factions and Ideas in Confederate Strategy* (Baton Rouge, 1973), 89.

Joseph E. Johnston. *Library of Congress*

Jefferson C. Davis. *Library of Congress*

sent through their commanders. The president's distrust of Johnston led him to appoint John Bell Hood to command one of Johnston's corps with instructions that Hood keep the administration apprised of Johnston's performance. The scheme produced unintended consequences when Hood undermined Johnston to secure command of the army for himself. Ironically, after having succeeded in his quest, Hood suffered the same fate. William Hardee, in command of a corps, allowed his anger at having been passed over for promotion in favor of Hood to influence the energy with which he executed his orders at Peachtree Creek and Bald Hill. Hardee's lethargy cost Hood opportunities to deliver a decisive blow against Sherman's forces.

Thus, Jefferson Davis's poor performance as commander-in-chief led to conflict and controversy among the members of the Confederate high command and played the primary role in Confederate defeat in the campaign for Atlanta. Moreover, the loss of Atlanta might very well have cost the Confederacy the war as it played a significant role in Lincoln's subsequent reelection.

In addition to analyzing the Atlanta campaign through a lens of Davis's failings, the present study provides several key points of departure from earlier interpretations of the campaign. First, it will provide a new assessment of Joseph E. Johnston as a commander. Traditionally Johnston has been characterized as overly cautious and unwilling to risk offensive action unless certain of success. Some scholars have emphasized his perceived caution by relating a story of a hunting expedition in which Johnston participated. His companions fired frequently at the various birds the troop came upon. Johnston, however, complained that the conditions were never favorable; either the birds were too low or too high. As a result, he never discharged his weapon and his reputation as an excellent shot remained intact. The episode, according to Richard McMurry, provides insight into Johnston's naturally cautious disposition. Steven Woodworth labeled Johnston "weak-kneed" and lacking the "inner strength necessary to lead an army." Albert Castel concluded that "prudence far outweighed boldness" in Johnston's "scale of military values."[3] Even Johnston's biographers have accepted the basic premise that Johnston favored defensive warfare.

The prevailing wisdom that Johnston preferred to operate on the defensive is the product of several factors. Johnston continually emphasized the disparity in

3 Richard McMurry, "The Enemy at Richmond: Joseph E. Johnston and the Confederate Government," *Civil War History* 27 (1981): 9. Steven Woodworth also makes note of the episode in his characterization of Johnston as a man whose "chief trait of personality was his fear of failure." See Steven Woodworth, *Jefferson Davis and His Generals: The Failure of Confederate Command in the West* (Lawrence, KS, 1990), 176; Woodworth, *Jefferson Davis and His Generals*, 178, 277; Castel, *Decision in the West*, 562.

strength between Union and Confederate armies in his communications with the Davis Administration, Louis Wigfall, and his wife, among others. He often claimed that offensive operations were hazardous under the circumstances. His postwar memoir articulated the same theme throughout. Further, his record during the war provides evidence of only two successful offensive strikes against the enemy. In the first case, at Manassas, he was never given proper credit for rushing his troops to the scene of the action. Rather, P. G. T. Beauregard and Thomas "Stonewall" Jackson garnered most of the praise for Confederate victory. Johnston's assault on the Federal left at the battle of Resaca, while successful in driving the enemy from its immediate position, did not result in a great victory and the army was forced to retreat the following evening. Further, the army's actual engagements during the campaign after Resaca were entirely on the defensive.

Another reason for the conventional characterization of Johnston as a cautious commander is the natural tendency to compare him with his successor in Virginia. After assuming command of Johnston's former army, Robert E. Lee demonstrated extraordinary acumen for offensive operations, even when he faced an enemy with a significantly larger army than his own. Lee was "audacity personified" and never complained about the number of troops available to him.[4] In their respective mythologies, Lee and Johnston, naturally have come to be seen as polar opposites. Lee, it seems was a tough act to proceed.

As a result, the customary interpretation of Johnston remains widely popular among historians of the Civil War. Nevertheless, throughout his career, and particularly during the Atlanta campaign, Johnston made numerous efforts to engage in both the strategic and tactical offensive. In the spring of 1862, he advocated a concentration of forces and an advance toward Washington rather than taking a defensive position on the Virginia peninsula. The Davis administration ignored his suggestion. In November of the same year, he again petitioned for a concentration of forces against Grant. Again, the president refused to support the plan which ultimately resulted in the fall of Vicksburg. During his campaign against Sherman in 1864, Johnston made several attempts to organize offensive action. He intended to deliver a second attack against the Federal left at Resaca until he discovered that the enemy had crossed the Oostanaula River and threatened his communications. Johnston's plans for an attack at Cassville against the divided Union army was well-planned and offered an excellent chance for success. Hood, however, failed to deliver the expected blow, and thereafter the relationship between Johnston and Hood deteriorated rapidly. On the morning of May 28 Johnston again hoped to

4 Lee's famous biographer, Douglas Southall Freeman, coined the phrase and inspired a book of the same name edited by Peter Carmichael.

John Bell Hood. *Library of Congress*

launch an attack against the Union left flank, but Hood failed once more. Finally, the preponderance of the evidence suggests that Johnston intended to assault the Federals once they crossed Peachtree Creek near Atlanta. Thus, while Joseph E. Johnston never approached Lee's aggressive record, he was not the cautious "weak-kneed" commander that many have claimed.[5]

A second point of emphasis in the present study is the role of Georgia governor Joseph E. Brown in the outcome of the Atlanta campaign. Few scholars have given much attention to the influence on the campaign of the feud between Brown and Davis. Only Mark Elam provides any significant analysis of the matter. He correctly concludes that animosity between the two executives resulted in the absence of a key militia force. Elam's analysis is premised on the notion that Brown should have supplied 40,000 militia troops, a number that Brown's muster rolls indicate was available to him. With such a large militia, Elam argues, Johnston could have extended his defensive lines in a manner that would have prevented Sherman's numerous flanking marches.[6] It was highly improbable, however, that Brown could have ever supplied all 40,000 militia that state muster rolls claimed were available. Even if he had, over half of the identified individuals were over the age of forty-five. Nevertheless, Brown certainly should have been capable of producing more than he did, and the Georgia militia's total absence from the front when the campaign began dramatically affected Johnston's ability to hold his positions at Dalton, Resaca, and Kennesaw Mountain.

This study also provides a complete reinterpretation of the affair at Cassville on May 19, 1864. At present, historical analysis of the day's events is unsettled though most rely on the diary of Lt. Thomas Mackall, the cousin of Johnston's aide-de-camp Gen. William Mackall. Scholars of the campaign have accepted Richard McMurry's assertion that the version of Mackall's diary that appears in *The War of Rebellion: A Compilation of the Official Records of the Union and Confederate Armies*, was a postwar production intended to promote Johnston's image after the close of hostilities.[7] Historians have generally rejected Mackall's claim that no Federal force ever appeared on the Canton Road. Scholars have therefore attempted to identify the strength and composition of the alleged Union column. The present

5 *The War of the Rebellion: A Compilation of the Official Records of the Union and Confederate Armies*, 128 vols. (Washington, D.C., 1880–1901), ser. 1 vol. 11, pt. 3, 477; hereinafter cited as *O.R.* All references are to Series 1 unless otherwise indicated; Woodworth, *Jefferson Davis and His Generals*, 178, 180–181; McMurry, "The Enemy at Richmond," 9.

6 Mark Elam, "The Road to Atlanta: The Role of Geography in Command and Decision Making During the Atlanta Campaign" Ph.D. dissertation, Florida State University, 1996, 232–258 and *passim*.

7 Richard McMurry, "The Mackall Journal and its Antecedents," *Civil War History* 20 (1974): 326–328.

study seeks to prove that Mackall was correct in his assessment and that there was no Federal presence on the road to Canton on May 19. Federal cavalry did appear on Hood's right flank along the Spring Place Road, but not in sufficient force to warrant Hood's withdrawal. The confusion between Hood and Johnston was the result of insufficient and disparate maps in possession of the Confederate high command. Confederate maps of the road system north of Cassville failed to identify the Spring Place Road and it was left unguarded by Wheeler's cavalry. The misunderstanding escalated thereafter and damaged the previously close relationship between the two men. From that afternoon forward, Hood began a campaign to secure command of the army for himself.

Analysis of Hood's role in the abandonment of the defensive position on the heights just south of Cassville offers another key point of departure from previous studies. Historians have generally accepted Hood's claim that the position, particularly on Polk's front, was exposed to enfilade fire from enemy batteries and was therefore untenable.[8] There can be no doubt that the sector in question sustained a punishing barrage from Federal artillery posted near the Female Seminary north of the town. Several Confederate officers including Hood, Polk, and Francis Shoup (Johnston's chief of artillery) met with Johnston on the evening of May 20 and insisted that the army withdraw from its position. Hood advocated strongly for the proposition. Johnston, however, believed that the troops stationed at that point in the line could have been protected either by digging traverses, or having them removed to the rear slope of the ridge until such time as the enemy advanced his infantry.

Most historians of the campaign have rejected Johnston's argument without considering sources other than those produced by Confederate officers present at the meeting. Nor have they reasonably considered the report of Samuel French, whose division occupied the point in question. He later claimed to have sustained only five wounded in the barrage. Further, Federal commentary on the position suggests that Johnston's assessment was correct. One such source is the diary of Orlando Poe, Sherman's chief engineer. Poe was so impressed by the works around Cassville that he made a sketch of the lines, something he did not do for any of the other Confederate defensive works throughout the campaign. Additionally, his journal entry notes that the works were too strong to risk a direct point attack, though he did suggest that they could have been turned with a flanking march. Oliver Howard also commented on the strength of the position in a postwar article

8 See, for example, Castel, *Decision in the West*, 204; Richard McMurry, *John Bell Hood and the War for Southern Independence* (Lincoln, NE, 1982), 108–109.

entitled "The Struggle for Atlanta."[9] Keeping Poe's and Howard's conclusions in mind, and considering that French sustained few casualties, Johnston's calculation that the lines could easily have been held seems reasonable. Nevertheless, Hood demanded that the army either abandon the works or launch an assault, something he knew Johnston would not do after the Federal forces were united again.

Hood's recommendation appears even more suspicious in the light of his orders to his aide, Col. Henry Brewster, on May 21. Hood sent Brewster to Richmond, with a letter that provided an account of the campaign thus far. If the content of Hood's message was similar to what Brewster told a social gathering soon thereafter, Hood was actively undermining his commander. Brewster claimed that Johnston had refused to take the offensive despite Hood's repeated appeals to do so—an odd statement considering Hood's actions at Cassville.[10] Consequently, when considered in their totality, Hood's behavior around Cassville suggests at the very least a deep-seated distrust of Johnston's ability to command, and perhaps his opening gambit to become the commander of the army.

The characterization of Hood's tenure as commander of the Army of Tennessee in and around Atlanta provides a final point of departure from much of the present historiography. Most scholars, as Brian Craig Miller has argued in *John Bell Hood and the Fight for Civil War Memory*, allow Hood's failures during his campaign into Tennessee to color their analysis of his generalship as a whole. As a consequence, Hood is generally portrayed as having exceeded his competence level as an army commander and that his planning and/or execution in the battles at Peachtree Creek, Bald Hill, and Ezra Church demonstrated that his appointment to the position was ill-conceived. Albert Castel has suggested, for example, that Hood lacked a sense of "realism" and tried to "do too much with too little." Stanley Horn criticized Hood for attempting to blame his defeats in the engagements around Atlanta on his subordinates and his soldiers' unwillingness to assault defensive works, and asserts that the general was "bewildered" during the final week of August.[11] The current study argues that Hood's plans were not only well designed, but that the failure to execute them falls primarily upon his lieutenants, most notably William Hardee. Hardee was angry at having been passed over by Jefferson

9 *O.R.* vol. 38, pt. 3, 899; Orlando Poe Diary, May 21, 1864, O. M. Poe Papers, Library of Congress; Oliver O. Howard, "The Struggle for Atlanta." *Battles and Leaders of the Civil War* (New York, 1956), IV:305.

10 *Mary Chesnut's Civil War*, ed. C. Vann Woodward (New Haven, CT, 1981), 616.

11 Brian Craig Miller, *John Bell Hood and the Fight for Civil War Memory* (Knoxville, TN, 2010), xviii–xix; Castel, *Decision in the West*, 562; Stanley F. Horn, *The Army of Tennessee: A Military History* (New York, 1941), 361, 367.

Davis for command of the army once he relieved Johnston. Hardee's refusal to follow Hood's clear orders was not something that Hood himself could control.

Even efforts to reassess Hood's tenure as commander of the Army of Tennessee in a more favorable light generally overlook the importance of Hardee's sluggishness and instead attribute Confederate defeat in the engagements around Atlanta to some shortcoming on Hood's part. Richard McMurry, for example, asserted that, while Hood had developed a good plan for the battle of Peachtree Creek, he should have been more involved in the supervision of the army's deployment. McMurry criticized Hood's decision to allow Benjamin Cheatham, new to corps command, so much independence. Cheatham, however, was not tasked with assailing the Union position as was another newly appointed corps commander, A. P. Stewart. Hood therefore wisely chose to observe the battle from Stewart's headquarters, rather than overseeing Cheatham's march to the Confederate right. Further, both Stephen Davis and Richard McMurry condemned Hood's decision to order the inexperienced S. D. Lee with two-thirds of the army to take possession of the crossroads at Ezra Church.[12] In reality, Hood had no other options and never intended that Lee engage in offensive operations. Clearly, Hood's performance as commander in the battles around Atlanta requires further investigation.

Lincoln and Davis: A Contrast in Leadership

The chief task of the present study is to identify the principal reason for Confederate defeat in the Atlanta Campaign. The answer is Jefferson Davis's failure to learn key lessons during the first three years of the war. In each case, the failure contrasted sharply with his counterpart, Abraham Lincoln. Davis never understood the advantages of centralizing command under one general-in-chief, relying instead upon a decentralized departmental structure. The design impeded Johnston's access to reinforcements from neighboring departments. Davis also allowed his personal friendship with or animus against other members of the Confederate high command to influence his policy-making decisions. Finally, Davis permitted and even promoted rancor and self-aggrandizement among members of the army's officer corps when he authorized direct communications between corps commanders and members of his administration. These three failings contributed to the increasingly dysfunctional nature of the Confederate high command in the West and all but guaranteed the fall of Atlanta and the final defeat of the Confederacy.

12 McMurry, *John Bell Hood and the War for Southern Independence*, 129, 134; Stephen Davis, *Atlanta Will Fall: Sherman, Joe Johnston, and the Yankee Heavy Battalions* (Wilmington, DE, 2001), 153.

Davis's shortcomings stood in stark contrast to Abraham Lincoln. Unlike Davis, Lincoln learned a series of valuable lessons during the first three years of the war. From the very beginning, Lincoln understood the need for a centralized command under one general-in-chief. Winfield Scott served in that capacity at the outset of hostilities, but his advanced age limited his usefulness. After appointing George B. McClellan to command the Army of the Potomac in late July 1861, Lincoln requested that McClellan present him with a grand strategy for all Union forces in the field. In doing so, the president was presumably hoping to find a replacement for the elderly Scott. McClellan's design proved to be haphazard and far too centered on eastern operations, thereby neglecting other theaters. Consequently, Lincoln determined to retain Scott as general-in-chief for the time being. By October, however, McClellan had convinced a congressional delegation that Scott's near "senility" made the performance of his job more difficult, and the congressmen demanded that Lincoln replace Scott with McClellan. Lincoln capitulated and appointed McClellan general-in-chief in addition to his duties as commander of the Army of the Potomac.[13] In doing so, Lincoln illustrated that political pressure could influence his decisions on military matters during the early stages of the war, a fault that he had overcome by the opening of the Atlanta campaign.

McClellan soon proved inept in his expanded role. He suggested that the president divide the Western theater into two separate departments and recommended that Henry Halleck command one and Don Carlos Buell the other. Though there was nothing inherently wrong with the proposal, once it was established, McClellan left Halleck and Buell to their own devices. In December McClellan fell ill and Lincoln took over responsibilities as general-in-chief. He wired both of his western commanders and discovered that they were not acting in concert and, in fact, were not even in communication with one another. Lincoln did not immediately strip McClellan of his expanded role, but McClellan's continued inability to oversee operations in both the Eastern and Western theaters, as well as reports of mismanagement of the Army of the Potomac, led the president to relieve him of his title of general-in-chief in March of 1862.[14]

From March until July Lincoln re-assumed the mantle of general-in-chief himself while he searched for a suitable replacement for McClellan. Eventually the president identified Henry Halleck for the position, believing that he had

13 T. Harry Williams, *Lincoln and His Generals* (New York, 1952), 3–4, 29–31; Donald, *Lincoln*, 318–319.

14 Williams, *Lincoln and His Generals*, 47, 53; *The Collected Works of Abraham Lincoln*, ed. Roy P. Basler, 8 vols. (New Brunswick, NJ, 1953), V:155.

demonstrated aptitude for strategic planning with the seizure of Fort Henry and Fort Donelson earlier in the year. Historian T. Harry Williams asserted that Halleck's tenure as general-in-chief demonstrated Lincoln's relentless effort to unify the command of his armies, but that it failed because Halleck avoided responsibility and instead burdened Lincoln with the difficult decisions.

When McClellan refused to advance throughout September and October of 1862, for example, Halleck exercised little control, yielding authority instead to Lincoln, who continually prodded McClellan to take the offensive. When Lincoln finally became exasperated with McClellan's inactivity and informed Halleck that he had the authority to remove McClellan as he pleased, Halleck refused to take responsibility for relieving the popular general. After Lincoln finally removed McClellan and replaced him with Ambrose Burnside, Halleck continued his hands-off approach and declined to comment on Burnside's operations near Fredericksburg. Further, Halleck had failed to provide Burnside with pontoon bridges in a timely fashion, a blunder that played a significant role in the decisive Confederate victory that followed. Lincoln chafed at Halleck's performance and informed him that "if in such a difficulty as this you do not help, you fail me in precisely the point for which I sought your assistance." As T. Harry Williams observed, the Union "was groping toward a modern command system" and the "trial of Halleck prepared the way for Grant."[15]

Despite his failings, Halleck had played a conspicuous role in promoting a unified command in the Western theater under Grant's direction in December 1862. In October, Lincoln had authorized John McClernand, a prominent Illinois Democrat, to recruit a force in the Midwest for the purpose of advancing on Vicksburg. The president failed to inform Halleck of the plan, thereby demonstrating that Lincoln lacked confidence that Halleck was suited for the office of general-in-chief. Lincoln's decision to keep Halleck in the dark concerning his plans for operations against Vicksburg illustrates that in late 1862 the president had not fully grasped the concept of unified command. Lincoln's secretive behavior increased the probability that he and Halleck might work at cross-purposes, a prospect that the office of general-in-chief was designed to prevent.

While McClernand raised his army, Grant proposed a plan for the reduction of Vicksburg which Halleck accepted. Halleck also discovered McClernand's designs, and preferring a West Point graduate to a political general, he advised Lincoln to combine all the forces in the region under Grant's leadership. Lincoln had already

15 Williams, *Lincoln and His Generals*, 313–314; Donald, *Lincoln*, 369–370, 409–410; Geoffrey Perret, *Lincoln's War: The Untold Story of America's Greatest President as Commander in Chief* (New York, 2004), 326.

developed a great deal of respect for Grant and accepted Halleck's proposal. Grant's capture of Vicksburg prompted Lincoln to increase Grant's authority even further. Lincoln established a new Division of Mississippi in October 1863 that combined the Departments of Ohio, Tennessee, and the Cumberland under Grant's unified leadership. Further, Lincoln permitted Grant a great deal of latitude with his new command, which Grant exercised almost immediately. He relieved William Rosecrans from command of the Army of the Cumberland and replaced him with George Thomas, the rock of Chickamauga.[16]

Early in 1864 Congress passed a bill reestablishing the rank of lieutenant general in the Army; Lincoln immediately nominated Grant and requested that he travel to Washington. Grant's promotion made him the highest-ranking officer in the Union army, thereby displacing Henry Halleck who could not serve as general-in-chief when another officer outranked him. Grant, wishing to take advantage of Halleck's organizational skills, requested that the War Department establish a new office of chief of staff and appoint Halleck to the position. The president demonstrated his immense trust in his newly appointed general-in-chief when he acquiesced to Grant's proposal despite Halleck's uneven performance in his former post. Once appointed to his new position, Halleck acted as a conduit between Grant and Lincoln. Halleck also facilitated communication between Grant and his subordinates in the West after he took up residence with the Army of the Potomac in Virginia.[17] Consequently, by the beginning of 1864, Lincoln had finally created a modern command system in the hands of a capable general-in-chief. Grant could direct the whole Union war effort and ensure that each theater of operations was engaged in the pursuit of his strategic vision.

In addition to Lincoln's effort to establish a unified command, the president also developed an aptitude for handling his generals during the war. At the outset of hostilities Lincoln often made appointments to military offices based upon political concerns rather than merit, a practice he later abandoned. In 1861 Lincoln used military patronage to generate political harmony in support of the war effort. He awarded commissions to both Republicans and Democrats. To keep the enthusiasm of Democrats high, Lincoln commissioned as generals several popular Democratic politicians including Benjamin Butler and John McClernand.[18]

He also appointed prominent anti-slavery Republicans, including John C. Fremont. Lincoln gave Fremont a great deal of latitude when he ordered him to

16 Williams, *Lincoln and His Generals*, 136, 191–193, 218–219, 284–285; Donald, *Lincoln*, 458.

17 Perret, *Lincoln's War*, 356, 359; Williams, *Lincoln and His Generals*, 301–302.

18 Ibid., 313–314.

go to St. Louis and organize an army on his own for the purpose of advancing on Memphis. Fremont's subsequent performance, however, demonstrated his ineptitude and Lincoln removed him from command. Nevertheless, political interests inspired the president to appoint Fremont to a second command in 1862. He failed again and was defeated by Stonewall Jackson at the battle of Cross Keys.[19]

The following year Fremont's supporters urged Lincoln to find another appointment for him. By that time, however, Lincoln had learned his lesson and was no longer willing to grant politicians commissions for military service unless they had already demonstrated ability on the battlefield. He had recently given opportunities to two other political generals, Nathaniel Banks and John McClernand, neither of which had borne fruit. Lincoln had hoped that they could open the Mississippi River, Banks advancing from the south and McClernand from the north. Yet Banks had accomplished nothing and McClernand had spent much of his time attempting to undermine Grant. Eventually Lincoln sent Charles Dana to investigate McClernand's activities and, upon receiving Dana's report, authorized Grant to remove him from command. Grant wasted little time and relieved McClernand promptly. In April 1864, after Richard Taylor defeated Banks in the Red River campaign, Lincoln accepted Grant's petition to replace Banks with Edward Canby. That Lincoln did so in an election year suggests that by that time Lincoln was willing to lose political support if it improved the North's chances to win the war.[20]

Lincoln also demonstrated a willingness to relieve generals he liked personally if their performance did not meet his standards. The president appointed John Pope to command the newly organized Army of Virginia in July 1862, and Pope and the president quickly developed a close relationship. In fact, while McClellan struggled on the Virginia peninsula, Lincoln made Pope his chief military advisor and sought guidance concerning the meaning of McClellan's communications to the administration. Lincoln found Pope such an agreeable companion that he was reluctant to let him quit the capital. However, after Lee defeated Pope at the battle of Second Manassas in August 1862, the president found it necessary to remove him from command. Lee's triumphant army that had driven McClellan from the peninsula and subsequently thrashed Pope now threatened the nation's capital. Lincoln believed that McClellan would be a better choice than Pope for the responsibility of organizing Union forces in the defense of Washington. The president reasoned that while McClellan had exhibited no capacity for offensive

19 Doris Kearns Goodwin, *Team of Rivals: The Political Genius of Abraham Lincoln* (New York, 2005), 394–395; Williams, *Lincoln and His Generals*, 77, 101.

20 Williams, *Lincoln and His Generals*, 217–218, 226, 230–231, 309–310.

warfare, his skills on the defensive and his superb organizational ability made him the right man for the present circumstances.[21] In doing so, Lincoln proved he was willing to replace a friend with someone he felt more suited to the task at hand.

In June 1863, Lincoln again relieved a general from command of the Army of the Potomac whom he personally liked. Joseph Hooker had sustained a humiliating defeat in May when Lee's army, approximately half the size of his own, trounced him at the battle of Chancellorsville. When the president learned that many of Hooker's senior subordinates no longer trusted him and that Hooker had no credible plans to oppose Lee's advance into Pennsylvania, the president replaced him with George Meade.[22] By early 1864 performance trumped political gain and personal friendship in Lincoln's decisions regarding the appointment and retention of generals in the Federal army.

The handling of generals who corresponded with the chief executive or members of their administration outside of the officially sanctioned chain of communication provided a final stark contrast between Abraham Lincoln and Jefferson Davis at the outset of the Atlanta campaign. According to established military protocol, subordinate officers were required to send all communications through their commander. Nevertheless, both Confederate and Union officers often ignored the code and directly communicated with their respective administrations. Lincoln found the practice objectionable and attempted to discourage it, believing that it caused unnecessary friction and led to the establishment of competing factions within the army's officer corps.

In the final days of 1862, in the aftermath of Ambrose Burnside's failed assault on Fredericksburg, Lincoln was confronted with discord within the Army of the Potomac's officer corps. William Franklin, a corps commander, and William Smith, in charge of a division, violated protocol and wrote the president that Burnside was failing in his capacity as commander of the army. Lincoln informed them that he would submit their ideas to his advisers, but he was not comfortable with their abandonment of proper channels. Soon thereafter, John Newton and John Cochrane, both of whom were Burnside's subordinates, arrived in Washington on leave and sought an interview with the president. They complained about Burnside's abilities and insisted that the army had no confidence in him. Lincoln was shocked and rebuked them for attempting to undermine their superior. Burnside's infamous Mud March in January 1863 only served to increase criticism of the commander among his officers. The discontent became so palpable that Lincoln was forced to

21 Donald, *Lincoln*, 361; Goodwin, *Team of Rivals*, 479.

22 Donald, *Lincoln*, 438, 440, 445.

replace Burnside and named Joseph Hooker as his replacement. Lincoln illustrated his exasperation concerning the army's high command when he handed Hooker a letter condemning his involvement in the matter. He reprimanded Hooker for his intrigues against Burnside, which had done "a great wrong to a brother officer." The president continued, "I much fear the spirit you have aided to infuse into the army, of criticizing their commander and withholding confidence from him, will now turn upon you."[23]

Lincoln's warning was prophetic, and in the weeks after Hooker's defeat at Chancellorsville, he too suffered from infighting and his subordinates' propensity to communicate improperly with the administration. Several officers either wrote or visited Lincoln and denounced Hooker's leadership. Many demanded his removal from command of the Army of the Potomac. Lincoln was not pleased with the situation as he did not want a repetition of Burnside's tenure. Nevertheless, the call for Hooker's removal continued to grow. Additionally, Hooker was unable to provide the president with a satisfactory response as to how he intended to confront Lee's advance into Pennsylvania. With the Army's officers complaining about their commander's incompetence and Hooker's inability to supply the president with a responsible plan of action against Lee, Lincoln replaced his friend with George Meade on June 28, 1863.[24]

Internal strife among Union officers was not limited to the Eastern theater of operations but occurred in the West as well. John McClernand blamed Henry Halleck for interfering with his organization of an advance against Vicksburg in December 1862. Halleck had convinced Lincoln to put Grant in charge of the expedition. Once McClernand discovered Halleck's role in the decision to award Grant overall command, McClernand wrote a letter to Lincoln demanding Halleck's removal as general-in-chief. Lincoln responded in January, having just dealt with infighting among the Army of the Potomac's officer corps that culminated in Burnside's replacement with Hooker. The president warned McClernand that he was not pleased with the internal divisions within the army's high command. He noted "I have too many family controversies, so to speak, already on my hands to voluntarily, or so long as I can avoid it, take up another."[25]

McClernand, however, ignored Lincoln's advice and continued to agitate against those he considered rivals. On March 15, 1863, he informed the president that Grant was a drunk and therefore unfit for his post. Halleck, possibly under

23 Ibid., 409; Williams, *Lincoln and His Generals*, 202,212–213; Donald, *Lincoln*, 411.

24 Williams, *Lincoln and His Generals*, 247, 251–259.

25 Ibid., 220–223; *The Collected Works of Abraham Lincoln*, ed. Roy P. Basler, VI:70.

Lincoln's direction, sent Charles Dana to investigate the charges. Dana, a former reporter, traveled under the cover of having been assigned by the War Department to investigate the paymaster service in the Western theater. Lincoln also sent his Adjutant General Lorenzo Thomas, who had the authority to relieve Grant if he found evidence substantiating the rumors of the general's alleged intemperance. Neither Dana nor Thomas found any support for McClernand's allegations. In fact, Dana criticized McClernand in a series of dispatches to the administration. As a result of these investigations, Secretary of War Edwin Stanton informed Grant that he had the authority to remove any officer that he wanted and that the government would support him in his decisions. Though Stanton did not name McClernand specifically, there was little doubt as to whom he was referring. Grant immediately relieved the politically powerful McClernand from his command.[26] Clearly, by the beginning of 1863, Lincoln had developed a distaste for the subversion of proper military protocol.

McClernand's removal also demonstrated that Lincoln was not above employing informants in an endeavor to discover his generals' competence for command. Lincoln wisely chose individuals to perform the service who had no personal interest in the content of their reports. Neither Dana nor Thomas stood to gain anything from Grant's removal. Dana was a civilian and Thomas never held field command during the war. They were impartial judges, unlike Jefferson Davis's primary informant during the Atlanta campaign, John Bell Hood.

While Lincoln learned important lessons concerning the advantage of a centralized command, the promotion of officers based on meritorious conduct, and the need to limit inappropriate communications, his counterpart did not. To begin with, Jefferson Davis never appreciated the benefits of a centralized command system. Instead, he favored a more localized system that emphasized autonomy for departmental commanders. Indeed, Davis usually allowed departmental commanders the final decision whether to send reinforcements from their army to another location.[27] Thomas Connelly and Archer Jones assert that several factors attracted Davis to a departmental system of command. First, the size of the Confederacy made it difficult to manage, particularly because of the inadequate railroads in the South. Each of the departments had its own Bureau of Supply that relieved the need for long-range shipment, and theoretically each bureau had a better understanding of local transportation systems than a central coordinator would have. The advantages of localized supply, however, did not mean

26 Williams, *Lincoln and His Generals*, 226–231.

27 Connelly and Jones, *The Politics of Command*, 89.

that a single individual could not oversee the strategic goals for each department. Davis, for the most part, seems to have ignored that possibility in deference to state and local politicians. Davis likely favored the departmental system as a way of pacifying local government officials who insisted that their own regional interests overshadowed the needs of others.

To his credit, Davis did realize that the multitude of departments established at the beginning of the war made reinforcement of threatened areas more difficult. In October 1861 he abolished the Department of Fredericksburg, the Department of Alexandria, and the Shenandoah Valley District and created the Department of Northern Virginia. Even so, the new department's commander, Joseph E. Johnston, could not order supplies or reinforcements from other sectors of Virginia, let alone other states. Then, after the battle of Shiloh in April 1862, Davis again abolished two departments and designed a new Second Department that incorporated most of Tennessee, Alabama, Mississippi, northwestern Georgia, and parts of Florida and Louisiana. The slow trend toward centralization received a boost in November when Davis appointed Johnston to departmental command over the armies of Braxton Bragg and John C. Pemberton. Indeed, by late 1862, Davis had established four primary departments—the Department of the Trans-Mississippi, the Department of the West, the Department of South Carolina, Georgia, and Florida, and finally the Department of Virginia and North Carolina.[28]

Grant's capture of Vicksburg in July 1863, however, reversed the president's course. Davis was so disillusioned with Johnston's performance that he returned to a policy of greater decentralization. Thereafter, whenever the Confederacy lost additional territory, Davis altered departmental commands by division rather than consolidation. Presumably, he believed that the local authorities could best handle Union advances into their region. In truth, the policy made any hope of Confederate victory much more difficult. For example, in late August 1863 Davis reorganized Braxton Bragg's department into the Department of Tennessee, which included Tennessee, small sections of Alabama and Mississippi, and eastern Louisiana. Even though Bragg was tasked with the defense of Georgia, the president assigned the state to P. G. T. Beauregard who commanded the Coastal Department (South Carolina, Georgia, and Florida). The reorganization seems particularly peculiar considering that Bragg's army was then encamped at Dalton in northern Georgia. As a result, Bragg's recruiting agents and commissary officers were greatly restricted in the performance of their duty. They could only operate in the vicinity around Dalton, slivers of Alabama and Mississippi, and eastern Louisiana. Federal control of most of Tennessee made it impossible to obtain forage or recruits from that state

28 Ibid., 90–91, 100, 124; Woodworth, *Jefferson Davis and His Generals*, 180–181.

and Beauregard retained authority over most of Georgia. By the time Johnston assumed command of the Army of Tennessee his department included northern Georgia but ended at Atlanta.[29] Thus, in the beginning of 1864 the Western theater was once again decentralized, and if Johnston hoped for reinforcements or cooperation from other commands he had to apply to Richmond and to his neighboring departments.

Perhaps the closest Davis came to creating any semblance of a unified command prior to the closing months of the war was in the appointment of military advisers—first, Robert E. Lee and, later, Braxton Bragg. Lee had authority to advise the president on general strategy, but he focused almost exclusively on the Eastern theater. Even after Lee's appointment to command the Army of Northern Virginia in June 1862, Davis relied heavily upon Lee for advice on matters concerning other departments. The advice Lee offered was generally eastern-centric and often designed to help his own army carry out his strategic goal. For example, in September 1862 Lee suggested that Bragg move the Army of Tennessee east to protect Richmond against a Federal concentration in Virginia. He repeated the request in December. In both instances, Union armies outnumbering Bragg by approximately 3 to 1 threatened Chattanooga. Clearly, Lee had little appreciation for the situation in the Western theater and apparently believed that the Federals were only capable of maintaining two fronts—northern Virginia and control of the Mississippi River. In fact, during the spring of 1864 Lee insisted that "the great effort of the enemy in this campaign will be made in Virginia." He believed that the Northerners intended to send portions of Sherman's army to Virginia, which would allow Johnston to advance into Tennessee. Contrary to Lee's assessment of the situation in the spring of 1864, Sherman counted almost 100,000 troops available for "offensive purposes." Johnston, meanwhile, confronted the Federals at Chattanooga with only 43,887 effective infantry, artillery, and cavalry.[30] Clearly, Lee proved ineffective as the president's advisor after he assumed command of the army in Virginia, particularly with respect to affairs in the Western theater. Though he remained influential in shaping Davis's policies, Lee's position was not comparable to the office that Ulysses Grant held in the Union army prior to the campaign season of 1864.

Davis appointed Bragg to the post of chief military advisor to the president on February 24, 1864. Bragg most certainly did not hold an office that bore any resemblance to a general-in-chief. Instead, for the most part, Bragg took on

29 Connelly and Jones, *The Politics of Command*, 153; Francis Shoup, "Dalton Campaign—Works at Chattahoochee River—Interesting History," *Confederate Veteran* III (1895): 265.

30 Connelly and Jones, *The Politics of Command*, 35, 38-39; *O.R.* vol. 32, pt. 3, 550–572, 676.

bureaucratic responsibilities and acted more as the president's chief of staff. He spent a great deal of time engaging in inspections which included field armies and their supply systems as well as the prisoner-of-war program and the conscription bureau. He did assume a strategic role in the coordination of troops in southern Virginia and the uppermost region of North Carolina, but he never attempted to influence events in northern Virginia, which remained strictly the province of Robert E. Lee.[31]

Moreover, Bragg's previous association with the Army of Tennessee did not help him to advise Davis on matters concerning that theater of operations. He believed that the army's poor record during his tenure as commander was the product of his subordinates' mistakes and ambitions rather than a result of his own failure. Bragg apparently considered the army more capable than it actually was. Almost immediately upon assuming his new post, Bragg began insisting that Johnston take the offensive. He ignored the fact that the army's humiliating defeat at Missionary Ridge in November 1863 had left it demoralized and severely weakened. Bragg's advice that Johnston advance also was contrary to his own policy after his victory at Chickamauga in September 1863. Rather than pursuing the course he now suggested that Johnston take, Bragg had remained atop Missionary Ridge, to starve the occupants of Chattanooga.[32]

In contrast to what Lincoln had achieved with the centralization of authority under Grant, Davis had decentralized his command structure in the West. Furthermore, Davis's appointment of Bragg to the role of military advisor, considering his ongoing feud with several of the officers serving in the Army of Tennessee, made him a poor choice for the position. Indeed, because the position had been vacant since June of 1862, when Lee had assumed command in Virginia, there was no reason to appoint Bragg in the first place. Davis's close personal friendship offers the only plausible explanation for Bragg's new assignment. If so, Davis's decision to make Bragg his military advisor offers insight into another key difference between himself and Lincoln.

In particular, the Confederate president's temperament affected his relationships with four of the prominent figures who were ultimately responsible for the outcome of the Atlanta campaign. Davis permitted his friendships with Braxton Bragg and John Bell Hood to influence his judgment on the condition of the army prior to

31 Judith Lee Hallock, *Braxton Bragg and Confederate Defeat*, 2 vols. (Tuscaloosa, AL, 1991), II:165–166, 181–182.

32 Thomas Lawrence Connelly, *Autumn of Glory: The Army of Tennessee, 1862–1865* (Baton Rouge, 1971), 278; Hallock, *Braxton Bragg and Confederate Defeat*, 189; Woodworth, *Jefferson Davis and His Generals*, 237.

the beginning of the campaign, as well as Johnston's performance as commander from May 7 until July 17. Conversely, the president's animosity toward Johnston and Georgia Governor Joseph E. Brown, which developed over the course of the war, made him less willing to accept their proposals or heed their advice.

Davis's close relationship with Braxton Bragg had caused him to excuse Bragg's poor performance as commander of the Army of Tennessee for more than two years. Davis had appointed Bragg to command believing him one of his best generals. Early in the war Bragg had proven adept at training raw recruits after secession, never complaining about his status behind the front lines. Further, Bragg had performed competently during the battle of Shiloh and the army's withdrawal to Mississippi thereafter. Davis considered him ideal for leading the western army. Yet Bragg demonstrated little strategic or tactical ability during his tenure. He lost at Perryville, Murfreesboro, and Missionary Ridge. Bragg's only victory, at Chickamauga, cost the Confederates more casualties than they had inflicted, and he failed to take advantage of William Rosecrans's flight to Chattanooga. Moreover, Bragg's penchant for blaming his subordinates for his losses resulted in deep discord within the army's officer corps. Bragg even attempted to fault others for his inability to take advantage of the Confederate victory at Chickamauga. Leonidas Polk bitterly lamented, "the truth is, General Bragg has made a failure notwithstanding the success of battle and he wants a scapegoat." Nevertheless, Davis's camaraderie with Bragg led him to sustain his commander despite his numerous defeats and his questionable management skills until the rout at Missionary Ridge. At that juncture Bragg's ineptitude became too difficult to tolerate even for Davis. Bragg's removal, however, did not end his legacy with the army. The split among the army's officers, those who supported Bragg against those who found him disagreeable and incompetent, remained even after Johnston took command.[33] Considering Bragg's extremely feeble record as a commander and his open hostility toward several officers still serving in the Army of Tennessee, his appointment as advisor, at least with respect to matters concerning his former army, was unwise.

Similarly, Davis's friendship with John Bell Hood influenced his perception of operations in the Western theater during the Atlanta campaign. Hood's insistence that the army could take the offensive in the spring of 1864 made Davis leery of Johnston's reports to the contrary. Hood sent Davis a series of reports after his arrival at Dalton suggesting that a reinforcement of between 10,000 and 15,000

33 William J. Cooper Jr., *Jefferson Davis, American* (New York, 2000), 395; Connelly, *Autumn of Glory*, 19–22, 68–91, and *passim*; Leonidas Polk to Wife, October 3, 1863, Leonidas Polk Papers, Library of Congress; Joseph E. Johnston to Louis Wigfall, Jan. 1864, Louis T. Wigfall Papers, Library of Congress.

troops would permit an advance into Tennessee. Though Hood's reports were inconsistent with others that the administration received, Davis willingly accepted their accuracy. Hood's ongoing communications with the president also affected Davis's perception of Johnston's conduct during the campaign. After the receipt of one such report he apparently exclaimed that Johnston would have to be removed. Further, Davis allowed his high opinion of Hood to influence Johnston's removal and Hood's promotion to command of the army.[34]

The president's relationship with Joseph E. Johnston prior to the spring of 1864 also affected the outcome of the campaign. The two men had become hostile in the wake of a dispute over Johnston's proper rank early in the war. Johnston's perceived lack of aggression during the Peninsula campaign in 1862 further irritated the president. The general's handling of the affairs around Vicksburg in the spring and early summer of 1863 exacerbated the tensions in their relationship to a breaking point. As a result, Davis refused to trust Johnston's assessment of the army's offensive capabilities for the upcoming spring campaign. He therefore did not order reinforcements to Johnston until the beginning of May, a decision that might have cost Johnston his strong defensive position at Dalton. Further, Davis became so dismayed with Johnston's retreat toward Atlanta that he refused to order Stephen D. Lee to strike William Tecumseh Sherman's supply line. With Johnston's army a few miles from Atlanta, Davis determined to relieve him from command despite Robert E. Lee's advice to the contrary.[35] Instead, Davis allowed his distrust of Johnston and his misplaced confidence in Braxton Bragg to influence the fateful decision to replace Johnston with Hood.

Davis also allowed his feud with Joseph E. Brown to influence decisions that changed the course of the campaign for Atlanta. During the first three years of the war the president and the governor had disputed numerous matters. Brown had complained about Davis's policies concerning recruitment of troops and the appointment of officers. The two executives had also argued over the acquisition of arms and ordnance. The dispute took on a new dimension of hostility in April

34 *O.R.* vol. 32, pt. 3, 606–608, 781; McMurry, *John Bell Hood and the War for Southern Independence*, 96; Jefferson Davis, *The Rise and Fall of the Confederate Government*, 2 vols. (1881; repr., New York, 1958), II:547–548; *The Papers of Jefferson Davis*, ed. Lynda Lasswell Crist, Kenneth H. Williams, Peggy L. Dillard, 13 vols. (Baton Rouge, 1999), X:434; Woodward, ed., *Mary Chesnut's Civil War*, 616, 635; *O.R.* vol. 38, pt. 5, 880.

35 Joseph E. Johnston, *Narrative of Military Operations: During the Late War Between the States* (New York, 1881), 71–72; *O.R.* vol. 11, pt. 3, 536, 543, 555; Woodward, ed., *Mary Chesnut's Civil War*, 482–483; Davis, *Rise and Fall of the Confederate Government*, II:557–560; Robert E. Lee, *Lee's Dispatches: Unpublished Letters of General Robert E. Lee, C. S. A., to Jefferson Davis and The War Department of the Confederate States of America 1862–65*, ed. Douglas Southall Freeman (1957; repr., Baton Rouge, 1994), 283–284.

1862 with the passage of the Conscription Act. That measure diminished Brown's responsibility for the recruitment of troops, a duty that gave the governor great delight, as it allowed him to boast about his prowess for the undertaking. Davis allowed his quarrel with Brown to upset him so much that he refused to release the Georgia State Guards after the battle of Chickamauga in September 1863. Brown warned that the administration's actions would diminish his ability to raise militia troops in the future. The following year Brown resisted the administration's establishment of a Georgia Reserve Force. Consequently, the Georgia militia was not prepared to assist in repelling Sherman's advance into the state until the end of June, when Johnston had already retreated to within twenty-five miles of Atlanta.[36]

Three years of war had not honed Davis's ability to manage his relationships with key members of the Confederate high command. In 1864 Davis allowed his friendships with Bragg and Hood to influence important personnel and strategic decisions. Meanwhile, his long-standing feuds with Johnston and Brown made cooperation difficult with both during the months immediately preceding the campaign, until Johnston's removal on July 17. Abraham Lincoln, on the other hand, had learned important lessons regarding the management of the Federal high command during the initial years of the conflict. By 1864 Lincoln no longer permitted political interests to dominate his appointment of general officers. Further, Lincoln had demonstrated that he was willing to relieve commanders whose performance suggested that they were unfit for their posts, even when the president found them personally appealing. He certainly was not willing to promote them to positions far above their ability, as Davis had done with Braxton Bragg.

Like the Federals, Confederate officers also engaged in communications that violated proper military protocol. Officers in the Army of Tennessee had corresponded with the administration as early as October 1862. Leonidas Polk, dissatisfied with Bragg's leadership, leveraged his friendship with Jefferson Davis to instigate communications with Richmond to undermine his commanding officer. Polk continued his letter-writing campaign until Davis finally removed Bragg in November of the following year. Edmund Kirby Smith also undermined Bragg when he sent an aide to visit Davis with a report that Bragg's incompetence was responsible for the Confederate defeat in Kentucky. Davis did little to discourage Polk or Smith from their smear campaign and might have unintentionally promoted it. Davis ordered Bragg, Polk, and Smith to Richmond and met with

36 *The Confederate Records of the State of Georgia*, ed., Allen D. Candler, 6 vols. (Atlanta, 1909–1911) III:37–39, 46–47, 75–76, 81, 83–84,104–106, 108–110, 177–78, 180, 431–432, 516, 521–522; hereafter cited as *C. R.* Ga; Joseph H. Parks, *Joseph E. Brown of Georgia* (Baton Rouge, 1977), 152, 198; Gustavas W. Smith, "The Georgia Militia About Atlanta," *Battles and Leaders of the Civil War*, vol. 4 (New York, 1956), 331–332.

each individually. At the conclusion of the meetings, Davis retained Bragg as commander of the army, but he also promoted Polk to lieutenant general under Bragg's command. Further, he allowed Smith to remain in command of the Department of East Tennessee and promoted him to lieutenant general as well.[37] Rather than rebuke either Polk or Smith, Davis promoted them, a clear sign that their behavior was acceptable.

William Hardee, in command of the Second Corps of the Army of Tennessee, made similar allegations against Bragg. Hardee routinely denigrated Bragg in front of the field and staff officers of his corps. In November 1862 he corresponded with William Preston Johnston, the president's aide, and asserted that Bragg should be replaced with someone more competent. Hardee's public professions and private communications were not lost on Davis, yet he again made little effort to curtail the activity.[38]

In January 1863, after Bragg's defeat at Murfreesboro, the feud between him and his subordinates once again became a matter of public record. Davis wired Joseph E. Johnston, then serving as departmental commander, to investigate the matter. Johnston realized that he would likely be Bragg's replacement if he reported that the situation demanded Bragg's removal. Not wanting to attain the position in such an unseemly manner, Johnston produced two reports exonerating Bragg. Consequently, Bragg remained in command and waged a public campaign against his subordinates who retaliated in kind. The dispute continued into October until the president finally intervened. Ultimately, Davis sustained Bragg and allowed him to reorganize the army, which included the removal of several of his critics in the officer corps. Polk was transferred to the Department of Alabama and Mississippi to serve as Johnston's second in command. Hardee, however, who had departed for Mississippi in the summer, was returned to the Army of Tennessee. Accordingly, the key conspirators in the anti-Bragg faction remained highly entrenched in important commands in the Western theater.[39] The message was clear: Corps commanders could publicly and privately undermine the army's commander without fear of any significant reprimand.

In February 1864, Davis demonstrated that two years of bitter strife among members of the Army of Tennessee's officer corps had not imparted to him the wisdom to restrain improper communications from subordinate generals. Instead, Davis decided to encourage such behavior. Since appointing Joseph E. Johnston to

37 Connelly, *Autumn of Glory*, 20–21; Cooper, *Jefferson Davis, American*, 402–403.

38 Connelly, *Autumn of Glory*, 21–22; Cooper, *Jefferson Davis, American*, 457.

39 Connelly, *Autumn of Glory*, 77–79, 87–91, 235–251, and *passim*; Johnston to Wigfall, Dec. 15, 1862, LC.

command his western army in December, Davis and Johnston had quarreled over whether the army was strong enough to advance into Tennessee. The president's long history with Johnston led him to distrust Johnston's characterization of the army's condition. Davis therefore seized the opportunity to appoint his friend, John Bell Hood, to a position as corps commander in Johnston's army. The evidence suggests that Davis instructed Hood to keep the administration apprised of the army's condition and perhaps even Johnston's conduct as commander.[40] Therefore, in addition to his duties as an officer, Hood became an informant.

The scheme offered considerable shortcomings. First, Davis was authorizing activity that had generated deep fissures in the Army of Tennessee's high command in the past. Hood's illicit correspondence with the administration threatened to resurrect the challenges that had plagued Bragg's term as commander. Second, and perhaps even more importantly, the arrangement provided Hood the opportunity to promote himself at Johnston's expense. He was aware of the strained relationship between Johnston and the president. Consequently, Hood undoubtedly understood that Davis would relieve Johnston if he believed the general incapable of defending Atlanta against Sherman's advance. Under those circumstances, Hood stood a reasonable chance of succeeding Johnston to command. When Johnston and Hood became engaged in a dispute concerning the events at Cassville on May 19, Hood embarked on a campaign to secure Johnston's removal and his own elevation to command of the army. Davis's decision to promote back-channel communications between a corps commander and his administration therefore produced unintended results when Hood began angling for Johnston's job. Indeed, Hood allowed his ambition to affect his conduct in the field. He failed to attack the enemy near Pickett's Mill on May 28 despite an opportunity to deliver a decisive blow. Hood also advocated the abandonment of strong defensive positions including those at Cassville and on the Chattahoochee River. Davis's encouragement of Hood to act as an informant resulted in Hood's perfidious behavior toward Johnston, which seriously undermined Confederate chances to defeat Sherman.

Thus, in the final analysis, the dysfunctional nature of the Confederate high command in the Western theater doomed its efforts in the spring and summer of 1864. The campaign for Atlanta demonstrated Jefferson Davis's primary failures as commander-in-chief. The Confederate president never developed an appreciation for the benefit of a centralized command under one general-in-chief. Instead, he adopted a departmental system that gave departmental commanders a great deal of autonomy. The decentralized system limited Joseph E. Johnston's ability to secure assistance from outside of his own department as Sherman

40 *O.R.* vol. 32, pt. 3, 606–608, 781; Woodward, ed., *Mary Chesnut's Civil War*, 616, 635.

advanced toward Atlanta. Further, Davis permitted his personal feelings to shape his policy making decisions and the way he handled his officers. His friendship with Braxton Bragg led to Bragg's appointment as the president's chief military advisor despite his unimpressive record during his tenure as commander of the Army of Tennessee. Considering Bragg's past performance and his ongoing feuds with several officers still serving in the army, the appointment was unwise. The president's dispute with Joseph E. Brown deprived Johnston of adequate militia which likely played a role in Johnston's failure to hold Dalton. Additionally, Davis allowed his poor relationship with Johnston to affect cooperation with his general from the time of Johnston's arrival at Dalton in December until his removal on July 17. Finally, Davis encouraged communications that violated military protocol when he instructed John Bell Hood to keep the administration informed regarding Johnston's conduct as commander. The scheme backfired when Hood used his back-channel communications to undermine Johnston to secure command of the army for himself. Jefferson Davis's performance as commander-in-chief therefore deserves primary blame for Confederate defeat in the Atlanta campaign of 1864.

Chapter 1

Structural Damages

Braxton Bragg's resignation in early December 1863 left Jefferson Davis with a quandary. Lieutenant General William Hardee, the army's most senior officer after Bragg's resignation, appeared the logical choice, and consequently Davis made an effort to secure his services as the new commander for the Army of Tennessee. To Davis's surprise, Hardee declined a permanent appointment, as he felt unable to serve the Confederacy successfully in that capacity. Instead, Hardee wished to remain in his present post as a corps commander and promised to faithfully serve Davis's future appointment to command the army. Hardee did accept temporary command of the army until the president could find a replacement. Davis hoped to convince Hardee that he should consent to the promotion and sent an aide, Preston Johnston, to persuade him to assume permanent command, but Hardee still refused.[1] Hardee's decision to decline the president's offer left Davis with few viable options to replace Bragg.

The structure of command within the Confederate military required that Davis give primary consideration to officers bearing the rank of full general, for which only four candidates, other than Bragg, were qualified. The list included Samuel Cooper, Robert E. Lee, P. G. T. Beauregard, and Joseph E. Johnston. Samuel Cooper was already sixty-five years old and had spent the war in an administrative capacity rather than commanding troops in the field. His advanced age and lack of battlefield experience made him a poor choice. With so few options available

1 *O.R.* vol. 31, pt. 3, 765; Hudson Strode, *Jefferson Davis: Confederate President*, 3 vols. (New York, 1959), II:502–503.

to him Davis briefly considered P. G. T. Beauregard for the vacancy. In fact, on December 3, 1863, Robert E. Lee proposed that if Beauregard were considered a suitable candidate for the position, Gen. Jeremy F. Gilmer might replace him as commander of the forces around Charleston.[2]

A long-standing feud, however, between Davis and Beauregard stemming from a disagreement after the First Battle of Manassas remained an obstacle to Beauregard's appointment. The quarrel had begun over the Confederate inability to take advantage of the victory at Manassas. It intensified during Beauregard's tenure in the Western theater in 1862 when Beauregard ordered a withdrawal from the fight at Shiloh despite the protestations of his subordinates. Soon thereafter, Beauregard retreated from Corinth without a fight and with no explanation. Then, in mid-June, he decided to vacation at the Bladen Springs resort north of Mobile. He claimed his poor health required attention, though he failed to ask the president for permission. Davis took the opportunity to remove Beauregard from command of the army and replaced him with Braxton Bragg.[3] Thus, Davis had already removed Beauregard as commander of essentially the same army, the Army of Tennessee, that in the wake of Bragg's departure needed a new chief. The elevation of Beauregard to the office would have placed Davis in the awkward position of admitting a mistake for relieving him in 1862. As a result, Davis was undoubtedly inclined to look elsewhere for Bragg's replacement. Though Davis generally exhibited poor management skills with individuals he found personally disagreeable, Beauregard's recalcitrant behavior warranted the president's ire.

After considering his options for a day or two, Davis decided to offer command of the Army of Tennessee to Robert E. Lee. Lee showed little enthusiasm at the suggestion. He responded that he would take the position "if desired," but that he doubted the wisdom of such a transfer. After all, he cautioned the president, the Army of Northern Virginia might suffer as a result of his departure. Notwithstanding Lee's objection, Davis ordered him to travel to Richmond in hopes that he could be convinced to assume command in Tennessee. During the week following Lee's arrival in the Confederate capital, he and Davis discussed the available alternatives for Bragg's replacement. After persuading Davis that he should remain in Virginia, Lee proposed that Beauregard assume command in the West. Davis declined and Lee suggested that Davis consider Joseph E Johnston for the position.[4]

2 Thomas Lawrence Connelly, *Autumn of Glory: The Army of Tennessee, 1862–1865* (Baton Rouge, 1971), 282; *O.R.* vol. 31, pt. 3, 779.

3 *O.R.* vol. 10, pt. 1, 410, 467, 569; Woodworth, *Jefferson Davis and his Generals*, 104–106.

4 Woodworth, *Jefferson Davis and his Generals*, 257–258; *O.R.* vol. 29, pt. 2, 866.

In addition to Lee, a number of other luminaries favored Johnston's appointment. On December 8, Davis's close friend Gen. Leonidas Polk recommended that the president offer Johnston the command. Polk cited support for Johnston from the army, as well as the country as a whole, and hoped that Davis could magnanimously look beyond his unpleasant past with the general. Brigadier General William Mackall, Johnston's close friend and subsequently his chief of staff, confirmed Polk's assessment of the mood of the army. Mackall wrote Johnston on December 9 that "the army wants you," and that "even Bragg's friends say that your presence would be worth 10,000 men."[5]

Politicians too hoped that Davis might appoint Johnston to command the army. Davis's secretary of war, James A. Seddon, voiced approval for Johnston's candidacy. In fact, a majority of the president's cabinet concluded that Johnston should replace Bragg. Furthermore, Johnston enjoyed a number of supporters in Congress, including Senator Louis Wigfall, who lobbied for Johnston's appointment. On one occasion Wigfall and several other legislators met in Seddon's office and solicited for their candidate.[6]

Friendship with Johnston was not the only motivation for Wigfall's efforts. In addition to his relationship with Johnston, Wigfall had developed considerable animus toward the president. The two vehemently disagreed over a bill Wigfall had introduced in the Senate in the fall of 1862 that permitted army commanders to choose their own staff officers. Because the officers would be awarded the rank of brigadier general, the proposal broke with the tradition that granted the power to appoint general officers to the president. Though the bill passed both houses of Congress, Davis vetoed it, thereby giving birth to a feud. Prior to the president's veto of the staff bill, the two men had enjoyed a close working relationship; Wigfall had routinely voted for confirmation of presidential appointments, for example. After the president's veto, however, Wigfall immediately changed course and challenged Davis's appointees regardless of their qualifications. The two disagreed on other matters as well, including military strategy and, in particular, the defense of the Trans-Mississippi. Wigfall hailed from Texas and thought the president too careless in his approach to the security of his state. The various disputes culminated

5 *O.R.* vol. 31, pt 3, 796–797; William Mackall to Joseph E. Johnston, Dec. 9, 1863, W. W. Mackall Papers, Southern Historical Collection, University of North Carolina.

6 Woodworth, *Jefferson Davis and his Generals*, 258; Gilbert E. Govan and James W. Livingood, *A Different Valor: The Story of General Joseph E. Johnston, C.S.A.* (New York, 1956), 238; Wigfall and Johnston were so close that the general had spent time convalescing in Wigfall's home after sustaining a wound at the battle of Seven Pines in June of 1862. See Craig Symonds, *Joseph E. Johnston: A Civil War Biography* (New York, 1992), 177; Connelly, *Autumn of Glory*, 282.

in Wigfall's accusation that Davis had engaged in "petty tyranny and reckless disregard of law and contemptuous treatment of Congress."[7]

Wigfall found several accomplices in his dispute with Davis including Senators Henry S. Foote of Tennessee and William L. Yancey of Alabama, who put aside their prewar quarrel to unite in opposition to the president. Consequently, a small but influential opposition to the president was in place by the close of 1863, particularly after the military reversals at Gettysburg, Vicksburg, and Missionary Ridge during the course of the year. A number of Johnston "supporters" emerged from this group and though they had no personal affinity for Johnston himself, they used the occasion as an opportunity to rile the president, who was known to have a strained relationship with the general. As a result, the congressional coalition that clamored for Johnston's appointment to command the Army of Tennessee was a combination of pro-Johnston and anti-Davis men. Their efforts proved successful as the president felt significant political pressure to appoint Johnston to command. With no other alternative and support for Johnston so strong, Davis ordered him to assume command of the Army of Tennessee, encamped at Dalton, Georgia, on December 16, 1863. On December 21, Richmond socialite and close associate of the president, Mary Boykin Chesnut, confided in her diary that "certainly Jeff Davis did hate to put Joe Johnston at the head of what is left of [the Army of Tennessee]."[8]

Johnston and Davis: A Marriage on the Rocks

The breakdown in command that ultimately doomed the Confederate efforts during the Atlanta campaign in 1864 had deep roots by the time Davis appointed Johnston to lead the Army of Tennessee. While his new appointment pleased Johnston, his optimism was tempered by what he expected to be a poor working relationship with the Confederate president. They had known each other during their time as cadets at the United States Military Academy at West Point, but their relationship while attending the academy remains something of a mystery. There is no credible evidence that the two developed a rivalry at that juncture, though there were spurious allegations that hostility arose from competition for the affection of

7 Symonds, *Joseph E. Johnston,* 178; Alvy King, *Louis T. Wigfall: Southern Fire-eater* (Baton Rouge, 1970), 159, 161, 178.

8 Foote and Yancey had clashed over the efficacy of secession prior to the war. See Symonds, *Joseph E. Johnston,* 179; Woodworth, *Jefferson Davis and his Generals,* 258; Davis, *The Rise and Fall of the Confederate Government,* II:547; *O.R.* vol. 31, pt. 3, 835–836; Woodward, *Mary Chesnut's Civil War,* 509. Chesnut's entry for December 18 opined that Lee was responsible for Johnston's appointment, though editor C. Vann Woodward noted that no other source made that claim.

a local young lady.[9] In all probability Johnston and Davis graduated from West Point harboring no ill will toward each other.

The first signs of a rift emerged over the issue of rank in the aftermath of the war with Mexico. Johnston entered the war as a captain, but his gallantry on the battlefield earned him two brevet promotions. First, at Cerro Gordo Johnston's superiors awarded him a brevet promotion to lieutenant colonel, thereby skipping over the rank of major. After the battle at Chapultepec Johnston again earned a brevet, which he thought made him a full colonel. After the war, Congress passed a new law providing that officers from the regular Army who had earned brevet promotion during the conflict, even in volunteer regiments, ought to retain their promotion on a permanent basis. Believing that the second brevet entitled him to the rank of colonel, Johnston was disheartened to learn that the *Register of Officers* listed him as a lieutenant colonel. The War Department claimed that Johnston's first brevet warranted the rank of major rather than lieutenant colonel, and that his superiors had made a mistake in granting him the higher rank after Cerro Gordo. Accordingly, his second brevet promotion only entitled him to the rank of lieutenant colonel. Johnston appealed the decision in March 1849, but then Secretary of War William L. Marcy rejected Johnston's petition, a ruling later confirmed by the Senate.[10]

Johnston refused to let the matter rest and on July 11, 1855, presented his case again, this time to the new secretary of war, Jefferson Davis. Davis determined that "the case had been decided by his predecessors and could not be reopened." Davis reaffirmed that decision in January 1856 when Johnston once again argued his cause.[11] Johnston's persistence demonstrates that he genuinely felt entitled to the rank of full colonel. The fact that Davis had twice rejected the argument surely irritated Johnston, but there is no record that this initial disagreement over rank led to open hostility between the two men.

In 1860 Johnston applied for the position of quartermaster general in the United States Army. His primary competition for the position was Albert Sidney Johnston (no relation), who enjoyed Jefferson Davis's support. It is uncertain whether Joseph E. Johnston learned that Davis backed another candidate, but considering the manner in which gossip traveled in social circles it seems likely that he did. If so, Johnston could not help but harbor at least an inkling of resentment

9 Govan and Livingood, *A Different Valor*, 14–15.

10 Symonds, *Joseph E. Johnston*, 89.

11 "Report on the Claim, April 15, 1858, of Lt. Colonel Johnston, 1st Cavalry, to the rank of Brevet Colonel," Papers of Joseph E. Johnston, box 1, folder 3, Swem Library, The College of William & Mary.

toward Davis. After all, Davis had twice rejected Johnston's application for the rank of colonel and subsequently had supported a rival candidate for the office of quartermaster general. Despite Davis's backing of an alternative aspirant, Johnston's friendship with John B. Floyd, who in 1860 held the position of secretary of war, landed him the office.[12] The promotion, however, did not elevate Johnston to a permanent rank of general within the army, as it only constituted a staff rank. Accordingly, Johnston remained a lieutenant colonel. The distinction between Johnston's staff rank and his line rank eventually became a factor in the pair's relationship after the first battle of Manassas.

Just prior to the battle at Manassas, Johnston sent a telegram to Davis requesting that the president identify whether he or General Beauregard would command once their forces were on the same field. Davis responded: "You are a General in the Confederate Army possessed of the power attaching to that rank." Davis then referred to Beauregard as a brigadier general, thereby implying that Johnston outranked Beauregard. The communication gave Johnston the impression that only Davis, as commander-in-chief, held a higher rank in the Confederate Army. Only days after the battle, however, Johnston felt his status challenged when Dabney Maury arrived at his headquarters with orders from Robert E. Lee that appointed him Johnston's adjutant general. Johnston asserted that the order was an "outrage," as he outranked Lee and despite his friendship with Maury he could not permit such a usurpation of his authority.[13] Johnston's animated reaction demonstrates a highly developed sensitivity over the matter of rank that likely dated to Davis's support for Albert Sidney Johnston's candidacy as quartermaster general, or perhaps even earlier to Davis's decision regarding Joseph E. Johnston's brevet rank.

In the following days the dispute over rank became even more intense. During that time Johnston received communications from Lee on formal stationery with a heading: "Headquarters of the Virginia Forces." Apparently a member of Lee's staff had crossed out Virginia, implying that Lee commanded all Confederate forces. Johnston complained to Adjutant and Inspector General Samuel Cooper that the orders were "illegal" and, therefore, he could not obey them. Johnston's telegrams to Cooper subsequently found their way to Davis's desk and aggravated the president. Davis attached a one-word endorsement to each communication, stating only:

12 McMurry, "The Enemy at Richmond: Joseph E. Johnston and the Confederate Government," 6; Connelly and Jones, *The Politics of Command*, 56–57; Symonds, *Joseph E. Johnston*, 91.

13 *The Papers of Jefferson Davis*, VII:254; Govan and Livingood, *A Different Valor*, 65, 66.

"insubordinate."[14] Though each man was clearly agitated by the other's conduct, their relationship had not yet become irreconcilable.

Still, the hostility continued to mount when the president officially decreed Johnston to rank fourth among full generals in the Confederate Army. In March 1861 the Confederate Congress had passed a law that established the criteria for ranking officers in the Confederate Army who had previously served in the United States Army. Section 5 of the law provided that: "the commissions issued shall bear one and the same date, so that the relative rank of officers of each grade shall be determined by their former commissions in the US Army." Davis implemented the law in August, after Johnston's protestations against Lee's "illegal" behavior. When Davis sent his nominations to Congress he assigned effective dates for each of the candidates, a clear violation of the statute that required the commissions to "bear the same date." According to Davis's submission, Samuel Cooper was the senior general with a rank to date from May 16. Meanwhile, Albert Sidney Johnston's rank was dated May 30. Both Cooper and Albert Sidney Johnston had been colonels in the US Army with Cooper's rank predating that of Johnston's. Davis next assigned an effective rank for Robert E. Lee to date from June 14, while Joseph E. Johnston's rank was dated July 4. Both Lee and Johnston had held a line rank of lieutenant colonel prior to secession, but Davis's assignment of dates meant that Lee was now the senior officer of the two. Only Beauregard, previously a major, lacked seniority to Joseph E. Johnston under Davis's interpretation of the law.[15]

The fact that Davis held this interpretation of the law might well have its origins in Johnston's "insubordinate" communications with Cooper in July. Otherwise, there was no reason to grant seniority to Lee over his fellow former lieutenant colonel Johnston. Davis's ranking of the generals by date conflicted with the statute upon which he based his authority. Moreover, the statute made no distinction with respect to staff grade or line grade. Because Joseph E. Johnston had held a commission as a quartermaster general in the US Army, the statute entitled him to the senior position in the Confederate Army. The most reasonable explanation for Davis's action is that Johnston's communications with the administration over the course of the previous month had irritated the president enough that he determined to take punitive action. A secondary reason for Davis's actions might have been that he hoped to make certain that Joseph E. Johnston would never outrank his close friend Albert Sidney Johnston, or for that matter Robert E. Lee,

14 Symonds, *Joseph E. Johnston*, 126; *O.R.* vol. 2, 1007; *The Papers of Jefferson Davis*, VII:335.

15 *O.R.* ser. 4, vol. 1, 164; Govan and Livingood, *A Different Valor*, 67; Woodworth, *Jefferson Davis and his Generals*, 176–177.

with whom he had developed a close working relationship while organizing the Confederate Army.[16]

Johnston balked at Davis's decision to rank him fourth among the generals. According to Johnston, his staff rank as a brigadier general entitled him to the most senior rank among those becoming full generals in the Confederate service. Johnston believed that Davis had snubbed him by failing to recognize him as the senior officer and angrily wrote Davis a letter expressing his indignation. Johnston's letter, dated September 12, conveyed his "surprise and mortification" at the president's interpretation of the law. He further claimed that the "proceedings are in violation of my rights as an officer" and asserted that "notwithstanding these nominations by the president and their confirmation by Congress, I still rightfully hold the rank of first general in the Armies of the Southern Confederacy." After making an impassioned argument as to why his rank as quartermaster general made him the senior ranking Confederate general, Johnston concluded that the president's interpretation "is a blow aimed at me only." Johnston later charged that Davis's interpretation had been "illegal and contrary to all the laws enacted to regulate the class of officers concerned."[17]

Davis considered Johnston's tone shocking. He read the communication to his cabinet and complained of its "intemperate" nature. Davis's terse response two days later suggests that the dispute over Johnston's rank had, by this time, produced a degree of mutual enmity between the two men. Davis called Johnston's language "unusual" and his arguments "utterly one-sided," and as "unfounded as they are unbecoming." In his postwar memoir Johnston attributed the origins of Davis's open antagonism toward him to their conflict over Johnston's place in the pecking order of the Confederate high command.[18] Nevertheless, despite the developing hostility between Davis and his general, the president retained enough faith in Johnston's abilities as an officer to keep him as commander of the Confederacy's primary eastern army.

If the question of rank was the genesis of the feud between Joseph E. Johnston and Jefferson Davis, it was not the only reason for their truculent association that eventually led to a collapse in leadership during the campaign for Atlanta. A dispute concerning strategy and tactics during the course of the war's first three years also added strain to their relationship. Johnston's evacuation of Harpers

16 McMurry, "The Enemy at Richmond," 7.

17 *O.R.* Ser. 4, vol. 1, 605; Johnston, *Narrative of Military Operations*, 71–72.

18 Cooper, *Jefferson Davis, American*, 364; *The Papers of Jefferson Davis*, VII:340; Johnston, *Narrative of Military Operations*, 73. Johnston's claim was based on information gleaned from mutual acquaintances in Richmond.

Ferry in June 1861 was the first of several episodes in which he and the president clashed over strategic and tactical matters. Before he left for Harpers Ferry in May, Johnston met with both Davis and Lee, who informed him of the importance of the assignment. They considered the position a "natural fortress" that commanded the entrance to the Shenandoah Valley from both Pennsylvania and Maryland and, consequently, a vital point of defense. Upon arrival at Harpers Ferry, Johnston made a reconnaissance of the surrounding area and came to a strikingly different conclusion. Both he and his engineers determined that the position "was easy to turn or invest," and thus offered none of the natural advantages that Lee and Davis had suggested.[19]

Johnston had good reason for concern, as the town of Harpers Ferry stood at the base of three imposing hills. Bolivar Heights, the least impressive of the three, peaked 200 feet above the confluence of the Potomac and Shenandoah rivers that bordered the town. Maryland Heights rose 840 feet above the rivers, while Loudoun Heights loomed 954 feet above any troops garrisoned in the town. If the enemy gained possession of one or more of the heights and placed artillery there, Johnston's command might have been trapped. Furthermore, the Potomac River was fordable at more than a dozen places, which meant that a Federal column could capture Winchester and thereby control the railroad and isolate any garrison remaining at Harpers Ferry. As historian Craig Symonds notes, Johnston would have needed to defend all three heights as well as all of the fords if he hoped to retain possession of the town.[20]

The political tension in Virginia exacerbated Johnston's problems. Loyalties to the Confederacy on the border were tenuous, and many Virginia troops under Johnston's command remained faithful to the Union. On the same day that Johnston arrived at Harpers Ferry, May 23, the people of Virginia ratified the articles of secession. Those with pro-Union sentiment quickly deserted, significantly weakening the force Johnston commanded. As a result, Johnston's entire command numbered only 5,200 men. To make matters worse, he discovered they were poorly equipped; some had arrived with no weapons, and those with muskets had no more than fifteen rounds of ammunition.[21]

With an enfeebled force and what he considered unfavorable topography, Johnston composed a series of communications to the administration in hopes of securing an order directing the abandonment of Harpers Ferry. On May 26,

19 Johnston, *Narrative of Military Operations*, 17.

20 Symonds, *Joseph E. Johnston*, 104.

21 Govan and Livingood, *A Different Valor*, 37; *O.R.* vol. 2, 880–881; Symonds, *Joseph E. Johnston*, 103.

Johnston insisted that the topography of the region required an additional 10,000 to 15,000 troops for adequate defense. Two days later he again emphasized the difficult terrain and his lack of strength, but this time added that he was "in the heart of a disloyal population." Johnston sent yet another telegram on June 6, in response to Lee, who had claimed that a loss of Harpers Ferry would damage Southern morale. Johnston suggested that if he remained in his current position, the Confederacy would likely lose five or six thousand troops, even more depressing to the Southern cause. The latest communication highlighted a fundamental difference between Johnston and Davis. Johnston considered the maintenance of the Confederacy's field armies paramount to the retention of territory. Meanwhile, Davis's position as president required him to consider the political consequences of the abandonment of regions deemed vital to the Confederacy's survival by political allies and enemies alike.[22]

Johnston's repeated requests for more specific orders caused some in the administration, including Adjutant General Samuel Cooper, to believe that Johnston's real purpose was to saddle the administration with the political fallout should he abandon Harpers Ferry. Cooper informed Johnston that the decision to retire from his post must fall on Johnston himself, based upon the circumstances on his front. Johnston immediately evacuated and on June 15 disavowed the notion that he ever intended the administration to bear the responsibility for the action. Johnston's withdrawal, however, did in fact create a stir in Richmond and led to some political backlash against the Davis administration. Davis, perhaps responding to political pressure, or perhaps irritated yet again with his commander, offered Johnston a backhanded compliment: he congratulated Johnston on breaking the line of the Baltimore & Ohio Railroad during his retreat.[23] In truth, considering the topographical and geographical weaknesses of Harpers Ferry, Johnston made a prudent decision. Nevertheless, in Johnston's first action as a commander of Confederate forces he had retreated and, consequently, set a precedent by which his future actions could be judged.

One month later, on July 18, Johnston embarked on a course that should have disabused people of the notion that he suffered from timidity and favored retreat as a first option. That morning, one hour after midnight, he received a telegram from General Cooper that informed him that a Federal army threatened

22 *O.R.* vol. 2, 880–881. Johnston estimated his own forces at that time at approximately 5,200 effectives; see Johnston, *Narrative of Military Operations*, 16; *O.R.* vol. 2, 889, 908; see Govan and Livingood, *A Different Valor*, 37.

23 *O.R.* vol. 2, 924, 929–930; John Jones, *A Rebel War Clerk's Diary at the Confederate States Capital*, ed. Earl Miers (1866; repr, Baton Rouge, 1993), 27; *The Papers of Jefferson Davis*, VII:208.

Beauregard at Manassas. The directive suggested that "to strike the enemy a decisive blow, a junction of all your effective force will be needed." It continued, "In all the arrangements, exercise your discretion." The order gave Johnston a dilemma as his army, then at Winchester, confronted a Union force under General Robert Patterson that numbered roughly 18,000 men. Should Patterson learn of Johnston's withdrawal, he might attempt an attack while the Confederates were on the move. The administration's order seemed to give Johnston discretion, and he might well have been tempted to leave a portion of his command as a rear guard against Patterson, should the latter attempt any advance. Instead, Johnston moved with his entire command that morning and left no rear guard to defend against Patterson. While Cooper had instructed him to send his sick and wounded to Culpepper, Johnston thought doing so would retard the movement of the rest of the army to Manassas. Instead, he decided to leave them at Winchester in the belief that Patterson would also move to Manassas when he discovered Johnston's departure from his front. Johnston acted boldly and decisively and managed to get his men to the rail station at Piedmont the following morning and from there his force boarded trains bound for Manassas Junction. Though Johnston's prompt response to Cooper's telegram played a significant role in the Confederacy's victory at Manassas, Johnston received few accolades. Instead, the press lauded Beauregard and dubbed him the champion of the battle. Moreover, Davis claimed that his own presence helped rally the troops and led to Confederate triumph.[24] As a result, Johnston's reputation remained in limbo.

The following year, after the dispute concerning rank, Johnston's perceived propensity to withdraw in the face of the enemy gave Davis further reason for alarm. Johnston's growing reputation for retreat, first demonstrated at Harpers Ferry, emerged again during the Peninsula Campaign in the spring of 1862. General George McClellan commenced the campaign, landing his Federal army of approximately 120,000 men on the Virginia peninsula east of Richmond. Davis subsequently directed Johnston to make defensive preparations and informed him that his sphere of command now included the Virginia peninsula.[25]

Johnston went to Yorktown to inspect the Confederate defenses. He came away decidedly unimpressed with the situation. Johnston believed that the low ground around the town was too soggy and worried that his troops would suffer

24 Davis, *The Rise and Fall of the Confederate Government*, I:346; Symonds, *Joseph E. Johnston* 113–114; 122–123; Johnston, *Narrative of Military Operations*, 33–37; Woodward, *Mary Chesnut's Civil War*, 109; Jones, *A Rebel War Clerk's Diary at the Confederate States Capital*, 35. In reality, Davis did not arrive at the battlefield until after the Federal rout.

25 Johnston, *Narrative of Military Operations*, 110.

from disease if forced to remain in that position for long. If so, their efficiency and morale would languish. He also believed that the terrain made it difficult for either side to attack the other and that the enemy's rifled artillery might prove decisive in a prolonged stalemate. Johnston soon expressed reservations about his prospects for success. In a meeting with the president, Robert E. Lee, and new Secretary of War George Randolph on April 14, he conveyed his apprehensions including a lack of proper fortifications in the Yorktown vicinity. Additionally, Johnston suggested that the sparse number of men to fill the fairly lengthy existing lines presented a problem. He also voiced anxiety over the Federal advantage in number and quality of cannons. Finally, Johnston feared that if he concentrated his forces near Yorktown the enemy might use its naval superiority and run a flotilla past the Confederate water batteries and land a strong infantry force in the Confederate rear.[26]

Davis, to the contrary, considered the abandonment of Yorktown and consequently the naval yards at Norfolk detrimental to the Confederate war effort. Randolph, who had served in the navy, also objected to a withdrawal from Norfolk. Lee too advocated a defense of the peninsula and insisted that its terrain narrowed the front and accordingly blunted the Union's numerical superiority. At the conclusion of the conference Davis announced his decision that Yorktown must be defended, and he directed Johnston to take command of the forces there.[27] Despite having inspected the Yorktown defenses himself and presenting a well-reasoned argument against retention of the position, Johnston had been overruled.

The president's decision deserves scrutiny because in the end it set Joseph E. Johnston up for failure. His decision to abandon Harpers Ferry, though sound tactically and strategically, set a precedent. During the Manassas campaign, Johnston had acted aggressively when he moved his forces from Winchester to Manassas, but Beauregard, Jackson, and Davis had claimed the lion's share of praise for the Confederate victory. Now Davis ordered Johnston to a position that could not possibly be used to stage an offensive against his foe. If the geography of the peninsula provided a narrow front and thus favored a defensive posture, as Lee had suggested, the same was true for the Union position. Any Confederate advance would be against a much larger Federal army defending a narrow front, with Union gunboats within supporting distance. Further, McClellan's army enjoyed the

26 Draft to Joseph E. Johnston, n.d., Correspondence to Wigfall 1863–1865, LC. Johnston's prognostication later proved accurate and a large number of Confederate soldiers fell ill while serving on the peninsula. See John Bankhead Magruder's telegram to Randolph on April 29, 1862, *O.R.* vol. 11, pt. 3, 475; Johnston, *Narrative of Military Operations*, 113.

27 Johnston, *Narrative of Military Operations*,115; Davis, *The Rise and Fall of the Confederate Government*, II:8.

advantage of rifled cannon, which meant that any prolonged stalemate inevitably benefited the Union with its advanced weaponry. Federal naval superiority meant that McClellan, as Johnston insisted, could transport his forces by river around Johnston's army if and when he became frustrated with a stalemate. Indeed, in his "Report on the Conduct of the War," Secretary Randolph admitted that Johnston had been accurate in his prognostication. Randolph went to Yorktown and found the Federals running transports up and down the James and York Rivers "mounted with the largest-sized guns, such as we could not compete with and made the position of Yorktown untenable."[28] Consequently, Johnston inevitably was forced to withdraw toward Richmond in hopes of successfully defending the Confederate capital. The perception that Johnston was a general too willing to retreat in the face of an enemy was all but guaranteed to gain credence as a result of the president's order that he defend Yorktown.

Johnston's combined forces in Yorktown numbered some 55,000 effective troops, the largest army the Confederacy had fielded to date. Nevertheless, the Confederates faced an army twice as large, and Johnston spent much of his time asking the administration to order the concentration of all Confederate forces, including any available reinforcements from the Carolinas. The presence of Irvin McDowell's Federal army, just north of Fredericksburg with approximately 40,000 men, meant that the administration was unwilling to send additional troops to Johnston. To do so would theoretically require the transfer of soldiers from north of Richmond employed in the defense against McDowell. On April 30 Johnston again proposed the concentration of all Confederate forces in the East. This time, however, he advocated that the combined forces take the strategic offensive and advance across the Potomac, presumably to march on Washington, D.C.. The same day, before Davis had ample time to respond to Johnston's new proposal, McClellan opened fire with his siege guns, and on May 1 Johnston decided to evacuate Yorktown.[29] Davis was taken by surprise and lamented that a retrograde movement from Yorktown would result in enormous loss of matériel, particularly unfinished gunboats. Despite the president's wishes to the contrary, Johnston felt compelled to retreat toward Richmond.

Presaging the dispute over departmental command during the Atlanta campaign, Johnston complained about his inability to transfer troops north of the capital to his own army as he withdrew up the peninsula on May 8. He argued

28 Davis, *The Rise and Fall of the Confederate Government*, II:93.

29 *O.R.* vol. 11, pt. 3, 456, 477. Robert E. Lee responded on May 1 that the president also favored taking the offensive. He did not, however, identify a specific plan, nor did he offer Johnston any reinforcements. See *O.R.* vol. 11, pt. 3, 485; Symonds, *Joseph E. Johnston*, 150, 152.

that because he seemed to be able to direct only those troops on the peninsula he should be "relieved of a merely nominal geographical command." Johnston's complaint suggests that the Confederate command structure was not only decentralized, but also disorganized at that juncture. Technically, the president had expanded Johnston's department to include the Departments of the Peninsula and Norfolk in addition to his own Department of Northern Virginia.[30] That there were so many departments in Virginia made it difficult for any commander to concentrate sufficient forces to confront a significant Federal presence. Moreover, while the administration had technically extended Johnston's department it had also interfered with the general's ability to direct operations. As a result, at least two people, Robert E. Lee acting on behalf of the administration and Johnston, were responsible for strategic decisions in Johnston's department.

Johnston's communication, requesting that he be relieved from his departmental command, illustrates his growing anxiety over the administration's unwillingness to concentrate all available Confederate forces in the East under his direction. The telegram also demonstrates a characteristic that Johnston exhibited on several occasions throughout the war: He often sought ways to minimize his own blame in the case of Confederate defeat. As departmental commander, critics would target Johnston if Union forces captured the Confederate capital. If Johnston exercised complete authority within the theater, such critics would be correct in their assessment. Johnston, however, believed that the administration had interfered with his ability to act as departmental commander and, consequently, did not want to be held accountable for any subsequent defeat.

Lee's response the following day likely produced more apprehension. Lee informed Johnston that two brigades from North Carolina were in transit, but that they were destined to reinforce the Confederate defensive lines near Gordonsville, northwest of Richmond.[31] Rather than concentrating forces under Johnston's command, the administration seemed intent on defending against Union threats wherever they materialized. Without reinforcements, Johnston continued to retreat in the face of McClellan's army.

Davis expressed only mild reservations about the speed with which Johnston withdrew from Yorktown and Norfolk. In fact, the inclusion of Randolph's testimony in his postwar memoir, that Union transports mounted with cannon made Confederate occupation of Yorktown untenable, suggests that Davis accepted the wisdom of Johnston's decision. Johnston's continued withdrawals nearly to the

30 *O.R.* vol. 11, pt 3, 485, 499; Johnston, *Narrative of Military Operations*, 109–110.

31 *O.R.* vol. 11, pt. 3, 501.

gates of Richmond went without any significant reprimand from the president. Instead, on May 11 Davis congratulated Johnston, stating, "I have been much relieved by the successes you have gained."[32]

The same communication, however, included a request that prompted a response from Johnston demonstrating that his simmering animosity toward the president was never far beneath the surface. Davis called Johnston's attention to a proposal made in the fall of 1861 to reorganize brigades and divisions by state. Davis claimed that "I have been much harassed and the public interest has certainly suffered by the delay to place the regiments of some of the states in brigades together." Davis had long hoped for a reorganization, but Johnston had at first objected and then had only slowly implemented the program. That Davis made the request with McClellan's army marching up the peninsula toward Richmond suggests that he was satisfied with Johnston's handling of the Confederate forces, as he made no comment to imply otherwise. Johnston, however, considered the request absurd and on the following day wrote to his wife: "I got yesterday one of the president's letters such as are written to gentlemen only by persons who cannot be held to personal accountability. I cannot understand the heart or principles of a man who can find leisure in times like these to write four pages of scolding to one whom he ought, for the public interest, to try to be on good terms with."[33]

On May 14 the president and Robert E. Lee visited Johnston at his headquarters. The conference lasted so long that the pair remained with Johnston overnight. During the meeting, Davis asked Johnston for details about his plans. Johnston's response demonstrates his irritation that the administration had not determined to concentrate all available forces in the East under his direction. Johnston said that because his strength was insufficient to launch an attack, he would wait for McClellan to take the offensive and hope that the Federals would make a mistake and thereby give him an opportunity to counterattack.[34] Johnston's answer apparently appeased the president, as he returned to Richmond the following morning.

As Johnston retreated toward Richmond, anxiety among the population and politicians increased dramatically. One observer, John Jones, bemoaned "is there no turning point in this long lane of downward progress? Truly it may be said that at

32 Ibid., 508

33 Ibid., 508; *The Papers of Jefferson Davis*, VIII:170; VIII:201–202; Davis made yet another request on May 29 with respect to the reorganization of Mississippi troops. Johnston responded the same day that he feared moving regiments from one point of his line to another so near the enemy. Symonds, *Joseph E. Johnston*, 134–135, 158.

34 Davis, *Rise and Fall of the Confederate Government*, II:101.

this moment, our affairs are in critical condition." Five days later, on May 19, Jones lamented that preparations were being made for the evacuation of Richmond. As he retreated, Johnston failed to provide information to the government as to his intentions in the face of a presidential inquiry regarding the affairs of the campaign. Davis decided to visit his commander's headquarters again and seek his counsel on May 20, 1862. He was surprised to find Johnston's army on the south side of the Chickahominy River on the very outskirts of Richmond. When Davis asked why the army was so close to the capital, Johnston responded that he thought the water of the Chickahominy posed a danger to the health of his men and had ordered the crossing on the supposition that a better source of water might be found on the south side of the river. He also asserted that the advantage of having the river to his front made the move advisable.[35] Johnston's last observation conforms with standard military doctrine that a river in an army's rear is an invitation to disaster when engaging in the tactical defensive, as it serves as a barrier to retreat if that army is defeated in battle. Nevertheless, the proximity of Johnston's army to the Confederate capital generated significant anxiety.

Davis continued to fear for the safety of Richmond and on May 22 rode out yet again in search of the army presumed to be near Mechanicsville. What he discovered distressed him greatly, as he found what he described as an army lacking both in organization and planning. Davis could not locate his commanding general, only adding to his dismay. Thereafter, Davis repeatedly requested information about Johnston's plans, while his commander offered ambiguous answers. Johnston later claimed that he "did not consult with the president as commander of the army because it seemed to me that to do so would be to transfer my responsibilities to his shoulders. I could not consult him without adopting the course he might advise, so that to ask his advice would have been, in my opinion, to ask him to command for me." In reality, it is likely that Johnston simply did not want to be overruled as he had been when he advocated the evacuation of Yorktown. Even with Johnston's unwillingness to reveal his strategy, Davis did not wish to remove him from command during "such an important campaign."[36]

Perhaps Johnston's equivocation on strategy influenced Davis's unwillingness to order reinforcements to the peninsula throughout the month of May. Finally on the 23rd, with the enemy closing in on Richmond, the administration informed

35 Jones, *A Rebel War Clerk's Diary at the Confederate States Capital*, 76, 77; Davis, *The Rise and Fall of the Confederate Government*, II:103.

36 Steven Newton, *Joseph E. Johnston and the Defensive Richmond* (Lawrence KS, 1998), 166; *O.R.* vol. 11, pt. 3, 536, 543, 555; Johnston to Wigfall, Nov. 12, 1863, LC; Davis, *The Rise and Fall of the Confederate Government*, II:88.

Johnston that General Benjamin Huger's brigade had been ordered to reinforce him. Also on the 23rd, Johnston discovered that a corps of McClellan's men under Maj. Gen. Erasmus Keyes had marched south of the Chickahominy River, while the rest of his army remained to the north. On May 27, Johnston learned that McDowell's army was moving south from Fredericksburg. To prevent the junction of McDowell and McClellan, Johnston decided to attack as soon as possible.[37]

By May 30 torrential rainstorms made the nearby fords nearly impassable, thereby stranding the Union corps under Keyes on the south side of the river without much hope of support from the rest of McClellan's army. Johnston devised a plan that envisioned three separate columns totaling approximately 30,000 men striking the Union force of about 15,000. Unfortunately for Johnston, Gen. James Longstreet, who was charged with delivering the decisive blow, marched his troops in the wrong direction. To make matters worse, Gen. Daniel Harvey Hill became impatient as Longstreet ambled about aimlessly on the wrong road and launched a premature attack. In the end, deficient leadership at the divisional level, inferior roads, bad staff work, vague orders, and poor weather marred the assault as no more than 14,000 Confederates attacked the Union position on May 31. In the midst of the assault, Johnston sustained a wound that incapacitated him and led to the elevation of Robert E. Lee to command the Confederacy's principal eastern army. In characterizing Johnston's conduct during the Peninsula campaign, one historian referred to him as "weak-kneed," an unfair charge considering the circumstances.[38] Johnston had little choice but to retreat toward Richmond in the face of the Federals' superior artillery and naval power that allowed them to dominate the James and York rivers. When McClellan finally gave him an opportunity to launch an attack Johnston did so at Seven Pines.

Interestingly, when Lee took command, the army at his disposal was significantly augmented with reinforcements from North Carolina, South Carolina, Georgia, and Stonewall Jackson's command in the Shenandoah Valley. In all, Lee's army increased to a total of about 92,000 men, nearly 40,000 more than Johnston led at Seven Pines. Afterwards, Johnston implied that had he been granted the opportunity to lead such a formidable force as the one Lee marshaled during the Seven Days battles from June 25 to July 1, he would have stood a similar chance of the success that Lee achieved when he drove McClellan back down the Virginia

37 *O.R.* vol. 11, pt. 3, 536; Joseph E. Johnston, "Manassas to Seven Pines," *Battles and Leaders of the Civil War* (New York, 1956), II:210–211; Symonds, *Joseph E. Johnston*, 161. McDowell returned to Fredericksburg the next day, but Johnston still planned an assault on Keyes.

38 Johnston, "Manassas to Seven Pines," 212.; Symonds, *Joseph E. Johnston* 163–165; Woodworth, *Jefferson Davis and his Generals*, 178.

peninsula.[39] Historians may justifiably wonder whether Johnston would have demonstrated the audacity Lee manifested during the Seven Days, but it is fair to suggest that his opportunity to defeat McClellan under such circumstances would have been significantly increased.

Perhaps a more important question concerns Davis's motivation for delivering reinforcements to Lee after he failed to extend the same courtesy to Johnston. Davis's unwillingness to accede to Johnston's repeated requests for reinforcements indicates that the president already held reservations about Johnston's willingness to take the offensive. Davis wasted little time in granting Lee more authority than his predecessor. On June 2, only two days after Johnston was wounded at Seven Pines, Davis gave Lee authority over the armies in eastern Virginia (Johnston's former army) and in North Carolina. The addition of troops from North Carolina gave Lee a larger pool from which to draw troops than Johnston had while in command on the peninsula. Yet Lee did not suggest any offensive action at that time. Lee's initial proposal, on June 5, called for sending reinforcements to Jackson in the valley to permit him to advance into Pennsylvania while Lee remained on the defensive in front of McClellan. The same communication insisted that Lee required 100,000 men to "resist the siege of Richmond, which perhaps would only prolong" the siege but not save the city.[40] If Lee's calculations were correct, Johnston had done a remarkable job on the Peninsula with about half as many men as Lee thought necessary for the capital's defense.

While he never regained command of what became known as the Army of Northern Virginia, the Peninsula campaign did not close the door on Joseph E. Johnston's career in the Confederate Army. In fact, despite the strained relationship between Johnston and his president, Davis continued to exhibit faith in Johnston's capability as an officer. Davis wrote to his wife in July 1862, "Genl. J.e. Johnston is steadily and rapidly improving. I wish he was able to take the field. Despite the critics who know military affairs by instinct, he is a good soldier, knows his troops, never brags even of what he did do and at this time would render most valuable service."[41] Clearly, in the summer of 1862, the relationship between Johnston and the president, while tense, remained viable.

In November 1862, after Johnston recovered from his wound, Davis appointed him to command the armies of Braxton Bragg in Chattanooga and John C. Pemberton in Vicksburg. In essence, Johnston held departmental command of

39 Stephen Sears, *The Gates of Richmond: The Peninsula Campaign* (New York, 1992), 195; Johnston, "Manassas to Seven Pines," 217; Johnston to Wigfall, Johnston to Wigfall folder, 1864, LC.

40 *O.R.* vol. 11, pt. 3, 571; Lee, *Lee's Dispatches*, 5–6.

41 *The Papers of Jefferson Davis*, VIII:265.

the Western theater. The arrangement suggests that Davis was considering moving toward a more centralized command system. Johnston, in a foreshadowing of the campaign for Atlanta, however, wasted little time in ruffling Davis's feathers in his new assignment. Upon his arrival at Chattanooga, Johnston immediately proposed a plan of action. His proposal echoed a plan Secretary of War George Randolph had offered prior to Johnston's arrival, advocating a unification of forces in the region for offensive maneuvers, which Davis had rejected. Davis was not opposed to such an offensive, but his displeasure with Randolph for issuing orders to Theophilius Holmes, commander of the Trans-Mississippi department, without running them by him first, precluded Davis from accepting the plan. In fact, the incident created such a disturbance within the administration that Randolph resigned his post on November 15. Johnston was fully aware that Davis had rejected the plan, having been informed by Randolph in a meeting on November 12.[42] Yet on November 24, the same day he officially received orders to take command of the departments then under Braxton Bragg and John C. Pemberton, he informed the administration of his intention to carry out the plan Davis had already rejected.

Johnston and Randolph believed that the army under Holmes in the Department of the Trans-Mississippi—not directly under Johnston's command—should be ordered to unite with General Pemberton's army in Vicksburg and attack the Federal army under Ulysses S. Grant. Davis's rejection of the Johnston-Randolph plan was strange considering his own communications with Holmes. Only one month earlier, on October 20, Davis had advocated cooperation between Holmes, Bragg, and Pemberton.[43] Yet Davis's rigid adherence to the departmental system meant that he was not willing to move beyond mere suggestions to departmental commanders unless he felt it absolutely necessary. He therefore rejected the Johnston-Randolph proposal in November.

Davis's trip to Vicksburg in December reminded him of the need for reinforcements to the theater should Grant commence an offensive. While touring the defensive works around the crucial Mississippi River bastion, the president observed firsthand the extensive nature of the lines. Johnston and Maj. Gen. Martin L. Smith, who were inspecting the fortifications along with Davis, insisted that a minimum of 20,000 more men were necessary to hold the lines of Vicksburg and Port Hudson to the south if Pemberton were to face Grant with an army in the field. Johnston once again urged the president to order troops from Holmes's

42 Woodworth, *Jefferson Davis and his Generals,* 180–181; Robert Garlick Hill Kean, *Inside the Confederate Government: The Diary of Robert Garlick Hill Kean, Head of the Bureau of War*, ed. Edward Younger (New York, 1957), 28–29.

43 *O.R.* vol. 17, pt. 2, 758; *O.R.* vol. 13, 890.

theater to Mississippi so that the combined force could take the offensive against Grant. Davis agreed to write Holmes, but in doing so merely requested that Holmes send 20,000 men, rather than ordering the transfer. Holmes considered the requirements of his own department more important and declined the president's invitation to detach such a large portion of the troops under his command.[44] As a result, the army under Pemberton remained woefully undermanned and incapable of taking the offensive.

Once again Johnston had promoted aggressive action and yet again he had been thwarted. He began to question his role as departmental commander and the level of authority the office held. In a letter to his friend Louis Wigfall he suggested that the commanders in his department (Pemberton and Bragg) were only nominally under his authority. Further, Johnston considered the administration's notion that he could personally take command of either of the two armies in his department "a very mischievous one in practice." The armies, he concluded, would thus have two commanding generals rather than one and could never effectively carry out a plan of operations, as the two generals might have very different ideas as to the proper course of action. Such an arrangement would also be personally demeaning to Pemberton or Bragg, who would have to accept a secondary role every time Johnston visited their army.[45] Additionally, Johnston noted that the administration expected him to take immediate command in the case of an emergency to either of the armies in his theater. He considered this a "ruinous" policy as it would be nearly impossible for him to "continue the system or plans of the other so well as that other [general]."

Finally, he argued that the two commands under his authority were so far apart that it was impractical to think that one could support the other in the event of a Federal advance. He complained that Lee's army in Virginia was closer to Bragg than Pemberton's forces were. Johnston suggested that reinforcements from Lee could reach Bragg in four days while it would take reinforcements from Pemberton at least six days to travel to Bragg's assistance. Any emergency that might necessitate a transfer of troops from Pemberton to Bragg or vice versa, "would certainly have passed long before their arrival." By March 4, Johnston learned that the Union army facing Bragg, under Gen. William Rosecrans, had received reinforcements from Virginia. Johnston hoped that Lee might send troops to Bragg to counter the movement.[46] Johnston understood that if Rosecrans could be reinforced from

44 Johnston, "Jefferson Davis and the Mississippi Campaign," *Battles and Leaders of the Civil War*, III:474; *O.R.* vol. 17, pt. 2, 783–784.

45 Johnston to Wigfall, March 4, 1863, LC.

46 Ibid., March 4, 8, 1863.

Virginia in four days (as he ultimately would be) a six-day transfer of soldiers from Pemberton's army to Chattanooga to counter the Federal concentration upon Bragg meant that Confederate hopes for success in the Western theater were tenuous.

To make matters worse, Davis adopted the harmful policy of permitting Bragg and Pemberton to communicate directly with the War Department thereby forgoing the customary practice that all such correspondence go through Johnston's headquarters. A practice that he perpetuated during the campaign for Atlanta when he instructed John Bell Hood to communicate directly with the administration regarding Johnston's performance as commander of the army. As a result, Johnston often remained unaware of the needs of the armies he purportedly commanded.[47] The arrangement did not comport with the administration's claim that Johnston held the highest military position in the Confederacy; if that were the case, both Bragg and Pemberton should have been ordered to follow custom and communicate through Johnston. Consequently, Johnston's uncertainty about the nature of his new position and the authority he wielded was well-founded. Even so, his multitude of complaints demonstrates that Johnston again desired to minimize his culpability in the case of Confederate defeat.

Jefferson Davis compounded Johnston's disquiet regarding his amorphous command when he ordered reinforcements from Bragg's army sent to Vicksburg without consulting his purported departmental commander. After traveling to Chattanooga to assess the situation for himself in December 1862, Davis determined that the Union army facing Bragg showed no signs of aggression. He therefore decided that a force of 8,000 should be sent to Pemberton. When Johnston learned of the president's decision, he objected under the belief that the Federal forces facing either Bragg or Pemberton would attack while the reinforcements were in transit. Johnston also lamented that Davis's decision meant that he could not hope to unite Holmes's and Pemberton's troops as his initial proposal envisioned.[48]

As was the case on the Virginia peninsula, the president's departmental system produced confusing results. Yet again, two individuals were responsible for directing operations within the department—Davis and Johnston. In this case, the president had not even informed Johnston of his decision to send 8,000 men from Bragg to Pemberton. Davis had further complicated the matter by permitting Bragg and Pemberton to communicate directly with the administration, leaving Johnston in the dark. Further, Davis's willingness to issue orders compelling the

47 McMurry, "The Enemy at Richmond," 9; Symonds, *Joseph E. Johnston*, 188.

48 *O.R.* vol. 20, pt. 2, 449–450; Johnston to Wigfall, Dec. 15, 1863, LC.

transfer of troops from Bragg illustrates that he was not afraid to use his presidential prerogative as commander-in-chief of the Confederacy's armed forces. Seen in this light, Davis's failure to do the same with respect to Holmes is puzzling. In any event, the contest over the proper locale from which to acquire reinforcements for Vicksburg increased the tensions between the two men.

This most recent confrontation between the president and his commander developed not because either man failed to appreciate the situation, but because of a failure in departmental design; a deficiency that Davis would manifest again during the Atlanta campaign. Had Johnston's assignment included Holmes's department, the outcome of the campaign might have been dramatically different. Indeed, Johnston persistently advocated a transfer of forces from the Trans-Mississippi to Pemberton's army so that the combined army could advance upon Grant. Davis's failure to include Holmes's department within Johnston's sphere of command hamstrung his general. War Bureau chief Robert G. H. Kean believed that Davis's "fatal notion of making each military department a separate nation for military purposes without subordination, cooperation, or concert," cost the Confederacy the state of Mississippi.[49]

In March 1863, in the aftermath of the Union victory at the battle of Murfreesboro between the forces of William Rosecrans and Braxton Bragg, the administration ordered Johnston to take charge of Bragg's army in Tennessee. Bragg had been summoned to Richmond and there was a movement afoot to have him replaced as commander of the Army of Tennessee. Johnston's presence with the Army of Tennessee meant that his ability to direct affairs in Vicksburg suffered greatly. Meanwhile, Davis continued to send orders to Pemberton via new Secretary of War James Seddon or Adjutant General Cooper without informing Johnston. Johnston considered the practice unacceptable and informed the War Department of his displeasure. Johnston's illness in April likely influenced Davis's practice of micromanaging affairs at Vicksburg. Johnston informed him that he was too weak to assume field command in Tennessee or to direct Pemberton's operations in Mississippi.[50] Even so, if Johnston truly held the highest position

49 Kean, *Inside the Confederate Government*, 72.

50 Johnston, *Narrative of Military Operations*, 163; Symonds, *Joseph E. Johnston*, 200, 202. Before Bragg was able to leave for Richmond his wife became ill with typhoid fever and he requested permission to stay with her. Johnston agreed, but formally took command of the army; Kean, *Inside the Confederate Government*, 50. Though Kean believed that Johnston was correct in the substance of his complaint, he thought Johnston's communication skills left much to be desired. Kean characterized the general as "a very little man" and "eaten up with morbid jealousy of Lee." See Kean, *Inside the Confederate Government*, 50; *The Papers of Jefferson Davis*, IX:137; Johnston to Wigfall, Nov. 12, 1863, LC.

in the Confederate military as Davis claimed, his refusal to consult with his chief general lacked professionalism and common sense.

In mid-April, Grant commenced his campaign against Vicksburg in earnest, but Johnston remained in his sickbed. By May 9 the situation for the Confederates in Vicksburg had become dire and Davis ordered Johnston to proceed immediately to Vicksburg and take command of the forces there, "giving to those in the field, as far as practicable, the encouragement and benefit of your personal direction." The directive reveals that despite the often fractious relationship between the president and his commander, Davis still considered Johnston an extremely capable officer. By the time Johnston arrived at Jackson on May 13 he faced a serious dilemma. Brigadier General John Gregg informed him that William T. Sherman and a force of four Federal divisions stood between his small army of approximately 6,000 men in Jackson and Pemberton's command, then at Edwards Station.[51] From the time of his appointment to the department, Johnston had sought to forge a combination of forces against Grant and he tried his best to accomplish that goal with the forces available to him in the region.

With the Federal force between Edwards Station and Jackson numbering approximately 20,000 men, Johnston could not hope to launch an assault with his own meager command Instead, he determined to unite the Confederate forces in the vicinity which, if accomplished, would have given him numerical superiority over Grant's combined army of approximately 33,000 at that time. Pemberton commanded 23,000 men then at Edwards Station with 8,000 additional troops in the garrison at Vicksburg. Meanwhile, Johnston expected reinforcements during the night of May 13, giving his own command approximately 15,000 troops.[52] A combination of Confederate forces would have given Johnston a significant numerical advantage over Grant.

As he had done at Manassas, Johnston acted boldly and ordered Pemberton to advance upon Sherman's rear with as many men as he could muster. Then Johnston would make an effort to cooperate with his own force in Jackson. Upon receipt of the order on the morning of May 14, Pemberton informed Johnston that he

51 Johnston, *Narrative of Military Operations*, 172; *O.R.* vol. 24, pt. 3, 870; *O.R.* vol. 24, pt. 1, 261. In "Jefferson Davis and the Mississippi Campaign," Johnston identified the force as belonging to James McPherson. See Johnston, "Jefferson Davis and the Mississippi Campaign," 478. In reality, the force standing between Johnston and Pemberton was a combination of two divisions from William Tecumseh Sherman's Corps and two divisions from James McPherson's Corps. See Michael Ballard, *Vicksburg: The Campaign That Opened the Mississippi* (Chapel Hill, NC, 2004), 274.

52 See *O.R.* vol. 24, pt. 3, 249 for the April 30 returns for Grant's army; Ulysses S. Grant," The Vicksburg Campaign," *Battles and Leaders of the Civil War*, III:495; Johnston, "Jefferson Davis and the Mississippi Campaign," 479.

would proceed immediately with his available force of 16,000 men. Another 1,500 soldiers, then fifteen to twenty miles behind his main column, would follow. He intended to leave a brigade at Big Black River Bridge and the garrison in Vicksburg in place to guard against any Union advance. Pemberton, however, failed to follow through with his promise. Rather than obeying his superior's order, Pemberton convened a council of war consisting of his general officers to assess the situation. After producing Johnston's order, Pemberton expressed opposition on the grounds that Johnston's proposal threatened the immediate security of Vicksburg. A majority of those present favored compliance with Johnston's directive, while a minority thought the army ought to seize the enemy's lines of communication along the road from Jackson to Port Gibson and compel Grant to attack them there. Pemberton determined to adopt the minority plan, in direct violation of his departmental commander's orders.[53]

That day, May 14, the Federals attacked Johnston at Jackson, who held them with his small force until Grant took advantage of his overwhelming numbers and ordered Sherman to march on the Confederate flank. With a threat to his flank and rear, Johnston abandoned Jackson and moved north toward Tougaloo. Despite the loss of Jackson, Johnston still hoped to unite Confederate forces in the region. On May 17 Johnston ordered Pemberton to evacuate Vicksburg and join his own army, thereby saving Pemberton's force from suffering a siege and ultimate capture. Johnston understood that the order would meet with hostility in Richmond, but he later recalled, "I was satisfied that the Confederacy could do without General Johnston, while I did not believe it could do without the veteran army under General Pemberton." Pemberton again ignored his superior's orders and decided to hold Vicksburg. At the time, Pemberton's actions provoked censure from the president. Davis endorsed a letter from Johnston that blamed Pemberton for failing to follow orders, thereby losing an opportunity to strike a crippling blow to the Federal forces.[54] Ultimately, Pemberton's actions resulted in a series of battles in which Grant drove his army into the defenses around Vicksburg. Yet again Johnston's inclination to unite all available forces and take offensive action, as he had advocated on the Virginia peninsula and again when appointed to departmental command in the West, suffered from forces beyond his control.

By the close of May, Grant's army near Vicksburg numbered about 50,000 and expected reinforcements. Indeed, reinforcements arrived so quickly that during the first week of June Grant's army stood at 77,000. To confront Grant, the

53 Ibid., 261–262.

54 Grant, "The Vicksburg Campaign," 505–506; *O.R.* vol. 24, pt. 1, 272; Govan and Livingood, *A Different Valor*, 225; Johnston, "Jefferson Davis and the Mississippi Campaign," 479.

Confederates now had 31,000 men under Pemberton in Vicksburg and around 23,000 under Johnston near Jackson, Mississippi.[55] In addition to numerical inferiority, the Confederates suffered from disrupted communications between the two commands (Johnston and Pemberton), as Grant's army had by that time encircled Vicksburg.

Johnston, concerned about the prospects for a successful conclusion to the campaign, sent a series of dispatches to the president requesting reinforcements. Davis responded by asserting that Johnston surely had greater numbers than he admitted and that the time to act was at hand, as the enemy would probably gain future reinforcements. Johnston persisted in requesting additional men, to which Davis responded that as theater commander he could order that troops be sent from Bragg's army in Tennessee. Johnston replied that such an action would result in the loss of Middle Tennessee, as Bragg could not hope to hold off the Federal army in his front under those circumstances. Johnston insisted that the administration, not he, must determine whether to lose Mississippi or Tennessee, and that he did not have the authority to make such a decision.[56]

Johnston's premise seems odd, as it was based on a false assumption. He erroneously claimed that the administration's act ordering him from Tennessee to Mississippi on May 9 constituted a permanent change in his status, and that he no longer commanded the department the administration had designed specifically for him in November and which included both Pemberton's and Bragg's armies. Rather, he now commanded only the "department of Mississippi." Neither Davis nor anyone else in the administration had ever suggested that in ordering Johnston to Mississippi he no longer held any responsibility for the Army of Tennessee. If the administration had never issued a specific order that changed Johnston's status, his interpretation makes little sense. In fact, on June 15 Davis explicitly informed Johnston that his interpretation lacked substance and that he remained in the capacity assigned him in November.[57] Johnston's refusal to order reinforcements from Bragg's army to Mississippi also contrasted with his philosophy that land could always be regained, and that the security of an army was more important than geographical concerns.

In reality, Johnston simply did not want to be held responsible for the political fallout should either Tennessee or Vicksburg be lost as a result of his orders. By

55 Samuel Carter III, *The Final Fortress: The Campaign for Vicksburg, 1862–1863* (New York, 239); Symonds, *Joseph E. Johnston*, 211; *O.R.* vol. 24, pt. 1, 222–223. According to Davis, Johnston's strength was closer to 32,000. See Davis, *The Rise and Fall of the Confederate Government,* II:412.

56 *O.R.* vol. 24, pt. 1, 194–195, 223–224, 226; Johnston to Wigfall, Aug. 12, 1863, LC.

57 Johnston to Wigfall, Aug. 12, 1863, LC; *The Papers of Jefferson Davis,* IX:218–219.

the middle of June, Johnston probably believed that Vicksburg was doomed to fall. He was not alone in that assessment. Ulysses S. Grant noted that he had "a large surplus of troops over what was required to make the investment complete," and that Sherman's line of defense against any enemy approaching from the east (Johnston) was virtually impregnable.[58] If Vicksburg fell, Johnston could place the blame squarely on Pemberton who had refused to follow his orders on either May 13 or May 17. Had he ordered troops from Tennessee and Rosecrans had then defeated Bragg, no one but Johnston would have been held accountable. Johnston undoubtedly considered himself in a position not of his own making and hoped to limit any damage to his reputation.

In hopes of salvaging the situation, Johnston continued to agitate for reinforcements in Mississippi. His repeated requests caused Davis some discomfort and prompted him to communicate that he was making every effort possible. In truth, Davis had not exhausted his options. The president's refusal to admit a mistake that led to the resignation of Secretary of War Randolph continued to plague the Confederate defense of Vicksburg. Richard Taylor, operating in Louisiana as part of the Department of the Trans-Mississippi, now under the command of Edmund Kirby Smith, reported on June 11 the availability of a large force along the west bank of the Mississippi for the purpose of defeating Grant. Taylor also suggested that there were then sufficient forces in the lower portion of the state to carry out an expedition against the enemy besieging Port Hudson. It is difficult to understand Davis's decision to ignore the availability of troops from the Trans-Mississippi. Robert Kean believed that the argument with Randolph in November caused the president's refusal to consider transferring troops from west of the Mississippi. For Davis to order Smith or Taylor to advance against Grant in June would be tantamount to an admission that he had been wrong in the first place.[59]

On June 15 Secretary of War James Seddon insisted that Johnston "hazard an attack," as the honor of the Confederacy demanded the retention of Vicksburg. Davis also demanded immediate action against the Union forces surrounding the Mississippi bastion. In spite of the administration's prodding, Johnston refused to attack an entrenched foe that outnumbered him more than two to one. Instead, Johnston conceived a plan that he hoped would save the army in Vicksburg. Johnston intended to divert Grant's attention with a feint, while Pemberton

58 Ulysses S. Grant to John M. Schofield, July 15, 1863, John M. Schofield Papers, Library of Congress.

59 Davis, *Jefferson Davis, Constitutionalist*, V:527–528; *O.R.* vol. 24, pt. 2, 461; Kean, *Inside the Confederate Government*, 80.

attempted to fight his way out of the city. On July 3, Johnston informed Pemberton that he hoped to commence the movement on July 7. Pemberton, however, surrendered the Vicksburg garrison to Grant the following day. Having learned of the availability of forces in the Trans-Mississippi, James Seddon commented that "there was more blame [for the loss of Vicksburg] on the command on the west than on the east side of the river."[60]

Nevertheless, Johnston's perceived failure to rescue Pemberton's besieged army gave Davis a scapegoat for the subsequent loss of the city. A paper war concerning the conduct of the campaign erupted between Davis and Johnston, the results of which further damaged their already troubled relationship. Mary Chesnut, whose husband served on Davis's staff, noted that "the president detests Joe Johnston for all the trouble he has given him and General Joe returns the compliment with compound interest. His hatred of Jeff Davis amounts to a religion." In fact, Davis was so angered over the loss of Vicksburg that when an acquaintance remarked that the city had apparently been lost for want of provisions, Davis replied curtly, "yes from want of provisions inside and general outside who wouldn't fight." Johnston harbored equally venomous feelings toward the president in the aftermath of the Vicksburg campaign. He chafed at the "slander of the 'organ' [presumably the administration] and underlings at the War Department." He referred to a letter from the president on July 15 as "the coolest piece of impudence I have ever read," which accused him of "various official sins of commission and omission."[61]

Pemberton added fuel to the fire when he submitted his report of the campaign blaming Johnston for the loss of Vicksburg. Johnston did not discover the existence of Pemberton's official report until September, when he read an article written by Pemberton in the Montgomery *Advertiser and Register* that made reference to the report. Johnston objected that Pemberton's failure to submit the report first to Johnston as his commanding officer deviated from standard procedure. Pemberton's claims incensed Johnston so much that he accused the former of engaging in "untruth and the great exaggeration," and having "published a false statement of a military matter."[62]

60 *O.R.* vol. 24, pt. 1, 227; Davis to Johnston, June 15, 1863, JP, WM; According to Johnston, Pemberton met with him after the fall of Vicksburg and in the presence of several other officers, including W. H. L. Walker, and Pemberton's own Inspector General, Lou Taylor, admitted that an attack against Grant would have been folly as he would have been able to repulse 100,000 men. See Johnston to Wigfall, Dec. 3, 1863, LC; *O.R.* vol. 24, pt. 3, 987; Kean, *Inside the Confederate Government*, 80.

61 Woodward, *Mary Chesnut's Civil War*, 482–483; Josiah Gorgas, Diary, July 17, 1863, Library of Congress; Johnston to Wigfall, Sept. 15, 1863, LC.

62 *O.R.* vol. 24, pt. 1, 249–295; Johnston to Wigfall, Nov. 26, 1863, LC; *O.R.* vol. 24, pt. 3, 1061.

Johnston's indignation at Pemberton's actions lacked authenticity as he had encouraged similar behavior from his own staff. On July 18, a letter signed "Vindicus" appeared in the *Memphis Appeal*, then published in Atlanta, which went to great lengths to defend Johnston's conduct during the campaign. In defending Johnston, the author lambasted Pemberton's refusal to follow orders and his subsequent retreat into the defenses of Vicksburg. Davis recognized that the details of the letter strongly suggested that the author had access to Johnston's headquarters. Consequently, the president sought to discover the culprit. Soon thereafter a copy of a similar letter rumored to have been authored by a member of Johnston's staff circulated in Richmond. Davis asked Johnston to explain and discovered that the author was Dr. David Yandell, Johnston's medical director, who also confessed responsibility for the original letter in the *Appeal*. Yandell insisted that the correspondence had been intended to remain private, but apparently Johnston encouraged a correspondent from the *Appeal* to copy the letter and publish it.[63]

By the end of the summer of 1863, the relationship between Joseph E. Johnston and Jefferson Davis seemed irreconcilable. Johnston's animus toward the president had originated in the dispute over rank that predated the war. Davis's rejection of Johnston's plans on the Virginia peninsula in 1862 exacerbated the general's distrust of the commander-in-chief. Finally, the Vicksburg campaign and the consequent fallout over blame for the loss of the Mississippi bastion cemented Johnston's negative opinion of Davis. Though Davis's hostility toward Johnston emerged only after the commencement of the war, it was no less palpable. Davis's discomfort with his general materialized first as a result of Johnston's complaints that Robert E. Lee lacked authority to give him (Johnston) orders. Davis's anger inspired his awkward interpretation of legislation granting him the power to name generals. He subsequently ranked Johnston fourth on the list of full generals despite the statutory guidelines that required otherwise. Johnston's refusal to communicate during much of his retreat up the peninsula in 1862 deepened the president's misgivings about his commander. Ultimately, Johnston's unwillingness to assault Grant at Vicksburg embittered the president, who blamed Johnston for the loss of the city. When Davis had no alternative but to appoint Johnston as commander of the Army of Tennessee in December 1863, the relationship between the two men afforded little encouragement for the upcoming spring campaign.

63 *The Papers of Jefferson Davis*, IX:314. See footnote 1; Rowland, *Jefferson Davis, Constitutionalist*, V:464–465.

Executives at Odds

Nor did the president's relationship with another prominent Confederate personality inspire optimism for the future. From the inception of the Confederate States of America, the struggle over the role and authority of the central government had plagued the Davis administration, and never more so than in its dealings with Joseph E. Brown, the governor of Georgia. Brown maintained a doctrinaire states' rights mantra throughout the war that routinely placed him at odds with the Davis administration. Within two months of Georgia's secession from the Union, the governor had leveled a multitude of complaints against what he deemed the administration's improper usurpation of state authority. Brown lodged grievances against the administration for a variety of abuses including the mustering and arming of troops, appointment of officers, and the passage of the Conscription Act. As the years passed, hostility between Governor Brown and President Davis rivaled that between the president and his primary commander in the Western theater, Joseph E. Johnston. With Sherman's army preparing to advance into Georgia in the spring of 1864, their mutual antagonism influenced the state's ability to repel the Federal advance. In particular, the dispute over the state militia deprived Joseph E. Johnston of a valuable resource against Sherman's repeated flanking movements.

As early as April 2, 1861, Brown had protested the administration's policy of mustering state troops into the Provisional Army of the Confederacy. The administration had called upon Brown to send troops to Pensacola, Florida, where they would be mustered into the provisional army. Brown objected and demanded that the central government muster the Georgia troops within the state borders. The administration responded the following day that it would not grant Georgia any special treatment that it did not extend to the other Confederate states, and consequently the Georgia troops could only be mustered into service upon arrival at Pensacola. On April 4, Brown informed the administration that he had managed to convince the troops to accept the administration's requirement in the face of "much difficulty." The Georgians apparently worried that some might not be accepted into the provisional army and would have to return home over a great distance. Brown refused to let the matter rest, however, and a week later insisted that future requisitions of state troops required that officials from the provisional army muster Georgia troops into service within state lines. The governor asserted that he wished to accommodate the Confederate government's troop requisitions, but that Georgia "insisted on having her rights respected."

Not only did Brown demand that the Confederate government muster Georgia troops within the state, he also continued raising troops in accordance with a Georgia law that conflicted with Confederate law. Brown knew that Section

4 of the Confederate legislation establishing the provisional army allowed forces tendered by states to "be received, with their officers, by companies, battalions, or regiments." Nevertheless, he persisted in organizing troops by brigades with the intention of forming two separate Georgia divisions under the command of his own appointees, Henry Jackson and William H. T. Walker. Secretary of War L. P. Walker rejected Brown's ploy and informed him on April 29 that "the organization of brigades and divisions belong to the president."[64]

The acquisition of arms also became a point of contention in the early stages of the conflict. With war on the horizon, Brown endeavored to secure adequate weaponry for state troops. His efforts included the purchase of muskets overseas, a practice that meant competition with agents in the service of the Confederate government. Davis considered the practice hazardous to the Confederacy when Brown's efforts caused an inflation in gun prices. The president's protests made little impression on Brown and he continued purchasing guns for state defense. In April 1862, Governor Brown charged the administration with the "illegal seizure" of 3,400 Enfield rifles from England belonging to Georgia. The administration expressed regret and promised to correct the mistake but noted that General Lee intended to arm Georgia regiments with the rifles. On May 7, 1862, Brown accused the administration of failing to compensate him for the Enfields and threatened that unless the Confederate government made good on its promise he would resort to counter-seizures as the only means of redress.[65]

The governor's clash with the administration did not end with the acquisition of weapons but carried over to their retention as well. In order to accelerate the establishment of an army, the Confederate Congress passed a law in mid-May 1861 that permitted a tender of troops directly to the Confederacy without the requirement to first tender to the state. Brown believed that the statute struck at the heart of the Confederacy and denied the rights of states. In a fit of jealousy over what he deemed a usurpation of constitutional authority, Brown determined to strike back and assert state sovereignty by any means available. The state, he reasoned, had equipped the recruits and now he demanded that those weapons remain in Georgia. The governor issued a proclamation in May 1861 stating that companies that tendered for service out of state could not take their muskets with them once they left Georgia. Secretary of War Walker offered the remaining muskets in the Confederate States arsenal in Augusta as compensation. Brown

64 *C. R. Ga.*, III, 37, 39, 46–47, 18–19; Parks, *Joseph E. Brown of Georgia*, 141; *O.R.* Ser. 4, vol. 1, 238.

65 Elam, "The Road to Atlanta," 239–240; *C. R. Ga.*, III, 177–178, 180. Apparently Lee did in fact issue the Enfield rifles to Georgia troops in Knoxville, Tennessee. See *C. R. Ga.*, III, 226.

rejected the proposal and claimed that the outdated conversion muskets left over in the Augusta arsenal failed to compensate the state adequately. As a result, many Georgia recruits arrived in Virginia without any weapons. The administration complained that it lacked the ability to arm the men upon their arrival in Virginia. Brown finally relented, to some extent, and agreed to send troops armed with 1842 model smoothbore muskets.[66] In so doing, Brown clearly hoped that all state-purchased rifled muskets would be used only for state defense. He also demonstrated his willingness to endanger the security of the Confederacy to prove a point about state sovereignty. Brown's policy was myopic and failed to consider that an insufficiently armed force in Virginia might very well result in the rapid loss of the upper South and leave Georgia on the front line of the conflict.

In the beginning of June 1861, Brown escalated the dispute when he threatened the arrest of any company that violated his orders and entered Confederate service with muskets taken from Georgia. The Georgia executive asserted that he was "anxious to have the spirit of insubordination to the state checked." The administration conceded and informed Brown that they would accept future tenders of troops to the provisional army even without weapons. Nevertheless, when the governor discovered that some muskets had slipped through his grasp, he demanded their return. On June 27, 1861, Brown informed the president that a company known as the Floyd Sharpshooters in transit to Virginia were in possession of state-purchased muskets in violation of his orders. He demanded that the president immediately send the weapons to Atlanta. Despite the fact that Brown permitted thousands of muskets to leave the state with troops he had expressly tendered to the Confederate service, he refused to abide weapons leaving the state without his permission. The dispute between Brown and Davis concerning the acquisition and distribution of weapons became public when Georgia and Richmond papers published stories on the matter. Brown objected and charged that the articles implied a lack of patriotism on his part, an allegation that the administration denied.[67]

Even when Davis attempted to ameliorate the deficiencies in militia armaments throughout the Confederacy, Brown impeded his endeavor. In the summer of 1863, the War Department recognized that militia regiments tasked with state defense lacked uniform weapons. Indeed, most regiments possessed an assortment of weapons often with varying calibers, which made supply difficult. To address

66 *C. R. Ga.*, III, 80–81, 89–90. The remaining muskets were converted flintlocks that had little value. Parks, *Joseph E. Brown*, 146.

67 *C. R. Ga.*, III, 92–93, 94–95, 98–99, 115; Parks, *Joseph E. Brown*, 152; Louise Biles Hill, *Joseph E. Brown and the Confederacy* (1891; repr, Westport, CT, 1939), 71.

the problem, the administration issued 1,500 Austrian Lorenz rifles to the state of Georgia. Rather than distributing the weapons to his militia, Brown retained almost all of them in case of future emergency. He issued only 100 of the rifles to the most poorly equipped of the militia companies.[68]

Yet another point of contention emerged during the first months of the war that centered on the appointment of officers. The Georgia governor never wavered in his commitment to organize troops for service in the Confederate army, but he insisted that the state reserved the authority to appoint officers to regiments proffered into Confederate service. On March 15, 1861, Secretary of War Walker accepted the governor's interpretation of the Confederate statute authorizing the requisition of troops, but only insofar as it concerned regimental officers for the 2,000 men that the Confederate government requested of Georgia. The president, Walker declared, would appoint general officers.[69] At the end of June, the administration called for the establishment of a reserve army corps of 30,000 soldiers and apportioned 3,000 of that number to Georgia. Additionally, the administration requested that the states only furnish organized companies rather than full regiments. The new requisition meant that state governors retained authority only for the appointment of junior officers and could not appoint regimental commanders.

Brown vehemently objected, but he agreed under protest to send the troops. Brown based his objection on the theory that the Confederacy could only raise troops through either individual enlistment in the regular army or requisitions on the states. He argued that those enlisted by way of requisition to the state were militia. Because they were militia, the governor retained the authority to appoint their officers.[70] Brown's assertion that any troops organized in Georgia and then tendered into Confederate service constituted militia played a pivotal role in the governor's interpretation of the Confederate Conscription Act.

The passage of the Conscription Act in April 1862 led to a much deeper rift between Davis and Brown than any previous argument. Brown asserted that the act was unconstitutional and propagated for the purpose of giving Davis power over state troops and authority to appoint officers. Brown claimed the legislation established the president as a military despot. In particular, Brown realized that the act meant that the states were no longer responsible for organizing regiments. Instead that task now belonged to Confederate military officers. Further, the Confederacy now had the power to take whatever manpower from the states that

68 William Harris Bragg, *Joe Brown's Army: The Georgia State Line, 1862–1865* (Macon, GA, 1987), 66.

69 *O.R.* Ser. 4, vol. 1, 166–167.

70 *C. R. Ga.*, III, 104–106, 108–110; Hill, *Joseph E. Brown and the Confederacy*, 55.

they deemed necessary—thereby leaving the state with few options in organizing its own defense. Davis went to great lengths to assuage Governor Brown's concerns with respect to conscription. In addition to corresponding with the Georgian, Davis sent envoys in hopes of convincing Brown that the need for soldiers outweighed the need for state sovereignty. Yet the act was more than just an attempt to shift authority to the central government; it was also an attack on the governor's pride. No longer was he responsible for the recruitment of Georgia troops, a task he relished. Brown incessantly bragged about the number of regiments he had raised, a duty the act transferred to Confederate recruiting officers.[71] Consequently, Brown considered passage of the Conscription Act a personal attack.

The governor opened his assault on the legislation on April 22, 1862, and continued his attacks through July. Brown contended that the Confederate Constitution reserved the recruitment and training of the militia to the individual states and that the power to appoint officers rested with the governor of each state. Further, the governor claimed that the power of Congress to raise armies did not encompass "armies composed of the whole militia of all the states." Brown insisted that the latter was precisely the manner in which Confederate armies had been recruited. Davis defended the law and noted that large majorities in both houses supported the legislation. The president provided a detailed response to each of Brown's claims and concluded that the governor erred in his interpretation of the law.

Brown, however, refused to relent without a fight. The governor claimed he would not throw obstacles in the way of enforcement, but neither would he assist the central government in its endeavor. Even so, he argued that state officers could not be held subject to the act. He therefore instructed militia officers to exempt themselves from conscription and threatened the arrest of any Confederate enlistment officer who disobeyed his edict. Secretary of War Randolph capitulated and exempted militia officers in all states of the Confederacy. The decision prompted a newspaper correspondent from the *Savannah Republican* to suggest that Randolph had yielded to a madman and that the governor's recklessness threatened civil war in Georgia.[72]

In September the Confederate Congress amended the conscription law and authorized the president to suspend the act anywhere he deemed enforcement impractical. The provision emboldened Brown, who demanded that Davis obtain Georgia troops only through requisition. In addition, he informed the president that he refused to allow enforcement of the second conscription act until such time

71 Parks, *Joseph E. Brown*, 198; Hill, *Joseph E. Brown and the Confederacy*, 79. See footnote 2.

72 *C. R. Ga.*, III, 192–198, 214, 233–246, 228–230; Hill, *Joseph E. Brown and the Confederacy*, 83.

as the Georgia legislature judged it appropriate. Davis took matters into his own hands and presented the case to the Georgia courts, and the state supreme court ruled in the president's favor. Brown thereafter attempted to convince the state legislature that outside influences had rendered the court's decision unenforceable, but a majority sided with the court. Having lost his argument, Brown remained petulant and exempted all state officers from conscription. The exemptions included individuals elected or appointed to inconsequential offices such as constable and public notary.[73] Though previous disagreements had caused friction between the Confederate president and the Georgia governor, the dispute over conscription virtually destroyed any hope for future cooperation. Furthermore, Brown's committed defense of state draft exemptions crippled the formation of the militia once Sherman advanced in the spring of 1864. The lack of Georgia militia severely hampered Johnston's defense against Sherman's flanking marches and played a significant role in the Union capture of Atlanta.

Consequently, as the year 1864 dawned, Jefferson Davis's poor rapport with both his chief general in the West and the governor of the state in which the campaign was likely to take place threatened to derail the Confederacy's hope for success. Davis's history with Johnston in particular revealed significant flaws in the president's leadership. Not only had Davis failed to establish a centralized command structure, he had interfered with Johnston's ability to conduct affairs in his own theater of operations. On the peninsula, Davis had deprived Johnston of access to troops in his theater. During Johnston's service as departmental commander in the West, Davis had again interfered. The result was a confusing system of command in which no one person seemed to possess final authority. Moreover, three years of war had produced a high level of animus between the president and his commander, particularly after the fall of Vicksburg. Yet Confederate prospects for 1864 depended largely on whether Davis and Johnston could work together and defeat William Tecumseh Sherman.

73 *O.R.* Ser. 4, vol. 2, 160; Hill, *Joseph E. Brown and the Confederacy*, 84, 85, 87–88; *C.R. Ga.*, II, 683–687.

Chapter 2

Reorganization of the Officer Corps: A Spy Is Born

Soon after designating Johnston as the new commander of the Army of Tennessee, Davis exhibited two salient characteristics that distinguished him from Abraham Lincoln. First, in February he appointed Bragg as his military advisor for no other discernible reason than their close relationship. While Lincoln had learned to promote officers based upon meritorious conduct and had even relieved generals with whom he had developed a close relationship, Davis permitted his loyalty to Bragg to influence his judgment. Bragg's poor performance while commanding the Army of Tennessee certainly did not entitle him to promotion to his new position. Furthermore, Bragg's temperament had generated hostility among many of the officers who had served under him. As a result, he was unable to provide impartial advice about his former army. In fact, Bragg's distaste for two of his former subordinates, Benjamin Cheatham and Patrick Cleburne, probably influenced the administration's unwillingness to promote them to corps command when Johnston sought to reorganize the army.

Second, Davis promoted the violation of the established protocol requiring all communications to go through the commanding officer. Davis's distrust of his new commander, particularly after Johnston refused to commit to an advance into Tennessee as the president desired, led him to promote John Bell Hood to corps command. Thereafter Davis instructed Hood to keep the administration advised regarding the strength and condition of the army. As a result, Davis created a scenario that threatened to undermine the relationship between two of the army's most important officers—Johnston and Hood. In fairness, Hood's record in the field merited his promotion. Though Hood's wounds, received at Gettysburg and

Chickamauga, had resulted in moments of melancholy, they did not, as some suggest, lead to chemical dependency, nor to any emotional instability that made him unfit for command. While Hood deserved his promotion, he certainly lost no opportunity to further ingratiate himself with the president and his advisors with a series of telegrams, as Davis had suggested, that grew increasingly self-serving as spring neared. Consequently, as the war entered its fourth year, Davis failed to learn the important lessons that Lincoln had during the course of the conflict. Indeed, Davis's personal incompetencies left the Confederate command structure vulnerable to future discord as the campaign commenced.

Johnston's Effort to Reorganize the Army

On December 31, 1863, Johnston advocated for a reorganization of his two existing army corps into three to improve maneuverability. He also recommended Maj. Gen. H. C. Whiting's appointment as a lieutenant general to command the proposed additional corps. The communication made no recommendation as to the other corps commanders. Clearly, Johnston intended Lt. Gen. William Hardee to remain in his position as a corps commander. Johnston conveyed his intention to retain Hardee in that capacity on January 16, 1864.[1] He failed to identify a candidate for the final corps commander in his initial communication with the administration, but the omission appears to have been by design.

Johnston apparently hoped that by designating Thomas Hindman as a corps commander in the official returns for the Army of Tennessee and in communications between himself and the administration that the president would accept Hindman as a *fait accompli*. Hindman had received an assignment from Hardee to temporary command of a corps, while the latter was acting as interim commander of the Army of Tennessee. Johnston hoped to make the appointment permanent. In his telegram on January 16, Johnston not only referred to Hardee as a corps commander, but Hindman as well.[2] Even so, Johnston made no official application to the administration requesting Hindman's appointment as corps commander. Presumably Johnston was attempting to elevate Hindman *de facto* to the position because he believed Hindman to be a political ally.

Johnston's effort seems rational considering the fallout from Bragg's tenure as army commander. Under Bragg's leadership the officer corps in the Army of

1 *O.R.* vol. 31, pt. 3, 882; *O.R.* vol. 32, pt. 2, 563–564.

2 The returns for January 20, 1864, list Hindman as a corps commander. See *O.R.* vol. 32, pt. 2, 586; Diane Neal and Thomas Kremm, *Lion of the South: General Thomas Hindman* (Atlanta, 1993), 181; *O.R.* vol. 32, pt. 2, 563–564.

Tennessee had fractured into two competing camps: those who openly supported Bragg and those who considered the commanding general personally distasteful and professionally incompetent. Johnston found the fissures in the officer corps abhorrent and commented that his army suffered from "having the only general officers in the Confederacy who practice here against each other the acts to which they were accustomed to resort in electioneering before the war." He was so worried about the situation that when he heard a rumor that Bragg might be sent back to the army as his chief of staff, Johnston complained to Senator Louis T. Wigfall that to do so would "put him [Bragg] in a position of more direct intercourse with his enemies than that which he left."[3] Obviously, Johnston hoped to eliminate the infighting and to restore a high level of camaraderie among his officers. Johnston's attempt to appoint Hindman permanently to corps command therefore made sense.

Hindman's arrival to the Army of Tennessee on August 13, 1863, meant that he had little time to become embroiled in the rift within the officer corps prior to the engagement at Chickamauga a month later. The schism itself had developed in the fall of 1862 and eventually resulted in a cadre opposed to Bragg that included Leonidas Polk, Daniel Harvey Hill, Patrick Cleburne, Benjamin Cheatham, and John C. Breckinridge. Therefore, Hindman played no role in the origin of the anti-Bragg element in the army. Though Hindman and Cleburne had cultivated a friendship while living in Arkansas prior to the war, Hindman's wounding at Chickamauga prevented him from prolonged exposure to the army's internal quarreling. The fact that Hindman played a limited role, if any, in the infighting that plagued the army's officer corps certainly appealed to Johnston. Johnston lamented to Louis Wigfall that if it were up to him he would "distribute the generals of this army over the Confederacy."[4] Clearly Johnston hoped to address the existing conflict among his subordinates. Hindman's elevation to corps command would serve that purpose.

In addition to Johnston's effort to establish Hindman permanently as a corps commander, his January 16 telegram to Richmond suggested that he hoped the administration might consider Maj. Gen. Mansfield Lovell as a candidate for corps command. Lovell was Johnston's friend and remained so after the war.[5] Further, Lovell had not previously served in the Army of Tennessee and consequently could not be identified with any of the factions within the army's high command. If the administration had accepted Johnston's proposal and elevated both Hindman

3 Johnston to Louis Wigfall, Jan. 1864, December 27, 1863 LC.

4 Connelly, *Autumn of Glory*, 20–21,75–76; Johnston to Wigfall, Jan. 9, 1864, LC.

5 *O.R.* vol. 32, pt. 2, 563–564. After the conclusion of the war Johnston wrote to Lovell lamenting his inability to have Lovell assigned to his army to "command a corps." See Joseph E. Johnston to Mansfield Lovell, March 29, 1869, Mansfield Lovell Papers, Library of Congress.

and Lovell to corps command, Johnston would have successfully orchestrated a reorganization of the army's hierarchy in a manner that limited the fallout from Bragg's tenure as commander.

The proposal, however, was not without its drawbacks. Johnston's attempt to promote Lovell demonstrated his general ignorance of political matters. He neglected to consider the political backlash that was likely if an unpopular general received promotion. And Lovell was unpopular. He had been born in the North and had commanded the Confederate garrison in New Orleans when it fell to the Union in 1862. Lovell's loss of New Orleans led to a court of inquiry. Though the court eventually exonerated him from most of the charges, his public image suffered. Davis, unlike Johnston, considered the political consequences of the appointment. In discussing the matter with his secretary of war, James A. Seddon, he assented to Seddon's judgment that a promotion of Lovell would lead to disharmony within the ranks of the army.[6] As a result, the administration rejected Johnston's application for Lovell.

Davis also declined to elevate Hindman to the status of permanent corps command. The president gave no explicit reason for rejecting Hindman. In fact, Davis never specifically refused Johnston's effort to promote Hindman. Rather, Davis remained silent on the matter altogether. In all likelihood, Hindman's advocacy of arming slaves led to Davis's reservations about his fitness for corps command. In April of 1863, Hindman had written to the *Memphis Appeal* in support of manumission for slaves who offered to serve in the Confederate military. He reasoned that the Federals' use of Black soldiers had so augmented their numerical superiority that the Confederacy needed to adopt a similar posture. The proposal met with fierce opposition from Southerners, many of whom considered the suggestion scandalous and perhaps even treasonous.[7] Johnston's attempt to promote Hindman to corps command therefore stood little chance of success.

On January 23, 1864, Johnston again requested that the administration consider his proposal. This time, however, he suggested that the promotion could be extended to whomever was best qualified, including major generals serving

6 Woodworth, *Jefferson Davis and his Generals*, 112, 261. Interestingly, Thomas Hindman served as the president of the court during its inquiry into Lovell's conduct. While the court reprimanded Lovell in characterizing his orders for the evacuation of Chalmette as a "serious error," they noted that he "displayed a great energy and an untiring industry in performing his duties," as well as exhibiting a "high capacity for command and the clearest foresight in many of his measures for the defense of New Orleans." The court's ruling, therefore, vindicated much of Lovell's conduct and gave Lovell no reason to harbor animosity toward Hindman. See *O.R.* vol. 6, 553–554, 643; Jones, *A Rebel War Clerk's Diary at the Confederate States Capital*, 330–331.

7 Neal and Kremm, *Lion of the South*, 114.

in the Army of Tennessee. In doing so Johnston appears to have abandoned concerns over personality conflicts (dating back to Bragg's tenure) to encourage the administration's acceptance of his reorganization of the army into three corps. The administration ignored Johnston's latest request, however, and instead suggested a reorganization of Kentucky troops into a single mounted infantry unit. The administration's proposition emphasized the political benefit of such a policy: A successful Kentucky unit might help to generate increased political support in this divided and turbulent region.[8] The communication made no reference to Johnston's request regarding either his applications for a new corps commander or his proposal that the army be reorganized into three corps.

As the administration bided its time making a decision with respect to corps commanders, Johnston carried out what reorganization he could. For example, he returned several Tennessee brigades to Cheatham's division, thus restoring it to its original composition. Bragg had removed these units from the division after the battle of Chickamauga, claiming that the division's composition promoted state pride rather than Confederate pride. Johnston's decision resulted in an impromptu celebration, as the division marched to Johnston's headquarters and cheered him loudly.[9]

Johnston scored a second small triumph when the Davis administration appointed Joseph Wheeler to command the army's cavalry corps. The Texas and Kentucky delegations in the Senate had held up Wheeler's confirmation in support of their own nominee, John Wharton. Many of Wharton's supporters also counted themselves Johnston allies *vis-à-vis* his quarrels with Jefferson Davis. Among them was Louis Wigfall, who stubbornly resisted Wheeler's appointment. Davis had sought Johnston's support in the matter, in hopes that he might convince Wharton's advocates to abandon their cause. Johnston informed Wigfall that Wheeler's reputation in the army justified the president's nomination. In reality, Johnston only supported Wheeler's nomination because he considered him the best of the three candidates under consideration, not because he believed that Wheeler possessed immense talent.[10] The restoration of Cheatham's division and Joseph Wheeler's appointment as cavalry commander were two of the few victories that Johnston enjoyed in his reorganization efforts.

8 *O.R.* vol. 32, pt. 2, 604, 615–616.

9 E. J. Harvie, "Gen. Joseph E. Johnston," *Confederate Veteran* 18 (1910): 522.

10 Johnston to Wigfall, Jan. 9,, April 1, 5, 1864, LC. As it turned out, Johnston's support of Wheeler was misplaced. Wheeler proved himself incompetent during the campaign. He was particularly ineffective in operations around Dalton and Cassville. Moreover, his raid in August failed to accomplish its purpose of damaging Sherman's communications, and at the same time deprived Hood of a sufficient cavalry presence in Atlanta. *O.R.* vol. 52, pt. 2, 606.

In most cases the administration ignored his suggestions, even when it came to the appointment of brigadier generals. A. P. Stewart's division also required attention. Stewart had recently received a new brigade from Alabama that needed a commander. Johnston, believing that Stewart favored Col. James Holtzclaw for promotion, traveled to Stewart's headquarters in search of confirmation. Having received affirmation from Stewart's staff officer J. C. Thompson that Stewart desired Holtzclaw's promotion, Johnston nominated him for the position. The administration once more ignored Johnston's request and instead promoted Col. Alpheus Baker, "a stranger," as one of Johnston's staff officers referred to him, to brigade command.[11] The administration's promotion of Baker over Holtzclaw seems odd, unless the relationship between Johnston and Davis is taken into consideration. The fact that Davis was apparently petulant enough to reject Holtzclaw in favor of the unknown Baker did not bode well for the campaign to come.

On February 8, Johnston again requested a response from the administration concerning the vacancy for a corps commander.[12] Finally, in mid-February, the administration answered with the appointment of John Bell Hood to command a corps in the Army of Tennessee. In promoting Hood, Davis overlooked two talented major generals already serving in the army, Benjamin Cheatham and Patrick Cleburne. Both had been part of the anti-Bragg contingent while Bragg was army commander. With Bragg now serving as the president's military advisor, it is not surprising that neither of the two received a promotion. Nevertheless, by January 1864, each had built an impressive resumé and deserved consideration for the post.

Cheatham had served with the army since Shiloh and had conducted himself admirably. Bragg, however, accused him of drunkenness at the battle of Murfreesboro and omitted him from the extensive list of officers commended for their action during the affair. Conversely, Leonidas Polk, Cheatham's corps commander, considered his action during the battle exemplary. In reality, Cheatham's behavior at Murfreesboro was at best erratic and probably his least effective performance as a commander. He may well have been inebriated, considering that a report surfaced after the battle that he had fallen off his horse. At the very least, Cheatham failed to advance his division at the appointed time and when he did so he sent his brigades forward in an uncoordinated fashion.[13]

11 J. C. Thompson to A. P. Stewart, Box 1, Folder 5, JP WM.

12 *O.R.* vol. 32, pt. 2, 698.

13 Connelly, *Autumn of Glory*, 84; William Polk, *Leonidas Polk: Bishop and General*, 2 vols. (New York, 1915), II: 312–313; Christopher Losson, "Major General Benjamin Franklin Cheetham and the Battle of Stone's River," *Tennessee Historical Quarterly* (Fall 1982): 286; Woodworth, *Jefferson Davis and his Generals*, 189.

Bragg's censure of Cheatham in his official report created a genuine controversy in the army's high command. Cheatham's political allies vigorously protested Bragg's criticism and Cheatham offered to resign. Though Bragg rejected Cheatham's resignation, the two continued their feud during the remainder of the war. Even so, Cheatham had performed well in the army's two most recent engagements. At Chickamauga, on September 19, Cheatham's advance foiled a Union flank attack. Then at Missionary Ridge, Cheatham's division was one of the few that had not fled in confusion. Rather, he held his position until night fell.[14] Nevertheless, considering Bragg's influence on the president, a promotion for Cheatham to corps command was unthinkable regardless of his generally successful record and his popularity with his men.

Like Cheatham, Patrick Cleburne's record throughout the war had earned him consideration for promotion to corps command. Not only had Cleburne distinguished himself as a divisional commander, but during the withdrawal from the disaster at Missionary Ridge, Bragg had placed him in command of two additional divisions to cover the army's withdrawal, a task he performed with great skill. Hence, he had already demonstrated the capacity to succeed as a corps commander under the most difficult circumstances. Cleburne so impressed his commanding general that Bragg commended him to "the special notice of the government" in his after-action report of the engagement.[15]

Despite his outstanding service, Cleburne stood little chance of receiving a promotion because of his involvement in the political machinations of the Army of Tennessee. Two things stood in his way. First, Cleburne had aligned himself with the anti-Bragg faction within the Army of Tennessee. When Bragg wrote to William Hardee in January 1863, after the battle of Murfreesboro, he suggested that he would resign his command if he had lost the army's confidence. Hardee responded that he had discussed the matter with Cleburne and Breckinridge (his divisional commanders) and all three concluded that Bragg should resign. Cleburne himself then informed Bragg that neither he nor his brigade commanders believed that the army remained confident in Bragg's leadership. After Bragg's dismissal from command of the army, Cleburne's criticism became more brazen. He spoke openly about Bragg's "military mis-management" during his tenure as commander.[16] Cleburne's rocky relationship with, and dismal assessment of, the president's

14 Connelly, *Autumn of Glory*, 85, 203, 275–276.

15 Woodworth, *Jefferson Davis and his Generals*, 261; *O.R.* vol. 31, pt. 2, 666.

16 William Hardee to Braxton Bragg, Jan. 12, 1863, William J. Hardee Papers, Alabama Department of Archives and History, Montgomery; *O.R.* vol. 20, pt. 1, 684; Craig Symonds, *Stonewall of the West: Patrick Cleburne and the Civil War* (Lawrence, KS, 1997), 182.

new military advisor made him an unlikely candidate for promotion despite his impeccable record as a commander in the field. Had Davis refrained from appointing Bragg to the post of his chief advisor, Cleburne would undoubtedly have received full consideration for corps command, as he deserved.

Bragg's new position, however, in combination with Cleburne's stance on slavery further ensured that Davis would not promote him to corps command. As early as April 1863, Cleburne contemplated the abandonment of slavery to secure Southern independence. He discussed the matter with St. John Liddell, one of his brigadier generals and a prominent Louisiana planter, who replied that he would willingly give up slavery in return for independence. The military reversals of 1863 caused Cleburne to again reflect on the question of slavery, as he, like his friend Thomas Hindman, considered the need for increased troop levels paramount. Also, like Hindman, Cleburne believed that the most effective measure to further that goal was to offer freedom to slaves who enlisted in the army. In December 1863, Cleburne devoted his time to the production of a document that promoted emancipation in exchange for military service. He asked his close friend and confidant Capt. Irving Buck for advice regarding a rough draft of the proposal. Buck concluded that Cleburne's scheme was controversial enough that it would likely bar him from promotion in the army.[17] Others, including Cleburne's chief of staff, Calhoun Benham, attempted to convince the general to abandon the idea. In fact, Benham considered the concept so upsetting that he requested a copy, if Cleburne persisted in the controversial endeavor, so that he could prepare a rebuttal.

Despite the mixed reviews Cleburne received, he determined to pursue the matter and requested that his corps commander, William Hardee, ask for a meeting of the army's general officers so that he could make his case. The meeting convened on January 2, 1864, at Johnston's headquarters at 7:00 p.m. Among those present were Hardee, Major Generals William H. T. Walker, Alexander Stewart, Thomas Hindman, Carter Stevenson, and Brigadier Generals Patton Anderson and William Bate. Cleburne read from his proposal arguing that adoption of the measure would, among other things, augment the woefully depleted ranks of the army as well as deprive the Union of the moral high ground, and "strip the enemy of foreign sympathy and assistance, and transfer them to the South." Though some, including Hindman, supported the measure, many did not.[18]

17 Symonds, *Stonewall of the West*,184; Samuel T. Foster, *One of Cleburne's Command*, ed. Norman D. Brown (Austin, 1980), 49.

18 Symonds, *Stonewall of the West*, 185–186; Russell K. Brown, *To the Manner Born: The Life of General William H. T. Walker* (Macon, GA, 2005), 196; Robert Durden, *The Gray and the Black: The Confederate Debate on Emancipation* (Baton Rouge, 1972), 59. Hindman was the only advocate present at the meeting. Others had either signed the document or expressed support and authorized

The harshest detractors were William Bate, Patton Anderson, and especially William H. T. Walker. While the other critics were content when Cleburne tabled his resolution and agreed to keep the matter quiet, Walker remained incensed. He believed that such sentiments would ruin the Southern war effort. Walker, therefore, pledged to inform the president and insisted that each of the generals present submit their conclusions on the matter in writing, which he would then forward to Davis. Five days after the meeting, on January 7, Walker met with his corps commander, William Hardee, to discover his views on the matter. Hardee declined to commit to either Cleburne's proposal or Walker's denunciation. Over the course of the following days, Walker gathered what evidence he could, including a copy of Cleburne's proposal, and responses from Anderson, Bate, Stevenson, and Stewart condemning the plan. Walker then sent the material to Richmond for the president's perusal.[19]

Davis, for his part, skillfully navigated a subject with potential to wreak considerable political havoc on his administration and within the officer corps of the Army of Tennessee. In essence, he determined to adopt the policy of the generals present at the January 2 meeting; he tabled the resolution and demanded silence from officers privy to Cleburne's plan. On January 23, Davis informed Walker that he considered the debate detrimental to the health of the Confederacy as a nation and that as a result "I have concluded that the best policy under the circumstances will be to avoid all publicity." The president also instructed Secretary of War James Seddon to make certain that Johnston understood that the administration insisted that officers in his army remain silent on the matter. Johnston dutifully adhered to Davis's wishes and ordered the suppression of the proposal itself and of any further discussion of its contents.[20]

The affair had officially ended, though it lingered in the mind of one influential member of the president's administration, Braxton Bragg. Bragg could not help but notice that the officers in favor of Cleburne's proposal also happened to have been his own staunchest opponents while he served as commander of the Army of Tennessee, while those opposed to Cleburne's measure had been his most ardent

---

Cleburne to use their names in support of his argument. The list included Daniel Govan, Mark Lowrey, Hiram Granbury, Lucius Polk (Cleburne's brigadier generals), and John Kelly. See Symonds, *Stonewall of the West*, 186.

19 Brown, *To the Manner Born*, 197, 200. While most objected to the entirety of Cleburne's proposition, Stewart at least considered the utility of using slaves as cooks and teamsters in the army, to allow whites serving in such capacities to move to the front lines.

20 *O.R.* vol. 52, pt. 2, 596, 606, 608.

supporters.[21] The timing of the incident all but ensured that Cleburne's candidacy for a position as corps commander would never find significant support from the administration. Johnston's latest application on January 23 to fill the voids in the army's leadership coincided with the administration's response to Cleburne's radical proposition. Bragg was faced with a reminder that the political divisions over his tenure as commander remained in effect and that Cleburne had not been one of his supporters. Meanwhile, Davis clearly considered Cleburne's idea to free slaves in return for service in the military unwise and politically divisive. To reward Cleburne after the general had placed Davis and the administration in a tenuous political position would be difficult. Consequently, despite his unparalleled record as a divisional commander in the Army of Tennessee and his handling of the rearguard at Missionary Ridge, Bragg's influence on Davis and political sensitivities precluded Cleburne's further promotion. Instead, the Davis Administration promoted John Bell Hood to fill the vacancy in the Army of Tennessee's high command.

John Bell Hood: The Kentucky Cavalier

Hood had developed a reputation as a ferocious fighter who relished offensive tactics, a trait the administration thought absent in Joseph E. Johnston and one that the president considered a priority for the spring campaign. Hood was a native of Kentucky, but he had served in the Second Cavalry in Texas where he had developed a taste for aggressive action. On one occasion, he pursued a band of native warriors that outnumbered his company by at least three to one over difficult terrain in the middle of the summer and which concluded in hand-to-hand combat. Prior to his service in Texas, Hood had graduated from West Point in 1853, ranking forty-fifth in a fifty-two member class.[22] While his contemporaries did not consider him an intellectual, Hood's battlefield exploits during the first three years of the war insured respect among his peers and his soldiers. In almost

21 Brown, *To the Manner Born*, 202.

22 John Bell Hood, *Advance and Retreat: Personal Experiences in the United States and Confederate Armies* (1880; repr., New York, 1993), 8–14; McMurry, *John Bell Hood and The War for Southern Independence*, 9. To be fair, a number of high-ranking Confederate generals and politicians failed to achieve distinction for their academic performance. Jefferson Davis, for example, ranked twenty-third in a class of thirty-three, William Hardee twenty-sixth in a class of forty-five and James Longstreet fifty-fourth in a class of fifty-six. Meanwhile, academic excellence at West Point did not always translate into battlefield success. Braxton Bragg, for example, graduated fifth in a class of fifty and is considered by most as one of the worst generals to serve in the war. See Brian Craig Miller, *John Bell Hood and the Fight for Civil War Memory* (Knoxville, 2010), 23.

every instance, he demonstrated an aggressiveness that few matched during the course of the war.

For example, at the battle of Gaines' Mill on June 27, 1862, Hood personally led his brigade in an assault that secured victory for the Confederacy. Until Hood's attack, the Confederates had been unable to drive the Union forces from their position, but Hood ordered his men to fix bayonets and charge rather than engage the enemy with their muskets when his men came under fire from the Federals. Hood's assault secured victory for the Confederates, but not without cost, as 572 of his 2,000 soldiers were either killed or wounded.[23] The maneuver demonstrated both his aggressiveness and his personal bravery, traits he continued to display during the course of Lee's campaigns in the summer of 1862.

Hood's exploits at Gaines' Mill won him promotion to divisional command. The division was relatively small, comprised of his own Texas Brigade and a brigade under the command of Evander Law. On August 30, Hood proved once again to be a dynamic leader on the battlefield as he led his men in a flank attack that ensured victory for Lee's army at the battle of Second Manassas. With two brigades under his command, Hood reported the capture of five cannons and fourteen stands of colors, which meant that he had driven at least that many regiments from the battlefield. Not only did Hood command his own division during the engagement, he also helped direct other troops during the fray.[24] Hood's attack, though wildly successful, resulted in fairly heavy casualties, with approximately one third of his 3,000 men either killed or wounded.

During the battle of Antietam on September 17, Hood cemented his reputation when he led his division of approximately 2,000 men in a counterattack against Gen. Joseph Hooker's assault on the Confederate left flank. Hooker was in the process of driving Stonewall Jackson from the field when Hood struck. The attack pushed the Federals through the famed Cornfield and was only halted when Union artillery concentrated on Hood's columns. The attack saved the Confederate left flank, but came with a fearful price, as Hood lost approximately half of his command in the process.[25] Hood's battlefield success in the summer resulted in his promotion to major general in October. The lesson for Hood was obvious: Aggressive action on the battlefield led to victory and promotion.

After the battle of Chancellorsville in May 1863, Robert E. Lee found himself in search of a new corps commander to replace the slain Stonewall Jackson. Lee

23 McMurry, *John Bell Hood*, 47–49; Castel, *Decision in the West*, 58.

24 Hood, *Advance and Retreat*, 37; McMurry, *John Bell Hood*, 55.

25 Castel, *Decision in the West*, 58.

considered Hood for the position along with Ambrose Powell Hill and Richard Anderson. Ultimately, Lee determined that Hill was his best option at the time. Still, he considered both Anderson and Hood as "capital officers" who would make good corps commanders in the future "if necessary."[26]

Gettysburg provided Hood's next opportunity to prove himself worthy of promotion. The battle demonstrated that he possessed an appreciation for tactical advantage in addition to an unparalleled talent for delivering an offensive strike. When he arrived at the location from which he was to begin his assault, his scouts alerted him to the Federal position on the Round Tops, the hills that dominated the terrain on the Union left flank. Hood realized that to attack as ordered would expose his right flank to fire from the Round Tops and make the success of his attack unlikely. Hood appealed three times to his corps commander, James Longstreet, for permission to move behind the hills and assault the Federal rear. In doing so, Hood exhibited an appreciation for maneuver, a skill he had not yet had the opportunity to demonstrate on the battlefield. When Longstreet rebuffed Hood's appeal, Hood protested, the only protest of his military service. Nevertheless, Hood launched his assault as directed but suffered a wound to his left arm soon after his division engaged.[27]

In September, Hood was transferred to the Western theater along with much of Longstreet's Corps and participated in the battle of Chickamauga. At Chickamauga, Hood commanded what was in essence a large corps that included the divisions of Joseph Kershaw, A. P. Stewart, Bushrod Johnson, and Thomas Hindman, in addition to his own. Along with the rest of the army, Hood assaulted the Federal position on the morning of September 20, 1863. During the attack, Hood sustained a wound to his right leg that resulted in amputation. For most soldiers, such catastrophic injuries ended military careers. Not only did such wounds limit a soldier's mobility, they often resulted in serious psychological damage that interfered with the victim's ability to execute his duty. Battle wounds sometimes resulted in a complete loss of mental faculties and on occasion landed the injured party in a hospital for the insane.[28]

26 *O.R.* vol. 25, pt. 2, 811.

27 Hood, *Advance and Retreat*, 58, 59. McMurry, *John Bell Hood*, 75. Most historians have wrongly concluded that the injury cost Hood the use of his left arm permanently. Recently discovered letters, however, suggest that Hood did indeed retain some use of the arm. See Stephen M. Hood, *The Lost Papers of Confederate General John Bell Hood* (El Dorado Hills, CA, 2015), 20.

28 Hood, *Advance and Retreat*, 63. The men of his beloved Texas Brigade raised approximately $5,000 to purchase an artificial leg from France, thereby demonstrating the depth of Hood's popularity among his men. See Miller, *John Bell Hood and the Fight for Civil War Memory*, 75; Eric Dean, *Shook Over Hell: Post-Traumatic Stress, Vietnam, and the Civil War* (Cambridge, MA, 1997), 122.

Though Hood never suffered such severe psychological effects, he certainly endured bouts of melancholy following the loss of his right leg and much of the use of his left arm. In December 1863, Hood routinely referred to his wounds in a self-deprecating manner. In one conversation he lamented, "this is the first house I have had myself dragged to," having required assistance to enter and exit his carriage. "I mean to be as happy a fool, well, as a one-legged man can be. So many strangers scare me always. I can't run now as I did before." Later in the month Hood again commented on his disability when he claimed engagements with four women, which he suggested was a "liberal allowance" for an individual who "cannot walk without help." On December 24, 1863, a member of Hood's staff, Henry Brewster, asserted that Hood "was in the habit of saying that he would not marry if he could any silly, sentimental girl who would throw herself away upon a maimed creature such as he was."[29] Clearly Hood's wounds damaged not only his body, but his psychological health as well. His most disparaging comments about his condition reflect a deep concern over his ability to engage in a romantic relationship with a woman.

Even so, fits of anxiety about his prospects for female companionship did not deter Hood from the pursuit of Sally "Buck" Preston, sister of Richmond socialite Mary Chesnut. The striking Preston attracted a number of suitors and inspired Hood to remark that he had "surrendered to [her] at first sight." Hood's pursuit of Preston did not end when he lost his leg after Chickamauga, as he continued his courtship of the belle during his convalescence in Richmond in the winter of 1863–64.[30] Hood's repeated efforts to attract the popular Buck Preston even after his catastrophic injuries suggests that while he endured periods of melancholy regarding his condition, he never allowed the injuries to define him.

Nor did he develop an addiction to alcohol or laudanum as some have speculated. Such charges have led to the conclusion by a number of historians that Hood was unfit for promotion to command of the Army of Tennessee when Davis elevated him to the position in July. Hood's subsequent failure to hold Atlanta and his failed campaign thereafter into Tennessee are often linked, in part, to his supposed addiction. There is no credible evidence to support these claims and Hood's acumen as an army commander deserves further investigation.

The first assertion that John Bell Hood attempted to medicate his physical and psychological wounds with an opiate did not appear until the middle of the twentieth century in Percy Hamlin's publication Old Bald Head: General R. S.

29 Woodward, *Mary Chesnut's Civil War*, 502, 509, 512.

30 Ibid., 565; McMurry, *John Bell Hood*, 83.

Ewell. Hamlin's allegation, however, lacked any substantiation as he failed to provide a source for the charge. Stephen Davis notes that subsequent authors have accepted Hamlin's contention, though they generally preface the assertion with words such as "perhaps" or "if."[31] Like Hamlin's claim, later charges that Hood used alcohol or laudanum failed to provide contemporary accounts in support of those allegations.

The only known extant account of Hood taking any opiates can be found in the medical journal of Dr. John Darby. Darby did prescribe Hood small amounts of morphine nightly to induce sleep after he had amputated the general's leg. As time passed, Darby reduced the doses. In fact, by November 10, 1864, about one and a half months after the amputation, Dr. Darby noted that Hood was able to sleep without the use of morphine. Subsequent entries mention the same, as well as the fact that Hood was able to walk (with the help of a prosthetic leg) across the room several times without pain or need of rest.[32] It would therefore appear that Hood's use of opiates ceased upon his recovery from surgery as there are no other first-hand accounts of Hood taking them.

If Hood had in fact resorted to either alcohol or opiates after his recovery from the amputation of his leg, one or more of his close associates would have undoubtedly mentioned his addiction in their correspondence, diaries, or memoirs. The fact that not a single associate did so provides strong evidence that the charge is erroneous. Both Jefferson Davis and Mary Chesnut became close friends of the general over the course of the war and neither observed Hood engaging in any addictive behavior.[33] Perhaps even more noteworthy is the fact that his associates in the army made no mention of addiction in their correspondence and diaries. Halsey Wigfall, who served on Hood's staff throughout the Atlanta campaign, made no reference to such behavior in his letters home to his family. Nor did Taylor Beatty, a member of the general's staff, record such activity in his diary of the campaign. Consequently, the allegation that Hood indulged in either excessive drinking or opiates and that his ability to command in the field was thereby affected, must be rejected. Rather, he, like many other Civil War veterans, carried on with his life despite the severity of combat wounds.

Indeed, as Richard McMurry noted, the Civil War produced a society that considered men visibly scarred from their wartime experience, by disfigurement or

31 Stephen Davis, "John Bell Hood's 'Addictions' In Civil War Literature," *Blue and Gray Magazine* (Oct. 1998): 28–29.

32 Hood, *The Lost Papers of Confederate General John Bell Hood*, 38.

33 Davis, "John Bell Hood's 'Addictions' In Civil War Literature," 30; Miller, *John Bell Hood and the Fight for Civil War Memory*, xx.

loss of limb, to be "manifestations of physical courage" and, thus, lionized in the community. Such men were so common that one civilian observed that she was familiar with soldiers having suffered all types of maladies and amputations except for blindness. Not only were such men common throughout the South, but even as the war neared its conclusion, they were celebrated as the idyllic heroes upon whom the fate of the Confederacy rested. On September 23, 1864, after the fall of Atlanta, Jefferson Davis promised the advent of a new aristocracy, one headed by wounded veterans.[34]

Though some men suffered debilitating mental anguish after sustaining combat wounds and required institutionalization, others demonstrated an ability to accept societal adulation for their sacrifice to the cause. Hood clearly belonged to the second category. Hood's frequent public appearances in Richmond social circles in December 1863 and January 1864 suggests, as Richard McMurry asserts, that Hood "accepted his fate [wounds] without bitterness." In fact, on Christmas Day 1863, Hood exhibited a remarkable ability to overcome any sense of loss in his relationships with the opposite sex. On the previous evening, Buck Preston had informed the general that there was "no hope" in his pursuit, as she was engaged to another man. Despite the setback, Hood attended festivities at the home of Mary Chesnut the following day and reveled in the reading of Tennyson's "Charge of the Light Brigade," which he heard for the first time. Hood's reaction to the reading provides evidence that his wounds did not alter his ardor for warfare, as "his eyes grew flaming, scintillating. And he made a gesture, which [James Chesnut] said was like the motion of a soldier receiving his orders in battle, at the end of every line."[35] Perhaps even more illustrative of his desire to return to the army, Hood actively campaigned for reinstatement to military command while he convalesced in the capital.

A Presidential Informant

Challenges to Johnston's command developed outside his purview even before the campaign commenced. During Hood's recovery in Richmond, he formed a close friendship with Jefferson Davis and his family. In fact, Hood and the

34 McMurry, *John Bell Hood*, 84; Woodward, *Mary Chesnut's Civil War*, 515; Miller, *John Bell Hood and the Fight for Civil War Memory*, 96.

35 McMurry, *John Bell Hood*, 84; Woodward, *Mary Chesnut's Civil War*, 516. Preston's engagement to another did not lead Hood to abandon his pursuit. He continued to court Preston and on Feb. 12, 1864, just before he left for Dalton, Hood convinced Preston to accept his own proposal. See Woodward, *Mary Chesnut Civil War*, 561–562. Preston ultimately abandoned the engagement to Hood and married another man.

president rode through the city together so frequency that observers commented on their blossoming friendship. The two developed a close enough relationship that Hood was given the use of the president's carriage. Additionally, Hood and Davis attended social gatherings and religious services together. The evidence suggests that while Hood developed a friendship with the president he hoped it might be of some benefit to himself professionally; his accolades for Davis during his convalescence demonstrate a degree of self-promotion. While visiting Mary Chesnut, he confessed that in a meeting with the president he had suggested that Davis's military credentials entitled him to take a field command himself.[36] The proposition was, of course, utterly unfeasible and could only have been intended to curry favor with the Confederacy's most powerful political figure.

Hood's effort to ingratiate himself with the president paid dividends. After Davis elevated Johnston to command of the Army of Tennessee, he discussed his strategic vision for the Western theater with Hood on at least one occasion. Davis revealed his intention to reinforce Johnston's army for an advance into eastern Tennessee early in the spring, with the object of marching to the rear of the Federal army, then at Chattanooga, and compelling it either to withdraw or to fight the Confederates in the open.[37] Clearly, Davis considered Hood to be a confidant worthy of discussions concerning future operations. Considering the pair's developing friendship and Hood's combat record during the war, Davis's selection of Hood to serve as a corps commander in the Army of Tennessee made a great deal of sense.

Though Johnston's recommendations for the corps vacancies fell upon deaf ears, he apparently approved of Hood's appointment. Having been informed of the administration's decision to elevate Hood to lieutenant general and transfer him to the Army of Tennessee to command a corps, Johnston telegraphed Richmond that "Hood is much wanted here."[38] The fact that Johnston demonstrated a penchant for discussing variety of military matters, including the relative strength of the armies and chances for success, with Hood upon his arrival, suggests that Johnston considered Hood's appointment to command in his army a positive development. Certainly Hood fit within the parameters Johnston had established in his initial

36 McMurry, *John Bell Hood*, 83; Woodward, *Mary Chesnut's Civil War*, 527, 565; Hood, *Advance and Retreat*, 67; Connelly, *Autumn of Glory*, 322.

37 Hood, *Advance and Retreat*, 67.

38 *O.R.* vol. 32, pt. 2, 763. Though Johnston appears to have been satisfied by Hood's promotion, Thomas Hindman was not. Hindman resented that Hood had superseded him to corps command and submitted his resignation to Jefferson Davis. Davis refused, and Hindman served as a divisional commander in Hood's Corps during the campaign. See McMurry, *John Bell Hood*, 98.

pursuit of officers to fill the army's vacancies on the corps level. Like Hindman and Lovell, Hood had no record with the Army of Tennessee and, therefore, had not participated in the political squabbling that had resulted in schism within the command structure over Bragg's conduct as army commander. Further, Hood's record during the war compared favorably to the performances of both Hindman and Lovell, making him a superior candidate for the position. Even so, his close association with Davis meant that Johnston could have viewed Hood's promotion with trepidation.

Johnston undoubtedly knew of Hood's friendly relationship with Davis through his own supporters in Richmond, yet he made no complaint about Hood's promotion. Furthermore, Johnston routinely discussed matters of military importance with Hood upon his arrival at Dalton, a practice he failed to engage in with his other subordinates. One theory as to why Johnston welcomed Hood and freely discussed strategic and tactical matters with his new subordinate was that he hoped to convince Hood that the Army of Tennessee suffered from deficiencies in both strength and logistical capabilities. If Johnston was successful in "educating" his new corps commander, Hood might then relay his findings to the administration.[39] Johnston would therefore be able to use Hood's close relationship to the president to serve his own interests.

Another interpretation of Hood's appointment was that Davis's assignment of Hood constituted an effort to keep him (Davis) advised of the condition of the army and Johnston's fitness to lead it: In essence, Hood would act as a spy. The suggestion that Davis sent Hood west to act as a spy first surfaced in the debate that emerged between Johnston and Hood after the war. A number of historians have since accepted the premise and dubbed Hood the president's "outside pet" or "mouthpiece," who "worked his way into the inner circle of the Administration with ambition aforethought" and "had been sent to keep an eye on Johnston." Historian Brian Craig Miller has asserted that Hood was under orders to report to the administration if he believed that Johnston was acting in a manner that damaged the likelihood of Confederate success.[40] Hood's continued correspondence with the administration after his arrival at Dalton undoubtedly influenced such interpretations of Davis's initial decision to promote Hood to

39 Castel, *Decision in the West*, 78.

40 Thomas R. Hay, "The Davis-Hood-Johnston Controversy of 1864," *The Mississippi Valley Historical Review* 11 (June 1924): 58; Richard O'Connor, *Hood: Cavalier General* (New York, 1949), 174; John Dyer, *The Gallant Hood* (New York, 1950), 228; Miller, *John Bell Hood and the Fight for Civil War Memory*, 108. Miller provides no direct evidence in support of his charge and seems to rely upon the fact that Hood began communicating with the administration soon after he arrived at Dalton.

the position. Still, other historians have offered alternative explanations for the president's appointment of Hood to corps command in the Army of Tennessee.

As Richard McMurry notes in *John Bell Hood and the War for Southern Independence*, Jefferson Davis made his initial decision to promote Hood to lieutenant general and place him in command of a corps in the Army of Tennessee while Braxton Bragg remained at the helm. Davis informed Bragg on October 29, 1863, of his intention and stated his confidence that Gen. John C. Breckinridge could serve in that capacity until Hood recovered from his wounds.[41] Clearly Davis intended to promote Hood to corps command in the Army of Tennessee long before Johnston took command. To suggest that the president ordered Hood to Dalton solely to act as a spy therefore strains credulity. Yet to assert that Davis's October decision to promote Hood meant that no such arrangement ever existed is also unconvincing.

Davis's telegram to Bragg in October 1863 demonstrates that the president considered Hood a rising star in the Confederate army and thought the general's record sufficient to warrant a promotion. At the time of the communication, Hood had not yet arrived in Richmond and had not yet begun the friendship that he cultivated with the president during the course of his recovery in the capital.[42] As the two men established their friendship during December 1863 and January 1864, Davis engaged in an argument with Joseph E. Johnston over the proper strategy for the upcoming campaign in the Western theater, a matter discussed in the following chapter. Davis hoped that Johnston's army would launch an offensive through eastern Tennessee, a strategy that Johnston considered ill-advised.

Between December 18 and 20, 1863, Johnston informed the administration that the army was unfit to assume the offensive as it lacked manpower and proper logistical support. Johnston reiterated his concerns about the condition of the army on January 2, 1864. At some point in mid-January, Davis informed Hood of his intention to reinforce Johnston so as to enable him to take the offensive into Tennessee.[43] Considering the president's hopes to regain Tennessee and his commander's perceived reluctance to assume the offensive, a tendency the president believed that he had demonstrated on the Peninsula in 1862 and at Vicksburg in 1863, it seems only natural that Davis requested Hood's assistance in assessing the army's capabilities once he arrived in Dalton. Moreover, the president's penchant for permitting his personal feelings regarding his officers to influence

41 McMurry, *John Bell Hood*, 88; *O.R.* vol. 52, pt. 2, 555.

42 Hood arrived in Richmond on Nov. 17, 1863. See McMurry, *John Bell Hood*, 80.

43 Johnston, *Narrative of Military Operations*, 265–266, 272–273; Hood, *Advance and Retreat*, 67.

his judgment undoubtedly played a role in his decision. As previously discussed, Davis's relationship with Johnston had deteriorated throughout the course of the war and had suffered its most serious setback after the loss of Vicksburg. During the Vicksburg campaign Johnston had similarly insisted that the administration provide him with significant reinforcements prior to any offensive he might want to take against Grant. To Davis the circumstances must have seemed eerily similar.

Consequently, while Davis clearly did not make his original decision in October 1863 to promote Hood to corps command in the Army of Tennessee to provide himself with a spy, he took advantage of the opportunity when the situation presented itself. Circumstances had dramatically changed since the previous October. By mid-January, Davis and Hood had developed a friendship and the president was unimpressed with Johnston's progress in Georgia. Davis had already sent his aide-de-camp, Col. Joseph Ives, to inspect the condition of the army in December, a decision that indicated he did not necessarily believe in the accuracy of Johnston's reports.[44] The opportunity to use Hood as a permanent informant certainly appealed to the president.

Hood's first communication with the president offers evidence that Davis did indeed intend that Hood provide him with information about the army's ability to conduct an offensive campaign. Hood opened his communication with a telling phrase: "I have delayed writing to you so as to allow myself time to see the condition of this army." Hood drafted the telegram on March 7, 1864, only one week after he had assumed his new duties at Dalton on February 28. His suggestion that there had been some delay in his writing to Davis is significant in two ways. First, the choice of the word "delayed" implies that Davis expected a report from Hood, otherwise there was no need for Hood to explain the timing of his message. Secondly, not only did Davis expect Hood to report back to the administration, he evidently intended that the communication from Hood would arrive promptly. The implication was that the president had expressed some urgency in the matter. Furthermore, the content of Hood's first telegram specifically addresses the conflict between Davis and Johnston over the condition of the army and its ability to conduct an offensive campaign. Hood claimed that the "addition of a few horses for our artillery will place this army in fine condition," and that a reinforcement of 10,000–15,000 additional troops would allow a move into Tennessee.[45] The language suggests that not only was reporting to the administration a feature

44 Johnston, *Narrative of Military Operations*, 267.

45 *O.R.* vol., 32, pt., 3, 606–607; McMurry, *John Bell Hood*, 93; Thomas Connelly and Stanley Horn have identified Hood's terminology as evidence of an arrangement between Hood and Davis to keep the president informed. See Connelly, *Autumn of Glory*, 322; Horn, *The Army of Tennessee*, 318.

of Hood's appointment, it had also become an important aspect of Hood's job description in light of the administration's conflict with Johnston over the impending spring campaign.

Thus, it seems clear that Davis had not learned a vital lesson in the first three years of the war. Unlike Lincoln, who by the spring of 1864 had managed to significantly reduce instances of communications that violated accepted military protocol, Davis encouraged the practice. Hood biographer Richard McMurry has argued that Hood's activity was not aberrant and occurred regularly during the course of the Civil War. McMurry observes that among Confederates the activity proved a common practice. As many as three other officers in Johnston's army wrote similar letters to Braxton Bragg while encamped at Dalton. On March 19 Maj. Gen. Alexander Stewart asked Bragg, "Are we to hold still, remaining on the defensive in this position until [the enemy] comes down with his combined armies to drive us out?" Apparently William Hardee also wrote a letter to Davis at some point in April expressing his view of the prospects for the spring campaign. Further, on April 16 Joseph Wheeler, in command of the army's cavalry, wrote to Bragg and suggested that 15,000 infantry and some cavalry would allow Johnston to assume the offensive.[46]

Nevertheless, Hood's correspondence featured one unusual quality: its volume. Unlike the others mentioned above, Hood wrote to the administration on multiple occasions between March 7 and April 13. In addition to his March 7 letter to the president, Hood wrote to Secretary of War James Seddon on March 10, and to Braxton Bragg on March 10, April 3, and April 13. The sheer quantity of communications as well as the nature of the information contained therein suggests that the administration anticipated that Hood would act as an informant once he arrived at Dalton. In his March 10 letter to Seddon, Hood wrote that he had "written these letters in thorough friendship and good feeling," and that he was "an earnest friend to the president and am ever willing to express to him my ideas in regard to the approaching campaign." Additionally, he once again conveyed confidence in the condition of the army.[47] The language suggests that Davis had expressed an interest in Hood's "ideas" and had requested that Hood keep him apprised of the army's condition and abilities. Though Hood's comments with respect to friendship hint at self-promotion, there is nothing in the letter that

46 McMurry, *John Bell Hood*, 97, 98; *O.R.* vol. 32, pt. 3, 781. This is from Hood's telegram to Braxton Bragg on Apr. 13, 1864, wherein Hood mentions a letter from Hardee to the president. The letter to which Hood referred, however, is not among the correspondence found in the president's possession. See *The Papers of Jefferson Davis*, X:334–339.

47 *O.R.* vol. 32, pt. 3, 606.

accuses Johnston of any misdeed. If Hood did engage in self-promotion he did not do so at Johnston's expense at that juncture.

In his communication to Bragg on March 10, Hood not only provided the administration with an assessment of the army's strength and condition, but also with his opinion regarding the proper course for the spring campaign. Hood suggested that an immediate concentration of forces would allow the army to advance against the Federals and to regain "lost territory." Failure to concentrate would result in inevitable retreat. Hood concluded his communication by noting that "I have written this letter after observing matters here and much thought upon it."[48] When considered in light of the ongoing dispute between Davis and Johnston over the army's offensive capabilities, the letter fits within the framework that Davis intended Hood to act as a conduit of information regarding the army's ability to advance into Tennessee. There was no overt self-promotion in the March 10 letter to Bragg, and it is likely that Johnston, had he seen it, would have approved of the assessment that the army needed reinforcements or would be compelled to retreat.

Hood's communications with the administration did not exhibit criticism of Johnston until April 3. In his letter to Bragg on that date Hood lamented, "How unfortunate for our country, it is for the generals in the field to fail to cooperate thoroughly with the authorities of the government and not act together." He continued, "from the recent acts of the president I appreciate his greatness even more than before." On April 13 Hood again wrote to Bragg stating that "I am sorry to inform you that I have done all in my power to induce General Johnston to accept the proposition you made to move forward. He will not consent." For a second time in as many letters he made every effort to flatter the president, claiming "in him [Davis] I have unbounded confidence."[49]

It is possible to brand Hood's April letters as his opening gambit to replace Johnston as the commander of the Army of Tennessee. Such an interpretation, however, is unwarranted. The campaign had not even begun and Davis could not remove the army's commander, without proof of misconduct or the army's loss of confidence in him, without a severe political backlash. Furthermore, to do so would require Davis to admit to a mistake in placing Johnston in command in the first place. Moreover, such an interpretation assumes a great deal of duplicity on Hood's part. After all, Hood and Johnston maintained a close working relationship throughout the early stages of the campaign. For example, on April 5 Hood wrote

48 Ibid., 608.

49 McMurry, *John Bell Hood*, 96; *O.R.* vol. 32, pt. 3, 781.

to Louis Wigfall that he was fond of his commanding general and that the two got along well together.[50] Their relationship only began to show signs of acrimony after the operations around Cassville on May 19.

Instead, as Richard McMurry argues, it is more likely that Hood's April communications suggest that he had simply lost patience with his commanding officer's refusal to advance into Tennessee. By April, Johnston had declined to endorse any of the multitude of plans of the administration, as well as those of a number of Confederate generals, including James Longstreet, Leonidas Polk, and P. G. T. Beauregard. Further, the April 13 telegram offers additional support for the conclusion that Davis had sent Hood west to act as an informant. Hood's claim that he had done everything in his power to convince Johnston to "accept the proposition you [Bragg] made," indicates that Hood considered the task of inspiring Johnston to move into Tennessee as part of his assignment.[51]

A fair interpretation of the available evidence suggests several important features of Davis's decision to elevate Hood to corps command in the Army of Tennessee. First, Davis's initial decision to appoint Hood was based solely on Hood's ability as a combat general and not to undermine Joseph E. Johnston. Davis clearly intended to promote Hood to the rank of lieutenant general prior to Johnston's replacement of Bragg as the army's commander. Second, once engaged in a debate with his new commander over the proper campaign strategy for spring, Davis instructed Hood to keep him informed of the army's condition and ability to conduct offensive operations. Hood's immediate and repeated communications with the administration provides strong evidence that Hood considered himself an agent of the president. Nevertheless, Hood's April communications with the administration should not be seen as an attempt to undermine Johnston as the army's commander.

As spring drew near, Johnston and the president continued to quarrel with one another. Johnston made repeated efforts to reorganize his army and appoint generals free of the political squabbling prevalent in the Army of Tennessee's officer corps during Bragg's tenure as commander. Davis considered Johnston's appointments unacceptable and refused to cooperate until he finally appointed John Bell Hood in February. In choosing Hood, Davis overlooked talented officers already serving in the Army of Tennessee including Benjamin Cheatham and Patrick Cleburne. In both cases, political considerations likely played a prominent role in the decision. Most notably, Davis's willingness to retain and promote officers he had befriended

50 McMurry, *John Bell Hood*, 97; H. J. Eckenrode and Bryan Conrad, *James Longstreet: Lee's War Horse* (Chapel Hill, NC, 1936), 292; Hood, *The Lost Papers of Confederate General John Bell Hood*, 146.

51 McMurry, *John Bell Hood*, 97; see *O.R.* vol. 32, pt. 3, 781.

despite their poor record during the war—in this case Braxton Bragg—influenced his evaluation of potential promotions. In selecting Hood, Davis chose a general with an impeccable record as a field commander. Despite Hood's severe wounds, he was neither psychologically incapable of serving as a corps commander, nor was he an addict as some have asserted. Hood's penchant for aggressive action appealed to the president, particularly after he and Johnston could not agree upon a strategy for the spring campaign. As a result, Davis instructed Hood to report on the condition and capability of the army. He therefore encouraged a behavior that Abraham Lincoln rightly believed was subversive to morale and produced animosity within the officer corps. The campaign had not yet begun, but the political tumult that had been so prominent under Bragg's leadership continued to haunt the Army of Tennessee as spring approached.

Chapter 3

Spring Plans: The Absence of a Unified Vision

President Jefferson Davis's encouragement of John Bell Hood's unconventional communications to the administration stemmed from a dispute between himself and Johnston over the proper course of action for the spring campaign in 1864. That dispute further illuminated two of the traits that distinguished Jefferson Davis from Abraham Lincoln. Without a central command, something that Lincoln had accomplished with the appointment of Ulysses Grant as general-in-chief, the Confederacy lacked the ability to implement a unified vision for both the Eastern and Western theaters of operations. In fact, the disagreement resulted in the submission of a plethora of schemes from all quarters of the Confederacy. Most of the submissions were poorly conceived. The one plan that offered the best hope for southern success fell victim to the president's habit of permitting his personal feelings to influence his judgment. The proposal called for P. G. T. Beauregard to advance with a sizable force into Kentucky and threaten Sherman's communications. If properly executed, the plan would likely have compelled Sherman to abandon Tennessee. Despite the proposal's reasonable chance for achieving success, Davis rejected it out of hand because it meant giving Beauregard, a general he detested even more than Johnston, a new field command. Thus, Davis's failure to recognize the advantage of a more centralized command system and his unwillingness to look beyond personal relationships with his generals posed considerable obstacles as the campaign season approached.

After promoting Johnston to command of the army, the Davis administration sent the new commander instructions, which he received upon his arrival at Dalton, Georgia on December 27, 1863. The communication urged Johnston to secure adequate supplies and to make every preparation necessary for resuming the offensive, particularly if the enemy exposed itself by separating its forces. Davis tempered his suggestion with the caveat that "while, however, these suggestions are ventured, your own experience and judgment are relied on to form and act on your own plans of military operations, and there will be the fullest disposition on the part of this department to sustain and cooperate with them." Davis's proposal, though subtle and seemingly deferential, clearly articulated his advocacy for offensive operations. Johnston wasted little time in responding to Davis's prodding and sent a return communication noting that the strength of the Federal army amounted to about 80,000 and that his own army was "far from being in condition to resume the offensive as it was deficient in numbers, arms, subsistence stores and field transportation." Johnston instead preferred to await the enemy's advance, repulse its assaults, and then counterattack. Johnston's strategy was based primarily on the condition and safety of his army in the field. His record as a commander had demonstrated that he was willing to relinquish territory in order to keep his army intact.[1]

Davis, on the other hand, developed his conceptual framework for the coming campaign with an eye to political as well as military ramifications. As a result, Davis's strategy for the 1864 campaign necessitated retention of territory still held by the Confederacy, as well as the recapture of territory (particularly Tennessee) then under Union occupation. Unlike Johnston, Davis routinely faced the wrath of governors and civil officials from across the Confederacy who petitioned him on behalf of their constituents. The prospect of recapturing lost ground appealed to Davis for another reason; it meant the supplies harvested from Tennessee farms could replenish the dwindling Confederate stores. The loss of Vicksburg and Port Hudson during the previous summer had deprived the South of access to agricultural produce from the fertile Trans-Mississippi. Davis hoped to offset his losses in the far west with the recapture of farmland in Tennessee. The problem of supplying the Confederate armies became increasingly desperate during the winter of 1863–64. Lee's Army of Northern Virginia had exhausted the available beef in that region and had begun to receive cattle from Georgia.[2] The transfer of beef from Georgia to Virginia necessarily diminished the supply available to Johnston's army at Dalton. Unless circumstances changed dramatically and the Confederacy

1 Johnston, *Narrative of Military Operations*, 263–266; Symonds, *Joseph E. Johnston*, 255. He had withdrawn on the Virginia peninsula and had recommended that Pemberton abandon Vicksburg to save the army defending the city.

2 Symonds, *Joseph E. Johnston*, 271; Woodworth, *Jefferson Davis and his Generals*,18; Davis, *The Rise and Fall of the Confederate Government*, II, 548; Elam, "The Road to Atlanta," 49.

acquired an additional supply source, both of its primary field armies faced the prospect of starvation.

In addition to potential political gains by the recapture of Tennessee, Davis believed that the state of enemy forces in the area was conducive to a Confederate offensive. Davis had received a report that the Federal strength in Chattanooga, Bridgeport, and Knoxville was lower than at any time since the battle of Missionary Ridge. Further, according to the report, the Federal cavalry, artillery, and train-horses were particularly deficient. The report Davis chose to rely upon for the formulation of his spring strategy stood in stark contrast to William Hardee's report made on December 17, 1863. Hardee, serving as the interim commander of the Army of Tennessee, suggested that enemy reinforcements in the region made offensive maneuvers impossible. Hardee also noted that his army required reinforcements and a more efficient supply system.[3] Despite conflicting reports, Davis determined to rely upon the former and ignore the latter.

On December 23, 1863, Davis wrote an optimistic letter to Johnston about the prospects for a Confederate invasion of Tennessee. Davis noted that intelligence received indicated that the condition of the Army "is encouraging and induces me to hope that you will soon be able to commence active operations against the enemy." Additionally, Davis stated that the loss from the battle of Missionary Ridge was minimal and the army had suffered little demoralization. The intelligence to which Davis referred came from reports generated by his aide-de-camp Col. Joseph Ives. These reports indicated that the army possessed ample artillery, horses, equipment, and transportation to carry out the movement into Tennessee.[4] Even so, Davis surely understood that the Army of Tennessee remained considerably outnumbered. Even if the information contained in the reports generated by the president's informants included some truth, the disparity in strength between the Federal army and the Army of Tennessee made offensive operations extremely difficult.

Johnston recognized the dangers inherent in an immediate advance under the prevailing circumstances and responded to Davis's suggestions on January 2, 1864. Johnston stressed that the recent returns indicated that his army numbered only 36,000 effective infantry and artillery while his opponent mustered 80,000 according to reports prepared by his predecessor, Braxton Bragg.[5] Clearly an

3 Davis, *The Rise and Fall of the Confederate Government*, II:547–548; *O.R.* vol. 32, pt. 3, 839–840.

4 Johnston, *Narrative of Military Operations*, 266–268.

5 Ibid., 272.

advance, even if the horses and transportation trains could sustain one, afforded slim hope for success without significant reinforcements.

During his first weeks in Dalton, Johnston endeavored to ascertain the condition of his army, which he found bore little resemblance to the force described in the president's letter of December 23. Despite his findings, Johnston waited two months before he informed the president of his conclusions. Johnston notified Davis on February 27 that much preparation was necessary for offensive operation. In particular, the army needed reinforcements, better transportation, artillery horses, and a new artillery commander. Johnston suggested that reinforcements might be procured by sending Longstreet to join him from east Tennessee together with any available troops from Polk's army in Mississippi and Beauregard's forces along the eastern seaboard. He also requested that Col. E. P. Alexander assume command of his artillery.[6]

Davis had been under the impression that his commander had spent the previous two months preparing for offensive maneuvers. The news that the Army of Tennessee still lacked sufficient transportation and artillery horses alarmed the president. On March 4, he directed Bragg to communicate the expectations of the administration to Johnston. Bragg instructed Johnston to take the offensive as soon as possible "for the movement [previously] indicated," and promised that the administration would furnish reinforcements when circumstances permitted. Bragg also relayed the administration's concerns over Johnston's assertion that the army lacked artillery horses. Bragg wrote: "the deficiency reported in artillery horses seems very large, and so different from the amount given by General Hardee on turning over the command, that hopes are entertained that there must be some error on your part."[7] Finally, he informed Johnston that Lee needed Alexander in Virginia and that General W. N. Pendleton would be ordered to assume the command of the Army of Tennessee's artillery.

Bragg's response befuddled Johnston. He knew nothing about any movement previously indicated as the communiqué suggested. In his reply, Johnston acknowledged his ignorance of any plan under consideration by the president.[8] Johnston understood that the administration desired a forward movement, but to his knowledge particulars about how he should achieve that goal remained undetermined. The impasse between Johnston and Davis set off a new flurry of communications reminiscent of the Vicksburg campaign. The tone of the new

6 Ibid., 279, 287–288.

7 *O.R.* vol. 31, pt. 3, 860.

8 Johnston, *Narrative of Military Operations*, 288–289, 290.

debate focused on two important and closely related issues. The first was the proper grand strategy for the coming spring campaign. The second concerned the actual strength and condition of the army, which affected its ability to successfully conduct operations, particularly the strategic offensive.

A Plethora of Plans

Bragg responded to Johnston that the administration indeed had a specific plan. The Davis-Bragg strategy for the spring of 1864 required Johnston to move to eastern Tennessee and link up with General Longstreet's corps of 15,000–17,000 men and another 15,000 furnished from the commands of Beauregard and Polk. The army was then to threaten Knoxville and force the Union army in Chattanooga to withdraw from its entrenchments or face having its communications cut off. Davis believed that the Federal forces at Knoxville were dependent on Chattanooga and that both relied upon Federal retention of Nashville. If the Confederates could interpose themselves between Knoxville and Chattanooga, the Federal army might assault the Army of Tennessee in order to maintain its communications. Should the enemy fail to give battle, the administration envisioned a rapid movement across the mountains from Kingston to Sparta. Such a movement would then allow the Army of Tennessee to enter country rich in sustenance and to threaten the Union force at Nashville. Davis also hoped that the desired movement would prevent Federal troops from boarding trains bound for Virginia. He considered gaining the initiative paramount.[9]

While the plan seemed sound initially and certainly more palatable than a direct advance on Chattanooga, it had several drawbacks. First, the mountainous topography in eastern Tennessee is not conducive to rapid or sustained movement despite the administration's assertions to the contrary. Davis apparently believed that the Western theater was similar to its eastern counterpart. He failed to recognize that the two theaters differed, particularly where supply was concerned. Armies operating in the East benefited from their proximity to abundant agricultural production in Virginia, the Carolinas, and Maryland. Consequently, the Army of Northern Virginia had been able to maneuver throughout Virginia, Maryland, and even into Pennsylvania without remaining on or near a railroad line. Armies in the West could not hope to supply themselves from the countryside while on the march. Settlement in the Western theater was sparse and provided limited

9 *O.R.* vol. 32, pt. 3, 614–615; Johnston, *Narrative of Military Operations*, 292–293; Davis, *The Rise and Fall of the Confederate Government*, II:548–549.

provisions for armies in the region. Western armies therefore relied upon railroads or rivers to connect them with depots for maintaining sufficient supply levels.[10]

Moreover, the terrain in eastern Tennessee, the avenue of Davis's proposed advance, posed a particular problem. Union Gen. Jacob Cox described the topography of the territory as inhospitable and suffering from inadequate country roads. Cox observed that the few existing roads were "scarce better than pack-mule tracks." Furthermore, the Federal campaign to take Knoxville, under Gen. Ambrose Burnside in the fall of 1863, had required a Herculean effort to transport artillery across the treacherous mountain passes. Cox asserted that "at the principal ascent of the mountain the teams of two or three guns had to be hitched to a single cannon to pull to the summit; and even these were aided by soldiers at the wheel." Burnside himself expressed concern over "the difficulty of transporting supplies" to his men in and around Knoxville. He feared that unless the Confederates could be driven south of their position at Dalton the railroad between Chattanooga and Knoxville could not be used to provide supplies for his column. Cox also noted that Confederate disruption of the railroad lines between Chattanooga and Nashville threatened the Federal garrison in Knoxville with starvation. In lieu of access to the railroad, Burnside suggested the establishment of a wagon train between Kingston and McMinnville.[11] The wagon train Burnside wanted never materialized, largely due to the poor condition of the roads and the mountainous terrain. The Union forces tasked with holding Knoxville, and with it eastern Tennessee, found themselves in dire circumstances as the winter set in.

By January 1864 the Confederate and Federal forces in eastern Tennessee had stripped the countryside of all available forage for either man or beast. The Union garrison in Knoxville faced severe food shortages, including the increasingly poor condition of the available cattle. Jacob Cox recorded that "it is literally true that it was the custom of the commissaries to drive the cattle over a little ditch in the field where they were corralled, and those only were killed which could not get over." Burnside's successor, Gen. John Schofield, fared no better. When he took command on February 8, he complained that the army in Knoxville had been living on half rations or less for some time and that of the 25,000 men in his command only 7,000 of them were fit for duty. Schofield lamented the condition of the army's animals and suggested that thousands of dead horses and mules lay

10 Paddy Griffith, *Battle Tactics of the Civil War* (New Haven, CT, 1989), 41.

11 Jacob Cox, *Atlanta* (New York, 1882), 2, 10–12; *O.R.* vol. 31, pt. 1, 680.

unburied around the town. He stated that of the 30,000 animals Burnside took with him into Tennessee only 1,000 remained capable of service.[12]

Confederates too recognized the supply deficiency in eastern Tennessee. In April 1864, Lt. Gen. Simon Buckner assumed command of Confederate forces in the region and informed the War Department that "it is almost entirely exhausted of supplies beyond the actual wants of its citizens." Buckner claimed that while he had 4,000 effective troops in his cavalry command, the horses were unfit for duty. In fact, the lack of forage in the vicinity led Buckner's predecessor to "disburse [the horses] over a wide extent of country, from the Big Sandy, in Kentucky, to near Asheville, North Carolina." As Mark Elam noted, if Buckner could not provide forage for his own command, he certainly could not hope to feed the thousands of additional animals that would arrive in the theater along with Johnston's forces.[13]

The Confederate advance into eastern Tennessee, as the Davis-Bragg plan required, stood little chance of success. The proposal called for rapid movement through a territory that lacked the resources to sustain an army operating a significant distance from its base of supplies. Unlike Virginia and Maryland where an army might requisition supplies from the local population, a large Confederate force advancing through eastern Tennessee could not rely on such methods. The low population density meant that the army could gather minimal forage even during the peak harvest season. The Davis-Bragg strategy called for Johnston to march into eastern Tennessee in early spring, well before harvest time. Further, the harsh winter and Federal presence in the region since October dramatically reduced the already limited forage available in the territory. Consequently, any Confederate movement through the area could not hope to support itself off the land. Johnston would be faced with a serious dilemma: either he could bypass Knoxville entirely and move into a position north of Chattanooga in hopes of finding adequate forage, or he could attempt to reduce the garrison at Knoxville. Both options presented significant danger.

If Johnston determined to advance into middle Tennessee north of Chattanooga he would be unable to receive supplies from Confederate commissary stores. The experience of the Federal garrison in Knoxville during the winter of 1863–64 demonstrated a lack of sufficient roads for the purpose of maintaining supply to a relatively small force. Burnside's force had amounted to approximately 25,000 men

12 Cox, *Atlanta*, 15. Those who could manage to hurdle the ditch were deemed sufficiently healthy, and consequently did not yet require butchering. John M. Schofield, *Forty-Six Years in the Army* (n.p., 1897), 41–42.

13 *O.R.* vol. 32, pt. 3, 803; Elam, "The Road to Atlanta," 47.

in October 1863.[14] According to the Davis-Bragg plan, Johnston would command over 70,000 troops. Not only would Johnston be responsible for nearly three times as many men as Burnside/Schofield, but he would also be much further from his base of supplies than the Federal garrison at Knoxville had been. Additionally, the movement would not displace the Union troops in Knoxville; instead it would allow them to harass and disrupt any attempt to supply Johnston's army via wagon train. Johnston would then be left with the hope that Sherman would abandon Chattanooga and pursue Johnston's army. Even then Sherman could resupply his army from the depot at Chattanooga while Johnston would be forced to obtain sustenance from the local farmers and communities, a difficult proposition due to the low population in the region. Sherman, on the other hand, might well leave an adequate force to defend Chattanooga and march south toward Atlanta with his remaining force. If Sherman chose the latter, the Confederacy would not be able to stop him. A movement into middle Tennessee would be a risk with serious consequences if Sherman did not act precisely as the Confederates intended.

Alternatively, Johnston's combined army could threaten Knoxville, as the Davis-Bragg design suggested. Like the move into middle Tennessee, the latter proposal had a number of flaws. The most objectionable aspect about any Confederate concentration on Knoxville was that such a movement would require a significant amount of time. The Federal garrison had withstood Longstreet's investment of the town from the middle of November until late December when Longstreet encamped in his winter quarters. There was no reason to believe that the arrival of Johnston's additional forces would compel Knoxville's immediate surrender. Neither Davis nor Johnston advocated a direct assault on a fortified city; Johnston's army would be forced into a siege unless Schofield abandoned the city prior to the Confederates' arrival. Even if Schofield retreated, however, Johnston's army would be in no condition to make a rapid advance from Knoxville. Few supplies remained in the city, and the countryside of eastern Tennessee had suffered from Federal occupation since mid-October. The poor condition of the roads meant that any advance would be slow, and the army could not hope to live off the land. Johnston would be forced to build a stockpile of supplies in Knoxville to serve as his depot for any movement into middle Tennessee. The process would take several weeks, if not months, and would provide Sherman with an opportunity to move toward Atlanta from his base in Chattanooga.

Accordingly, the Davis-Bragg plan for the upcoming spring campaign was poorly designed and destined to fail. Davis was blind to the difference in the conditions between the Eastern and the Western theaters of operations. Having

14 *O.R.* vol. 31, pt. 1, 680.

observed Robert E. Lee maneuver his army through Virginia and Maryland, he believed similar activities could be undertaken without much difficulty in the West. Braxton Bragg, having served as commander of the Army of Tennessee, should have alerted the president to the distinctions between the two theaters of operations. Perhaps he believed that the Perryville campaign in 1862 proved that such a maneuver was possible.

However, the proposed plan for the spring of 1864 faced obstacles that the advance into Kentucky two years earlier did not. The most notable difference between the campaigns was the Confederate point of departure. In 1862, Bragg had moved north from Chattanooga, while Gen. Kirby Smith marched into Kentucky from his base in Knoxville. Both commands benefited from having a supply depot (in Chattanooga and Knoxville) to their rear without fear that supply routes might suffer molestation from Federal forces. Furthermore, the campaign commenced in the middle of August when soldiers on the march could expect to supply themselves with corn, apples, and other provisions from the surrounding countryside. Even so, Kirby Smith commented on the difficulty of his advance from Knoxville to Richmond, Kentucky. Smith suggested that his march was one of the most difficult of the war; his troops were subjected to great hardship including poor roads, minimal water, and only green corn and unsalted beef to eat. Smith made his march with about 12,400 men, a force significantly smaller than the proposed advance under the Davis-Bragg plan.[15] Bragg should have known that the success of his 1862 campaign owed much to variables not present in 1864. While the condition of the roads in eastern Tennessee had not changed, the availability of provisions and the number of troops requiring them would be dramatically different. Bragg failed in his capacity as military advisor to the president when he neglected to inform Davis of the distinct differences between the Eastern and Western theaters of operation and ignored the striking dissimilarity between the Perryville campaign and the proposed plan for the spring.

Upon receipt of the Davis-Bragg plan, Johnston wrote to Bragg on March 19, detailing his objections including concerns regarding the maintenance of communications and the ability to supply the army. Johnston proposed that reinforcements should be sent to him at Dalton for the purpose of a defensive stand against the enemy, followed by a counterattack. If this did not meet with the administration's approval, Johnston proposed that Polk's Army of Mississippi reinforce his own and together march into western Tennessee through Alabama in order to draw the Federal army out of its strong entrenchments around Chattanooga. Johnston presumed that a forward movement to Ringgold and

15 *O.R.* vol. 26, pt. 2, 935; *O.R.* vol. 26, pt. 1, 776.

thence on to Cleveland held the best chance for success should the administration insist on offensive operations.[16]

Johnston's fallback plan, an advance through Alabama into western Tennessee, offered a far greater opportunity for success than did the Davis-Bragg design. The roads were easier to traverse because they lacked the numerous mountain ranges present in eastern Tennessee. Furthermore, no significant Federal or Confederate forces operated in northern Alabama during the winter of 1863–64, so the region had not been stripped barren of supplies. Still, a Confederate invasion of Tennessee through Alabama faced the difficulties of a large army operating in a territory with low population. Johnston's men could hope for considerably less forage than their counterparts in Lee's army. Another fault with the plan was that it, like the Davis-Bragg plan, relied on Sherman to behave in a manner consistent with Confederate objectives. Should Sherman determine to leave an adequate force in Chattanooga and march on Atlanta with his remaining troops, the Confederacy could do nothing to stop him. Though Johnston's proposal for an offensive afforded more hope of success than the Davis-Bragg strategy, his preference for making a defensive stand remained the best option under the circumstances.

As the dispute between the president and Johnston over the proper course of action for the spring campaign escalated, others also offered their suggestions for offensive operations into Tennessee.[17] Only one of them had any real hope of success and that was the second of two proposals offered by James Longstreet. Undaunted with objections to his initial proposition and eager to play a principal role in the upcoming campaign, Longstreet proffered a second plan of action. His new proposal envisioned a unification of his own command with P. G. T. Beauregard's troops in Abingdon, Virginia. Initially, Beauregard's troops could concentrate in Greenville, South Carolina and acquire the necessary supplies for an advance into Kentucky by way of Pound Gap. According to Longstreet, the force would number approximately 40,000 infantry and artillery and thus compel the Union to abandon all or most of Tennessee. Should the Federals attempt to concentrate their forces on the invading army under Beauregard, Longstreet asserted that Beauregard could maneuver into Tennessee and unite with Johnston. He calculated that the transfer of a division from Polk's command in Mississippi to South Carolina would compensate for the troops headed north with Beauregard. Further, troops from Mobile could be transferred to Atlanta if Johnston moved

16 *O.R.* vol. 32, pt. 3, 653–654; Johnston, *Narrative of Military Operations*, 294–296; *O.R.* vol. 32, pt. 2, 559–560, 603–604, 644–645; Davis, *The Rise and Fall of the Confederate Government*, II:549.

17 A detailed analysis of Leonidas Polk's plan and James Longstreet's first plan may be found in Appendix I.

north into Tennessee. The plan apparently received the support of Robert E. Lee, who assisted Longstreet in his effort to convince Davis to adopt the strategy. The fact that Lee considered the plan worthy of support suggests that it promised a legitimate chance for success.

The proposal, however, met with criticism from Johnston. Johnston argued that the Federals enjoyed the protection of interior lines and could concentrate more easily on any isolated Confederate force. He further asserted that Grant's return to Tennessee indicated that the primary Union effort in the spring would surely target Atlanta. Consequently, Johnston maintained that reinforcements and supplies should be sent to him at Dalton as soon as possible to defeat the inevitable Union advance upon that position.[18]

Davis too had reasons to reject Longstreet's second proposal, though Davis's objections stemmed from personal animosity rather than discomfort with the strategy Longstreet advocated. On March 25 the president informed Longstreet that the railroad could not support the troop movement of Beauregard's men into South Carolina as Longstreet wanted. According to Davis, such a movement threatened to interrupt the supply of corn to Lee's army in Virginia. Davis's contention was unreasonable; surely Lee's army could survive on half rations of corn for a few days. Davis went on to argue that Longstreet's proposal left the coastal defenses too weak and stripped Atlanta of the ability to defend itself.[19] Again, Davis's contention lacked merit. If the Confederacy launched an invasion of Kentucky, the Rebels would claim the initiative and the Federals would be forced to react to their opponents. As a result, the Union would be hard-pressed to defend Kentucky from a large field army and at the same time press an attack on the Confederacy's coastal cities. The president's claim that Longstreet's plan would endanger Atlanta was patently absurd. Davis himself sponsored a plan that required Johnston to evacuate Dalton and move through eastern Tennessee, a move that would enable Sherman to advance on Atlanta if he chose to ignore the threat that Johnston's army posed to his rear. Longstreet's proposal allowed Johnston to remain in Dalton, between Sherman and Atlanta. In reality, Davis refused Longstreet's proposal out of spite against Beauregard.

The relationship between Beauregard and Davis had deteriorated ever since the aftermath of the first battle of Manassas in 1861. Beauregard's conduct after the battle of Shiloh in 1862 had further incensed the president. Indeed, it is safe to assert that Davis promoted Johnston to command of the Army of Tennessee only

18 *O.R.* vol. 32 pt. 3, 640–641, 637, 653.

19 Ibid., 675.

because he detested Johnston less than Beauregard. To have accepted Longstreet's latest plan would have elevated Beauregard to *de facto* command of a major field army, a proposition Davis clearly disliked. Consequently, he rejected a plan that presented the best opportunity among all those proffered for a spring offensive.

The fact that Robert E. Lee supported Longstreet's strategy for the spring indicates that the plan was not without merit. First, the plan addressed the most glaring deficiency in the previously considered spring offensives. Beauregard's army would advance with adequate supplies from its starting point in Abingdon, Virginia. Additionally, the plotted course of the army's advance meant that it would not encounter a terrain stripped bare of forage due to the presence of Federal or Confederate forces over the course of the winter. Nor would the garrison in Knoxville pose a significant threat to Beauregard's supply line. Once in Kentucky, Beauregard would have access to the forage available in that state and could recruit troops to swell his ranks.

Further, the commitment of 40,000 troops ensured that the army would gain Kentucky with little trouble, as no Federal force in the vicinity could hope to match its numbers. With the addition of soldiers recruited from Kentucky, the Confederate force would pose a serious threat to the Union occupation of Tennessee. At a minimum the Federal garrison at Knoxville under Schofield would need to abandon its position and move to Nashville to protect the supply depot there. Nashville served as the largest army depot in the country with massive warehouses often covering entire city blocks. The depot at Nashville provided Sherman's army with its source of supply. If Nashville could be threatened with siege, Sherman's supplies would be in jeopardy. Even if Schofield were able to reach Nashville before Beauregard, his force no longer numbered 25,000. On March 14, Grant ordered the Ninth Corps from Schofield's army to the east. As a consequence, Schofield only commanded two infantry divisions with approximately 7,000 effective men and an additional 2,000 cavalry. Upon discovery of Schofield's diminished army, Sherman ordered the addition of a third division. That division consisted of 5,000 new recruits untested in battle.[20] Even with a third division, Schofield's army lacked the manpower to oppose the Confederate force envisioned in Longstreet's latest plan. If Beauregard and Longstreet moved into Kentucky and then threatened Nashville, Sherman would probably have needed to abandon Chattanooga.

On May 1 the Federal troops in the Western theater remained widely dispersed and vulnerable to Longstreet's proposed plan of action. Sherman's force in Chattanooga consisted of approximately 73,000 soldiers in the Army of the Cumberland, under the command of Gen. George Thomas. General James

20 Castel, *Decision in the West*, 88, 92; *O.R.* vol. 32, pt. 3, 67.

McPherson and his Army of the Tennessee, with 24,500 men, remained in Huntsville, Alabama until the beginning of May.[21] If the Confederate invasion of Kentucky commenced in late April, as Longstreet suggested, Union forces in the region faced a dilemma. To defend Nashville against a Confederate army numbering between 40,000 and 45,000 infantry and artillery, Sherman would be forced to bolster Schofield's command significantly. Since many of Schofield's troops were raw, a reinforcement of fewer than 40,000 would have been insufficient. A transfer of that many troops to Nashville would have left only about 30,000 men to defend Chattanooga and offered an opportunity for Johnston to besiege the remaining garrison. Sherman could order McPherson to march from Huntsville to Chattanooga to compensate for the reduction of his forces there. To do so, however, exposed McPherson's army to an attack if Johnston decided to interpose himself between McPherson's line of march and Chattanooga. Consequently, unless Sherman decided to move north with his entire command with both McPherson and Thomas, he courted disaster. If Sherman chose the prudent course of action and marched north with the Army of the Cumberland and the Army of the Tennessee, Johnston could take Chattanooga without a fight.

Longstreet's second suggestion for taking the offensive in the spring gave the Confederacy its best hope for success and is likely the reason that Lee chose to offer his support. The plan addressed the problem of supply, one of the primary drawbacks to the Davis-Bragg strategy. Additionally, the number of troops allotted to the invasion force under Beauregard meant that Sherman needed to respond aggressively. Sherman, however, would not have the option to march on Atlanta, as Johnston's army still stood in his way at Dalton. Sherman's only real alternative would be to concentrate on Beauregard, which meant the abandonment of Chattanooga and Knoxville. Further, by the time Sherman concentrated his forces and advanced on Beauregard, the latter could withdraw to Abingdon if necessary. Even if Beauregard were forced into battle, his army would have adequate strength to defend itself. Finally, Longstreet's strategy would have allowed the Confederates to take the initiative and recover much of Tennessee. The fertile farmland in the middle of the state offered the Confederacy a replacement for the loss of the Trans-Mississippi during the summer of 1863. It also provided the administration with political capital. Politicians in Tennessee and Alabama could all claim victory as Federal forces would no longer occupy their states. Georgians too stood to benefit with the threat of imminent invasion removed. Nevertheless, Davis refused to adopt the plan and offered a bevy of weak objections to it. Davis's personal animosity toward Beauregard offers the only reasonable explanation for his

21 Castel, *Decision in the West*, 112; *O.R.* vol. 32, pt. 3, 536.

behavior. The president permitted a personal grudge to prevail over sound strategy and political expediency.

None of the proposals for the spring campaign were perfect and some were without any merit at all. The Davis-Bragg plan was the worst of the lot. The evidence clearly demonstrates that an advance through eastern Tennessee carried too great a risk; a large force could not be adequately supplied. Further, the plan called for Johnston to evacuate his position at Dalton, thereby providing an opportunity for Sherman to move on to Atlanta unmolested. Longstreet's initial proposal mirrored the Davis-Bragg strategy and so too deserves criticism. Johnston's own proposal for offensive operations was the best of those plans that advocated the northward advance of the Army of Tennessee. The army would at least have an opportunity to supply itself. Still, Sherman would be given the chance to decide for himself whether he wanted to move on Atlanta. Considering his decision to march to the sea at the conclusion of the Atlanta campaign, Sherman appears to have had little compunction in requiring his army to subsist off the land. Longstreet's second plan offered the best opportunity for Confederate success by a large margin. Johnston could remain between Sherman and Atlanta while a second sizable army moved into Sherman's rear and endangered his supply line.

Unfortunately for the Confederacy, the plan also meant Beauregard's return to the field—a proposition Jefferson Davis could not stomach. Clearly the dispute over the proper course of action for the spring campaign generated a disagreement between the administration and the Confederacy's top lieutenant in the West. The dispute hinged on whether Johnston's army remained capable of invading Tennessee after the disaster at Missionary Ridge in November 1863.

Condition of the Army of Tennessee

Despite his rejection of Longstreet's plan, Davis remained committed to offensive operations in the Western theater as soon as conditions permitted. His belief in the efficacy of aggressive action came not only from political concerns, but also from the impression that the condition of Johnston's army allowed for a movement into Tennessee. The president and his administration believed that the Army of Tennessee was in good condition even after the fiasco at Missionary Ridge. According to reports, the army's strength would be recouped with the addition of one or two brigades from the Department of Mississippi and the arrival of stragglers and convalescents. Further, Davis received reports that suggested that the army had adequate artillery as well as sufficient ammunition and supplies. Davis's aide, Col. Joseph Ives, had visited Dalton and informed the president that forces there appeared ready for battle. In fact, on December 11 Hardee informed the president that the army was "in good spirits, the artillery re-organized and equipped . . . and ready to fight." Though Hardee's communication on December 11 presented the picture of an army ready for action, his earlier report on December 4 indicated that the army lacked offensive punch, numbering a mere 30,127 effective infantry and artillery. Hardee had also complained about the state of supply on December 3 when he informed Johnston, then in command of the department, that without the supply of more meat "it will be impossible to hold this army together."[22]

On December 17, Hardee sent a telegram to the War Department that clearly contradicted his earlier assessment that the army was ready for action. The communication, like the December 3 telegram to Johnston, emphasized inadequacy in the army's supply. In it he stated: "To enable this army to take the field, reinforcements are necessary . . . but in our present condition it is necessary to avoid a general action." Further, "the question of supplies, both for men and animals, presents a source of infinite trouble." Finally, and perhaps most importantly, Hardee informed Davis that the Federals' recent reinforcements dispelled any hope of offensive action on the part of the Army of Tennessee.[23]

Davis chose to ignore Hardee's protestations of December 17 and focus instead on his December 11 communication and Colonel Ives's report. On December 23, Davis sent a telegram to Johnston stating his understanding of the condition of the army in Dalton. The president insisted that the evidence available to him led him to believe that the army could soon take the offensive. Davis claimed that the letter from Bragg received soon after the battle of Missionary Ridge indicated that the army sustained few casualties and remained in fighting condition. He also referenced the report from Colonel Ives that suggested that the material condition of the army "was not unfavorable." To bolster Ives's account, Davis cited the report of the chief of ordnance that the artillery was well equipped with guns, horses, and ordnance. The infantry too was well supplied with weaponry and ammunition. The president claimed that with stragglers and convalescents returning to the ranks and the addition of cavalry from east Tennessee he expected Johnston's army to exceed the number of troops available to any Confederate army since the start of the war. Davis closed with the observation that Hardee's communication of December 11 indicated the readiness of the army for the upcoming campaign.[24] The president failed to mention Hardee's subsequent communication to the contrary. Rather, he relied upon the information that best suited his hope for the spring.

22 *O.R.* vol. 31, pt. 3, 781, 783, 810, 865, 860; Castel, *Decision in the West*, 32. There is nothing in the record, however, that indicates Johnston passed Hardee's December 3 message to the president.

23 *O.R.* vol. 31, pt. 3, 839–840.

24 Ibid., 856.

In reality, the army at Dalton bore no resemblance to the one described in the president's missive. On January 2, Johnston informed Davis that the recent returns revealed only 36,000 effective infantry and artillery. Though that figure was significantly higher than the 30,127 Hardee had reported in early December, it compared unfavorably to the size of the army during the Chickamauga campaign. Moreover, Lee's armies routinely numbered significantly more troops than those available to Johnston at Dalton. Even at the close of April Johnston's army mustered only 40,000 effective infantry and artillery, including 1,500 troops under the command of Gen. George Cantey, recently arrived from Polk's army in Mississippi. An additional 8,500 cavalry were present for duty, only 2,400 of whom were effective due to the poor condition of their horses. The difficult campaign that extended into the winter of 1863–64 left the troopers with few serviceable mounts. In fact, many of the troopers had returned to their homes in search of new horses for the upcoming campaign.[25] Certainly most convalescents and stragglers had returned to the army by April, which meant that the only way to increase the Army of Tennessee's ranks was reinforcement from another theater of operations. As a result, Davis clearly erred in his calculation that the army might exceed any previous Confederate army during the war.

It was not due to a lack of effort on the part of its new commander that the Army of Tennessee remained relatively weak. Upon his arrival at Dalton, Johnston had diligently sought ways to improve the strength and morale of his army. Though Davis advocated an advance into Tennessee, Johnston feared that the condition of his army would prevent even an effective defense against a Union advance from Chattanooga. On January 6, Johnston informed his confidant, Senator Louis Wigfall, that Sherman's arrival from Mississippi had augmented the Federal force arrayed against him by 25,000 men. To enhance his own troop strength Johnston advocated that Wigfall propose a bill to the Congress allowing for the impressment of slaves into the army. Johnston believed that slaves could be substituted for soldiers engaged in detached service and those on extra duty who worked as cooks, engineer laborers, and pioneers. Johnston asserted that more than 10,000 men could be added to the front line if slaves replaced them.[26]

In addition to his effort to increase the size of his force, Johnston worked diligently to procure supplies. Two obstacles made his task more difficult. First, Georgia began furnishing Lee's army with beef during the winter of 1863–64. Consequently, the Army of Tennessee was forced to share beef rations with the army

25 *O.R.* vol. 32, pt. 2, 510; *O.R.* vol. 32, pt. 3, 866; Castel, *Decision in the West*, 110.

26 Johnston to Louis Wigfall, Jan. 6, 1864, LC.

in Virginia. Further, economic interests compelled Johnston's army to compete for access to the railroad. The government's transport of cotton from Georgia to Wilmington, North Carolina interfered with the army's ability to access supplies. The managers of the Georgia Railroad complained that they lacked the fuel to meet the government's cotton demands as well as the army's supply demands. Johnston became so frustrated with the railroad service that he claimed, "if the enemy manages railroads no better, as far as the defensive is concerned we may take away our troops."[27] Nevertheless, Johnston's efforts to supply his men over the course of his first few months in command made a positive impression on the troops.

Ambrose Doss of the 19th Alabama infantry regiment cheerfully wrote to his wife on January 27 that his rations were acceptable. They included "plenty of bread, three quarters of a pound of beef and several other little nourishments including rice and sugar." Sometimes the men even received "a little hog meat." In addition to securing satisfactory forage for his army, Johnston instituted a policy of fair food distribution. During Bragg's command, officers generally fared far better than enlisted men. Under Bragg officers were permitted to befriend commissaries and quartermasters and thereby obtain the best available provisions. Johnston ordered that rations be distributed evenly between officers and enlisted men.[28]

Not only did soldiers receive food from the commissary, but they also managed to secure food from the local population and in the form of care packages from home. For example, Lt. A. J. Neal was delighted that he had purchased one hundred pounds of flour and fifteen old hens that produced four eggs a day from a local farmer. In addition to receiving meat from his wife, Pvt. Ambrose Doss also purchased one hundred dollars' worth of meat between January and the beginning of March. Other soldiers also received packages from home to supplement their diet. Spencer Welch, an army surgeon, wrote to his wife in January thanking her for her shipment. Welch listed sweet potatoes, ten gallons of kraut, ten gallons of molasses, forty pounds of flour, twelve pounds of butter, a ham, and a side of bacon, among other things.[29]

In addition to his efforts to secure proper rations for his troops, Johnston instigated other reforms as well. He began by extending amnesty to all absentees, a policy that increased the army by 649 soldiers. Johnston also established a system of furlough lotteries that proved highly popular. A furlough was granted to one

27 Elam, "The Road to Atlanta," 49; Johnston to Wigfall, Jan. 1864, LC.

28 Ambrose Doss to Sarah Doss, Jan. 27, 1864, Ambrose Doss Letters, Kennesaw National Battlefield Library (KNBL); A. J. Neal to Ella Neal, March 8, 1864, A. J. Neal Letters, KNBL.

29 Neal to his mother, Feb. 3, 1864, Neal Letters; Doss to wife, March 3, 1864, KNBL; Spencer Glascow Welch, *A Confederate Surgeon's Letters to his Wife* (1911; repr., Marietta, GA., 1954), 88–89.

out of every twenty-five men and one of ten men in those units that reenlisted for the duration of the war. J. W. Ward commented that "the prospect of obtaining immediate furloughs endured many of the men to reenlist."[30]

Johnston also oversaw a building project with each brigade constructing its own church. Randall Gibson's brigade from Louisiana erected two churches, one Protestant and one Catholic. General Patrick Cleburne even used the churches as a schoolhouse to teach members of his command to read and write. Further, Johnston saw to the acquisition of proper clothing and footwear for his soldiers. On March 8 Halsey Wigfall, serving on Hood's staff, noted that the men "seem well clothed and shod and there was more the look of uniform about their appearance than I have seen since I have been in the army." Johnston's insistence on frequent drill further helped to transform the army. Prior to Johnston's arrival the infantry received little or no training on the firing range. Johnston ordered that marksmanship be made a priority. On March 21 Halsey Wigfall expressed to his mother that officers with previous service in Lee's army considered the Army of Tennessee superior in their drill. In totality, Johnston's measures transformed the dispirited army he inherited after its loss at Missionary Ridge. As early as January the men had gained confidence in their new commander. Johnston inspired so much enthusiasm that one Tennessee regiment even volunteered for a term of 99 years or until the end of the war.[31]

Despite Johnston's extraordinary efforts, serious obstacles remained. In particular, the condition of the animals and the artillery improved little over the course of the winter. Upon elevation to command of the army, Johnston attempted to improve the condition of both artillery and cavalry horses. He ordered that horses be sent throughout the region to areas with adequate forage. Sherman's raid on Meridian in late February, however, forced Johnston to recall most of his cavalry and artillery. Lieutenant A. J. Neal of the 1st Florida Artillery lamented that the horses improved while at Kingston but suffered some while in close proximity to Dalton. In particular he noted that half of the "long forage" was spoiled. On March 14 Halsey Wigfall observed that "the horses are in bad order." Further the army's artillery appeared more suited for a war waged a half a century earlier. Many batteries still operated 6-pound and 12-pound howitzers, guns that were outdated

30 Larry J. Daniel, *Soldiering in the Army of Tennessee: A Portrait of Life in a Confederate Army* (Chapel Hill, NC, 1991), 138; J. C. Thompson to A. P. Stewart, Box 1, Folder 2, JP WM; Daniel, *Soldiering in the Army of Tennessee*, 138.

31 J. C. Thompson to A. P. Stewart, Box 1, Folder 2, JP WM; Halsey Wigfall to Louis Wigfall, March 8, 21, 1864, LC; Arthur M. Manigault, *A Carolinian Goes to War: The Civil War Narrative of Arthur Middleton Manigault, Brigadier General, C.S.A.*, ed. R. Lockwood Tower (Columbia, SC, 1983), 188.

even at the beginning of the war. Nevertheless, Johnston took what measures he could to reform that branch of service. He reorganized the artillery into regiments, one for each corps and one in reserve.[32]

Undoubtedly Johnston's performance had done much to restore the army's condition. By the middle of March the men were receiving adequate rations, the furlough system and church construction had improved morale, and Johnston had increased the army's drill efficiency. Even so, the April returns demonstrate that the army numbered less than 44,000 men. Despite Johnston's best efforts to supply his army, he lacked the manpower to advance into Tennessee as the president envisioned. The poor condition of the army's transportation vehicles and horses for both the artillery and the cavalry also stood in the way of a forward movement.

As the spring approached, Johnston continued to request reinforcements to hold his position at Dalton. Davis, however, did not believe that Johnston's army lacked the ability to make offensive maneuvers. On March 7 Davis had received a communication from Gen. John Bell Hood that indicated the army was in magnificent spirits and only required an additional 10–15,000 men to advance into Tennessee. Based on Hood's report, Davis refused to send Johnston any reinforcements unless Johnston agreed to accept the administration's proposal for an advance through eastern Tennessee. On March 12 Davis informed Johnston that if he agreed to execute the Davis-Bragg strategy he would receive an additional 32,000 men from Polk, Beauregard, and Longstreet. Four days later, Johnston again cited supply problems as an impediment to the proposed invasion. Johnston argued that the army remained deficient in artillery horses and transportation. He further asserted that he had not yet been able to secure the surplus of stores necessary for an advance.[33]

Embroiled again in an argument over the spring campaign strategy, Johnston sent his assistant, Adjutant General Benjamin Ewell, to Richmond to persuade the administration. Ewell arrived in the capital on April 13 and met with Davis. Ewell stated that Johnston did not oppose an offensive movement *per se*, though this was disputable considering Johnston's communication of March 19 that called for a defensive stand followed by a counterattack. Ewell argued that Johnston only opposed the administration's plan of action for an advance into eastern Tennessee. In response, Davis gave Ewell an ultimatum; Johnston would receive 15,000 reinforcements only if he agreed to take the offensive. Davis also demanded that Johnston respond to the offer of reinforcements by the following

32 Neal to father, March 3, 1864, KNBL; Halsey Wigfall to Louis Wigfall, March 14, 1864, LC.

33 *O.R.* vol. 32, pt. 3, 606–607, 615, 636–637; Hood, *Advance and Retreat*, 92; Johnston, *Narrative of Military Operations*, 298.

day or face revocation. Interestingly, Davis's proffered reinforcements no longer matched the numbers indicated in the March 12 communication, which had suggested Johnston could expect as many as 32,000 additional men. Perhaps the administration believed Hood's assessment that reinforcements totaling 10–15,000 were sufficient for an advance. Hood made his observations to the president in a letter penned on March 7. It is likely that Davis did not receive the letter prior to the administration's March 12 communication to Johnston offering substantially more reinforcements. Having received Hood's assessment, Davis and Bragg might have determined to send a portion of the 32,000 elsewhere. In fact, on April 11 the administration ordered Longstreet from eastern Tennessee back to Virginia.[34]

In addition to Hood's letter, Davis had received similar reports from other sources, which likely influenced the administration's ultimatum. On March 29 Brigadier General William Pendleton, sent by the administration to assess the condition of the Army of Tennessee, reported that the army's artillery corps, once the horses recovered from a difficult season, would prove satisfactory and capable of contributing. Further, a report dated April 11 from Davis's aide, Col. Arthur Cole, disputed Johnston's claims concerning the condition of his field transportation. Cole observed that any deficiencies were Johnston's fault, considering his past service as the Quartermaster General of the United States Army. Cole attributed the deficiencies to the season and believed the situation reparable.[35]

A second report from Pendleton, containing Bragg's notations, contradicted Johnston's estimation of the enemy strength. Pendleton had met with Johnston on April 15 to discuss the possibility of offensive operations. During the meeting, Johnston relied on the testimony from his cavalry chief, Gen. Joseph Wheeler, who estimated the Federal forces at approximately 103,000 men. Pendleton generated a report of the meeting and sent it to Davis, who then forwarded it to Bragg. Bragg returned the report with notations that insisted that Wheeler had overestimated the Federal strength. According to Bragg, the Union army consisted of no more than 70,000, of whom only 60,000 were serviceable.[36]

Bragg was not alone in his assessment. Hood also miscalculated Sherman's strength. In a March 17 letter to the president, advocating an advance, Hood asserted that the men were well fed and well clothed, in high spirits and "eager for the fray." He noted that the Army mustered approximately 40,000 men and that a junction with Polk would bring the total to 60,000, giving the Confederates a 10,000 man

34 Castel, *Decision in the West*, 100; *O.R.* vol. 32, pt. 3, 772.

35 *O.R.* vol. 32, pt. 3, 686, 773–774.

36 Johnston, *Narrative of Military Operations*, 301; Castel, *Decision in the West*, 103.

advantage over their opponents. If Bragg and Hood were correct, the addition of only 15,000 men to the total of the Army of Tennessee's April returns showing an effective total of 43,887 in all branches of service would put the Confederates on an equal footing with Sherman's army. In reality, Wheeler's estimate of the enemy was far closer to the truth, as the Army of Tennessee confronted approximately 100,000 men within the combined armies under Sherman.[37]

In any event, Johnston's reply to Davis's ultimatum was both late and vague, claiming that "assuming the offensive must depend on relative forces. I shall be ready to do so whenever they warrant it." To Davis's credit, he did not withdraw the offer of reinforcements as indicated in his ultimatum. Nevertheless, circumstances in Virginia eventually required the administration to concentrate on the campaign in the Eastern theater, thus effectively ending the dispatch of Longstreet's Corps to Johnston. Davis's decision to concentrate on the situation confronting Lee's army in late April 1864 illustrates his belief that the Federal army did not possess the ability to mount dual offensives, one in the East and one in the West. Soon, he discovered that they could. In fact, on May 6, Davis ordered General Polk to turn command of the Department of Mississippi over to General S. D. Lee and proceed to Dalton with Loring's division and any other available troops to meet the threat posed by Sherman's advance toward Rome.[38]

In his postwar defense, Davis claimed that because Johnston proved unwilling to carry out the administration's initial plans for an offensive into eastern Tennessee, the Federal army managed to create combinations rendering the Davis-Bragg plan impractical. Consequently, Davis asserted that he took "prompt measures to enable General Johnston to carry out immediately his own proposition to strike first at Ringgold and then at Cleveland." Davis also argued that while Johnston's proposed offensive held less promise than his own, it "might have been attended with good results had it been properly executed."[39] The record, however, indicates that Davis took no such measures. The president's first attempt to send reinforcements for the purpose of executing Johnston's proposed offensive occurred on May 6. Davis issued the order only after Sherman began his advance toward Dalton and Rome and two months after Johnston mentioned the possibility of an invasion of western Tennessee. Davis had been given ample opportunity to take the necessary steps to ensure the success of Johnston's plan to strike at Ringgold.

37 Jones, *A Rebel War Clerk's Diary at the Confederate States Capital*, 350; *O.R.* vol. 32, pt. 3, 207–210; Sherman, *Memoirs of General W. T. Sherman*, 472–473.

38 *O.R.* vol. 32, pt. 3, 781; Castel, *Decision in the West*, 101; Joseph Parks, *General Leonidas Polk C.S.A.: The Fighting Bishop* (Baton Rouge, 1962), 373.

39 Davis, *The Rise and Fall of the Confederate Government*, II:549–550.

Davis's failure to lend prompt assistance can be seen in his own admission that, when Sherman began his advance, Johnston's army mustered less than 50,000 men.[40] Further, his statement that Polk's command was then en route (on May 1) is simply false. Clearly, Davis's efforts to effectuate Johnston's proposal lacked the promptness he asserted and made it nearly impossible for his general to properly execute his (Johnston's) plan.

Prior to Johnston's assumption of command of the Army of Tennessee he and Davis viewed each other with suspicion. Their relationship only grew more tenuous over the course of the winter of 1863–64. Davis remained adamant throughout the course of the winter and into the spring that the Army of Tennessee was capable of offensive operations. Even though he received conflicting reports on the condition of the army, the president insisted that Johnston move into eastern Tennessee. The stalemate between the president and his commander in the West highlighted each of the key traits that distinguished Davis from his counterpart, Abraham Lincoln. Davis did not appreciate the advantage of a centralized command, and as a result the Confederate leadership could not produce a unified vision for the upcoming campaign season. Davis's distaste for Beauregard caused him to reject a proposal that offered the Confederacy a reasonable prospect for success. Finally, the president's dispute with Johnston had resulted in his encouragement of inappropriate communications between John Bell Hood and the Davis administration.

Johnston too found reasons to reject each of the offensive proposals. Most of his complaints were well founded. The system of supply left much to be desired as railroad cars in Georgia shipped Georgia beef to Virginia and often transported cotton to Wilmington rather than forage to Dalton. Moreover, Davis's plan offered little chance for success and Johnston knew it. As the spring campaign season loomed and the Federal advance became a certainty, Jefferson Davis and Joseph E. Johnston continued to discover new reasons to harbor distrust.

40 Ibid.

Chapter 4

Dalton to Adairsville: Maps, Militia, and Maneuver

As the campaign season in spring 1864 neared, a combination of factors threatened the Confederate defense of Georgia. The limited number of troops that Johnston had to defend against Sherman's seemingly overwhelming numbers constituted one problem. The dispute over the proposed spring offensive exacerbated the long-standing feud between Jefferson Davis and his chief lieutenant in the Western theater of operations. With Johnston unwilling to advance into eastern Tennessee, Davis refused to send reinforcements to Dalton. As a result, the personal quarrel between the two meant that Polk remained in Mississippi until Sherman commenced his advance on Dalton. Though both Johnston and Davis deserve blame for the impasse, Davis's proclivity for permitting his feelings to influence his decisions clearly affected the time-table for Polk's arrival in Georgia. By the time Polk arrived, Johnston had already lost possession of his defensive line along Rocky Face Ridge. Had Polk been present, Sherman's flanking maneuver would have been much more difficult, maybe impossible. Thus, Johnston's poor relationship with the president and both men's unwillingness to compromise deprived Johnston of the use of approximately 20,000 troops at the beginning of May 1864.

With Polk still in Mississippi, the Georgia militia could have filled the void to some extent. The conflict between Jefferson Davis and Georgia governor Joseph E. Brown eventually culminated in mutual hostility over the passage of the Conscription Act. After that, the governor had made every effort to impede enforcement of conscription in Georgia by granting exemption to state officeholders. The policy resulted in thousands of draft-eligible men escaping conscription.[1] Thereafter, the administration's handling of the Georgia State Guard following the battle of Chickamauga so distressed Governor Brown that he refused to cooperate with the administration in raising a reserve force in the months preceding Sherman's invasion of Georgia. The absence of militia may also have contributed to Johnston's retreat from his defensive line along Rocky Face Ridge.

In addition to the president's ineffective handling of his relationships with Johnston and Brown, the Confederates in the West suffered from a shortcoming not of Davis's making; William Tecumseh Sherman possessed an advantage not only in manpower but also in information. Over the course of the war, the Union army developed technologically advanced mapmaking capabilities, while Southerners could boast only of Jedediah Hotchkiss and D. B. Harris. Sherman's Army Corps of Engineers produced accurate maps for the entire army, giving Federal officers a uniform set of maps. Meanwhile, Confederate divisional and corps commanders manufactured their own maps, often resulting in discrepancies from one map to another. Indeed, some Confederate maps lacked critical topographical features, an oversight that may well have cost them their strong defensive position near Dalton.

Without Polk or the militia to guard his left flank and with deficient maps, Johnston was forced to rely on a depleted cavalry corps. The cavalry, under the command of Joseph Wheeler, failed to provide accurate information regarding Federal activity on Johnston's left. Johnston's lethargic response to what little information Wheeler's cavalry provided allowed Sherman to outflank his position around Dalton. In the aftermath of his timid performance near Dalton, Johnston launched a daring assault on Sherman's forces at Resaca when presented with the opportunity. Johnston planned a second attack, but circumstances prevented its execution. The geography around Resaca rendered the Confederate defensive position perilous and forced Johnston to retire southward toward Calhoun. Insufficient maps, however, plagued the army's movement south and resulted in the abandonment of Calhoun and Adairsville.

Maps

Three years of war had taught both sides that accurate maps were vital. In describing the Peninsula campaign of 1862 Confederate Gen. Richard Taylor commented that "The Confederate commanders knew no more about the topography of the country than they did about Central Africa. Here was a limited district, the whole of it within a day's march of the city of Richmond . . . and yet we were profoundly ignorant of the country, were without maps, sketches,

1 *C.R. Ga.*, III, 506–507.

or proper guides." A Confederate engineer in charge of the Map Reproduction Office in Richmond quipped that when Lee took command of the Army of Northern Virginia in June 1862, not a single useful map of the region existed. The Federals fared no better, and the evidence suggests that neither side possessed detailed maps early in the war. In 1861 the Topographical Bureau produced maps based on a variety of sources that included Revolutionary War memoirs, travel accounts, and local histories, a practice that indicates the lack of accurate cartographic information available to the Federal government at the outset of the war. As the war progressed both sides sought to remedy the situation, though the North had a decisive advantage with two government agencies responsible for the production of maps.[2]

With equipment and bureaucracy already in place, the Union mapmaking effort improved rapidly and by 1864 had produced 43,000 maps for Federal armies. Sherman in particular understood the need for accurate maps. Prior to the commencement of his campaign for Atlanta, Sherman ordered Col. William Merrill, chief engineer of the Topographical Department, Army of the Cumberland, to prepare a map that would be used by all officers under his command. Merrill enjoyed access to an extremely well-equipped map department. Despite being far removed from the nation's capital, Sherman's map office "had a printing press, two lithographic presses, one photographic establishment, arrangements for map-mounting, and a full corps of draftsmen and assistants."[3] Though the Federals enjoyed the advantage in technology, Sherman's army found itself operating in enemy territory. Consequently, the Union soldiers possessed little knowledge of the terrain they would encounter during the campaign.

Merrill's use of James R. Butt's "Map of the State of Georgia" as a basis upon which to build his campaign map helped the Federals to overcome their topographical shortcomings. Merrill, his staff, and Federal cavalry then made a practice of cross-examining locals, refugees, prisoners, merchants, and spies about the surrounding country. The answers helped Merrill "elaborate" on Butt's production and construct a more accurate map of the region. According to Thomas Van Horne, who served with the Army of the Cumberland, the process improved the quality of the army's maps immeasurably. In fact, Butt's "Map of

2 Richard Taylor, *Destruction and Reconstruction: Personal Experiences of the Late War*, ed. Longmans Green and Co. (n.p., 1955), 99; Albert H. Campbell, "The Lost War Maps of the Confederates," *The Century Magazine* 35, no. 3 (Jan. 1888): 480; Philip Muntz, "Union Mapping in the American Civil War," *Imago Mundi: A Review of Early Cartography* 17 (1963): 90–91. The Coast Survey, and the Corps of Topographical Engineers, were already in operation at the beginning of the war.

3 Richard Stevenson, "Mapping the Civil War," *Civil War Times Illustrated* (Nov.–Dec. 1992): 62; Thomas Van Horne, *History of the Army of the Cumberland* (Cincinnati, 1875), II:456.

the State of Georgia" failed to identify the existence of Snake Creek Gap, the passage that Sherman's army ultimately used during its march around Johnston's left flank. Only through interrogation did the Federals learn of its existence and add its location to the master campaign map that was then distributed throughout the army. At the commencement of the campaign the Topographical Department distributed 4,000 copies of campaign maps to Sherman's brigade, division, and corps commanders in anticipation of his advance upon Atlanta.[4]

Sherman's campaign map became less accurate as his army moved further south, but it still proved useful because of its uniformity. Officers could use the lettering on the map or lot numbers to guide their movements. For example, on May 10 Maj. Gen. James McPherson ordered a subordinate to "Post one of your regiments on the mountain toward the east end of the gap, not far from the letter M or O in the word mountain east of Villanow." On July 17, as his forces neared Atlanta, Sherman informed Maj. Gen. George Thomas, commanding the Army of the Cumberland, that Maj. Gen. John Schofield would move toward Peach Tree Road and "take post about lots 239, 247, and 272, with pickets forward as far as 196." The lots to which Sherman made reference were, like Butt's "Map of the State of Georgia," the fruit of prewar endeavors. The northern part of the state had been divided into townships and sections as part of the Cherokee Purchase. The Office of Topographical Engineers of the Army of the Cumberland ordered its scouts and agents to stop at every house and discover the precise number of the section and township lot each rested upon, thereby giving it an advantage when constructing the campaign map.[5]

As a result, even when roads or rivers were depicted inaccurately on the common campaign map, the Federal armies under Sherman could still effectively coordinate their maneuvers. If all else failed, each of Sherman's subordinate officers could at the very least understand the nature of his orders even when the designated road or ford could not be found. The officer could travel in a general direction, based upon "lots" and know that others were able to do the same thing.[6]

4 Elam, "The Road to Atlanta," 87; Van Horne, *History of the Army of the Cumberland*, II:457–458. The informants were not always volunteers. Sometimes Federal officers rounded up local farmers and questioned each separately under threat that if their answers differed one or more of them might be shot. See Earl B. McElfresh, *Maps and Mapmakers of the Civil War* (New York, 1999), 51–52; *O.R.* vol. 38, pt. 1, 137.

5 *O.R.* vol. 38, pt. 4, 129; *O.R.* vol. 38, pt. 5, 159; McElfresh, *Maps and Mapmakers of the Civil War*, 65. This information was available to the Confederates as well, although they failed to make much use of it.

6 Van Horne, *History of the Army of the Cumberland*, II:458.

Sherman did his best to help Merrill improve the accuracy of the army's maps as he moved south. Scouts and topographers routinely traveled deep into enemy territory, often requiring cavalry escorts. On occasions when they avoided detection the topographers could verify accuracy or update any erroneous information in a leisurely manner. If the detail encountered Confederate opposition, the cavalry escort made every effort to distract the enemy's attention while the cartographer or scout gathered whatever information he could until forced to retreat. Sherman considered the effort to supplement the accuracy of the army's campaign map so important that he issued general orders facilitating the endeavor on May 31. The orders insisted that "No topographical engineers shall be employed as an aide-de-camp or in any other duty than in making purely military surveys." He also advised that all corps, division, and brigade commanders assist the topographers to "work in harmony and for the benefit of the whole army."[7]

Once scouts and cartographers gathered more accurate information about the topographical features of the surrounding countryside as the army moved south, they sent it back for inclusion in revised campaign maps. Sherman ordered that lithographic presses be moved as close to the front as possible to assure that the process would be carried out swiftly. The updated maps were then distributed to generals throughout the army, though uniform distribution was not always possible. For example, on July 17 two Federal units arrived at the same location, causing some confusion, whereupon they discovered that one of them had not received the updated map.[8] Even while operating deep within enemy territory, Sherman's officers had access to fairly reliable maps thanks to the dedication of the commanding general and the energy of the Topographical Department.

Conversely, Johnston's army lacked sufficient resources and could not match the accuracy or the output of the Union map-making enterprise. In fact, Braxton Bragg had assigned a mere four officers to the task of mapping the country between Dalton and Atlanta in November 1863. Even so, Mark Elam has suggested the Confederates in the Western theater did have one significant advantage: at the outset of the campaign they occupied the entire state of Georgia and could make maps of the terrain without interference from the enemy. Yet because they had only taken up their position near Dalton after their defeat at Missionary Ridge in November 1863, the Army of Tennessee's engineers lacked a detailed knowledge of the region and had little time to rectify the situation before the start of campaign

7 Elam, "The Road to Atlanta," 89; *O.R.* vol. 38, pt. 4, 371.

8 Elam, "The Road to Atlanta," 84; *O.R.* vol. 38, pt. 5, 62, 165.

season.[9] Nor could the Confederates in the West count on an advanced mapmaking department, such as the one organized under Sherman's command.

Indeed, the western Confederate cartographic capabilities paled in comparison to their eastern compatriots in the Army of Northern Virginia. In Virginia, the Engineer Bureau collected maps produced by Jedediah Hotchkiss for Stonewall Jackson and D. B. Harris for P. G. T. Beauregard, as well as captured Federal maps. By the close of 1862, the Bureau was able to provide Lee a set of lithographed maps of Virginia for distribution throughout his army.[10] Lee had ample opportunities to use the maps of Virginia, as he spent the overwhelming majority of the war within state lines. Only Lee's brief forays into Maryland in September 1862 and Pennsylvania in the summer of 1863 took his army outside of Virginia. Consequently, the army's cartographers, including the famed Hotchkiss, had nearly two years to produce accurate maps of Virginia prior to the commencement of the spring campaign in 1864. These detailed maps of Virginia undoubtedly helped Lee achieve success on the battlefield while confronting Grant's army from the beginning of May until the siege of Petersburg in June.

By contrast, the Army of Tennessee's maps were inferior and lacked uniformity. The Engineer Bureau limited its mapping efforts to Virginia and parts of North Carolina, which meant that Johnston's army was forced to rely solely on its own cartographers. Nevertheless, that did not prevent Johnston from securing adequate maps of Georgia, particularly around the army's base of operations in Dalton. Johnston arrived at Dalton in late December and had approximately four months to produce sufficient maps of the region prior to the beginning of the campaign in May. Yet the extant Confederate maps of the area suggest a lack of industry on the part of the army's cartographers. The maps generally provided insufficient detail and indicate that the Confederates possessed only a moderate understanding of the topography between Chattanooga and Atlanta. Further, Confederate maps varied, sometimes significantly, depending upon the party responsible for the map's production. Unlike Sherman's army, which depended on a central mapmaking department, Confederate generals often produced their own maps. For example, Henry Clayton, a brigadier general in Hood's Corps, appears to have collected maps from a number of sources including Joseph Wheeler and his corps commander. Any map that he received from Hood, however, could not have come into Clayton's possession prior to the middle of April because Hood apparently

9 Wilbur Foster, "Battle Field Maps in Georgia," *Confederate Veteran* 20 (1912): 369; Elam, "The Road to Atlanta," 79, 81.

10 James L. Nichols, *Confederate Engineers* (Tuscaloosa, AL, 1957), 81–86.

did not acquire a map of North Georgia until then. Meanwhile, Leonidas Polk employed his own cartographer, Walter Morris.[11]

At times the maps failed to identify key geographic features. For example, Johnston's own campaign map reproduced in his postwar memoir identifies neither the passage through Rocky Face Ridge, three miles due west of Dalton, nor Dug Gap three and a half miles southwest of the town. General Joseph Wheeler, chief of the army's cavalry, possessed a faulty map as well. Despite the reputation that he produced the best maps in the entire army, Wheeler's map of Dalton and its surrounding topographical features apparently failed to identify the existence of Snake Creek Gap.[12]

The error proved critical when Sherman's army marched through Snake Creek Gap and around Johnston's left flank. Wheeler was not the only general who possessed a map that bore no indication of Snake Creek Gap. The gap was also missing from the map belonging to Henry Clayton. Clayton's map of Dalton clearly pinpoints the locations of the other gaps in Rocky Face Ridge.[13] There is a dotted line running in a southeasterly direction in the bottom left-hand corner of Clayton's map that may represent Snake Creek, but it is not labeled as such. Nor is there any specific indication of the presence of a gap as there is for Montgomery (Mill) Gap and Dug Gap. Indeed, each of the other gaps is represented with heavy shading on either side, a characteristic absent from the point at which the dotted line cuts through Rocky Face Ridge.

11 Campbell, "The Lost War Maps of the Confederates," 480; Elam, "The Road to Atlanta," 86; Hood, *The Lost Papers of Confederate General John Bell Hood*, 196; Hood, *Advance and Retreat*, 116. The handwriting on Clayton's maps suggests at least three authors and possibly a fourth.

12 Elam, "The Road to Atlanta," 86; Robert Davis Jr., "Every Crossroads and Farm: Confederate General Henry DeLamar Clayton's Civil War Maps of Northwestern Georgia," *The Georgia Historical Quarterly* 82, no. 1 (Spring 1998): 154. Wheeler's report of his command's activities between May 6 and June 1 provides evidence that he remained ignorant of Snake Creek Gap throughout the opening phase of the campaign. The report mentions the battle at Dug Gap on May 8, but no reference to any gap south of that location appears in the report. Instead, Wheeler made a passing reference that he "also developed the fact that all but two divisions of the enemy had turned our left flank, moving toward Resaca." See *O.R.* vol. 38, pt. 3, 944–945.

13 Clayton's map of Dalton was published in Robert Davis Jr.'s, *Every Crossroads and Farm: Confederate General Henry DeLamar Clayton's Civil War Maps of Northwest Georgia*, 156. Clayton possessed copies of a number of Wheeler's maps in addition to his own, probably obtained from corps' headquarters. The map of the area around Dalton appears to be his own (from headquarters), as the handwriting differs from maps prepared by Wheeler's chief cartographers John M. Stewart and J. S. Tyner. The map identifies Mill Gap as Montgomery Gap, though its location indicates that it is one and the same.

If the line was meant to represent Snake Creek, even that depiction was inaccurate, as Snake Creek terminated just west of the gap. The dotted line on Clayton's map connects to what appears to be other bodies of water west of Rocky Face Ridge. Because Clayton served under Hood and most likely received his map of the region from Hood's headquarters, a letter from Halsey Wigfall may provide evidence that the dotted line was not intended to depict either Snake Creek or Snake Creek Gap. Wigfall, who served as a member of John Bell Hood's staff, described the army's position in great detail, but his letter made no mention of Snake Creek Gap.[14] As a result, it seems fair to say that a number of Rebel maps were deficient, and it is likely that at least some Confederates did not know that a passageway around their left flank existed until the Federals under the command of James McPherson marched through the gap on May 8.

Another instance in which a Confederate map lacked an important attribute can be seen in a comparison of Polk's and Clayton's maps of the region around Kennesaw Mountain. A map produced by Wheeler's engineer John Stewart and part of Clayton's collection, identifies an unfinished railroad between Lost Mountain and Kennesaw Mountain. Conversely, Polk's map of the same region, contains no information pertaining to its existence. Considering that unfinished railroads often made for good defensive positions, Polk's map, like Wheeler's and Clayton's maps of Dalton, fails to identify an important topographical feature. Clayton's map of the Kennesaw region also provides the location of farms in the area, a quality missing from Polk's map.[15] Further, Clayton's map identifies the names of several roads including Cassville Road and Roswell Road, while Polk's map does not.

The plethora of names for the four passages through Rocky Face Ridge complicated the situation created by the disparate maps possessed by the Confederate high command at the outset of the campaign. In fact, each of the routes through the ridge went by at least two names. The northernmost gap, through which the Western & Atlantic Railroad ran, has been called both Mill Creek Gap and Buzzard's Roost. The passage three miles due west of Dalton was named Montgomery Gap, Mill Gap, or Rays Gap. Dug Gap, approximately three and a half miles southwest of Dalton, was also referred to as Babb's Gap and Villanow Gap. Some apparently called Snake Creek Gap by the alternate name of Snead Gap. The inconsistency in names may well have been a contributing factor

14 Halsey Wigfall to Louis Wigfall, May 1, 1864, LC.

15 Polk's map of the Kennesaw Mountain area is part of the collection housed at the Kennesaw National Battlefield Park Library and was likely produced by Walter Morris who served as Polk's chief engineer. The farms are depicted on Clayton's map are identified for the purpose of requisitioning supplies, particularly for the army's animals. See McElfresh, *Maps and Mapmakers of the Civil War*, 15, 17.

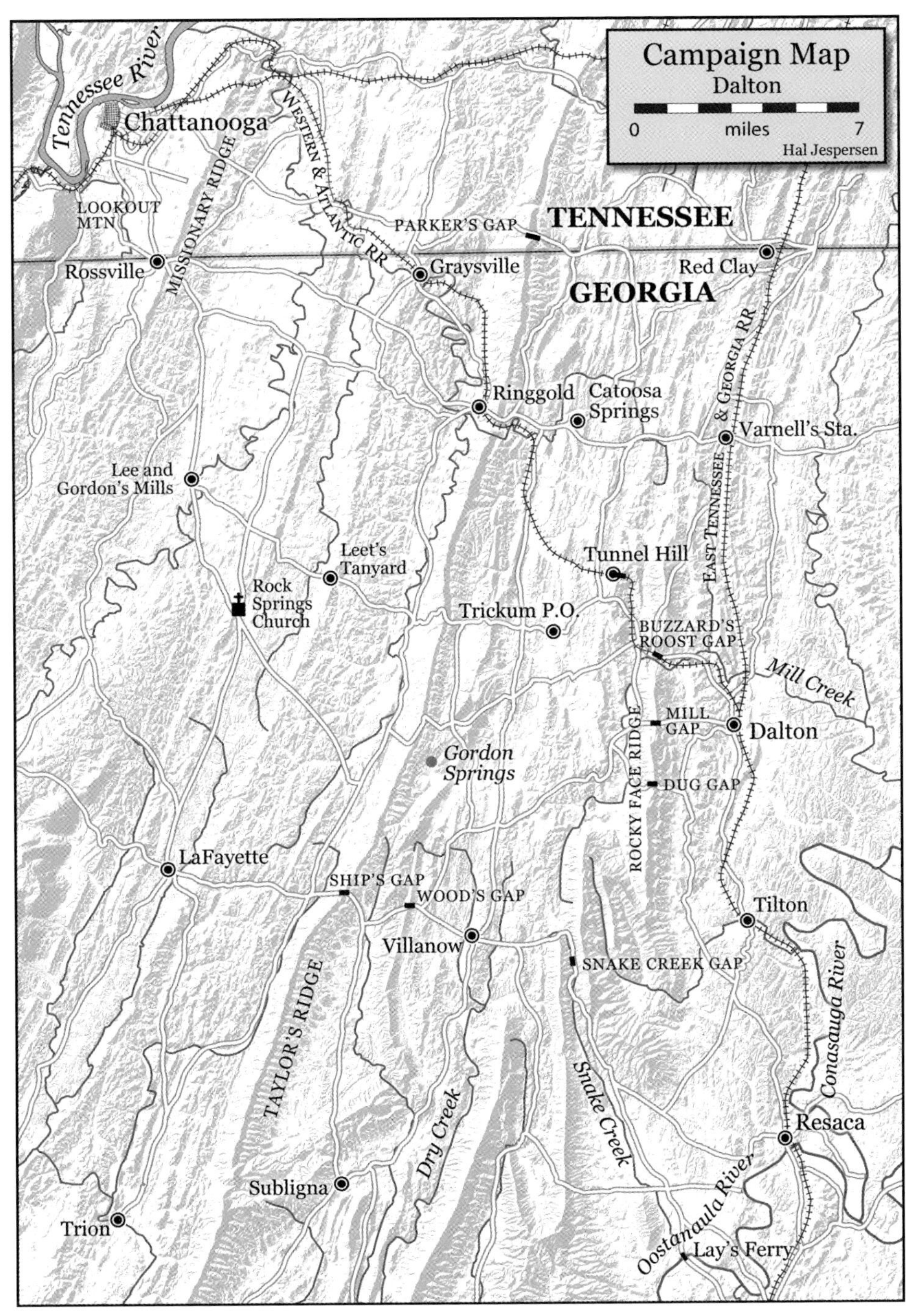
Campaign Map
Dalton
0 miles 7
Hal Jespersen
Tennessee River
Chattanooga
LOOKOUT MTN
MISSIONARY RIDGE
WESTERN & ATLANTIC RR
PARKER'S GAP
TENNESSEE
GEORGIA
Rossville
Graysville
Red Clay
EAST TENNESSEE & GEORGIA RR
Ringgold
Catoosa Springs
Varnell's Sta.
Lee and Gordon's Mills
Leet's Tanyard
Tunnel Hill
Rock Springs Church
Trickum P.O.
BUZZARD'S ROOST GAP
Mill Creek
MILL GAP
Dalton
ROCKY FACE RIDGE
Gordon Springs
DUG GAP
LaFayette
SHIP'S GAP
WOOD'S GAP
Tilton
Villanow
SNAKE CREEK GAP
TAYLOR'S RIDGE
Conasauga River
Snake Creek
Dry Creek
Resaca
Sublligna
Oostanaula River
Trion
Lay's Ferry

to the Confederate failure to defend Snake Creek Gap. According to Johnston's chief of staff, William Mackall, the gap was left unguarded because the result of an unnamed officer failed to obey orders. Though Mackall did not identify the culprit, he was probably referring to Joseph Wheeler who had been ordered to scout the area.[16] Considering that Wheeler's maps did not identify the location of Snake Creek Gap in tandem with the multitude of names given to the passages through Rocky Face Ridge, it seems entirely possible that whoever Wheeler may have sent in that direction simply made a mistake and went to the wrong location.

To make matters worse, inadequate map-making supplies limited the Confederacy's production of finished maps, particularly in the West. By the close of the war's second year Confederate engineers had exhausted the domestic supply. The limited quantity of available supplies often meant that junior officers possessed only crude sketches rather than detailed maps. As a result, regimental commanders and sometimes even brigade commanders relied upon vague descriptions and poor diagrams when carrying out the orders of superior officers.[17] Thus, the Confederates entered the Atlanta campaign with a significant cartographical disadvantage. The army's high command possessed disparate maps, some of which lacked crucial topographical features. The plight of junior officers was significantly worse, as many had no maps at all.

Militia

Insufficient maps were not the only challenge the Confederacy faced in the Western theater in 1864. Political discord involving the Georgia governor and the Confederate president also affected Johnston's defense of the state. In the fall of 1863, the debate between Brown and the Davis administration shifted from

16 In some cases, maps failed to identify the passage identified as Montgomery Gap, Mill Gap, or Rays Gap. Richard McMurry, "The Opening Phase of the 1864 Campaign in the West," *The Atlanta Historical Journal* 27 (Summer 1983): 5. On May 7, Johnston's Chief of Staff William Mackall ordered the Second Arkansas Rifles to take position in Villanow Gap, the same gap identified on Clayton's map as Dug Gap. See *O.R.* vol. 38, pt. 4, 673, *Richmond Daily Dispatch*, May 12, 1864. The multitude of names and the fact that existing Confederate maps differ on the number of passages through Rocky Face Ridge has led to confusion even among historians. Mark Elam, for example, identifies Buzzard's Roost and Mill Creek Gap as separate entities. Richard McMurry suggests that only three gaps passed through the ridge, recognizing only Mill Creek Gap (Buzzard's Roost), Dug Gap, and Snake Creek Gap. See Elam, "The Road to Atlanta," 116; McMurry, "The Opening Phase of the 1864 Campaign in the West," 5; Richard McMurry, "Rocky Face to the Dallas Line: The Battles of May 1864," *The Blue & Gray Magazine* 6 (1989): 17; *O.R.* vol. 38, pt. 3, 721; Irving A. Buck, *Cleburne and His Command* (Jackson, TN, 1959), 208; *O.R.* vol. 38, pt. 4, 664, 672, 673, 692.

17 Nichols, *Confederate Engineers*, 87–88; Jack Coggins, "The Engineers Played a Key Role in Both Armies," *Civil War Times Illustrated* 3 (Jan. 1965): 43.

conscription to militia service. In June, the administration had requested that states establish a reserve corps that could respond to Federal raids more effectively than the militia. Militia units had to be assembled and discharged according to the prevailing laws which often meant delay. Brown responded that he could raise a sufficient force but that he preferred that it be done under state law. Brown informed the administration that a number of companies had responded to his recent proclamation calling for volunteers for state defense. He added that if the central government was amenable to the arrangement, he could organize 8,000 men for six months duty by August. In an emergency, he would then tender the units to the administration so long as the president retained their organizational structure.[18]

The governor's rejoinder to the administration's appeal was characteristic of Brown's temperament and political dogma. If the reserve force were mustered under Georgia militia laws, Brown would retain the authority to appoint officers and determine whether to organize the units into companies, battalions, regiments, brigades, or even divisions. Conversely, if the reserve force were organized under congressional law, authority transferred to the administration. Unwilling to cede power to the central government, a chief tenet of his doctrinaire states' rights principles, Brown proved yet again incapable of compromise. The administration accepted Brown's proposal, though Secretary of War James Seddon remarked that the initial plan, which contemplated the establishment of a reserve corps, provided more flexibility than the militia laws allowed. The congressional law provided for a longer term and permitted temporary service while, according to Seddon, the militia laws did not. He warned that the militia, once tendered to the administration, would be "continuously in the field" until their terms expired.[19]

Brown, having secured a small victory in his ongoing battle with the administration, followed through on his promise and organized the Georgia State Guard, which terms of service required an emergency before it could be called out.[20] In mid-September 1863, William Rosecrans's Federal army crossed into northern Georgia, thereby constituting a sufficient emergency, and the administration called upon the State Guard to assist in the state's defense. The Army of Tennessee defeated Rosecrans on September 19–20 at the battle of Chickamauga and the Union forces retreated to Chattanooga on September 21. The emergency had passed, yet the administration refused to discharge the State Guard. On September 25 Brown requested that Davis release the State Guard from service so that the

18 *C.R. Ga.*, III, 339–344, 348.

19 Ibid., 348–349.

20 Elam, "The Road to Atlanta," 238.

men might return to their farms and harvest their crops. He further noted that unless the farmers could sow wheat the harvest for 1864 would suffer. Finally, Brown argued that if the president failed to release the guardsmen they would be unlikely to extend their commitment beyond six months once their enlistment expired in February. The administration ignored Brown's appeal and kept the State Guard on duty.[21]

On November 12 Lt. Col. M. W. Lewis of the 9th Regiment, Georgia State Guards, informed Brown that the guardsmen considered their prolonged service an injustice and suggested that if they were not released, they would likely disregard any future militia mobilization. Fearing the state's inability to muster militia during the next emergency, Brown again petitioned the administration for their release from duty. Brown lamented that "these troops have now been about two months in service, when there was no enemy upon the soil of Georgia and no raid making its way into her territory." The governor asserted that the administration's policy of retaining the State Guard in the field violated the "letters and spirit of the contract," under which the men had entered Confederate service.[22]

The administration did not respond until January 13, 1864, when James Seddon inquired whether the governor might authorize the use of the State Guard for the relief of P. G. T. Beauregard in South Carolina. The application infuriated Brown who lambasted the administration for failure to "keep its faith" with the Georgia guardsmen. Brown again assailed the central government for keeping the men on active duty with no imminent threat to the state of Georgia. Seddon retorted that the situation on Georgia's borders had remained perilous throughout the previous six months and therefore necessitated the State Guard's continued field service.[23] Seddon's claim lacked merit and Brown knew it, setting the stage for continued hostility and halfhearted cooperation during future emergencies.

Perhaps in anticipation of Brown's reticence, Davis authorized the establishment of the Georgia Reserve Force according to the guidelines set forth the previous June which Brown had rejected. The reserves would only be called upon in case of emergency and provide temporary service. Those required to serve included men between the ages of 17–18 and 40–45, as well as Confederate soldiers who had previously been detailed to work in munitions factories and similar tasks. The idea made perfect sense; what did not was Davis's appointment of Howell Cobb

21 *C.R. Ga.*, III, 339–344, 418–419.

22 Ibid., 431–432, 434–437.

23 Ibid., 459; *O.R.* ser. 4, vol. 3, 165.

as commander of the reserve corps. The history of mutual enmity between Brown and Cobb rivaled the governor's relationship with the president.[24]

Cobb wasted little time in antagonizing his longtime adversary. On April 21, 1864, Cobb wrote Brown and alluded to the governor's recent speech in which he had proclaimed anxiety over the election of a number of able-bodied young men to "inferior county, district, or militia offices," thereby exempting them from military service. Brown, in his speech, had suggested that older men ought to fill those positions. Cobb then cited an act of Congress that only allowed exemptions for officeholders necessary to the administration of state affairs. He subsequently inquired whether 2,000 justices of the peace and 1,000 constables were necessary, considering the suspension of most court activities. Cobb also questioned the appointment of 3,000 militia officers even though no militia units were then organized.[25]

Brown responded on May 5 with his usual states' rights diatribe, insisting that the state legislature's declaration exempting all state officers trumped the congressional act Cobb had cited. Brown admitted that most of the officers were able-bodied men but insisted that most of the justices of the peace and the constables were farmers and needed to harvest their crops. In defending his policy, the governor even asserted that no emergency existed and that "We are in no danger of subjugation."[26] Brown's claim that no peril then threatened the safety of the state was patently absurd; that very day Sherman commenced his advance on Johnston's army encamped at Dalton.

The real reason Brown rejected Cobb's request for troops was twofold. First, he clearly harbored resentment over the administration's refusal to disband the Georgia State Guard after the battle of Chickamauga.[27] The second reason reflected Brown's obsession with maintaining his own authority. So long as military units were organized under state militia laws, Brown retained the authority to appoint officers, determine organizational structure, and call them to duty. Under the act providing for the Reserve Force, however, the Davis administration made those decisions. Consequently, Brown again let his vanity and devotion to states' rights color his approach to defending the state against the impending Federal advance.

Howell Cobb and Joseph E. Brown continued their dispute throughout most of the month of May. Cobb impugned Brown's patriotism, while Brown labeled

24 Bragg, *Joe Brown's Army*, x; Parks, *Joseph E. Brown of Georgia*, 285–286.

25 *C.R. Ga.*, III, 503, 504–507.

26 Ibid., 516, 521–522.

27 Ibid., 521.

Cobb a hypocrite. All the while Sherman pushed Johnston deeper into the state. Finally, on May 18, Brown issued a proclamation that called upon state officials between the ages of eighteen and forty-five to report to Maj. Gen. H. C. Wayne in Atlanta for the purpose of repelling the enemy from the state. The governor threatened severe penalties for failure to obey his orders promptly. The only permissible exemptions were for those whose duties attached to the statehouse, penitentiary, courts, and state roads. Cobb dryly observed that when he had called upon Brown for cooperation in the establishment of the Reserve Force, the governor had insisted that all state officers, both civil and military, had been needed for the proper administration of state affairs, a policy his May 18 proclamation clearly abandoned.[28]

Brown had spent much of the war shielding state residents from the conscription law. His opposition to what he believed to be an unconstitutional encroachment upon states' rights had blinded him to the exigency of the circumstances. Further, Brown's anger at the administration for keeping the Georgia State Guard in the field after the Confederate victory at Chickamauga continued to influence his policymaking decisions. Consequently, he delayed calling up the militia until Johnston's army had retreated approximately forty miles from its starting position at Dalton. Had Brown swallowed his pride and aided in the organization of the Reserve Force, Johnston might have held his position at Dalton indefinitely, or at least for an extended period. Instead, thousands of able-bodied men remained far behind the front lines as Sherman began his advance from Chattanooga on May 5, 1864.[29] Thus, at the outset of the campaign the Confederate army under Joseph E. Johnston suffered from inadequate maps and could not hope to augment its strength with the addition of a sizable body of militia.

Dalton, Resaca, and Retreat

Nevertheless, the position Johnston's army occupied near Dalton offered a great deal of security. Rocky Face Ridge covered approximately twenty miles,

28 Ibid., 530, 546, 563; *C.R. Ga.*, II, 703.

29 As previously noted, Howell Cobb estimated that Brown had exempted at least 6,000 able-bodied Georgia citizens that held low level political offices, or superfluous militia commands. See *C.R. Ga.*, III, 502–507. In reality Cobb severely underestimated the number of available white males between the ages of sixteen and sixty. In December 1863, Brown persuaded the Georgia assembly to pass legislation reorganizing the state militia. In furtherance of the new law, enrollment officers scoured the state and enrolled 41,398 individuals, 16,500 of whom were between the ages of seventeen and forty-five. See William Robert Scaife and William Harris Bragg, *Joe Brown's Pets: The Georgia Militia, 1861–1865* (Macon, GA, 2004), 4–5.

starting about seven miles northwest of Dalton and running south nearly to the Oostanaula River. Its height was nearly as impressive as its length, measuring about 700 feet above the surrounding valleys. Only four passages allowed access through the ridge: Buzzard's Roost, Mill Gap, Dug Gap, and Snake Creek Gap. The Western & Atlantic Railroad ran through Buzzard's Roost approximately three miles northwest of Dalton. Meanwhile, Mill Gap lay about three miles west of the town. Dug Gap was situated roughly three and a half miles southwest of Dalton. A road from Dalton to Villanow intersected Dug Gap, presumably the reason for one of its alternate names. Finally, Snake Creek Gap ran eleven or twelve miles south of Dug Gap and passed through the southern end of Rocky Face Ridge.[30]

The strength of the position inspired awe from Confederates and Federals alike. Halsey Wigfall called it impregnable. He commented on its natural strength and noted that the army had fortified the gaps. So strong was the position that Wigfall expressed hope that the "Yankees" would be "ever senseless enough to attack," and if they did they would find themselves "more cut to pieces than they have ever dreamed possible." Major J. C. Thompson in A. P. Stewart's division also considered the position a natural fortress. Thompson suggested that Stewart's construction of a dam that could flood the gap when attacked made the location impervious to assault. Sherman too considered the Confederate's line of defense along Rocky Face Ridge impenetrable. Like Thompson, he believed that the abatis and dams made an already naturally strong defense impractical to attack. Further, Sherman's chief engineer Orlando Poe suggested that the Rocky Face line presented "a very strong position and if the rebels had been at all stubborn they would have given us a great deal of trouble." Perhaps the ultimate compliment came from Federal infantry tasked with assaulting the Confederate lines, who nicknamed the position the "Georgia Gibraltar."[31]

In spite of the abundant testimony that Rocky Face Ridge provided an admirable defensive line for Joseph E. Johnston's army, the Confederate commander later claimed otherwise. In his postwar reminiscence he asserted that the line at Dalton had little to recommend it and that it displayed neither "intrinsic strength nor strategic advantage." He further suggested that he only retained his defensive position at Dalton for fear of the administration's response

30 See Campaign Map of Dalton, p. 89. McMurry, "The Opening Phase of the 1864 Campaign in the West," 5; McMurry, "Rocky Face to the Dallas Line," 17. In some places the ridge towered as much as 1,500 feet above the valley floors. Elam, "The Road to Atlanta," 116.

31 Halsey Wigfall to Louis Wigfall, May 1, 1864, LC; Halsey Wigfall to Charlotte Wigfall, March 21, 1864; J. C. Thompson to A. P. Stewart, Box 1, Folder 5, JP WM; *O.R.* vol. 31, pt. 1, 63; Poe to wife, May 7, 1864, LC; McMurry, "Rocky Face to the Dallas Line," 18.

to a retrograde movement.[32] While encamped at Dalton, however, Johnston made no complaint about the strength of his defensive position along Rocky Face Ridge. It is probable that Johnston concocted his ambivalence toward the position after the war to hide his embarrassment for having lost such a strong line of defense as rapidly as he did. Johnston's troop dispositions, however, provide evidence that he held the same opinion of Rocky Face Ridge as Wigfall, Thompson, Sherman, Poe, and the legion of Union soldiers who, as previously mentioned, had dubbed it the "Georgia Gibraltar."

The Crow Valley, northwest of Dalton, represented the only real weakness of the Confederate defensive line. After all, the valley on the north side of the Western & Atlantic Railroad was the only part of the Confederate defensive position that did not require attackers to assault a mountain pass. Accordingly, Johnston placed a significant portion of his army in the valley to defend against an attack from the north. Johnston assigned the responsibility of defending Crow Valley and the northernmost portion of Rocky Face Ridge to John Bell Hood, an indication that he considered Hood his most reliable subordinate at that juncture. Hood posted two divisions of his corps in Crow Valley to defend against an attack from the north. He placed a third division on the north of Rocky Face Ridge around Buzzard's Roost. When the Federals approached on May 7, Johnston ordered both William Bate's division and Benjamin Cheatham's division from Hardee's Corps to reinforce Hood. Johnston held Hardee's remaining divisions under Patrick Cleburne and William H. T. Walker in reserve near Dalton.[33]

Johnston was so concerned with the one weakness in his line that he overcompensated for its defense and left no Confederate troops guarding Mill Gap, Dug Gap, or Snake Creek Gap. Presumably he thought that he could dispatch men to those locations rapidly if the Federals threatened any of them. Johnston believed that Joseph Wheeler's cavalry had established pickets in position to guard against Federal penetration into the valley west of Rocky Face Ridge and would send word in time for him to march troops to the threatened location.[34] Because the defense of a narrow front, in this case two mountain passes, required fewer troops, Johnston surely felt that a sufficient number of troops could be found among the

32 Johnston, *Narrative of Military Operations*, 277–278.

33 McMurry, "Rocky Face to the Dallas Line," 18; *O.R.* vol. 38, pt. 3, 760–761; Joseph E. Johnston, "Opposing Sherman's Advance to Atlanta," *Battles and Leaders of the Civil War* (New York, 1956), IV:263.

34 Exactly when Johnston became aware of Snake Creek Gap is not entirely clear, though he was made aware of its presence prior to Sherman making use of it to turn Johnston's flank. *O.R.* vol. 38, pt. 4, 664, 668.

reserve divisions encamped in Dalton. Johnston's conviction that he could respond rapidly to a Union advance into the valley west of Rocky Face Ridge was inaccurate. Instead, poor reconnaissance and a misinterpretation of Sherman's grand strategy hampered his ability to hold his position against Sherman's flanking maneuver.

Civil War armies depended upon the cavalry to keep them apprised of their enemy's whereabouts, yet Johnston's cavalry at the outset of the campaign lacked an essential component—healthy mounts. During Braxton Bragg's tenure as commander of the Army of Tennessee he had ordered most of the cavalry into eastern Tennessee. The unforgiving terrain there wreaked havoc on the horses and though the cavalry returned to the army in the spring, it was in extremely poor condition. As a result, Johnston had little choice but to send a large portion of his cavalry to the rear for rest, recuperation, and recruitment. In the army's April 30 returns Johnston listed the total effective strength of his cavalry at only 2,640 men. In fact, though Maj. Gen. William Martin's division counted nearly 2,000 officers and enlisted men present, none could be considered effective because of the poor condition of their mounts.[35] The deficiency in cavalry, therefore, severely impaired Johnston's ability to stay abreast of his enemy's movements as Sherman's combined armies began their advance upon Atlanta.

Johnston's miscalculation as to Sherman's intentions exacerbated the problem. As Johnston's deployment of his infantry suggested, he deemed a Federal approach from the north through Crow Valley a near certainty. To confront Sherman's expected advance, Johnston ordered the bulk of Wheeler's depleted cavalry to observe Union activity near Tunnel Hill. Johnston posted only one under-strength cavalry brigade on his left toward Dug Gap.[36] Clearly his primary concern was that Sherman would strike his right flank.

Still, Johnston did express occasional anxiety about the safety of his left flank, and in particular he worried for some time that the enemy might advance upon his left by way of Rome, approximately forty-four miles southwest of Dalton. If Sherman managed to place his army at Rome, he would threaten the Confederate communications and interpose the Federal army between the Army of Tennessee and its base in Atlanta. On April 22, a Confederate scout reported that between 10,000 and 15,000 Federals were in Decatur, Alabama, rumored to be headed for Rome. There is no direct evidence that Johnston received the report himself, but based on circumstantial evidence it seems likely that he did. Bragg's telegram to Polk the following day requesting that Polk send a division to reinforce Johnston

35 Connelly, *Autumn of Glory*, 330; *O.R.* vol. 32, pt. 3, 801.

36 *O.R.* vol. 32, pt. 3, 810–811; McMurry, "The Opening Phase of the 1864 Campaign in the West," 17.

suggests that the entire Confederate high command was aware of the threat to Johnston's left. Nevertheless, the fact that the Army of Tennessee numbered only 43,375 at the close of April meant that Johnston needed to concentrate his army where he thought an attack was most likely.[37] If Johnston, however, had access to an additional force he might well have placed it on his left. Unfortunately, Joseph E. Brown's quarrel with the president meant that the Georgia militia was not available, though it was sorely needed.

Johnston's troop dispositions for those forces that arrived from other departments in early May demonstrate his eagerness to bolster his left flank. On May 7, James Cantey's brigade arrived at Resaca from Mississippi as did two regiments of Daniel Reynolds's brigade from Mobile. Johnston first ordered Cantey to Dalton, but then countermanded the order and directed that he remain at Resaca, an indication that Johnston felt increasingly insecure about his left flank. He also directed J. A. Williams to move Reynolds's contingent to Villanow (Dug) Gap, thus extending the left of his lines around Dalton. In addition, Johnston remained apprehensive about Rome, and upon learning that Polk and approximately 14,000 additional men were on their way to join him from Mississippi, he instructed Polk to concentrate there. Clearly Johnston hoped to augment his left even while reports of an advance upon his right trickled into headquarters.[38] Consequently, it seems likely that any available militia would also have been posted on the left. In fact, Dug Gap and Snake Creek Gap afforded ideal locations for the posting of militia troops.

Defense of a mountain pass, even when carried out by unseasoned troops, provides the defenders with an extraordinary advantage over any assaulting force. Though Leonidas and his Spartans had left the most enduring legacy at Thermopylae, history is littered with similar exploits. Indeed, Federal assaults on Buzzard's Roost and the lightly defended Dug Gap on May 8 proved to be one-sided affairs despite the fact that at Dug Gap the Union force numbered 4,500 while the Confederates only deployed about 1,000. Even with a substantial numerical advantage, the Federals suffered 357 casualties, fifty of whom were captured, while the Confederates lost only twenty men. The narrow front of mountain passes intrinsically favored the defenders, who also had the advantage of being able to shoot down on their opponents. Further, the positions at Dug Gap and Snake Creek Gap provided no opportunity for the Federals to attempt a flanking maneuver, thereby necessitating a frontal assault. Colonel W. C. P. Breckinridge

37 *O.R.* vol. 32, pt. 2, 644, 698; *O.R.* vol. 32, pt. 3, 801, 811–812.

38 *O.R.* vol. 38, pt. 4, 673–675; Mackall Diary, May 4, 5, 7, 1864, JP WM.

of the 9th Kentucky Cavalry described Dug Gap as a "mere road cut out of the mountain-side and really needed no breastworks, for the natural palisades and contour of the mountain rendered easy its defense by resolute men." Snake Creek Gap, according to Breckinridge, was a "narrow defile" and "capable of impregnable defense."[39] Without concern for the safety of their flank and rear defending troops, even untested militia units could be counted on to hold such positions until the arrival of veteran reinforcements.

When Brown finally called out the Georgia militia units they proved useful despite their limited numbers. Only 3,000 assembled in Atlanta after Brown's May 18 summons. They did not see action until the end of June, when Johnston ordered them to guard his left flank at Marietta. Though their own commander, Gustavus W. Smith, considered their chances for success limited, they surpassed his expectations and fought off each Union advance until faced with a much larger force. In fact, they engaged veteran Federal troops in "open country," a much more difficult landscape than the defense of a mountain pass. The militia responded so well to their first encounter with enemy forces that Johnston lauded their effort. Joe Brown's policy of shielding so many young able-bodied men from conscription likely played a role in the Georgia militia's success. Unlike other state militias that relied upon sixteen-year-old boys and men between the ages of forty-five and fifty, Georgia could rely, at least in part, on men in their twenties and thirties.[40] It is not unreasonable, then, to suggest that the militia, had it been called out in April in anticipation of Sherman's advance, could have rendered admirable service in defense of Dug and Snake Creek gaps.

Unfortunately for Johnston, no militia were available in early May, and he was forced to rely upon Wheeler's depleted cavalry command for the information necessary to make adequate troop deployments. Wheeler's poor performance during the first week of May made Johnston's task more difficult. In his report on the campaign Wheeler claimed to have established pickets as far south as Ship's Gap, a passage through Taylor's Ridge and on the road to Snake Creek Gap. If he had done so, and the scouts had remained in that location, no Federal forces could have approached Snake Creek Gap without detection. It is likely that either Wheeler never ordered troops to that location, or he recalled them soon thereafter. By May 1, Johnston's concern for the safety of his left prompted him to order Wheeler to observe the Tennessee River from Bridgeport to Gunter's Landing and report any

39 Castel, *Decision in the West*, 134; W. C. P. Breckinridge, "The Opening of the Atlanta Campaign," *Battles and Leaders of the Civil War* (New York, 1956), IV:278–279.

40 Gustavus W. Smith, "The Georgia Militia About Atlanta," 331–332; *O.R.* vol. 38, pt. 5, 867–868; Scaife and Bragg, *Joe Brown's Pets*, 4–5.

Federal activity to the commanding officer at Rome. Johnston repeated the request three days later on May 4. These orders illustrate Johnston's concern regarding the rumored buildup of Union forces in Decatur. For the most part, however, Wheeler's scouts provided minimal information regarding Union movements on Johnston's left. In fact, on May 6 Thomas Mackall, on Johnston's staff, commented that "Not a thing has been ascertained by Wheeler's cavalry—inactive."[41]

While Johnston directed Wheeler to keep him informed of Federal activity in the direction of Rome, reports of an increased enemy presence north of Dalton flowed into army headquarters. By May 5 scouts confirmed the presence of Federals at Ringgold and Red Clay, and on May 7 at Varnell's Station. These reports seemed to substantiate what Johnston had anticipated, that Sherman intended to advance through Crow Valley on Johnston's right flank. Johnston's assessment was mostly accurate, and Sherman advanced two of his three combined armies in that direction. Major General George Thomas and his Army of the Cumberland advanced upon Ringgold and then Tunnel Hill, while Maj. Gen. John Schofield's Army of the Ohio moved on Red Clay and Varnell Station.[42] The third of Sherman's armies, the Army of the Tennessee, under Maj. Gen. James McPherson, headed in a different direction, first to Lee and Gordon's Mills and then on to Lafayette.

Johnston received only minimal intelligence concerning McPherson's movements, yet there was enough information that Johnston should have acted more aggressively on his left flank. On May 4 scouts informed Johnston's headquarters that the Federals in north Alabama (McPherson's men) were "leaving for Dalton as rapidly as possible." As a result, Johnston should have known that the threat to Rome by way of a Union advance through Alabama was significantly diminished. Then on May 7 Johnston received intelligence that a division of McPherson's army was near Lafayette, with the rest to follow. Johnston appears to have understood the threat to his left, but he still considered Rome the likely target. Johnston apparently deemed his orders to Polk to concentrate at Rome that same day sufficient to meet McPherson's movement.[43] He did not consider McPherson's presence in Lafayette a menace to either Dug or Snake Creek Gaps, or he would have ordered troops to those locations. Johnston's erroneous belief that the southernmost passages through Rocky Face remained safe from McPherson's army was the product of substandard reconnaissance.

41 *O.R.* vol. 38, pt. 3, 944. Confederate cavalry could not have been present at Ship's Gap on the evening of May 7, as McPherson reported his cavalry securing the passage that night. See *O.R.* vol. 38, pt. 4, 67; *O.R.* vol. 38, pt. 4, 656, 660; Mackall Diary, May 6, 1864, JP WM.

42 Mackall Diary, May 4, 5, 7, 1864, JP WM; Castel, *Decision in the West*, 123.

43 Mackall Diary, May 4, 7, 1864, JP WM. *O.R.* vol. 38, pt. 4, 675.

Wheeler's poor performance undoubtedly played a vital role in Johnston's continued ignorance regarding Union activity southwest of Dalton. Johnston's chief of staff William Mackall repeatedly ordered a reconnaissance of the region. On May 5 Mackall instructed Wheeler to "acquire the most authentic information of the present position of the enemy this side and to the east of Taylor's Ridge." Mackall clearly meant that Wheeler should scout the west side, otherwise the order was redundant. Mackall reiterated the instruction early on the morning of May 7, only this time he was even more specific. He informed Wheeler that Johnston wanted him to leave a "body of cavalry in the valley west and south" of Dug Gap. That afternoon, having heard nothing from Wheeler, Mackall notified the cavalry commander that Johnston believed that it was "absolutely necessary" to send a reliable officer with his command into the valley south and west of Mill Creek Gap.[44]

Wheeler finally responded, though Col. J. Warren Grigsby's Kentucky brigade did not arrive at Dug Gap until well after dark. By midnight on May 8, Col. W. C. P. Breckinridge of Grigsby's command had established pickets in front of the gap and sent scouts into the valley south of their position. It had taken Wheeler an entire day to act upon Johnston's order, first issued at seven in the morning. Though Grigsby dispatched scouts to the south of Dug Gap, the darkness precluded them from providing thorough intelligence to headquarters until daylight on May 8. At 11:00 p.m. Johnston received a report from a scout who had just returned from Lafayette. The scout informed the Confederate commander that he had found no Federal activity in the town. The report apparently convinced headquarters that the enemy had concentrated its forces between Tunnel Hill and Ringgold. What Breckinridge discovered the following morning, however, should have alarmed Johnston and motivated a redistribution of his available forces toward his left flank. At daylight Breckinridge encountered "very large bodies of troops" on "all the roads leading to the south," and wired the information to headquarters at 10:15 a.m.[45] Breckinridge's account of activity in the area clearly contradicted the information obtained the previous evening. At 1:30 p.m. Breckinridge reported a force of approximately 10,000 Union troops moving along the valley between Taylor's Ridge and Rocky Face Ridge.

To confront the Federal activity on his left, Johnston reacted tentatively. At noon on May 8, Johnston instructed Cantey to remain at Resaca and hold his brigade ready "to take cars." Johnston further ordered that Cantey closely observe

44 *O.R.* vol. 38, pt. 4, 664, 672–673.

45 Breckinridge, "The Opening of the Atlanta Campaign," 278; Mackall Diary, May 7, 1864, JP WM; *O.R.* vol. 38, pt. 4, 677.

the "approaches in front of Villanow and Lafayette." Johnston's orders to Cantey constitute his only conceivable instructions to any infantry command for the defense of Snake Creek Gap. Yet it was impossible for Cantey to hold his men in readiness for boarding railroad cars in Resaca, while at the same time establishing a defensive line in Snake Creek Gap. At best, Cantey could post a few scouts at the eastern end of the six-mile-long defile. Certainly he could not have hoped that a picket posted on the gap's western approach would be able to relay information of a Union advance to Resaca in time to enable the brigade's redeployment for a successful defense of the southernmost passage through Rocky Face Ridge. Moreover, Cantey was new to the area, having just arrived from Mississippi, and probably did not know of the existence of Snake Creek Gap until May 9.[46] It is probable that he did not even have maps of the region. Despite the imminent threat to his left at Snake Creek Gap, Johnston made no further troop dispositions to meet it until late in the evening. Instead, Johnston became fixated with the defense of his right flank.

Johnston behaved exactly as Sherman hoped that he would. At 11:00 a.m. a member of Johnston's staff recorded that the enemy was "all here" and that the right of their line extended only to the south of Trickum.[47] Apparently Johnston believed that the Northerners Breckinridge had identified earlier in the day represented the far right of the Federal line. To divert Johnston's attention from Snake Creek, Sherman ordered assaults at Buzzard's Roost and Dug Gap. As a result, any hope of further reconnaissance south of Dug Gap ended around 2:00 p.m. on May 8, when John Geary's division of Joseph Hooker's Corps advanced into the valley west of the gap and drove Grigsby's command into the defile. With the rest of Wheeler's cavalry operating on Johnston's right flank and Grigsby occupied in the defense of Dug Gap, Johnston remained ignorant of Union movement south of Dug Gap.

Johnston did not attempt to strengthen his left until late afternoon when he ordered two brigades of Cleburne's division to Dug Gap. Cleburne did not arrive until after dark when he positioned his troops to defend against any further Union attacks. Only after Cleburne's arrival did Johnston order anyone to Snake Creek Gap. The duty fell to W. C. P. Breckinridge, whose regiment had been on continuous duty for over twenty-four hours. Breckinridge moved out at approximately 10 o'clock, but poor roads and insufficient guides slowed his progress. Breckinridge reached the eastern mouth of Snake Creek Gap the following morning at dawn

46 *O.R.* vol. 38, pt. 4, 678–679; Wilbur G. Kurtz, Sr., "Why Was Snake Creek Gap Left Un-Guarded? An Episode of the Retreat of the Confederate Army of Tennessee from Dalton, Georgia, May, 1864," Mss 130, Box 36, Folder 11, Atlanta Historical Society.

47 Mackall Diary, May 8, 1864, JP WM.

only to discover McPherson's Corps in possession of the passage.[48] McPherson's capture of Snake Creek Gap threatened Confederate control of the railroad at Resaca through which provisions for the army at Dalton traveled.

Yet the Confederates did not immediately abandon their position at Dalton. Thomas's approach to Buzzard's Roost and Schofield's advance toward Crow Valley so impressed Johnston that he remained confident that Sherman's real objective was his right flank. Consequently, Johnston spent most of May 9 in Crow Valley with Hood in expectation of a Union attack on that portion of his line. Only after nightfall did Johnston return to headquarters and discover the telegrams from Cantey at Resaca and William Martin, posted along the Oostanaula River, reporting a heavy enemy presence advancing on Rome or Resaca. Finally Johnston considered the possibility of a genuine threat to his left and ordered Hood to Resaca with three divisions, one from his own corps and two from Hardee's corps.[49] Johnston's decision to send Hood to Resaca with two of Hardee's divisions demonstrated once again that he trusted Hood more than any of his other officers at that point in the campaign.

Early on the morning of May 10, Hood wired headquarters that "Resaca all right, hold on to Dalton." Considering that Hood did not leave for Resaca until late in the evening on May 9 and his communication reached headquarters at approximately 8:00 a.m. the following morning, it seems unlikely that he performed any meaningful reconnaissance. In fact, McPherson's entire corps still threatened Resaca and the Western & Atlantic Railroad from its position in Snake Creek Gap. McPherson had emerged from the mountain passage the previous day only to find a force of unknown strength behind trenches in defense of Resaca. Worried that Johnston might send the bulk of his army to strike his flank and unable to identify the composition of the troops entrenched in front of him, McPherson opted to return to Snake Creek Gap and await further developments. Yet Hood made no mention of McPherson's presence in his dispatch to headquarters, unless his mention of an enemy column in Snickers Gap was meant to identify Snake Creek Gap. Instead, Hood insisted that Johnston should "look out for Dug Gap." Hood then returned to Dalton with the belief that Sherman intended to focus his primary attention on the Confederate right. On the afternoon of May 10, Johnston's headquarters received word of Polk's arrival in Rome and that scouts had found no enemy activity between Rome and Villanow. Further, the Federals

48 *O.R.* vol. 38, pt. 3, 721–722; Breckinridge, "The Opening of the Atlanta Campaign," 279.

49 McMurry, *John Bell Hood and the War for Southern Independence*, 102; Mackall Diary, May 9, 1864, JP WM; Johnston, *Narrative of Military Operations*, 307.

in Snake Creek Gap appeared interested in fortifying their position rather than advancing upon Resaca.[50]

Throughout the evening of May 10 Johnston remained convinced that Crow Valley was Sherman's principal point of emphasis in his effort to dislodge the Army of Tennessee from its position near Dalton. Several factors led the Confederate commander to his conclusion. First, he had thought a Union advance from that direction most likely at the outset of the campaign, a belief that influenced his assessment of the limited intelligence reports received during the first days of the campaign. Additionally, the poor performance of his cavalry, which likely never established pickets west of Ship's Gap, enabled large Federal columns to operate on his left flank without his knowledge. Finally, while an enemy column had emerged from Snake Creek Gap and advanced upon Resaca, the presence of Cantey's small force convinced the Union commander in charge of that force to return to the safety of the gap. The Federal behavior suggested that the column on Johnston's left lacked sufficient numbers to successfully assail Cantey. Hood's report the following day seemed to confirm that impression as did Polk's telegram suggesting no enemy between Rome and Villanow. Therefore, Johnston seems to have judged McPherson's advance diversionary and an attempt to convince him to strengthen his left, thereby making an attack on his right more likely to succeed.

The following day produced a great deal of confusion at Johnston's headquarters. At 9:00 a.m. Cantey notified Dalton that a large Federal force threatened his position at Resaca. Johnston ordered Polk from Rome to Resaca, as well as Hindman's division which had just returned with Hood. Hood also retraced his steps to Resaca and wired headquarters at 3:00 p.m. that no enemy was within four miles of the town. A scout, however, contradicted Hood's assessment and reported the presence of 30,000 Union soldiers between Snake Creek Gap and Resaca. With conflicting information as to the enemy's troop dispositions, Johnston repositioned his own army to defend against a strike at either flank. Johnston's new alignment suggests that by the evening of May 11 he finally realized that the Federal maneuvers on his left flank represented more than a mere feint and jeopardized his position at Dalton. Only three divisions remained in defense of Buzzard's Roost and Crow Valley, while a portion of Polk's Corps held Resaca with two additional divisions within supporting distance. Then on May 12, Wheeler's reconnaissance alerted Johnston that the majority of Sherman's armies

50 Mackall Diary, May 10, 1864, JP WM; *O.R.* vol. 38, pt. 4, 106. As previously mentioned, the Confederates defending Resaca were mostly from James Cantey's brigade recently arrived from Mississippi. Also, if Hood 's reference to Snickers Gap was intended to identify Snake Creek Gap, it provides further proof of the inconsistent cartographical enterprise that plagued the Army of Tennessee.

had abandoned their positions around Dalton and were in motion for Snake Creek Gap.[51] The danger to his communications compelled Johnston's withdrawal from his position around Dalton and his concentration at Resaca.

Johnston's failure to cover Snake Creek Gap is puzzling. In his memoir, in response to the charge that he acted late in his concentration at Resaca, Johnston claimed that he had examined the terrain around Dalton and calculated the time necessary for the enemy to flank the Confederate position through Snake Creek. If Johnston is taken at his word, he clearly understood the inherent danger in leaving the gap unguarded, making the failure to do so incomprehensible. Additionally, the inherent defensive strength of Snake Creek Gap required a minimal force to hold it until reinforcements could arrive should the Federals attempt an assault. According to W. C. P. Breckinridge, the position, if guarded by a mere 250 men, was impregnable. Patrick Cleburne roundly criticized the failure in his after-action report of the operations between May 7 and May 27. Cleburne commented that the retrograde movement to Resaca became necessary "by the untoward circumstances of Snake Creek Gap not being occupied," thus permitting McPherson to outflank the Confederates. Cleburne observed that the commanding general (Johnston) could not have failed to appreciate its importance. Cleburne surmised that "its loss exposed us in the outset of the campaign to a terrible danger, and on the left forced us to retreat from a position where, if he [the Union army] adhered to his attack, we might have detained the enemy for months."[52]

The fact that the Confederates left Snake Creek Gap undefended was so mystifying that some historians have questioned whether Johnston knew of the gap's existence. The evidence does not present a clear answer, but it is likely that he did. First, the road from Dug Gap to Villanow, which gave Dug Gap one of its alternate names (Villanow Gap), also connected to the road through Snake Creek Gap. There can be no doubt that Johnston knew about Dug Gap and also about Villanow. According to W. C. P. Breckinridge, both Dug Gap and Snake Creek Gap were well known to both armies, as well as the public roads that ran through each of the gaps. Consequently, it seems logical that anyone who was familiar with the road from Dug Gap to Villanow, as Johnston was, would also be knowledgeable about the road through Snake Creek Gap that intersected the Villanow Road. Though the poor maps of the region suggest that a number of high-ranking Confederates were ignorant of the passage through Snake Creek, others, including Breckinridge were familiar with it. A. P. Stewart, upon observing

51 Mackall Diary, May 11, 12, 1864, JP WM; *O.R.* vol. 38, pt. 4, 698, 703.

52 Johnston, *Narrative of Military Operations*, 316; Breckinridge, "The Opening of the Atlanta Campaign," 278; *O.R.* vol. 38, pt. 3, 721.

Union maneuvers on his front on May 5, remarked that the enemy was "moving down Sugar Valley with the design to get into our rear at Resaca." Because Snake Creek Gap provided the only entrance into Sugar Valley, the comment indicates a knowledge of the defile. Patrick Cleburne also knew about the existence of the passage through Rocky Face Ridge's southern end. Finally, Lt. Thomas Mackall's diary entry on May 8 specifically mentions Grigsby's orders instructing him to march on Snake Creek Gap that evening.[53] Though the evidence is not conclusive, the preponderance of the data supports the conclusion that Johnston was familiar with Snake Creek Gap.

Whether Johnston would have remained in his defensive position around Dalton for months had he defended Snake Creek Gap as Cleburne suggested cannot, of course, be determined. Yet the rapidity with which the Army of Tennessee was dislodged assuredly affected the timetable for the campaign. If the Confederates hoped for Lincoln's defeat in the November election, they needed to retain possession of Atlanta. Sherman's ability to outmaneuver Johnston and force him from the protection of his mountain fortress within a few days after the outset of the campaign therefore boded poorly for Confederate desires to defeat Sherman's army in the field and Lincoln at the ballot box.

The ensuing battle of Resaca was, in some ways, a microcosm of several of the salient themes of the present study. Johnston, when presented with an opportunity to act aggressively, did not hesitate and planned two separate assaults. Further, the commanding general again relied upon Hood to facilitate the most critical task on the battlefield, thereby demonstrating that Johnston clearly placed more trust in Hood during the first phase of the campaign than he did in his other corps commanders. Despite Johnston's aggression, Jefferson Davis found yet another way to goad his general when he intimated that Johnston's *inactivity* threatened Lee's army in Virginia. Finally, the absence of the state militia in combination with the topographical features of northern Georgia forced Johnston's redeployment of his army south of the Oostanaula River.

At Resaca, Johnston's defensive position seemed to invite disaster with the confluence of the Oostanaula and Connasauga rivers to his rear. If Sherman launched a successful attack, the retreating Confederates would have few escape routes. Sherman thought it unlikely that Johnston would defend the town and

53 McMurry, "Rocky Face to the Dallas Line," 18; Kurtz, "Why was Snake Creek Gap Left Un-Guarded?"; *O.R.* vol. 38, pt.4, 673, 677–678; J. C. Thompson to A. P. Stewart, Box 1, Folder 5, JP WM; *O.R.* vol. 38, pt. 3, 721; Mackall Diary, May 8, 1864, JP WM. The entry is from the official version of the diary that can also be found in the *O.R.* Richard McMurry has asserted that the "official" version was a postwar elaboration of another document or documents. A more detailed discussion on the veracity of the "official" version of the Mackall diary can be found in Appendix II.

ordered an attack at daybreak against what he believed was the Confederate rearguard. What the Federals encountered, however, was Johnston's entire army entrenched upon a ridge northwest of the town. Johnston rested his left flank on the Oostanaula River and from there his line ran north almost to the Connasauga. The steep banks of Camp Creek ran across most of the Confederate front and proved a difficult obstacle when the Northern troops attacked on the morning of May 14.[54]

The Union attack fizzled out by 3:00 p.m. in total failure and provided an opportunity for a Confederate counterattack. On the previous afternoon Hood had directed Wheeler to send a force of cavalry to protect his right flank and to scout the area. After the Federal advance on May 14, the Confederate scouting parties on the right discovered that the Union left flank was vulnerable to a counterattack. At four o'clock Johnston ordered Hood to attack the Federal flank as soon as possible in an effort to cut Sherman off from his only line of retreat through Snake Creek Gap. Johnston's attack at Resaca does not fit the popular perception that he was fundamentally conservative and lacked the willingness to engage in offensive action. Sherman's army still numbered over 100,000 men and even with the arrival of a portion of Polk's Corps the Confederates mustered approximately half that number.[55] Despite the vast disparity in numbers, Johnston proved willing to launch an attack when presented with an opportunity to strike a decisive blow.

Historians have largely ignored the fact that Johnston displayed a level of audacity at Resaca that conflicts with traditional interpretations of his character. Even Johnston's biographers failed to recognize that Johnston attacked an army nearly twice the size of his own. One of Johnston's primary critics overlooked the attack altogether in his description of the affair at Resaca.[56] The risk was even greater than it might appear upon first glance. If Johnston's forces were defeated, a Union counterattack could drive the retreating Confederates into the Oostanaula River. Nevertheless, Johnston made a calculated gamble and ordered the assault.

To augment the strength of the onslaught, Johnston ordered three brigades from Walker's division of Hardee's Corps and one brigade from Loring's division of Polk's Corps to his right. Thus Johnston had once again entrusted Hood with the most critical responsibility on the battlefield and placed soldiers from other corps under his command. Hood's assault drove the Union left some distance

54 *O.R.* vol. 38, pt. 4, 170; Elam "The Road to Atlanta," 7.

55 *O.R.* vol. 38, pt. 4, 708–709; Johnston, *Narrative of Military Operations*, 310–311; Castel, *Decision in the West*, 153.

56 See Symonds, *Joseph E. Johnston*, 281–285; Govan and Livingood, *A Different Valor*, 269–270; Woodworth, *Jefferson Davis and His Generals*, 275.

to the rear before a Federal battery and the advance of a division from Hooker's Corps checked the Rebels' momentum. Had Stewart's division not moved too far to the right and therefore missed most of the fighting, the Confederate success could have been even greater. Pleased with Hood's accomplishment on the Union left, Johnston determined to renew the attack in the morning. The goal remained the same: to drive the Federal army to the west and seize Sherman's escape route through Snake Creek Gap.[57]

Later that evening, news that Sherman had secured a lodgment at Lay's Ferry across the Oostanaula caused Johnston to call off the plans for a renewed assault on the Federal left. Johnston ordered Walker's division to defend against the Union crossing of the Oostanaula and instructed his chief engineer to lay a pontoon bridge of his own across the river east of the railroad bridge in case he needed to evacuate Resaca to protect against the Federal flanking maneuver. The report of the Federal crossing at Lay's Ferry was accurate. Around four o'clock in the afternoon, Thomas Sweeney's division of McPherson's army forced a crossing of the ferry against a small force of Confederate cavalry. Sweeney, however, heard that Confederates threatened his rear and had returned to the north side of the Oostanaula until the following day.[58]

That night Johnston received a telegram from Richmond that impugned his conduct as commander of the Confederacy's principal western army. Davis asserted that Johnston's inactivity had permitted Sherman to reinforce Grant's army in Virginia. Davis's acerbic communication advised Johnston that if he could not prevent Sherman from reinforcing Grant he could at least inform the administration as soon as forces departed from Sherman's army en route to Virginia. Sherman, however, had not reinforced Grant as Davis claimed, and the rebuke seemed particularly unwarranted considering Johnston's assault on the Union left earlier in the day. The following morning, Johnston inspected his lines and waited for news regarding the rumored Federal crossing of the Oostanaula at Lay's Ferry. At 10:00 a.m. Johnston returned to his headquarters and replied to the president's charges. Johnston asserted that "we are assembled in the presence of the whole force of the enemy assembled from Tennessee and North Alabama. I think he [Sherman] cannot re-enforce Grant without my knowledge, as my whole line is engaged in skirmishing. Yesterday he made several assaults that were repulsed."[59] Clearly, the president's reprimand irritated the general. Johnston had acted aggressively, in

57 Mackall Diary, May 14, 1864, JP WM; Castel, *Decision in the West*, 164–166.

58 Johnston, *Narrative of Military Operations*, 312; *O.R.* vol. 38, pt. 3, 399–400; Poe to wife, May 15, 1864, LC.

59 *O.R.* vol. 38, pt. 4, 705, 712.

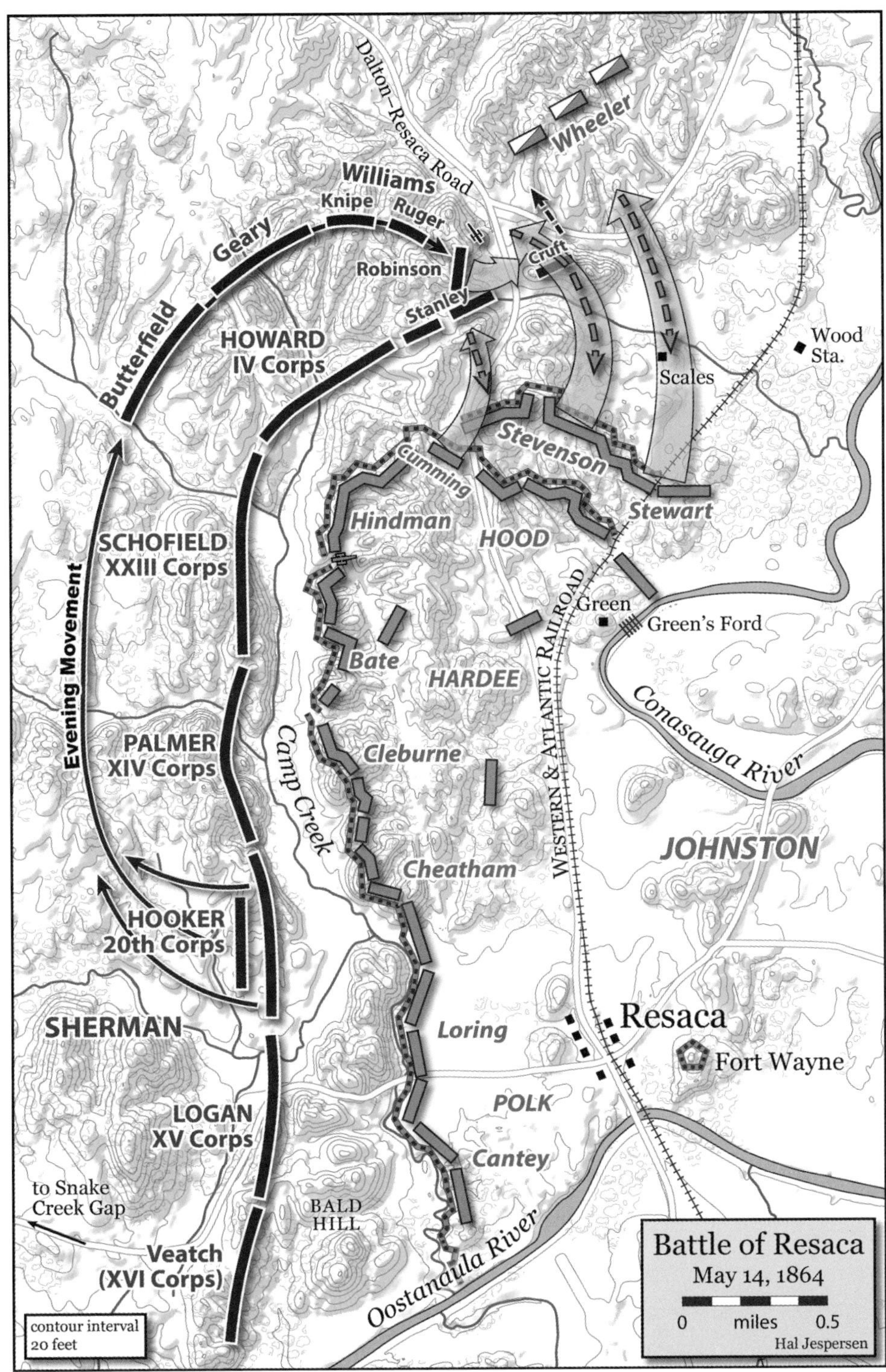
Dalton–Resaca Road
Wheeler
Williams
Knipe
Ruger
Geary
Robinson
Cruft
Stanley
Butterfield
HOWARD
IV Corps
Wood
Sta.
Scales
Stevenson
Cumming
Stewart
Hindman
HOOD
SCHOFIELD
XXIII Corps
Green
Green's Ford
WESTERN & ATLANTIC RAILROAD
Bate
HARDEE
Conasauga River
Evening Movement
PALMER
XIV Corps
Camp Creek
Cleburne
JOHNSTON
Cheatham
HOOKER
20th Corps
SHERMAN
Resaca
Loring
Fort Wayne
POLK
LOGAN
XV Corps
Cantey
to Snake
Creek Gap
BALD
HILL
Veatch
(XVI Corps)
Oostanaula River
contour interval
20 feet
Battle of Resaca
May 14, 1864
0 miles 0.5
Hal Jespersen

accordance with the president's oft-espoused tactical preference, and received a reprimand as his reward.

During the afternoon, Sherman launched another attack on Johnston's lines, which the Confederates resisted, giving Johnston a new opportunity. At approximately the same time that the Federal force withdrew from its attack, Johnston received a report from Walker indicating that the rumored threat to Lay's Ferry was no longer present. Johnston immediately ordered a renewal of Hood's attack on the enemy left and again provided Hood with units from other corps. As his telegram to the president indicated, Johnston planned his second attack with the knowledge that he faced Sherman's entire force and that his own army remained heavily outnumbered. In doing so, Johnston displayed a level of aggression not commonly attributed to him. Just as the attack got underway, however, Walker reported a strong Federal presence on the south side of the Oostanaula.[60]

With Sherman's lodgment across the Oostanaula, Johnston felt compelled to withdraw his army toward Calhoun, an action that might have been unnecessary if Brown had called out the militia early in the spring. Sweeney's seizure of Lay's Ferry faced little opposition because most of Wheeler's cavalry had operated on Hood's right during May 14 and 15. That limited the number of troopers available to guard against Union passage of the river on Johnston's left. Defense of fords and ferries is similar to the defense of mountain passes and consequently ideal for unseasoned militia troops. Once the militia joined Johnston's army and he established a defensive line along the Chattahoochee River in July, Johnston deployed them at river crossings, including Turner's Ferry and the railroad bridge. Considering his use of the militia in July, it seems probable that Johnston would have employed them in a similar fashion had they been available at Resaca. A force of 3,000 or 4,000 entrenched defenders, even untested militia, would have made the capture of Lay's Ferry a far more difficult proposition for the Union attackers. At the very least, the addition of a militia force to Walker's division on the evening of May 14 would have secured Johnston's left flank long enough to enable him to attempt a second assault on the Federal left the following day. Assuming only half of the militia made its way to the front in time to assist Johnston in early May, Johnston could have extended his defensive lines an additional two to three miles on the south side of the river, giving him an opportunity to attack Sherman on the north side.[61]

60 *O.R.* vol. 38, pt. 4, 705, 712, 713; *O.R.* vol. 38, pt. 3, 981.

61 *O.R.* vol. 38, pt. 4, 708–709; Smith, "The Georgia Militia About Atlanta," 332–33; Henry Stone "From the Oostanaula to the Chattahoochee," *The Atlanta Papers*, ed. Sydney Kerksis (Dayton, OH, 1980), 94–95. As previously mentioned, Brown's enrollment officers had identified 16,222 able-

Even with militia, however, Johnston could not have held his line at Resaca for an extended period thanks to the geography of north Georgia. The river systems in Georgia, like most in the Western theater, offered only minimal advantage for armies operating on the strategic defensive. Most of the rivers in the Western theater ran on a north-south axis, unlike those in Virginia. The width of rivers in Georgia also differed dramatically from those in Virginia, where Lee's army had held the enemy at bay for two years. In Virginia, Lee could establish strong defensive lines along the Rappahannock, Rapidan, North Anna, South Anna, and the James Rivers. Each of the Virginia rivers was wider, deeper and had higher bluffs than their counterparts in Georgia. The James River, for example, was about 700 yards in width and 15 fathoms in depth at the point where the Federals made their crossing. By comparison, the Chattahoochee, the most impressive river in Georgia, measured approximately 150 yards at one Union crossing point. Furthermore, the river courses in the two theaters of operation significantly differed. In Virginia the rivers were fairly straight, which allowed for a rapid flow of water, making them more difficult to cross. Conversely, in northwestern Georgia the numerous hills and valleys resulted in waterways with multiple twists and turns. Accordingly, Georgia rivers and creeks built up considerable deposits of silt that stemmed the flow of water and also produced a larger number of shallow spots, making Georgia waterways more fordable.[62]

At Resaca, the Oostanaula makes turns to the south just east and west of the town, thus providing more opportunity for the buildup of silt and debris. Within a ten-mile span southwest of the Federal position at Resaca, the Oostanaula takes several additional turns and includes a ferry at Calhoun.[63] If Johnston wished to remain at Resaca, he would have needed to cover the Lay's and Calhoun ferries as well as any shallow points along the river in the vicinity. Even with a sizable militia turnout, Johnston could not have hoped to hold miles of river frontage southwest of Resaca, as well as the ridge north of the town. Therefore, while the availability of militia would have permitted Johnston to launch his second planned attack against the Union left, it would not have allowed him to remain at Resaca very long.

---

bodied men between the ages of seventeen and forty-five. See Scaife and Bragg, *Joe Brown's Pets*, 5; Griffith, *Battle Tactics of the Civil War*, 129. Griffith notes that while there was no consensus as to how many troops were needed per yard, commanders generally employed somewhere between 2.5 and 5.

62 Elam, "The Road to Atlanta," 19–20, 121; Warren Wilkerson, *Mother May You Never See the Sights I Have Seen: The Fifty-Seventh Massachusetts Veteran Volunteers in the Army of the Potomac, 1864–1865* (New York, 1990), 167; *O.R.* vol. 38, pt. 2, 403.

63 See Resaca to Cassville, p. 113.

On the evening of May 15, then, Johnston had little choice but to withdraw toward Calhoun. Both Hardee and Hood performed admirably during the battle, but Polk's under-strength corps (some of his troops were still in transit from Mississippi) had conceded ground to the Federal advance. As a result, Johnston could not safely strip his line north of Resaca to bolster Walker's division sufficiently to allow Walker to take the offensive against the Union column south of the Oostanaula. Around midnight the army crossed the Oostanaula and headed south. Interestingly, Johnston assigned Hardee's Corps rear-guard duty.[64] Apparently, Hardee's stout defense against Federal attacks during the previous two days had impressed the commanding general enough to warrant that responsibility.

The following two days again demonstrated the Confederates' cartographical deficiency. Johnston retreated to Calhoun with the intent of establishing a defensive line in the vicinity of the town. Upon his arrival, Johnston discovered a large creek, the Oothcalooga, that impeded his ability to deploy troops in a contiguous line. The size of the creek restricted communication between forces positioned on opposite sides of the water. The potential isolation of forces on either side rendered the defense of Calhoun hazardous.[65] Johnston's cartographers apparently had not identified the creek as a hindrance to establishing a strong defensive position. The poor quality of the maps meant that Johnston was, in a sense, retreating blindly, not knowing where he might find the next defensible position on the road between Resaca and Atlanta.

Having been thwarted at Calhoun, Johnston determined to redeploy near Adairsville, ten miles to the south, where his map suggested that the terrain offered a favorable line of defense. The map depicted a relatively narrow valley bordered on both sides by formidable ridges that would make the position hard to flank. This information too proved inaccurate, as the valley was much broader than the maps had indicated. The width of the valley floor meant that Johnston could not sufficiently defend the valley and the heights on both sides.[66] Sherman could easily take possession of whichever ridge Johnston left unguarded and post his superior artillery corps in a position that commanded the valley.

On the evening of the seventeenth, Johnston met with Hardee and Hood to discuss the army's options. During the day scouts reported that McPherson's army had gone to Rome, thereby weakening Sherman's force. Additionally, a division of Polk's cavalry under Brig. Gen. William Jackson had arrived from the

64 Johnston, *Narrative of Military Operations*, 314.

65 Ibid., 319.

66 Ibid., 319–320.

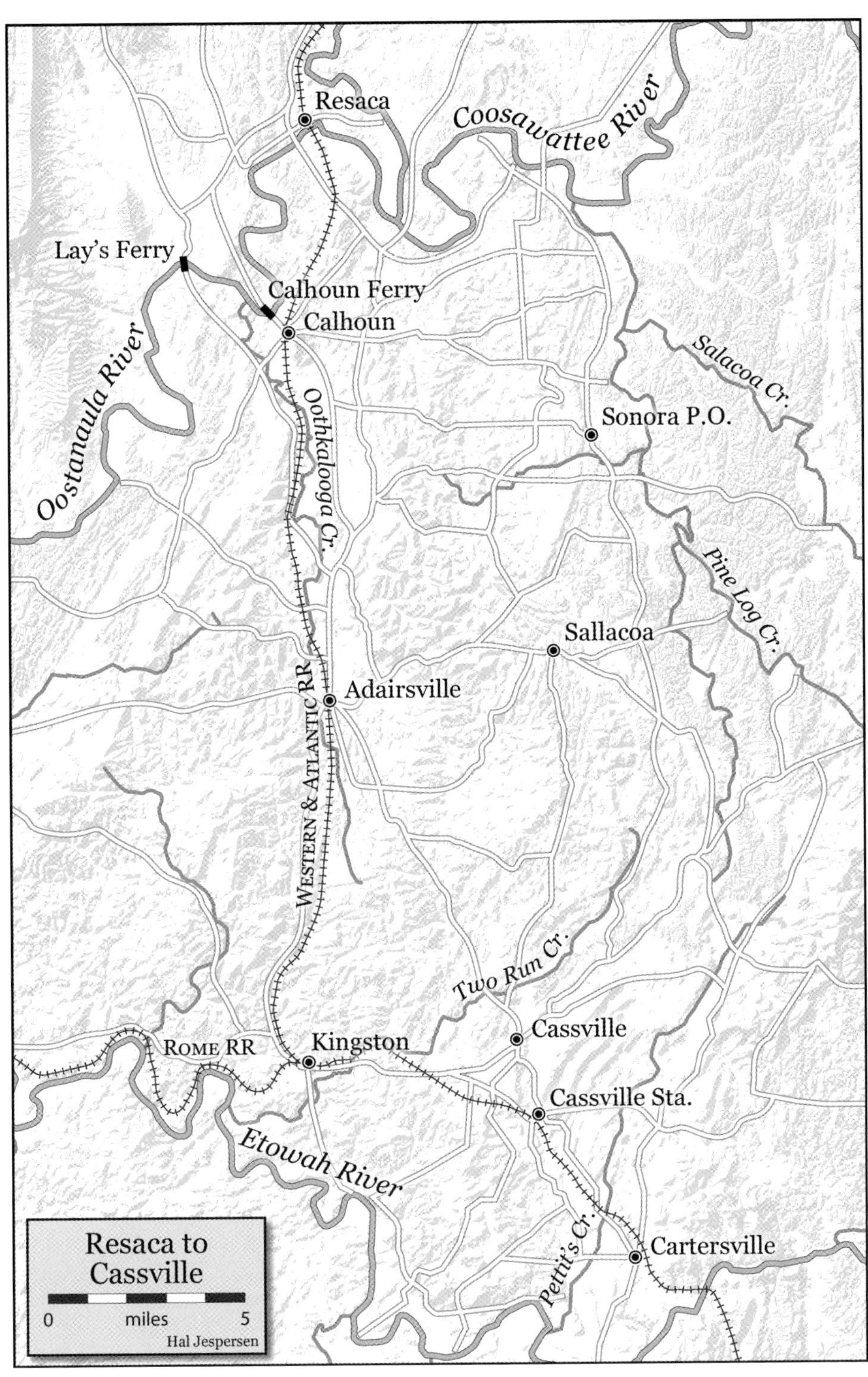
Resaca
Coosawattee River
Lay's Ferry
Calhoun Ferry
Calhoun
Oostanaula River
Oothkalooga Cr.
Salacoa Cr.
Sonora P.O.
Pine Log Cr.
Sallacoa
Adairsville
Western & Atlantic RR
Two Run Cr.
Cassville
Rome RR
Kingston
Cassville Sta.
Etowah River
Pettit's Cr.
Cartersville
Resaca to Cassville
0 miles 5
Hal Jespersen

Department of Mississippi, increasing Johnston's numbers and giving him greater parity with his adversary. Under the circumstances, Hardee advocated that the army remain at Adairsville and confront the enemy. Hood advised that the army continue its withdrawal southward toward the Etowah River.[67] Johnston decided to retire toward Cassville where he believed that the system of roads into the town offered him an opportunity to strike his enemy while it was divided. The following morning Johnston put his plan in motion and the Army of Tennessee made its way toward Cassville in hopes of springing the trap on their foe.

The opening phase of the campaign had begun very poorly for Johnston and the Army of Tennessee. Johnston's loss of the army's defensive position around Dalton ranks as one of his worst performances while serving as a Confederate officer. Johnston's misapprehension of Sherman's strategic plans influenced his timid response to reports of Federal activity on his left flank. Insufficient maps undoubtedly contributed to the rapid loss of a nearly impregnable position. Personal acrimony involving Johnston, Davis, and Brown further hampered the Confederate defense of Rocky Face Ridge, as it meant that neither Polk nor the state militia were available to Johnston during the first few days of the campaign. Finally, the condition of the cavalry's horses and the lethargy of their commander, Joseph Wheeler, doomed Confederate efforts to retain their mountain stronghold. At Resaca, Johnston redeemed himself and demonstrated a willingness to act much more aggressively, for which he is rarely given credit. The geography around Resaca, however, made defense against Sherman's flanking attempt almost impossible and compelled Johnston's withdrawal from the town. Flawed maps forced the army's continued retrograde movement from Calhoun, Adairsville, and eventually toward Cassville. Nevertheless, the army's spirits remained high, causing one newspaper correspondent to opine that the men were optimistic of success and that Johnston had Sherman precisely where he wanted him.[68] Though the reporter knew nothing of Johnston's plans, he was accurate in his assessment. The Confederates did indeed have Sherman where he wanted him, headed into a well-planned trap north of Cassville.

67 *O.R.* vol. 38, pt. 3, 704. In reality, the Union force headed for Rome only consisted of one division each of cavalry and infantry. See *O.R.* vol. 38, pt. 4, 227, 235; Mackall Diary, May 17, 1864, JP WM.

68 *Richmond Daily Dispatch*, May 24, 1864.

Chapter 5

Controversy at Cassville

May 19, 1864, was a pivotal day for the Confederate high command. Until that time Johnston and his corps commander John Bell Hood had maintained an affable rapport. Though the relationship did not transform overnight, the events at Cassville created a fissure that permanently changed the course of their association and damaged the trust between the two men. Once that occurred, Hood used his back-channel communications with the Davis administration to criticize Johnston's tenure as commander and complain about Johnston's alleged inaction. As a result, Jefferson Davis's policy of advocating improper communications between Hood and the administration had unintended consequences—Hood began undermining his commander likely in hopes of securing the position for himself. The consequences proved catastrophic for Confederate success in the West.

Johnston's decision to launch an assault near the town of Cassville on May 19, 1864, likely arose from a combination of factors. First, all three of his corps commanders favored a halt to the continuous retreat from Dalton to Cassville. John Bell Hood had advocated an offensive posture from the time he assumed command of his corps. Though he never offered a specific plan of action prior to the Federal advance on Rocky Face Ridge, he left no doubt as to his preferred method of warfare. Like his mentor Robert E. Lee, Hood believed in bold strokes, something not well suited for defensive warfare. Leonidas Polk also found offensive action more amenable to his tastes. He had, after all, produced a plan to take the offensive in the early spring before the Federals could initiate their move south. Finally, William Hardee, the most cautious of the three, hoped to give battle at

Adairsville and expressed his dissatisfaction with the retreat from that place.[1] Cassville offered an opportunity to satisfy Johnston's lieutenants.

Moreover, the road system between Adairsville and Cassville provided the Confederates with an opportunity to strike Sherman's forces while they were on the move. The Rebels had marched south on three roads. Hardee had taken the Kingston-Cassville Road that angled southwest to Kingston and then east into Cassville. Polk and Stevenson's division of Hood's corps had traveled on the Adairsville-Cassville Road that led south from Adairsville and straight into Cassville. Hood's other two divisions had moved south toward Cassville on the Ironton/Sallacoa Road that was to the east of Adairsville. The Confederate high command anticipated that Sherman would likewise divide his army on its approach to Cassville. If the Confederates could concentrate their forces on one of the Union columns as it moved south, they stood a reasonable chance of winning a substantial victory.[2]

In addition to the advantage offered by surprise attack, the Confederates enjoyed another benefit from the proposed engagement near Cassville. The number of troops available to Sherman had decreased while Johnston's army had recently received reinforcements. On the evening of May 17 Sherman had ordered a cavalry division under Gen. Kenner Garrard to destroy the railroad between Rome and Kingston. Sherman not only lost a cavalry division for the purposes of the raid, but an infantry division under the command of Jefferson C. Davis also marched on Rome on the seventeenth and remained there the following day. Meanwhile, on May 18 the last of Polk's troops, two brigades of Samuel French's division, arrived from Mississippi and joined Johnston's army near Cassville. French's brigades headed through Rome and escaped toward Kingston via railroad cars just as Davis advanced upon the town. As a result, Johnston enjoyed a parity in numbers not present at any other point during the campaign, and the greatest Confederate army ever massed in the Western theater.[3]

There is some controversy regarding who originally designed the Confederate plans for an offensive strike on the morning of May 19. Both Johnston and Hood later claimed to have devised the scheme and historians are split on the matter. Robert Jenkins has recently made a strong case that Johnston did not conceive the

1 See Appendix I; Mackall Journal, May 17, 1864, *O.R.* vol. 38, pt. 3, 982.

2 Robert Jenkins, *The Cassville Affairs: Johnston, Hood, and the Failed Confederate Strategy in the Atlanta Campaign, 19 May 1864* (Macon, 2024), 114.

3 *O.R.* vol. 38, pt. 4, 227, 235; Samuel G. French, *Two Wars: An Autobiography* (Nashville, 1901), 194; Castel, *Decision in the West*, 198. According to Castel's calculations, the Army of Tennessee numbered between 70,000 and 74,000 men at that time.

plan on May 17 while the army was in Adairsville as he (Johnston) claimed in his postwar memoir. Nevertheless, it is entirely possible that Johnston designed the attack while in Cassville on May 18. The fact that he made no mention of it at the time does not rule out the possibility since Johnston was notoriously secretive. It is also possible, if not likely, that Johnston and Hood formulated the plan together. Up to that point in the campaign, the two had been close confidants. Hardee was convinced that not only did Johnston frequently consult Hood on strategic matters, but that Hood likely had an oversized influence on Johnston's decisions.[4] The fact that both insisted on authorship of the plan until their deaths suggests that they both likely had a hand in conceiving the design.

Regardless, early on the morning of May 19 Johnston distributed an order commending the army for its courage and informing the troops that he intended to turn upon the enemy and give them battle. Johnston then ordered Hardee to deploy his corps facing the road to Kingston just southwest of the town. Polk was to deploy east-west across the Adairsville-Cassville Road directly in the path of any Federal column marching south along that road, and Hood deployed just to the east of Polk.[5] Hood's precise location has been difficult for historians to determine with accuracy. As discussed in the previous chapter, the commanders in the Army of Tennessee did not operate with a common set of maps. The available evidence suggests that the disparity and defectiveness in maps led to confusion about Hood's exact whereabouts as well as the whereabouts of the Federal column that struck his flank and rear on the morning of May 19. In turn, that misunderstanding played an integral part in the dispute that later emerged between Hood and his commander.

A Missed Opportunity: The Assault That Never Was

As the Confederate high command met to discuss their options for confronting Sherman's armies at Cassville, they were unaware that their maps were missing a key feature. None of the Confederate maps accurately reflected the road system north of Cassville. While the Rebels were aware of the Kingston-Cassville Road, the Adairsville-Cassville Road, the Ironton/Sallacoa Road, the Pine Log Road and the Canton Road, they were entirely ignorant of the Spring Place Road. The latter of which lay between the Ironton/Sallacoa Road and the Pine Log Road. That ignorance meant that Wheeler and his cavalry failed to provide a proper screen and it was down this road that Federal cavalry made contact with Hood's column

4 Jenkins, *The Cassville Affairs*, 22–32; Hardee to wife, June 12, 20, 23, 1864, ADAH.

5 *O.R.* vol. 38, pt. 3, 704; *O.R.* vol. 38, pt. 4, 728; Johnston, *Narrative of Military Operations*, 320.

while it was moving into position to deliver the planned assault. The encounter disrupted the Confederate offensive and has caused controversy ever since.[6]

As the morning dawned on May 19, Hardee established a defensive position astride the Kingston-Cassville Road to defend against any Federal advance from Kingston. Polk, meanwhile, moved his corps along the Adairsville-Cassville Road about a mile northwest of the town. The two corps (Hardee and Polk) took up positions nearly two miles from one another, The distance between Hardee and Polk meant that it was difficult for either to support the other. Nevertheless, Johnston proved willing to take that risk if it meant an opportunity to concentrate the bulk of his forces on an unsuspecting enemy moving down the Adairsville-Cassville Road and, or the Ironton/Sallacoa Road. Two Run Creek impeded Federal forces attempting to attack Hardee's right flank and the general had demonstrated a capacity for acting on the defensive during the engagement at Resaca.[7]

Hood was then to move into position on, or near, the Ironton/Sallacoa Road in anticipation of the planned assault. According to Hood, he rode at the head of his corps to the designated position and found it in possession of Confederate cavalry. Hood commented that there were no signs of the enemy on the Ironton/Sallacoa Road when he arrived at that location. While waiting for his corps to file into position, Hood claimed that a Federal column appeared on the Canton Road to his rear and right.[8] That a Union force appeared to the right and rear of Hood's corps is undoubtedly accurate. Hood, however, was inaccurate when he asserted that it struck his corps along the Canton Road. As a result of his erroneous contention scholars have constructed a historiography that attempts to identify the mythical Federal column that assailed Hood from the Canton Road.

Richard McMurry is rather noncommittal in identifying the Union force and its exact location. He does not, in any of his publications, assign a specific Northern

6 Jenkins, *The Cassville Affairs*, 86–90.

7 Johnston, *Narrative of Military Operations*, 320–321; In a letter home dated May 16 William Mackall had noted that Hardee "had behaved very handsomely [at Resaca] and raised himself very much in my opinion." It seems likely that Mackall reflected the views at army headquarters. See William Mackall, *A Son's Recollections of His Father* (New York, 1930), 210.

8 The Ironton/Sallacoa road has also been identified as the road to Mosteller's Mill and the road to Spring Place. See Castel, *Decision in the* West, 199; Richard McMurry, "Cassville," *Civil War Times Illustrated* (Dec. 1971): 4–9, 45–48; Johnston, *Narrative of Military Operations*, 321. Johnston apparently did not know the precise name of the road, but his description of a road about a mile east and parallel to the Adairsville-Cassville Road is consistent with the Ironton/Sallacoa Road. Furthermore, the campaign map reproduced in Johnston's memoir depicts only two roads leading into Cassville from the north. See Johnston, *Narrative of Military Operations*, 320. One road enters Cassville directly from Adairsville. The other is unnamed, but identical to maps depicting the same road and identifying it as the road to Sallacoa; Hood, *Advance and Retreat*, 334.

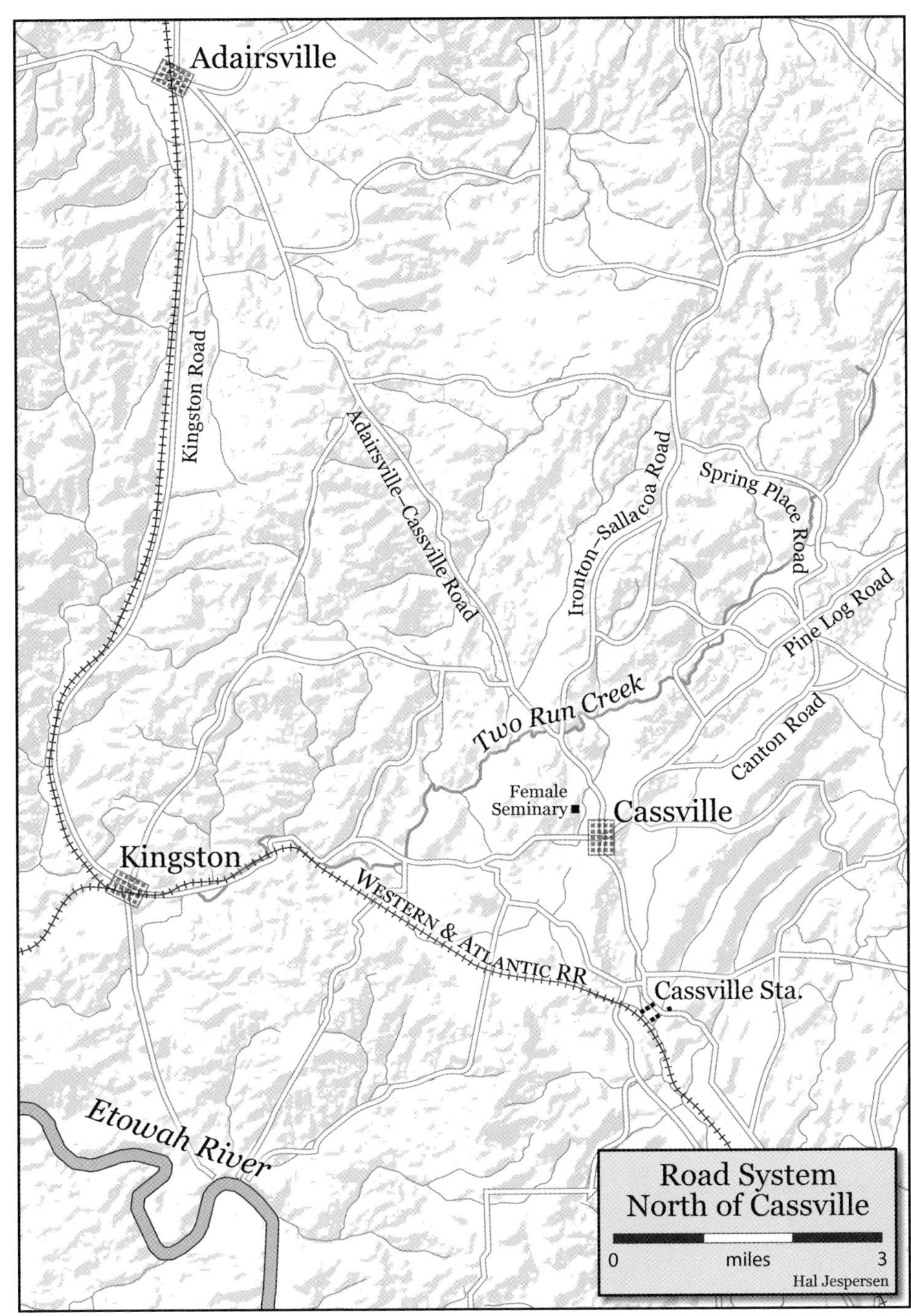
Adairsville
Kingston Road
Adairsville–Cassville Road
Ironton–Sallacoa Road
Spring Place Road
Pine Log Road
Two Run Creek
Canton Road
Female Seminary
Cassville
Kingston
Western & Atlantic RR
Cassville Sta.
Etowah River
Road System North of Cassville
0 miles 3
Hal Jespersen

unit to the Canton Road. Instead, he asserts that a Federal column appeared to the east of Hood's Corps. McMurry alludes to the possibility that they were either an unknown body of cavalry or possibly infantry units from Hooker's Corps.[9] However, no existing reports or communications of any kind provide evidence that any unit from Hooker's Corps ever appeared as far east as the road to Sallacoa, let alone even further east. Federal columns moving down that road necessarily approached Hood from the north and northeast, not the east.

Three other historians, Albert Castel, Stephen Davis, and Craig Symonds, have offered a specific identity for the presumed body of Northern troops. Albert Castel correctly identifies the positions of most of the Federal forces on the morning of May 19. Castel properly identifies the IV Corps, under Maj. Gen. Oliver Howard, and the XIV Corps, under Maj. Gen. John Palmer, headed toward Cassville along the Kingston-Cassville Road. Castel's observation that the XX Corps under Maj. Gen. Joseph Hooker marched down the Adairsville-Cassville Road, while the XXIII Corps under Maj. Gen. John Schofield moved south along the Ironton/Sallacoa Road appears consistent with reports found in the *Official Records*, though Schofield shifted to the Adairsville-Cassville Road on the morning of May 19. In his attempt to identify the presumed Federal presence on the Canton Road, however, Castel mistakenly suggests that the Union column consisted of cavalry divisions of Edward McCook and George Stoneman.[10]

Reports from the *Official Records* demonstrate that McCook served as a screen for Schofield, who, as noted above, was nowhere near the Canton Road on May 19. During the previous afternoon McCook informed Schofield that he was eight miles from Adairsville and eleven miles from Cassville. He further noted the presence of Confederate cavalry in the direction of Cassville and suggested that "if I am to march toward Cassville I desire at least a section of my battery to accompany me." The communication establishes two important facts. First, McCook operated under the direction of Schofield as the Federal army moved toward Cassville. Second, he was in the vicinity of Adairsville and headed toward Cassville, not Canton. Lieutenant Colonel Horace Lamson's report provides further evidence that McCook was operating north of Cassville on the nineteenth. According to Lamson, in command of the second brigade of McCook's division, his brigade camped near the forks of Adairsville and Cassville roads on the evening of May

9 McMurry, "Cassville," 8. Also see McMurry, *John Bell Hood and the War for Southern Independence*, 108; Richard McMurry, *Atlanta 1864: Last Chance for the Confederacy* (Lincoln, NE, 2000), 81.

10 Schofield's precise order of march remains uncertain. It appears that he did in fact march down the Sallacoa Road, but the movement commenced well after noon and after Hood retreated to a ridge in the rear of Cassville. See *O.R.* vol. 38, pt. 4, 255–256; Castel, *Decision in the West*, 199, 201.

18. The following morning his unit moved six miles toward Cassville, encountered a Confederate column and engaged in a sharp skirmish.[11] The description is consistent with a movement down either the Ironton/Sallacoa Road or the Spring Place Road. It is not consistent with a movement eastward toward Canton and then westward again back toward Cassville. Consequently, it is impossible that McCook and his column appeared on the road to Canton at any point during May 19.

The assertion that George Stoneman advanced on the Canton-Cassville Road also finds no support in the *Official Records*. Indeed, the *Official Records* sustain the contention that Stoneman moved down either the Ironton/Sallacoa Road or the Spring Place Road with McCook. McCook specifically reported that he "formed a junction with Stoneman, who acted as support," and the two divisions marched down to Cassville on the nineteenth. Regrettably, Stoneman produced no reports regarding his activities near Cassville on that day, but he had been ordered by Schofield to keep west of Pine Log Creek on May 17. A communication from Schofield to Sherman on the evening of the nineteenth, confirms that Stoneman operated in tandem with McCook during the day. Schofield reported that Stoneman and McCook spent the day skirmishing with a Confederate infantry division "which now appears to be about due north from Cassville and not more than a mile from that place."[12] Consequently, it is not possible that McCook and Stoneman approached Cassville by way of Canton. Both divisions approached Cassville from the north at the head of the XXIII Corps.

Castel is not alone in his effort to discover the identity of the presumed force on the Canton Road. Stephen Davis, in *Atlanta Will Fall*, comes close to analyzing correctly the Federal approach to Cassville. He assigns both McCook and Stoneman to the Ironton/Sallacoa Road. Unfortunately, Davis spends little time on the controversy, only noting that a disagreement between Hood and Johnston emerged after the war regarding the presence of a Union force on Hood's flank and rear. He concludes by suggesting that "modern scholarship tends to favor Hood," but does not make any reference to the Canton Road.[13]

Craig Symonds contends that a portion of Gen. Daniel Butterfield's infantry division appeared on the road. Presumably, Symonds draws his conclusion from Hood's memoir. According to Hood, a postwar conversation with a General Carson of the Union army revealed that Butterfield's command was responsible for the movements along the Canton Road. The claim lacks any support from the

11 *O.R.* vol. 38, pt. 4, 223, 241; *O.R.* vol. 38, pt. 2, 781.

12 *O.R.* vol. 38, pt. 3, 766; *O.R.* vol. 38, pt. 4, 256.

13 Stephen Davis, *Atlanta Will Fall: Sherman, Joe Johnston, and the Yankee Heavy Battalions* (Wilmington, DE, 2001), 55–56.

evidence found in the *Official Records*. In fact, every report produced by an officer from Butterfield's Division proves that he spent the day on the Adairsville-Cassville Road. According to these same reports, Butterfield's division acted as the army's extreme left flank on the morning of the nineteenth. Rather than straying eastward off of the Adairsville Road, Butterfield angled to the west when he discovered Confederates in his front. He recognized the hazardous situation in which he found himself and hoped to move closer to his supporting columns.[14] Consequently, the contention that Butterfield appeared on the Canton Road must be rejected.

Finally, Robert Jenkins addressed the controversy in his recent publication *The Cassville Affairs* and comes closest to correctly identifying the Union forces and where they were when they made contact with Hood on the morning of May 19. Making use of Joseph Johnston's and Joseph Wheeler's maps, Jenkins noted that the Confederate maps of the region were defective. Johnston's map, found in his *Narrative of Military Operations* is devoid of any topographical features north of Cassville and east of the Ironton/Sallacoa Road. While Wheeler's map does include most of the road networks northeast of Cassville, it is missing the Spring Place Road. Jenkins asserts that as a result, Wheeler failed to provide a cavalry screen along the Spring Place Road, which allowed Federal cavalry under McCook to assail Hood's corps as he moved into position to launch his offensive. Unfortunately, Jenkins does not limit the Federal cavalry probe to the Spring Place Road. Rather, he argues that a portion of McCook's column managed to make its way to the Canton Road and briefly assault the rear of Hood's corps that was still marching along that road. In doing so, Jenkins provides support for Hood's claim that a body of the enemy made an appearance to his rear along the Canton Road.[15]

While Jenkins's contention that McCook's division struck Hood along the Spring Place Road is accurate, there is no evidence that any of the Union cavalry troopers made it as far as the Canton Road and skirmished with Hood's rear guard there in the morning. Jenkins refers to a report of Maj. David Briggs of the Second Indiana Cavalry in support of his assertion. Briggs stated that upon encountering the enemy (Hood) he and his men were ordered to advance in line of skirmishers and lost one man who was wounded in the action. Briggs then

14 Symonds, *Joseph E. Johnston*, 293; Hood, *Advance and Retreat*, 104; *O.R.* vol. 38, pt. 2, 77, 309, 361, 380, 437, 464, 170, 376. See also Hood, *The Lost Papers of Confederate General John Bell Hood*, 96–98. Hood reproduces a letter from Paul Oliver of Butterfield's command. In the letter, Oliver mentions his movement down "the road" while Butterfield maneuvered the rest of his force along Two Run Creek to cut the railroad. A look at the map reveals that "the road" must have been the Adairsville-Cassville Road.

15 Johnston, *Narrative of Military Operations*, 321; Jenkins, *The Cassville Affairs*, 86–90, 138–140; Hood, *Advance and Retreat*, 334.

reported that his regiment retired. Briggs's account squares with McCook's report of the brief engagement that occurred between his division and Hood's corps on the morning of the nineteenth. Briggs then stated that after his withdrawal he was ordered (most likely by McCook) to move to the right and take possession of a gap in the mountain. From the new position in the gap, Briggs claimed to have made a "bold and desperate charge." Presumably, it was this last claim upon which Jenkins relies when he places the Second Indiana on the Canton Road during the morning hours. McCook's report of the affair, however, asserted that the charge of the Second Indiana took place during the afternoon.[16] When considering that Briggs's account mentioned that his regiment repositioned itself into a gap in the mountain before making their attack in tandem with McCook's report, it seems clear that the charge did not occur during the initial encounter between McCook's division and Hood's corps. Consequently, it is clear that Hood erred in his claim that the enemy assailed him from the Canton Road on the morning of May 19.

Each of the foregoing attempts to reconcile the reports concerning the affair at Cassville has yielded a confusing and largely inaccurate analysis. While it is universally accepted that a Federal column came into contact with Hood's corps on the morning of May 19, the composition of that force and the precise location that it struck Hood is still a matter of debate. As a result, Hood's reports as to the location of his own troops and that of the enemy's require reinterpretation.

As the sun rose on May 19, 1864, Joseph E. Johnston's prospects for a signal victory looked promising. The Army of Tennessee mustered a larger host of effective fighting men than ever before. Sherman had responded precisely as Johnston hoped and divided his forces, half following Hardee from Adairsville toward Kingston and the other half following Hood and Polk from Adairsville to Cassville. Sometime between seven and eight o'clock in the morning Johnston issued his general order that generated the desired response—enthusiasm throughout the army. As the morning progressed, Hardee deployed his troops upon a ridge about two miles west of Cassville and astride the road to Kingston with open fields of fire to his front. He proceeded to strengthen his position with the construction of rail barricades with Two Run Creek acting as an anchor for his right flank.[17] His position, though held by a single corps, appeared capable of holding off a Union advance from Kingston until the afternoon, unless the Federals attacked in force at an early hour.

16 Jenkins, *The Cassville Affairs*, 140; *O.R.* vol. 38, pt. 2, 785, 751–752. Jenkins mentions that W. H. Underwood of the Second Indiana cavalry was wounded during the charge, but Briggs's report stated that Underwood was wounded while the unit advanced as skirmishers, not during the charge.

17 *Memoirs of General W. T. Sherman*, ed. Charles Royster (New York, 1990), 505; *O.R.* vol. 38, pt. 4, 220–221, 233; *O.R.* vol. 38, pt. 3, 705, 715, 983; *Richmond Daily Dispatch* July 16, 1864; *O.R.* vol. 38, pt. 1, 192.

If the Federals failed to press an early attack, Polk and Hood would have the time necessary to conduct their assault on the Union troops advancing from the north. At the same time Hardee formed on the road to Kingston, Johnston directed Hood to form his corps along the Ironton/Sallacoa Road. As Hood marched his men to the Ironton/Sallacoa Road, Polk assembled his Corps astride the Adairsville-Cassville Road approximately two miles northwest of Cassville. Johnston had set his trap; now he waited to see if Sherman would fall for it.

After the battle of Resaca, Sherman and his staff thought it unlikely that Johnston intended to make a stand north of the Etowah River. When Johnston's army vacated Adairsville on the evening of the seventeenth Sherman felt confident in his assessment of the situation. His directive to George Thomas on the night of the eighteenth demonstrates that he did not expect his adversary to turn on him with any significant force before he crossed the Etowah about eight miles south of Cassville. Sherman advised Thomas to press the pursuit of Johnston and "follow his well marked trail." Sherman then sent a dispatch to Schofield ordering him to follow Hooker as he marched his corps south of Adairsville. The communication speculated that he did not think Johnston would give battle north of the Etowah, but that if Johnston could be forced to do so "we must do it, even at the hazard of beginning battle with but part of our forces."[18] That, of course, is exactly what Johnston hoped for. Unfortunately for Johnston, things did not work out precisely as he had anticipated. Even so, the Federal approach to Cassville offered the Confederates an opportunity to deliver a substantial blow to their foe.

The Union advance against Hardee's position proved much more listless than Sherman's dispatch to Thomas portended. Howard's IV Corps led the Federal advance toward Kingston at five in the morning but did not arrive at Kingston until a little after eight. There it encountered some Confederate cavalry and was forced to deploy and did not drive off the enemy until approximately nine o'clock. Thereafter, the corps proceeded in the direction of Cassville. When the lead division of the corps, under Maj. Gen. David Stanley, encountered Hardee's line it halted and waited for support from Maj. Gen. John Newton. Newton did not form his column until almost one o'clock in the afternoon. The Union infantry then waited for their artillery to probe the Confederate lines before advancing upon Hardee at approximately two o'clock in the afternoon. One Confederate officer observed that the Federals seemed confused in taking their positions and lamented that the Confederates had failed to assault their bewildered enemy.[19] Clearly the sluggish

18 Poe to wife, May 16, 1864, LC; *O.R.* vol. 38, pt. 4, 233, 242.

19 *O.R.* vol. 38, pt. 1, 858; *O.R.* vol. 38, pt. 3, 715.

Union advance from the direction of Kingston provided Johnston the opportunity that he sought north of Cassville to deliver a crushing defeat to the Federals advancing from Adairsville.

As Howard's men progressed slowly along the road from Kingston, Butterfield's division of Hooker's Corps advanced at the head of the Union column moving south from Adairsville along the Adairsville-Cassville Road. The lead brigade under the command of William Ward began its march within four miles of Cassville. They soon confronted what they perceived to be the Confederate rear-guard and steadily pushed forward until they encountered a larger force of Confederates. Here the brigade halted and waited for support. Colonel James Wood, also in command of a brigade in Butterfield's division, moved forward under orders to make a reconnaissance toward Two Run Creek, on Ward's right. In the process of making the reconnaissance Wood came into contact with an enemy force about half a mile from the creek and "in dangerous proximity" of his left flank.[20] Wood quickly withdrew his brigade to a defensive position. According to Wood, he withdrew not only because he faced a large Confederate force to his front and left flank, but also because his division lacked support from the remainder of the corps. He complained that the division (Butterfield's) received no support on the right from the second division, nor on the left from the first division, as the orders (as he understood them) had indicated.

At this time the Confederates opened an artillery barrage upon both Ward and Wood. Ward soon realized, like Wood, that he faced a large force of Confederates, not just a rear-guard, and that the situation might prove hazardous. Butterfield, recognizing the danger, redeployed the brigade further to the west, closer to James Wood's brigade that had moved up in support of Ward. Butterfield's division remained at its new position until about four o'clock when the other two divisions of the corps finally arrived and the whole body moved forward toward Cassville together.[21] The fact that Butterfield's division remained relatively isolated for such an extended period demonstrates that the planned offensive, if executed properly, offered a considerable opportunity for the Army of Tennessee. Had Hood's and Polk's corps advanced as intended they faced only one division. At the very least, the Confederates should have been able to destroy Butterfield's command and might well have been able to defeat the remainder of the XX Corps in detail as each division arrived on the field of battle. Not only was such a scenario a distinct possibility, it was, in fact, fairly likely.

20 *O.R.* vol. 38, pt. 2, 361, 437. This was undoubtedly Polk's Corps, the same troops Ward encountered.

21 *O.R.* vol. 38, pt. 2, 437, 376.

Richard McMurry argues that the attack probably would not have been capable of overwhelming both Hooker and Schofield before elements of the IV and XIV Corps came to their rescue. He bases his conclusion on Johnston's *Narrative of Military Operations*, in which Johnston explained his decision to withdraw to the heights beyond Cassville. Johnston claimed that he did not countermand Hood's retreat because by the time he learned of Hood's action, the Federal forces on the Kingston Road threatened Hardee's position. Johnston's assertion, however, fails to comport with the evidence available in the *Official Records*. As noted, the Federal advance along the Kingston Road halted until two o'clock in the afternoon and only threatened Hardee when they pushed forward at that late hour. Therefore, both Hooker and Schofield remained isolated from the remainder of the Union army until the afternoon. An assault, if conducted as planned, promised to decimate the Federal forces north of Cassville. Hooker's Corps was strung out all along the Adairsville-Cassville Road. Two divisions, including Butterfield's, had advanced in the direction of Cassville while the third division remained several miles back.[22] The rough terrain also made the Union position more perilous. Though both sides faced the same landscape, the Confederates, had they launched their offensive, would at least have had the benefit of having already formed their lines, while the bulk of the Union forces had not yet done so. The task of formation into line of battle was necessarily complicated by the nature of the terrain, thereby giving the Confederates a distinct advantage in such an encounter.

Equally propitious for the Confederate assault was the progress of Schofield's XXIII Corps. Schofield had not continued his march from Mosteller's Mill, his campsite of the previous evening, southward along the Ironton/Sallacoa Road toward Cassville. Instead, he had moved to the Adairsville-Cassville Road and waited for Hooker's last division to move out. Only after receiving orders from Sherman at about half past noon did Schofield contemplate any movement. Even then he informed Sherman that he would move "as soon as the road is clear," and endeavor to "get on the road to the east [Sallacoa] as soon as I can and keep my communication with General Hooker." Thus, the Confederates had an opportunity to destroy Hooker's first two divisions in detail and then move upon his only remaining division and Schofield's command. The attack could have been made without any danger of Federal infantry threatening the Confederate flank on the Ironton/Sallacoa Road, as Schofield did not move his command to that road until sometime in the afternoon. Despite a most auspicious beginning to May 19 for the

22 McMurry, "Cassville," 9; Johnston, *Narrative of Military Operations*, 322; *O.R.* vol. 38, pt. 4, 255. Johnston likely mentioned Federal pressure on Hardee to exculpate his own failure to halt Hood's retrograde movement.

Confederate cause, the advance of Federal cavalry under McCook and Stoneman down the Spring Place Road, which had been left unguarded by Wheeler's cavalry, terminated the Confederate attack before it even commenced.[23]

According to Hood, he was in the process of deploying his troops when a body of enemy troops appeared on his flank along what he mistakenly thought was the Canton Road. He confessed later, in his report at the close of the campaign, that he thought the enemy column likely consisted of cavalry units. Taylor Beatty, a member of Hood's staff, also thought that the enemy force was cavalry. In this assessment both men were correct. The cavalry divisions of McCook and Stoneman, as discussed earlier in this chapter, accounted for the Federal presence on Hood's flank. However, they appeared along the Spring Place Road, not the road to Canton as Hood asserted. Hood ordered Hindman to "send out a body of skirmishers to find out who they were." The appearance of the Federals necessarily slowed Hood's progress. Hood's postponement in launching the designed assault left Johnston anxious about the day's prospects. To expedite the attack, Johnston ordered William Mackall to investigate the delay. Mackall reached Hood at approximately 10:20 and found him withdrawing his corps. Mackall, despite not having seen the enemy for himself, sent word back to headquarters that the Federals were threatening Hood's flank on the Canton Road. Mackall's communication accepted two key principles without question. First, he believed that a Northern column menaced Hood's flank. That assertion, of course, was accurate. Second, Mackall's dispatch did not question the location of the Federal forces. Hood had reported them on the Canton Road and that is precisely what Mackall communicated to Johnston. That assertion, however, was inaccurate. Upon hearing the news, Johnston expressed disbelief, stating that Confederate cavalry occupied the Canton Road and reported no Federal presence. Johnston then lamented that if the report were true (Federals on the Canton Road), Hood would have to retire.[24] Hood needed no encouragement; he had withdrawn almost upon first contact.

Hood claimed that the appearance of the enemy on the "Canton Road" compelled him to withdraw his corps to the rear. Further, he maintained in his postwar memoir that the enemy opened fire on him immediately with artillery and musketry, forcing him to deploy a line of skirmishers from Hindman's division.

23 *O.R.* vol. 38, pt. 4, 255–256; Jenkins, *The Cassville Affairs*, 138.

24 *O.R.* vol. 38, pt. 3, 635; Colonel Taylor Beatty, Diary, May 19, 1864, Southern Historical Collection, University of North Carolina; Hood, *Advance and Retreat*, 102; Mackall Journal, May 19, 1864, *O.R.* vol. 38, pt. 3, 983; W. W. Mackall, "Memoranda of the Operations at Cassville on May 19, 1864," *O.R.* vol. 38, pt. 3, 622.

Hood's report from the field shortly after the affair at Cassville, however, indicated minimal action took place on his front on May 19. Indeed, Hood recounted only slight skirmishing. Hood's acknowledgment that his corps was so lightly engaged is revealing. If Hood genuinely believed that a strong enemy column threatened his flank and rear, he made no effort to meet such a menace. Hindman's division, once formed, quickly drove off McCook's cavalry. The engagement was so brief that the report of Brig. Gen. Edward Walthall, who served in Hindman's division, made no reference of an encounter with enemy cavalry whatsoever. McCook himself reported that as soon as the Confederates advanced in a division front upon his troops he felt compelled to withdraw.[25] Having driven back the Federal cavalry, Hood made an extraordinarily strange decision; he withdrew his corps to the rear.

Hood apparently made his retrograde movement before discovering the identity and strength of the foe he reported on his flank and rear. If Hood had ascertained the enemy strength on his flank and then withdrew only after discovering that a division or more of infantry imperiled his advance position, his retreat would make sense. Instead, his retreat occurred almost immediately after the skirmishing commenced. Hood admitted that Johnston's chief of staff, Gen. William Mackall, appeared almost simultaneously with his decision to deploy skirmishers from Hindman's division. Moreover, Col. Taylor Beattie of Hood's staff recalled that the retrograde movement (back to Polk's right) began soon after Hood and Mackall spoke to one another.[26] General Mackall possessed no authority to change Hood's alignment. Consequently, it seems likely that Hood made the decision and, as a result, Johnston's hope to strike an offensive blow dissolved.

Perhaps the greatest oddity of the affair is that Hood's failure to engage the Union force on the Adairsville-Cassville Road seems inconsistent with his character. Hood had demonstrated throughout the war that he preferred to deliver smashing offensive assaults upon the enemy. In August 1862 Hood delivered a crushing blow on the Federal left flank at Second Manassas. On the evening of the twenty-ninth he ordered his command to "push forward and attack the enemy." When Union troops crested a ridge near Groveton to his immediate front he ordered Brig. Gen. Evander Law to charge them. The following day Hood led the Confederate attack, often blazing ahead with such speed that his commanding general, James Longstreet, repeatedly requested that he halt and wait for the rest of the corps. The savagery of the assault cost Hood nearly 1,000 casualties in his

25 Hood, *Advance and Retreat,* 100; *O.R.* vol. 38, pt. 3, 761, 798; *O.R.* vol. 38, pt. 2, 752.

26 Hood, *Advance and Retreat,* 100–103.

division.[27] At Second Manassas, Hood acted without hesitation, always opting to attack aggressively whatever enemy he encountered. He continued to exhibit such ferocity whenever the opportunity presented itself.

Less than three weeks later at Sharpsburg, Hood led his division, counting approximately 2,300 muskets, in a desperate counterattack against Federal troops in Miller's cornfield. As he ordered his troops forward, he informed one of Stonewall Jackson's aides that he required reinforcements or else he would be forced back, "but I am going on while I can!"[28] During his advance, Hood exposed the right flank of his division to the main Union line. Yet, the threat to his right flank had absolutely no effect on the force with which he delivered his blow. In fact, Hood failed to make any dispositions that defended his division from a counter-stroke along his right flank. Though Union shot and shell decimated Hood's division in the assault, the experience did little to change Hood's predilection for offensive warfare. Even at Gettysburg, when he deemed the attack on Little Round Top injudicious, he carried out his orders.

Hood's actions at Gettysburg starkly contrasted with his inaction at Cassville. At Gettysburg, much like Resaca, Hood ordered a thorough reconnaissance of the ground in his front. At Cassville he failed to make any reconnaissance. At Gettysburg Hood obeyed his superior's orders and made an assault on a position he later described as "seemingly impregnable." At Cassville he withdrew his corps without consulting his commanding general. Hood's behavior at Cassville seems almost inconceivable considering his previous track record. His gallantry in battle had cost him most of the use of his left arm and required the amputation of a leg but had never yet caused him to lose his nerve. Steven Woodsworth, in *Jefferson Davis and His Generals*, characterized Hood's performance as panicked and the product of his short tenure as a corps commander.[29] Woodsworth's critique ignores Hood's successful handling of a corps both at Chickamauga and at Resaca. As a result, the charge that Hood suffered from a lack of experience which accounted for his erratic behavior at Cassville goes too far.

Rather, Hood's performance in the morning hours of May 19, 1864, might simply be described as his most lackluster of the war to date. He had performed well in virtually every capacity and on every battlefield until that time. He was not in over his head as a corps commander, as Woodworth suggests, but on that morning he made a series of poor decisions. Common sense would dictate that

27 John Hennessy, *Return to Bull Run: The Campaign and Battle of Second Manassas* (New York, 1993), 289, 292; *O.R.* vol. 12, pt. 2, 605; Hood, *Advance and Retreat*, 36; *O.R.* vol. 12, pt. 2, 560.

28 Stephen Sears, *Landscape Turned Red: The Battle of Antietam* (Boston, 1983), 198.

29 Hood, *Advance and Retreat*, 58–59; Woodsworth, *Jefferson Davis and His Generals*, 276.

Hood fully identify the strength and composition of the force on his flank. Once this task was accomplished, he could have deployed a brigade across the Spring Place Road, thus securing his flank from the cavalry probe, and turned his attention to administering the anticipated assault. At the very least he should have waited for instructions from Johnston before making his retrograde movement. His decision to retreat without consulting his commander deserves censure.

It is possible that Hood became so agitated with what he perceived as a failure on Johnston's part to secure the Confederate flank with a cavalry detachment that he abandoned the assault. Colonel Beatty complained that the Federal approach upon the corps' flank constituted the "second or third time since [the army] left Dalton that enemy have gotten up on us without our knowing anything of it."[30] Clearly a member of Hood's staff considered the failure to secure the army's flanks an ongoing problem and probably considered Johnston responsible. It is not unreasonable to think that Hood shared the same opinion and that Beatty's diary entry reflected the mood at Hood's headquarters.

In fact, Hood was not the only Confederate commander who turned in a poor performance on the morning of May 19. Johnston too merits blame in the affair. Johnston had ordered Wheeler and his cavalry to cover the Federal advance from Adairsville, but he apparently failed to advise him to cover the Spring Place Road. While neither Johnston or Wheeler possessed accurate maps of the road system northeast of Cassville, Johnston should have made it clear to Wheeler that he needed to be certain that all of the approaches to Cassville were properly screened. After all, the Confederates had already lost their defensive line atop Rocky Face Ridge due to Wheeler's poor performance. Considering that a quick reconnaissance of the road network north of Cassville would have revealed the existence of the Spring Place Road and that the Confederates reached Cassville on May 18, Johnston demonstrated poor judgment for failing to order his cavalry to scout the area. Wheeler's report of the day's action indicates that he remained completely unaware of the existence of Spring Place Road and consequently, of McCook's and Stoneman's approach. Further, as Thomas Connelly noted in *Autumn of Glory*, Johnston responded to the news of Hood's retreat inadequately. Rather than sending a staff officer to instruct Hood to conduct a proper reconnaissance of the enemy to his front, he simply accepted the report and reorganized the alignment of his troops accordingly.[31] As a result, it is fair to assign blame for the failure of the planned Confederate assault at Cassville to both Johnston and Hood.

30 Beatty Diary, May 19, 1864, UNC.

31 *O.R.* vol. 38, pt. 3, 946; Connelly, *Autumn of Glory*, 348.

Regrettably for the Confederate high command, the afternoon and evening proved equally discouraging.

Advance, Remain, or Retreat?

After having failed in his attempt to deliver a significant strike against the Union army north of Cassville, Johnston repositioned his army along a ridge just southeast of the town. The movement was conducted in some confusion and in the face of "considerable skirmishing and artillery." Here he established strong defensive works and hoped that Sherman might launch an attack that evening, or perhaps the following day. As his army strengthened the defenses, Johnston rode the length of his lines with his chief of artillery, Brig. Gen. Francis Shoup. Shoup identified a 150–200 yard space along Maj. Gen. Samuel French's divisional front that jutted out and formed a salient. Shoup considered the spot vulnerable to enfilade fire from a hill approximately half a mile beyond the position. In response, Johnston identified a series of nearby ravines that he believed offered adequate protection for the troops should the Federal artillery open on the location.[32] Several officers, including Hood, disagreed with Johnston's contention. A hastily drawn map fueled the dispute.

General Polk's engineer, Capt. Walter Morris, made a hurried reconnaissance of the Confederate works during the evening and produced a map consistent with his observations. The map later found its way into Hood's memoir. Hood used Morris's map to justify his assertion that neither he nor Polk could withstand any serious artillery barrage the following day. Morris's map depicted the Confederate line running east to west with Hood's Corps adjoining Polk's Corps at an angle with Hardee to the west of Polk. The map also depicted the deployment of Federal forces at a somewhat higher elevation than the Confederates. According to Hood, the point at which his corps joined Polk's right was untenable.[33]

In his memoir, Hood solicited a report on the matter from Morris, who claimed that the right of Polk's line could not have been held and that traverses would have been to no avail. Morris declared that the "opposing ridge [Union position] passed on a line about 23 degrees south of west, forming an angle with General Polk' s line of defense of about 25 degrees, and forming something less of an angle with Lieutenant General Hood's line." Accordingly, the angle was so severe that both Polk and Hood would likely have sustained severe enfilade fire

32 Mackall Diary, May 19, 1864, JP WM; Johnston, "Opposing Sherman's Advanced to Atlanta," 268.

33 Hood, *Advance and Retreat,* 111–112, 106.

from enemy batteries posted on the opposing ridge line. Morris emphasized the danger by alleging that the enemy enjoyed the advantage of a higher position that would allow them to deliver a "plunging fire from twenty to sixty feet and sweeping through the ravine, and across the rear of the ridge to a distance of about a thousand feet."[34] If Morris's observations were accurate, the Confederate position to the rear of Cassville had little to offer. Yet other maps suggest a completely different picture.

Wilbur Kurtz studied the area around Cassville during the 1920s and 1930s before time and modernity had stripped the landscape of the scars of war. Kurtz identified Johnston's defensive works on a ridge east of Cassville. The ridge runs north to south in a slightly westerly direction so that it terminates almost directly south of the town. Kurtz also located the Union position on a ridge northwest of Cassville. If Kurtz was accurate in his placement of Union forces, their position did not give them the advantage of being able to fire from a higher position, as both ridges are at the same elevation.[35] Consequently, according to Kurtz's findings, the Confederates would not have suffered from the plunging fire that Morris described. Further, Kurtz's map does not depict the sharp angles between Hood's and Polk's corps found in Morris's map. Kurtz discovered a small salient on the extreme right of Polk's Corps, but that is the only point on his map that might be considered perilous to its occupants. A second map confirms Kurtz's general findings.

Orlando Poe, Sherman's chief engineer, made a sketch of the defenses after the Confederates abandoned them on the night of May 19. The sketch appears on the first pages of his field diary found in the Library of Congress. Poe made no other sketches of Confederate defensive works during the campaign, suggesting that those found at Cassville impressed him more than any other. In fact, Poe observed that the Confederate lines "were strong to resist a direct front attack."[36] Poe's sketch appears to support Kurtz's findings. His rendition of the Confederate lines does not illustrate any sharp angles of which Hood complained on the night of the nineteenth. Poe's map does depict a slight salient at about the same point that Kurtz identified. The weight of the evidence, therefore, challenges Hood's belief that his corps and Polk's troops held positions that could not be defended. Hood primarily based his reasoning on Morris's findings made at a late hour as the sun set. Conversely, Kurtz had several years to study the topography around Cassville

34 Ibid., 112–113.

35 McMurry, "Cassville," 9, 47.

36 Poe Diary, May 21, 1864, LC.

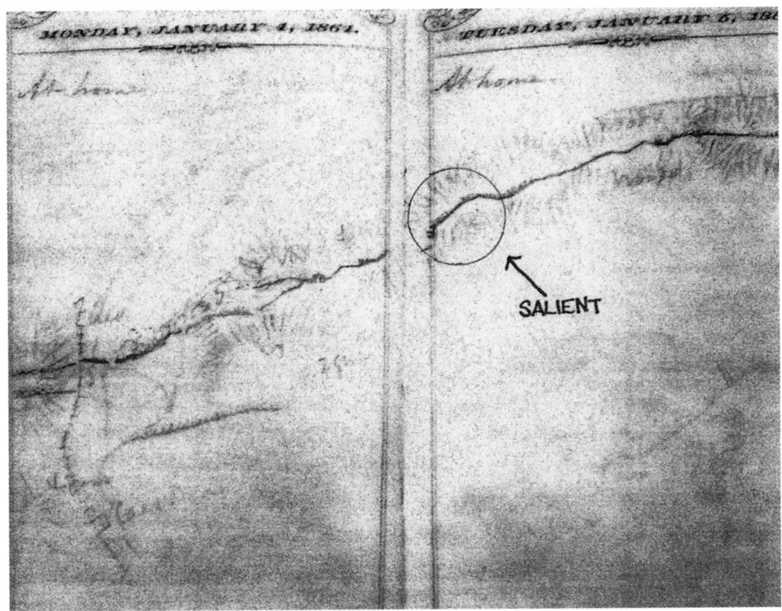

This map is from Poe's field diary, housed in the Library of Congress.

Photo taken by Dennis Conklin

and his findings concur with Poe's, who enjoyed the benefit of full daylight when making his sketch.

As previously mentioned, the Federal advance in the late afternoon caused confusion among the Confederate ranks. Howard's Corps drove eastward along the Kingston Road while Hardee's men made a stubborn defense. At about six o'clock Howard established a forty-gun battery to dislodge the remnants of Hardee's Corps positioned in a stand of woods west of the Confederates' new position. The barrage produced a "raking effect upon the flank of the rebels." Hardee subsequently redeployed his corps alongside Polk and Hood on the ridge east of Cassville. Meanwhile the Federal artillery approaching from the north had unlimbered along a parallel ridge north and west of the town and commenced firing upon the Confederate lines (Polk and Hood) at approximately four o'clock. The extant reports suggest that the artillery duel that ensued favored neither side. As the opposing artillerists dueled, the Union infantry filed into the valley between the two ridges.[37] Hood's and Polk's men occupied themselves by either

37 Fullerton Journal, May 19, 1864, *O.R.* vol. 38, pt. 1, 859; *O.R.* vol. 38, pt. 1, 495; *O.R.* vol. 38, pt. 2, 484–485; Hood, *Advance and Retreat,* 105; Johnston, "Opposing Sherman's Advanced to Atlanta," 268.

strengthening the defenses or sheltering themselves from the Federal artillery. The Confederate reports, however, do not support the contention that the Union artillery wreaked havoc, as Hood later insisted.

Hood argued that he personally observed the destruction wrought by enfilade fire on his own and Polk's lines. Though Hood undoubtedly endured a storm of artillery fire as he rode along his lines, his recollection of the affair deserves examination. While Hood frequently reviewed his corps on horseback, his injuries meant that he could not dismount. In the early spring a staff member recounted in a letter home that Hood often rode as many as twenty miles without dismounting.[38] Hood surely remained on horseback during his inspection of the Confederate lines. Furthermore, the fading sunlight necessarily diminished his capacity to investigate. As a result, he could not have made a thorough or precise assessment of the defensive position on his evening ride.

The available Confederate reports support the proposition that the Union artillery had minimal effect. The vast majority do not even mention an artillery barrage let alone a severe bombardment. Only a few reports mention the Federal cannonade and the contents of these are revealing. General Edward Walthall recalled heavy shelling but did not comment on its severity. Colonel William Brantly, serving in Walthall's brigade, claimed that the artillery was "most furious," and that his unit lost one man killed and three wounded. These casualty figures are not particularly acute. Lieutenant Colonel Campbell of the 13th Louisiana recorded that his regiment endured a heavy shelling but that it lasted only a brief time. Most telling is the report of Maj. Gen. Samuel French, of Polk's Corps, whose division, according to Hood, occupied the most perilous portion of the Confederate line. French reported the bombardment and noted that his division "sustained a loss of 0 men killed and five wounded."[39] In view of the minimal number of casualties in the most vulnerable location along the Confederate defenses, Hood's assertion that the works could not be held appears unfounded.

In fact, the salient at Cassville compared favorably to the salient held by the Federal Army of the Potomac at Gettysburg, which endured one and a half hours of artillery bombardment prior to the Confederate assault on the third day of the battle. Under those circumstances, the Union infantry removed themselves to the opposite side of the ridge and suffered relatively few casualties as a result.

38 *O.R.* vol. 38, pt. 3, 635; Halsey Wigfall to mother, March 21, 1864, LC.

39 See for example *O.R.* vol. 38, pt. 3, 715, 798, 802, 806, 809, 818, 826, 830, 833, 840, 860, 867, 875, 899. Thirty years later French recorded that his division had nine men wounded during two hours of shelling. See Samuel French, "Joseph E. Johnston's Campaign in Georgia, Criticisms of Gen. S. G. French," *Southern Historical Society Papers* 22 (1894): 9.

In addition, the Confederate defensive position at Kennesaw Mountain later in the campaign included a salient similar to that at Cassville. T. H. Maney's brigade occupied the salient at Kennesaw and held the position throughout the battle despite its flawed features. Not only did Maney defend a salient, but the lack of trees in the vicinity exacerbated his problem. The abatis in front of his works was insufficient compared to the rest of the Confederate line. Further, he faced a landscape that provided shelter for advancing Federal columns, as the ground in front of his position sloped in such a way as to create a blind spot for Maney's brigade. Nevertheless, Maney held his position throughout multiple attacks. If anything, the Confederate position at Cassville was more defensible than Maney's at Kennesaw. Orlando Poe thought so, as did O. O. Howard who later declared the Confederate defenses east of Cassville admirable and that their evacuation had been accomplished by a flanking maneuver. A Confederate officer writing to Lieutenant General Stewart after the war echoed Howard and Poe. He noted that the works around Cassville were the strongest position he ever saw during the war.[40] Even so, Hood insisted that Johnston evacuate the defenses east of Cassville.

After dining with his staff, Johnston visited Polk's headquarters at the invitation of his lieutenants. There he met with both Polk and Hood and others including French and Hardee, though Hardee arrived late while French left early. Hood stated that he and Polk could not hold their lines if attacked in the morning because of enfilade fire from enemy artillery already in position. In support of the claim, Hood produced Walter Morris's map as proof of their desperate situation. Both Johnston and French recalled that Hood took the lead in advocating a change of position, and French claimed that Polk was not nearly as "strenuous" in support of abandoning their present lines. Apparently Hood proposed attacking the Federals in the meeting, while Polk advocated a withdrawal of the army. Johnston contested both proposals, as did Hardee upon his arrival.[41]

Historians have generally accepted Hood's argument that the position was indefensible. Albert Castel characterizes Hood's argument as "powerful," and though rejected by Johnston for a while, ultimately persuasive. Richard McMurry admits that little evidence exists regarding the conference on the night of the nineteenth. Nevertheless, he agrees that the available evidence corroborates Hood's

40 Castel, *Decision in the West*, 313; Howard, "The Struggle for Atlanta," 305; Report of Major J. C. Thompson to A. P. Stewart, Box 1, Folder 5, JP WM.

41 Mackall Journal, May 19, 1864, *O.R.* vol. 38, pt. 3, 984; Johnston, *Narrative of Military Operations*, 323–324; French, *Two Wars*, 198; French, "Joseph E. Johnston's Campaign in Georgia, Criticisms of Gen. S. G. French," 4; Castel, *Decision in the West*, 205; McMurry, "Cassville," 47.

version of events.[42] In support of that assertion, McMurry relies on a postwar letter from Capt. Walter Morris to Polk's son. Though the letter may authenticate Hood's narrative of the conversation, its foundation remains flawed. Morris, after all, was responsible for the production of an inaccurate map upon which Hood's argument rested.

Hood's reliance on the Morris map was the second time that day that he acted with faulty intelligence. Hood began the day under the belief that a Federal cavalry column assailed his corps from the Canton Road, when in reality McCook's column operated on the Spring Place Road. The error was almost assuredly the result of faulty maps in the possession of the Confederate high command. That misunderstanding likely influenced the course of the discussion at Polk's headquarters that night. Johnston, as the Mackall journal indicates, suspected that no Federal forces had operated along the Canton Road that morning.[43] It is likely that he conveyed his apprehension that a Union column had advanced from that direction during the evening meeting. For his part, Hood knew that an enemy force had descended upon his flank and the suggestion that they had not insinuated that he was both a liar and a coward for having retreated. Considering Hood's well-known reputation as a passionate individual, the implication that he had either lied or behaved in a timorous fashion could not have given him cheer. Furthermore, if Hood shared Beatty's reservations regarding the recent success of Federal columns to approach Confederate positions undetected, then Hood had even more reason to be incensed.

Perhaps the combination of his apprehension about the prospects for his commander to secure the army's flanks and the insinuation that he had failed in his duty earlier in the day prompted his bellicose response that the army should advance to the attack in the morning. Most of the available evidence suggests that Hood alone advocated such a policy. In any event, the argument between Johnston and Hood lasted for at least an hour. Johnston eventually capitulated and ordered a retreat, later claiming that a lack of confidence among the army's leadership (Hood and Polk) rendered the position untenable.[44] In reality, as the Kurtz and Poe maps demonstrate, and the extant Confederate reports confirm, the defenses

42 Castel, *Decision in the West*, 205; McMurry, "Cassville," 47; McMurry, *John Bell Hood and the War for Southern Independence*, 109.

43 The official version of the diary is strongest in this regard, but even the field diary suggests that Johnston thought the report inaccurate.

44 Johnston claimed that Hood argued in favor of a retreat across the Etowah. See Johnston, *Narrative of Military Operations*, 324. According to a member of Polk's staff present at the meeting, however, Hood favored an attack. See McMurry, "Cassville," 47. Because Polk's staff member had nothing to gain from making such an observation, it should be believed. A postwar letter form Walter

east of Cassville provided as much shelter for the occupants as any other during the campaign and perhaps the entire war. Yet the army marched southward once again, this time over the Etowah, ever in search of greener pastures.

Johnston, likely with Hood's help, had designed a plan to catch the Union army divided. Sherman behaved precisely as the Confederates had hoped he would and separated his army in pursuit of the Rebels. The Federal army approached Cassville lethargically both from Kingston and from Adairsville. Howard's Corps did not vigorously pursue Hardee until mid-afternoon. Howard's caution provided a distinct opportunity for Polk and Hood to deliver a decisive strike against Hooker and Schofield. Indeed, Hooker advanced his column in piecemeal with his divisions separated in such a way as to invite destruction. Schofield, meanwhile, loitered in the rear waiting for Hooker's final division to move forward down the Adairsville-Cassville Road. McCook's probe down the Spring Place Road, however, disrupted Johnston's plans.

As McCook marched toward Cassville, Hood moved in the direction of the Ironton/Sallacoa Road with the intention of launching his flank attack, as directed, from that location. Upon arrival he encountered the lead elements of McCook's column on his right flank. Hood's response to McCook's approach proved a dismal failure. Hindman's division quickly dispatched the Federal menace, but Hood determined to withdraw without ascertaining the size or composition (cavalry, infantry) of the Federal force along the Spring Place Road. He compounded his error when he informed Johnston of a Union column on the Canton Road. Johnston correctly surmised that the report was in error. Unfortunately for the Confederates, neither Hood nor Johnston realized that the error originated not with the assertion of a Federal presence, but with Hood's belief as to where the Federals appeared. While Hood deserves blame for his immediate withdrawal and misunderstanding of his location, Johnston also failed when he did not advise Hood to maintain his position and attempt to ascertain the strength of the Northerners on his flank. As a consequence of poor performances by both Hood and Johnston, the Confederates fell back to a defensive position on the ridge east of Cassville.

Once entrenched on the ridge, two points of contention led to a Confederate withdrawal from the position. First, Walter Morris's map convinced Hood and Polk that they occupied untenable positions. The evidence demonstrates that Morris's calculations were inaccurate. Hood and Polk did not adjoin at sharp angles, nor was the Confederate position at a lower elevation than the ridge upon which the Federal batteries unlimbered. Rather, the extreme right of French's

---

Morris suggests that Polk too was in favor of Hood's proposed advance. See Hood, *The Lost Papers of Confederate General John Bell Hood*, 93.

division occupied a slight salient and reports from the officers present suggest minimal exposure. Nevertheless, Hood could only rely on the evidence available to him at the time. He endured a barrage of artillery when riding along his lines in the evening. Further, he had no way of knowing that Morris's estimation of the defensive works wrongly depicted the junction of his own corps with that of Polk. A sharp exchange between Hood and his commanding general followed. It would seem likely that the matter of a Federal presence along the Canton Road became a point of contention during the evening meeting. Hood probably felt aggrieved by the insinuation that he had acted timidly in the morning and, consequently, advocated an assault on the following day. Neither Polk nor Hardee joined Hood in the proposal and so Johnston determined to withdraw south of the Etowah.

The day had begun with Johnston and Hood as close confidants; it closed with the two at odds. Johnston suspected that Hood had fabricated the report of a Federal column operating on the Canton Road. Johnston's suspicion is clearly manifested in his report on the campaign, his postwar memoir, and his staff's recollection of the day's events.[45] At the same time, Hood knew that a Union force had threatened his flank. Indeed, he probably considered its appearance without warning an indication that his commanding officer was not up to the task. Hood undoubtedly understood that Johnston had received his account with skepticism. The dispute between the two men did not immediately destroy their relationship, but it certainly caused a rupture that led to distrust and eventually to animosity. Moreover, Hood benefited from an outlet not available to most officers. He could address his growing lack of confidence in the army's commander to the president. After all, Davis had invited him to communicate directly with the administration. As a result of the affair at Cassville and Davis's invitation to engage in unconventional communications, Hood commenced a campaign to have Johnston relieved of his command.

45 See Mackall Diary, May 19, 1864, JP WM; W. W. Mackall, "Memoranda of the Operations at Cassville on May 19, 1864," *O.R.* vol. 38, pt. 3, 622, 983; Mackall Journal, May 19, 1864.

Chapter 6

Cassville to the Chattahoochee and Johnston's Removal

Within two days of the army's retreat from Cassville, Jefferson Davis's scheme to use Hood as an informant manifested itself in a way the president could not have intended. Hood sent an aide, Henry Brewster, to Richmond with instructions to report to the president concerning the conduct of the campaign to date. The evidence suggests that Brewster's account was intended to discredit Johnston's handling of the army. Hood's communications with the administration had therefore taken on a new tone. Prior to May 21, Hood's messages had avoided overt criticism of his commander; now, in the wake of Cassville, Hood changed course and disparaged his chief. Moreover, when considered in light of Hood's subsequent performance near Pickett's Mill and along the Chattahoochee River, his latest communication suggests that he not only intended to undermine Johnston, but that he likely hoped to secure command of the army for himself. Certainly Davis did not intend that open communications between Hood and the administration destabilize the command structure and reduce the commanding general's ability to confront Sherman's advance. Nevertheless, such an outcome was foreseeable. Indeed, Davis's counterpart, Abraham Lincoln, understood the perils inherent in the enterprise and had counseled his generals against it.[1] Davis, however, continued to permit and even encourage the activity.

In addition to Davis's receipt of communications outside of the chain of command, the army's retreat south toward Atlanta exposed the president's other primary failures as commander-in-chief. The absence of a centralized command

1 Williams, *Lincoln and his Generals*, 202, 212–213; Donald, *Lincoln*, 411.

impeded cooperation among members of the Confederate high command. The parochialism intrinsic to the president's departmental system meant that Johnston could not deploy a cavalry raid against Sherman's supply line. Johnston requested S. D. Lee to assist in the endeavor, but Lee considered the defense of his own department more important. The departmental system also hindered Johnston's construction of defensive works around Atlanta, as the necessary labor force (slaves) belonged to planters who resided in P. G. T. Beauregard's department. Finally, the president's willingness to allow his personal relationships with his subordinates to influence his judgment played a decisive role in the outcome of the campaign between Cassville and the Chattahoochee. Davis's distrust of Johnston made him less compliant with the general's request for a raid against Sherman's communications from another department. Further, his friendship with Braxton Bragg blinded Davis to the possibility that Bragg was not qualified for his new post as military advisor, and most definitely not competent to make a determination about Johnston's possible removal from command of the army.

From Cassville to the Chattahoochee

After the withdrawal from Cassville, where Johnston had issued orders that he intended to stand and fight, the first signs that his soldiers' morale was beginning to suffer emerged. William Mackall noted that the troops had been in good spirits until the retreat from Cassville, but that the failure to follow through with the general order suggesting that the army would give battle "impaired [the] confidence" of the men. William Norrell of the 10th Georgia commented in his diary: "It is now 13 days since we began to march 12 of which has been in the retreat." Norrell further remarked that most of his fellow soldiers believed that Johnston had intended to lead Sherman south of the Etowah River, "hence his show of fight and then rapid retreat." Lieutenant A. J. Neal of the Marion Light Artillery stated that some of his fellow soldiers believed that Johnston would fall back all the way to Atlanta. Neal had more confidence in his commander and thought that he would engage the enemy somewhere between Allatoona and Marietta and that they would then "race for Tennessee."[2]

Though some in the army conveyed apprehension regarding the retrograde movements, Georgia newspapers continued their overt support of Johnston's performance that most had demonstrated since his appointment to command the Army of Tennessee. The *Atlanta Appeal* claimed that the citizens of Georgia had

2 Mackall Diary, May 20, 1864, JP WM; William O. Norrell, Diary, May 20, 1864, Kennesaw Mountain National Battlefield Library; Neal to Father, May 20, 1864, KNBL.

no cause for concern "on account of these moves on the military chess-board." The correspondent insisted that Atlanta would never fall to the "ruthless invaders," so long as the citizens did their duty. A reporter from the *Atlanta Intelligencer* attempted to bolster confidence among the state's populace with the suggestion that though the army continued southward it "remained in buoyant spirits" and "there is no sign of disorder or straggling." Meanwhile, the *Southern Watchman* of Athens proclaimed that "not a shadow of despondency clouds the manly, confident faces of the sturdy line, and every eye sparkles defiance." The correspondent could not speculate as to when Johnston would give battle, but he declared that whenever he did victory was assured and that "Atlanta is much more secure than the Confederate capital."[3]

Davis, like some in the army, held less sanguine views of Johnston's performance than the general's boosters in the press. After hearing that Johnston had abandoned Resaca, the president expressed "disappointment" and informed him that the reinforcements sent from Mississippi and Alabama gave him ample strength to "achieve important results."[4] The communication was Davis's second rebuke in the span of a week, and like the telegram to Johnston at Resaca it clearly shows that Davis thought Johnston was shy of engaging the enemy. Johnston did not appreciate the president's insinuation that his actions had been uninspiring since abandoning the defensive line near Dalton. He had launched one attack at Resaca against an army twice the size of his own and had intended to risk a second assault the following day until he learned that a sizable Federal column threatened Calhoun to his rear. Further, Johnston's well-conceived plans to attack Sherman's divided army at Cassville went awry primarily because the president's own acolyte, John Bell Hood, had failed to deliver the expected blow and had later argued against holding the defensive line south of the town.

Johnston responded to the president's criticisms the next day, May 21. The general noted that he had "earnestly sought an opportunity to strike the enemy," but that the direction of the railroad, the enemy's flanking maneuvers, and their strong defensive positions made offensive operations "too hazardous."[5] Johnston's communication gave the impression that he had acted entirely on the defensive. His message likely contributed to the president's long-held suspicion, developed

3 *Atlanta Appeal*, May 24, 1864. The author was optimistic that a significant number of able-bodied men would answer Governor Brown's call for militia; *Atlanta Intelligencer*, May 25, 1864; *Southern Watchman*, May 25, 1864.

4 *O.R.* vol. 38, pt. 4, 725.

5 Ibid., 736.

during the Peninsula and Vicksburg campaigns, that his general lacked the requisite aggression.

The same day that Johnston emphasized the difficulty in striking the enemy in his telegram to the president, Hood dispatched an aide to Davis with a message that undoubtedly offered an unfavorable assessment of Johnston's activities since the opening of the campaign. Since Sherman's advance on the Confederate position at Dalton, the army, and especially Hood, had been perpetually in motion. On May 21 Johnston established a strong defensive position near the town of Allatoona that resembled their starting position at Dalton. At Allatoona the Western & Atlantic Railroad cut through the Allatoona Mountains at Allatoona Pass. Like Dalton, the position offered Sherman little choice other than a flank march to the east or west. As a result, the Confederates could finally rest for a few days, which allowed Hood the occasion to apprise the administration regarding the campaign to date. That he did so at the first opportunity since the commencement of the campaign offers further evidence that Davis intended Hood to act as an informant as part of his assignment to corps command in the Army of Tennessee. Even so, Hood's prior communications with the administration in March and April had been innocuous enough to deliver by telegram. His May 21 message, however, required delivery in person, a practice that suggests the need for secrecy. Further, considering Johnston's penchant for complaining to anyone who would listen whenever the administration challenged him, it seems likely that Hood had caught wind of the president's latest reprimand and shaped his message accordingly.

Colonel Henry Brewster, a volunteer on Hood's staff, was charged with delivering Hood's letter to the president. Hood explained that the colonel "has been with us since we left Dalton and can give you an account of the operations of this army since the enemy made their appearance in our immediate front." Hood further suggested that "I think it would be well for you to have a conversation with him in relation to our affairs."[6] If Brewster gave the same account to the president that he did to a gathering at Mary Chesnut's home, and there is no logical reason to think otherwise, Hood's appraisal of Johnston's conduct as commander was disingenuous at best and perhaps his opening gambit to replace Johnston as commander of the Army of Tennessee. Brewster told the guests at Chesnut's home that Johnston did not fight at Dalton because "he had no plan" and that Dalton represented the army's best "stand." He labeled Johnston "overcautious" and asserted that both "Hood and Polk wanted to fight."[7]

6 *The Papers of Jefferson Davis*, X:434.

7 Ibid.,434; Woodward, *Mary Chesnut's Civil War*, 616.

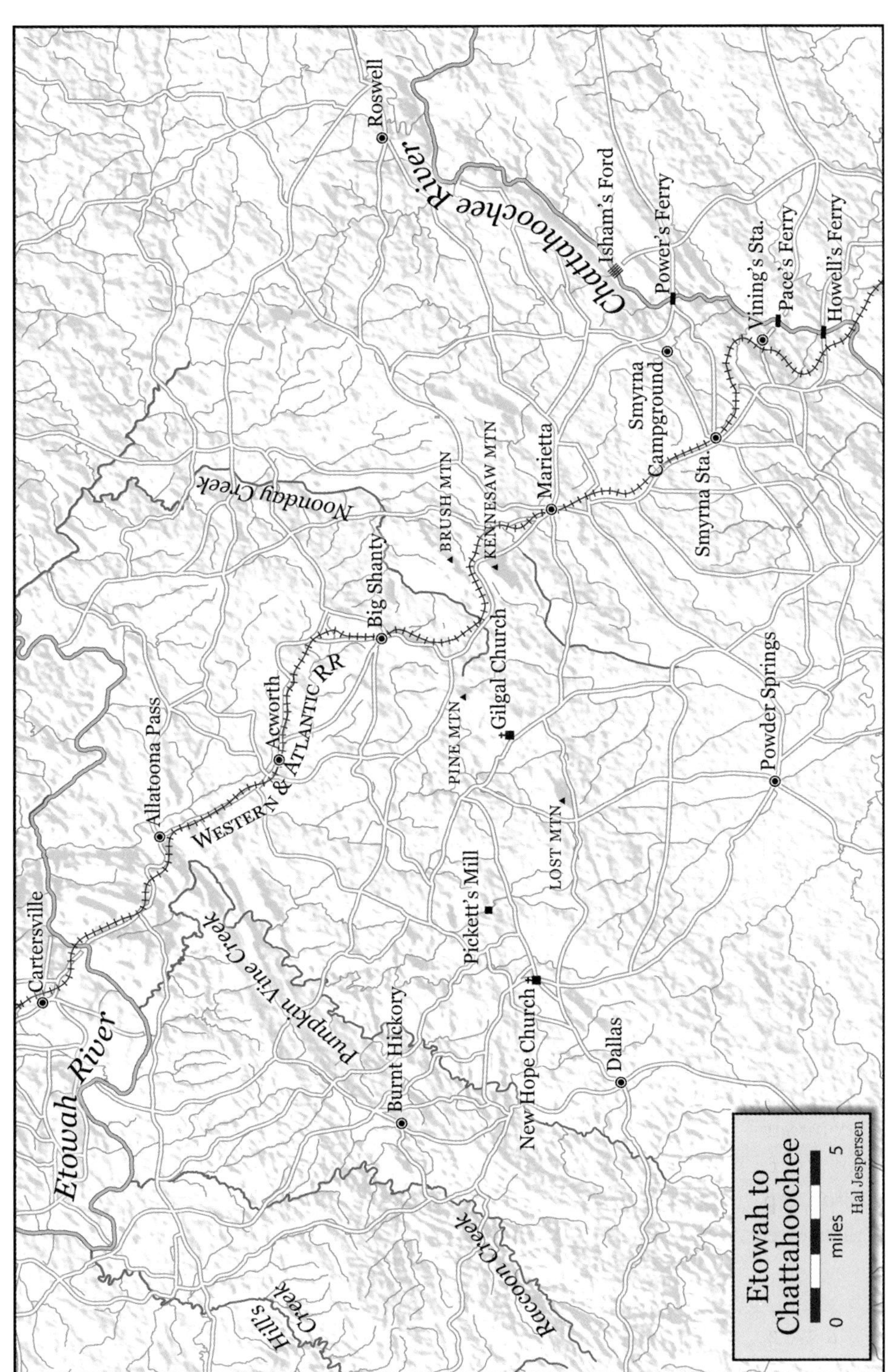
Etowah to Chattahoochee
0 miles 5
Hal Jespersen
Roswell
Chattahoochee River
Isham's Ford
Power's Ferry
Vining's Sta.
Pace's Ferry
Howell's Ferry
Smyrna Campground
Smyrna Sta.
Marietta
KENNESAW MTN
BRUSH MTN
Noonday Creek
Big Shanty
Gilgal Church
PINE MTN
LOST MTN
Powder Springs
Acworth
Allatoona Pass
WESTERN & ATLANTIC RR
Pickett's Mill
Cartersville
Etowah River
Pumpkin Vine Creek
Burnt Hickory
New Hope Church
Dallas
Raccoon Creek
Hill's Creek

Brewster further suggested that Hood's and Polk's friendship with the president meant that Johnston distrusted them and refused their council. Hood, Brewster claimed, was acting as the army's "reserved corps," and Johnston's delay in engaging the enemy was "breaking Hood's heart." According to Brewster, his conversation with the president led Davis to exclaim that Johnston should be replaced, though not with Hardee or Polk. Clearly, Hood had sent Brewster to Richmond to curry favor with Davis while at the same time undermining the president's already unstable relationship with Johnston. Otherwise, Davis's response that Johnston must be replaced makes little sense.[8]

Most of Brewster's claims were patently false. While Johnston's performance at Dalton during the first week of the campaign deserved criticism, the subsequent engagements at Resaca and Cassville provided evidence of Johnston's tactical skill as well as his willingness to commit to offensive operations. Brewster's allegation that Johnston refused Hood's counsel strains credibility. William Hardee, for example, later alleged that Johnston not only consulted Hood, but that Hood was responsible for most of the army's strategy. Richard McMurry has noted that Hood and Johnston spent much of their time together during the initial phase of the campaign. Entries in the diary of Thomas Mackall support McMurry's contention. Further, Mackall's diary identifies several instances where Johnston sought Hood's advice on strategic and tactical matters.[9] Brewster's statement that Hood's Corps acted as the army's reserve also appears groundless. Johnston had routinely given Hood and his corps the most critical tasks on the battlefield, including the assignment of delivering each of the planned offensives, first at Resaca and then at Cassville.

Thus, the events at Cassville dramatically altered the relationship between Joseph E. Johnston and John Bell Hood. Prior to Cassville the two men had acted in concert and Johnston relied heavily on his lieutenant. The proceedings on May 19, however, irrevocably damaged their confidence in one another. Johnston did not believe the accuracy of Hood's report that a Federal force had threatened his flank from the Canton Road. Hood, almost assuredly operating with a different map than his commander, had witnessed the Union cavalry descend upon Hindman's

8 Woodward, *Mary Chesnut's Civil War*, 616, 635; Brian Craig Miller, Albert Castel, and Craig Symonds have suggested that Brewster made the same representations to Davis that he did to the guests of the Chesnuts. Richard McMurry, on the other hand, believes that the substance of Brewster's report to the president remains a mystery. See Miller, *John Bell Hood and the Fight for Civil War Memory*, 114; Castel, *Decision in the West*, 211; Symonds, *Joseph E. Johnston*, 295–296; McMurry, *John Bell Hood and the War for Southern Independence*, 110.

9 Hardee to wife, June 12, 20, 23, 1864, ADAH; Richard McMurry, *John Bell Hood and the War for Southern Independence*, 103; Mackall Diary, May 2,9,14,17,18,1864, JP WM.

right flank from a road he believed led to Canton. Hood could not have appreciated Johnston's implication that either he had been deceived by a false report or had invented the affair to excuse his precipitous retreat.[10] As a consequence, disparate maps seem to be at the root of the disagreement between the two men and radically altered the course of the campaign. Hood's dispatch of Brewster to Richmond marked the breaking point. Since his assignment to the Army of Tennessee, Hood's communications with the administration might have been self-serving and indicative of his wish to take the offensive, but they did not directly denigrate Johnston's handling of the army. Brewster's report to the president, however, almost assuredly targeted Johnston's competence as commander. Though Hood's earlier telegrams might have exaggerated the army's offensive capabilities, they did not present demonstrably false accusations, a characteristic common to Brewster's claims. Hood, therefore, had embarked on a new course and likely hoped that in the event of Johnston's removal he would be given command of the army.

In the aftermath of Cassville, Johnston, like Hood, lost faith in his once-trusted collaborator. As Richard McMurry noted, after May 25 Johnston and Hood spent little time together. Not only did they spend significantly less time in each other's company after Cassville, Johnston immediately began to rely on Hardee to confront Sherman's ceaseless flanking marches. The strength of the Confederate defensive line at Allatoona meant that Sherman would likely avoid assaulting the army in its present position. Accordingly, Johnston instructed Wheeler to observe Sherman's activities and keep him abreast of Federal movement east or west of Allatoona. Wheeler's lack of enterprise once again disappointed Johnston. On May 23 Wheeler reported that local civilians believed that Sherman was retreating. Brigadier General Samuel Ferguson, however, informed headquarters that heavy columns of dust could be seen to the west and that Federal infantry were moving in that direction. Rather than sending Hood to meet the Union menace on his left as he had previously done, Johnston ordered Hardee to march southwest toward Dallas, Georgia.[11]

10 Johnston sent a telegram to Davis on May 20, asserting that Hood had been deceived and that "when the mistake was discovered it was too late to resume the movement." See *The Papers of Jefferson Davis*, X:433.

11 McMurry, *John Bell Hood and the War for Southern Independence*, 114. McMurry observed that after May 25 Hood rarely appeared in Thomas Mackall's diary and that when he did it was only to mention the movements of his corps. McMurry posits several possibilities as to what fractured the previously close relationship between the two men. He identifies Cassville and New Hope Church on May 28 as potential flash-points, as well as the prospect that Johnston had learned about Hood's various communications with the administration. Johnston, *Narrative of Military Operations*, 325; Mackall Diary, May 22, 23, 1864, JP WM. Ferguson commanded a cavalry brigade in William Jackson's division recently arrived from Mississippi.

On the morning of May 25 Hardee established a defensive line in the vicinity of Dallas. Polk took position next to Hardee and Hood formed on the right of Polk. The formation mirrored Johnston's previous dispositions with Hood and Hardee covering the army's flanks. The army's alignment at Dallas indicates that while Johnston no longer favored Hood above his other commanders, he still trusted Hood and his corps more than Polk. In the late afternoon Hooker's Federal corps, numbering approximately 16,000 men, advanced upon New Hope Church. Stewart's division of Hood's Corps, with about 4,000 men, confronted the Union onslaught. Johnston, who was then at Hood's headquarters, inquired as to whether Stewart wished him to send reinforcements, an offer Stewart deemed unnecessary. By 7:30 p.m. the Northerners withdrew and a drenching rain began pelting the battlefield. Hooker had sustained approximately 1,600 casualties while Stewart claimed to have lost between 300 and 400 men. The one-sided victory gave the Confederates reason to celebrate for the first time since Sweeney's advance across the Oostanaula had forced the evacuation of Resaca. Despite the heavy rain, Stewart's men gave a "prolonged cheer of victory." Johnston lodged at Hood's headquarters that night, a decision that some historians offer as evidence that the two remained on friendly terms.[12] It is likely, however, that Johnston stayed with Hood that night because the inclement weather made a return trip to army headquarters unpalatable.

The two armies spent the following day building entrenchments and adjusting their troop dispositions. In the morning, Johnston observed that Sherman's lines extended farther to his right than they had the previous evening. To confront the new threat Johnston ordered Patrick Cleburne's division of Hardee's Corps to the extreme right of the Confederate line. The placement of Cleburne on Hood's right provides some support to the proposition that Hood no longer enjoyed Johnston's full confidence. Rather than shifting the whole army to the right and maintaining its present alignment, a feasible maneuver considering that Union troops did not advance against any Confederate positions that day, Johnston chose to augment Hood's position with the army's most famed division. In fact, much of the Union maneuvering occurred on the Confederate left with McPherson's army advancing into Dallas during the afternoon.[13] Nevertheless, despite Federal activity on his

12 Castel, *Decision in the West*, 221, 225–226. That Johnston took an active role in the deployment of Hood's Corps with Hood present could be seen as evidence of a strained relationship. *O.R.* vol. 38, pt. 2, 14; *O.R.* vol. 38, pt. 3, 818; Mackall Diary, May 25, 1864, JP WM; Symonds, *Joseph E. Johnston*, 298; McMurry, *John Bell Hood and the War for Southern Independence*, 110, 114.

13 Johnston, *Narrative of Military Operations*, 328; Buck, *Cleburne and his Command*, 218; *O.R.* vol. 38, pt. 1, 316–317, 321.

left, Johnston stripped Hardee of his most trusted division in the effort to secure his right wing under Hood's command.

On May 27 Johnston again exhibited a willingness to attack his enemy when he thought the opportunity presented itself. Sherman, focused on dislodging Johnston from his lines near Dallas and New Hope Church, determined to make an assault on the Confederate right flank. The Union commander believed that Johnston intended to retire toward the Chattahoochee River and that he faced only a fragment of the Confederate army. Oliver O. Howard, tasked with making the attack, assigned Thomas Wood's division to carry out Sherman's orders. The Confederates soon detected Wood's movement, and Cleburne reported that the Federals were moving in force on the army's right. Johnston seized upon the opportunity in the belief that Sherman was abandoning his lines and moving back to the east. The Confederate commander hoped that he could catch Sherman as he moved his army out of its entrenchments and ordered Hardee and Hood forward. The attack encountered stiff resistance and Johnston quickly learned that Sherman remained in force on his front. Realizing that the Union movement signaled an advance against his flank, rather than a retreat, Johnston ordered Stewart's division to support Cleburne on the army's right. That afternoon Wood assailed Cleburne and suffered a bloody repulse, sustaining 1,400 casualties compared to the Confederate loss of 388.[14] Though Johnston had not caught Sherman's army on the move as he had hoped, he had once again won an uneven contest and thwarted his foe's flank attack.

During the night Wheeler informed Hood that Sherman's dispositions exposed his left flank, prompting Hood to request permission to march to the rear of the Federal position and launch an attack. In a conference with his three corps commanders, Johnston listened to Hood's suggestion and subsequently ordered him to carry out the proposed assault. Johnston instructed Hood to march his corps during the night and assail the Federal flank at dawn, and he suggested that Hardee and Polk move forward once Hood commenced his attack. Johnston had drastically changed the nature of the intended advance. Rather than a limited attack on an isolated enemy force, Johnston determined to deliver a general assault along his entire line once Hood advanced upon the Union left.[15]

14 *O.R.* vol. 38, pt. 3, 322; Castel, *Decision in the West*, 229–230; Buck, *Cleburne and his Command*, 219; Castel, *Decision in the West*, 231. The order indicates that three weeks of campaigning had given Johnston a better feel for the capabilities of his subordinates. With the Federals threatening his right flank he placed the indomitable Cleburne and Stewart, who had just proven himself at New Hope Church, in the path of the enemy advance. *O.R.* vol. 38, pt. 1, 196; *O.R.* vol. 38, pt. 3, 726.

15 Hood, *Advance and Retreat*, 120. There is some dispute concerning the date of the proposed movement. In their memoirs both Hood and Johnston claimed that the maneuver occurred the night

Wheeler's report that a Federal force had crossed Little Pumpkin Vine Creek (also called Pickett's Mill Creek) and isolated itself from the rest of the Union army was only partially accurate. Three regiments of Union infantry had crossed to the east side of the creek during the afternoon and evening engagement. The creek, though, posed no real impediment to their reinforcement. In fact, the three Federal regiments made their way across the creek without difficulty when they were ordered to secure the flank of the Thirty-Seventh Indiana early in the evening of the 27th. Indeed, they did so under fire from Confederates on the east side of the waterway. The Confederates had also traversed the creek earlier in an assault upon the Union left before the Northerners extended their line across Little Pumpkin Vine. Therefore, even if Federal troops had moved to the east side of the creek, Sherman could reinforce them if necessary. Regardless, the Union troops withdrew to the west side of the waterway after the cessation of battle on the night of May 27.[16] The Confederates, unaware of the Union withdrawal, continued with their preparation for the early-morning assault.

Precisely when Hood embarked on his movement against the enemy left is unclear, as was the composition of the force he took with him. Hood later claimed that he commenced "after night" and approached the designated position from which to launch his attack at dawn. His account also implied that he made the march with his whole corps. The extant Confederate reports do not support Hood's assertion. Only two of his three divisional commanders, Alexander Stewart and Carter Stevenson, submitted accounts of their activities during the month of May, but neither made any mention of marching toward the Federal left on the evening of May 27 or the morning of the 28th. Regimental and brigade reports from three of the four brigades in Stewart's division make reference to a change of position on the morning of May 28, but only one account mentions the prospect of delivering an attack. Further, Hardee's Assistant Adjutant General, Henry Hampton, recorded in his journal that only a portion of Hood's Corps moved in the direction of the Federal left. As a result, Hindman's division was the only element of Hood's Corps

of May 28–29. Thomas Mackall, who served on Johnston's staff, and Taylor Beatty on Hood's staff, however, recorded in their diaries that the attack was to be made on the morning of the 28th. Albert Castel, Richard McMurry, and Craig Symonds all accept the 27–28th as the proper time frame. See Hood, *Advance and Retreat*, 120–121; Johnston, *Narrative of Military Operations*, 333; Mackall Diary, May 28, 1864, JP WM; Beatty Diary, May 27, 1864, UNC; Castel, *Decision in the West*, 242–243; McMurry, *John Bell Hood and the War for Southern Independence*, 111; Symonds, *Joseph E. Johnston*, 299; Johnston, *Narrative of Military Operations*, 333. In support of his contention that he intended a general assault, Johnston reproduced a letter that William Hardee sent him after the conclusion of the war that substantiated Johnston's assertion. See Johnston, *Narrative of Military Operations*, 334.

16 *O.R.* vol. 38, pt. 1, 606, 605. The Confederates were dismounted cavalry that Wheeler had positioned on Cleburne's right. *See O.R.* vol. 38, pt. 3, 948; *O.R.* vol. 38, pt. 1, 605–606.

that could have begun its march on the night of May 27. It is likely that Hindman started for the Union left at some point during the late hours of the 27th, as William Loring of Polk's Corps reported occupying Hindman's former position that night.[17] At best then, Hood could only have hoped to make the assault at the appointed time with a third of his men.

The distance of Hood's march, like its timing and strength, remains somewhat mysterious. Hood made no reference to the matter other than to say that he departed "after night" and arrived near dawn. His statement implies that his column marched for at least four or five hours, a time frame that would allow for the movement of an equal number of miles over the rough terrain of north Georgia. Johnston later claimed that Hood had marched between eight and ten hours and the next morning was still "at least six miles from the Federal left, which was little more than a musket-shot from his starting point." If Johnston's assertion is to be believed, Hood and Hindman must have gotten lost during the night, though no reports of such a fiasco appear in the record. It seems more likely that Hood managed to maneuver Hindman's division to the designated point of assault at dawn or soon thereafter. Considering Hindman's location at nightfall on the 27th, he needed to march between three and four miles in order to reach the site of the planned assault. Only after his arrival with Hindman did Hood order the better part of Stewart's division to march to the scene of the intended attack.[18] The belated movement of Stewart's brigades meant that Hood could not have possibly made the assault at the appointed time.

As the morning wore on, Johnston waited in vain for the start of the expected advance. At approximately 9:00 a.m. a messenger from Hood informed the army's commander that the Union left no longer extended beyond Little Pumpkin Vine Creek. Instead, the courier asserted, the enemy had established defensive works on the west side of the creek, thereby making an assault against the new Union position too perilous. Hood was correct; after midnight the Federals had withdrawn to the west side of the creek and constructed defensive works. Had Hood investigated more closely, however, he might have discovered that the new Union entrenchments

17 Hood, *Advance and Retreat*, 121; *O.R.* vol. 38, pt. 3, 636. Albert Castel has accepted Hood's claim, while Richard McMurry asserted that Hood moved out on the morning of May 28. See Castel, *Decision in the West*, 242–243; McMurry, *John Bell Hood and the War for Southern Independence*, 111; *O.R.* vol. 38, pt. 3, 813, 818, 833, 846, 855–868. The report of Robert Keen of the 20th Louisiana is the only one that suggests that the movement might have been made with the intention of assaulting the enemy. Marcellus Stovall and his regimental commanders did not report moving toward the right at all on the 28th. *See O.R.* vol. 38, pt. 3, 824–831; *O.R.* vol. 38, pt. 3, 706, 875.

18 Hood, *Advance and Retreat*, 121; Johnston, "Opposing Sherman's Advance to Atlanta," 270; *O.R.* vol. 38, pt. 3, 833, 846, 855–868.

extended only about half a mile north of his own position and could easily be turned if desired. (See Map of Pickett's Mill.) Furthermore, William Carlin's brigade, occupying the extreme Union left, advanced approximately a quarter of a mile in a "single line" early on the morning of May 28, thereby abandoning the protection of their fortifications.[19]

After the war, Hood argued that in addition to the enemy entrenchments, the creek itself presented a difficult obstacle. His contention seems unlikely when considering the available evidence. The creek today is a shallow meandering waterway and easily passable in multiple places. (See image of Little Pumpkin Vine Creek on page 152.) Moreover, on May 27, 1864, at least three Federal regiments traversed the stream with minimal effort.[20]

Attempting to explain Hood's unwillingness to assault the Federal position on the morning of May 28 must be done in light of Brewster's mission to the president. Likely, Brewster had by that time reached Richmond and informed Davis that Johnston refused to take offensive action in spite of Hood's persistent pleas. It must be remembered that Hood had initially proposed an attack upon what he believed to be an isolated Federal command, not against the entire Union line as contemplated under Johnston's alteration of the plan. Hood had probably hoped to win a quick victory over a relatively small enemy force that would increase his renown in the army and perhaps his credibility with the president. His decision to march against the Federal left with only one division suggests that he might never have intended to initiate a full-scale assault. After all, if such an attack was successful on the heels of Brewster's report it might render the aide's undertaking moot. When Hood finally discovered that the enemy no longer occupied the east side of the creek and that he could not hope to achieve an easy victory, he apparently saw no upside in pursuing the attack according to Johnston's design.

Even if one assumes that Hood was not angling for command of the army, his behavior on the morning of May 28 seems peculiar. First, he marched only a portion of his command to the designated starting point for the attack. If he intended to carry out the tactical vision of his commander and instigate a general assault, his entire corps ought to have been on hand in the early morning hours. Stevenson, by all accounts, remained in his defensive lines some three miles distant from Hood's location east of Pickett's Mill. Stewart's three brigades only moved

19 Mackall Diary, May 28, 1864, JP WM; *O.R.* vol. 38, pt. 1, 606, 615; *O.R.* vol. 38, pt. 1, 529. Pickett's Mill State Park ranger, James Wooten, asserted that Hood could have easily flanked the Federal position on the morning of May 28. The entrenchments are still visible and indicate that a short march northward from Hood's location would have rendered them unsafe for their occupants. James Wooten, interview by author, Pickett's Mill State Park, October 13, 2011.

20 Hood, *Advance and Retreat,* 121; *O.R.* vol. 38, pt. 1, 606.

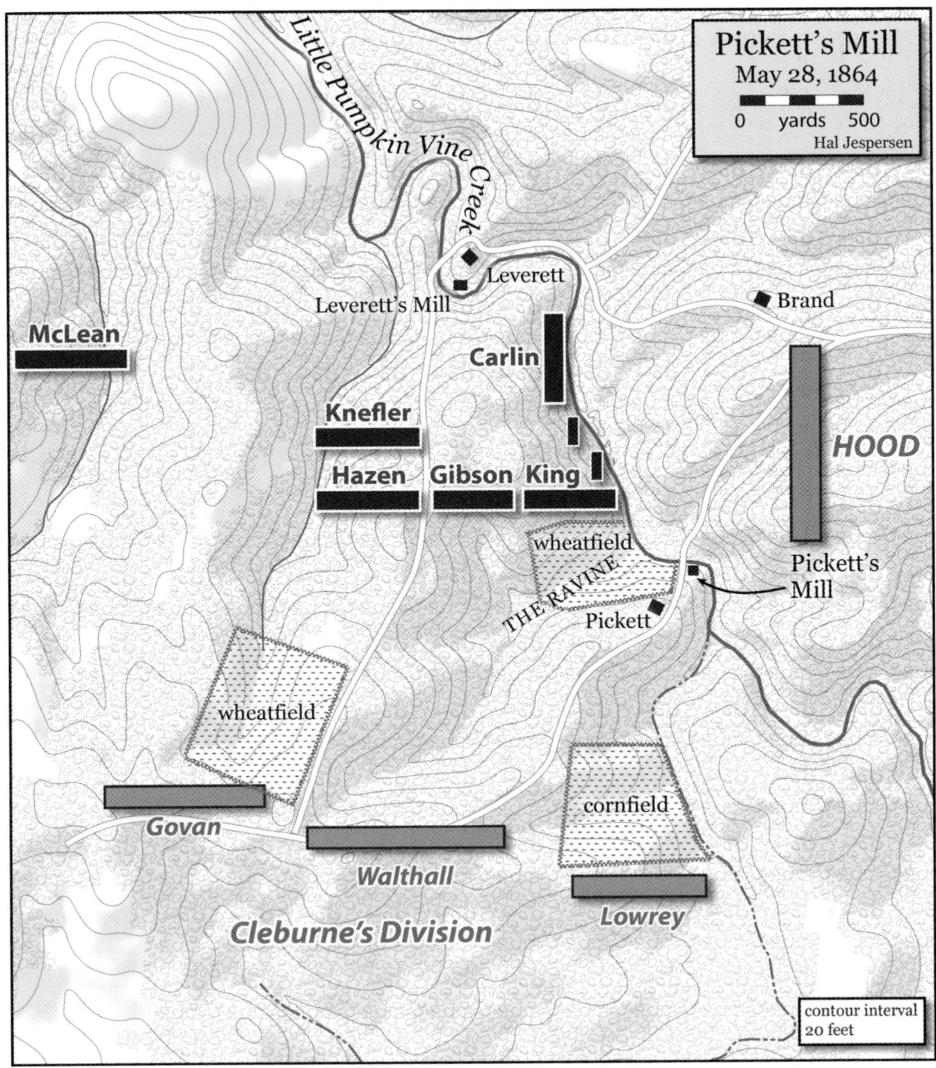

toward the Confederate right in the morning and there is no indication in their after-action reports to suggest that they departed before sunrise. Considering the treacherous terrain, they could not have been within supporting distance of an assault for at least two hours and possibly more.[21]

Further, Hood apparently made no effort to reconnoiter the Northerners' position once he reached the designated starting point for his attack. If he had, he

21 The brigades of Stewart's division began their march approximately three and a half or four miles from their destination. Wood's Federal division required more than four hours to cover a similar distance over nearly identical terrain. See *O.R.* vol. 38, pt. 1, 377; Castel, *Decision in the West*, 230.

Little Pumpkin Vine Creek. *Daniel Vermilya and James Garfield*

would have discovered the meager defensive works guarding the extreme Union left. General Richard Johnson, in command of the division defending that sector of the Federal lines, remarked that his position "was an exceedingly bad one, but it seemed impractical to correct it." Hood might have also learned that Carlin had moved out of his entrenchments and formed in a single rank on a nearby ridge. Hood's inactivity is in stark contrast to his behavior during the battle of Resaca. In both cases, the proximity of Wheeler's cavalry gave him the ability to direct a thorough reconnaissance of the enemy position. He did so at Resaca and discovered the enemy flank unguarded; at Pickett's Mill Hood did nothing. Hood reached his position just east of Pickett's Mill at dawn and did not inform Johnston, less than two miles away, that the enemy position could not be assailed without great risk until midmorning.[22] The hours between his arrival and his dispatch at 9:00 a.m. provided ample opportunity for Wheeler's cavalry to discover the

22 *O.R.* vol. 38, pt. 1, 523; Mackall Diary, May 28, 1864, JP WM. Johnston was at Cleburne's headquarters on the morning of the 28th.

weakness in the new Union defensive position had Hood ordered a reconnaissance. Yet Hood made no effort to probe the Federal line for a weakness or discover the strength of the force opposing him.

Hood's behavior at Pickett's Mill was not characteristic of his long service as a Confederate officer, nor was it indicative of his aggression during the opening phase of the campaign. Throughout the war, Hood had been known for his tenacity when engaged in offensive action, a trait that he exhibited at Resaca. The events at Cassville, however, had clearly affected Hood and altered his disposition. Only two explanations account for his erratic performance at Pickett's Mill. Either Hood's dispute with Johnston at Cassville so poisoned their relationship that thereafter he sought Johnston's removal as commander of the army and sent Brewster to Richmond in furtherance of that endeavor. Or he did not wish Johnston removed, but the affair at Cassville resulted in a loss of trust between the two men that caused Hood to act cautiously, a trait previously foreign to his temperament.

Johnston's and Hood's fractured relationship probably deprived the Army of Tennessee of a significant victory at Pickett's Mill on May 28. Not only were the Union entrenchments susceptible to a minimal flank march, but only two fresh brigades under the command of Richard Johnson occupied the ground to Hood's front, with Carlin's brigade having left the safety of its works. Wood's division held the ground to Johnson's right, but it had suffered 1,400 casualties during the battle the previous afternoon and evening. Moreover, Johnson and Wood were badly isolated from the rest of Sherman's army. Oliver Howard commented that Nathaniel McLean's brigade moved to the west during the night of May 27 in an effort to connect with the rest of the army which left Wood and Johnson in a precarious position.[23] If Hood had performed with his usual pre-Cassville energy, the Confederates could easily have destroyed two of Sherman's divisions and in the process attained greater parity in the comparative strength of the two armies.

Despite the setback caused by Hood's highly questionable behavior, Johnston set to work on devising an alternative plan. After receipt of information, later proved inaccurate, that the Federals near Dallas were moving north, Johnston ordered that Hardee instruct General William Bate on the Confederate left flank to reconnoiter the Union works on his front. Bate ordered a reconnaissance as planned and instructed the dismounted cavalry brigade under Frank Armstrong, loaned to him for the expedition, to advance the head of the infantry and determine the strength of the enemy line. Only if the Federals were in the process of withdrawing were the brigades of Bate's division to be sent forward. Armstrong soon encountered a strong enemy presence. Bate quickly realized that the Union

23 *O.R.* vol. 38, pt. 1, 195.

troops remained on his front in great strength and dispatched orders canceling the charge. For some unknown reason the brigades of Jessie Finley and Joseph Lewis advanced toward the enemy line. The ensuing slaughter claimed between 1,000 and 1,500 Confederates including 51 percent of Lewis's brigade. Lewis's soldiers blamed Bate for the disaster, believing he was responsible for the notion that only a skirmish line held the enemy defenses. As a result, Bate's troops no longer trusted their commander and ridiculed him "from all sides and quarters," particularly those in Lewis's brigade. From that point forward, the capacity of Bate's division to deliver an effective assault was substantially diminished, a characteristic that later manifested itself during the battle of Peachtree Creek.[24]

Despite Bate's defeat at the battle of Dallas, Johnston's performance since his arrival at Allatoona deserves praise. He had thwarted Sherman's flanking effort at Dallas and defeated Federal assaults at New Hope Church and Pickett's Mill. Further, Johnston had demonstrated aggression on the morning of May 27 when he believed Sherman was in the process of abandoning his position, and again that night when he ordered a general assault for the following day. Johnston's aggression was not lost on the enemy. In a letter to his wife on May 30, Orlando Poe described the Confederate attacks as persistent.[25]

On June 1 Johnston informed the administration that the army was in excellent condition and had defeated the enemy in a series of "partial engagements," that when combined "amounted to a battle." If Johnston hoped to earn the administration's confidence for his conduct thus far, Bragg's response the following day deflated such aspirations. Bragg suggested that Lee, like Johnston, had not engaged in a general battle *lately*, but that "in a series of partial engagements he has greatly damaged the enemy."[26] Bragg's telegram reminded Johnston that the administration held Lee in high esteem for his ability to deliver punishing blows to the enemy, a distinction that Johnston could not claim, despite his repeated efforts at Resaca, Cassville, and Little Pumpkin Vine Creek.

The administration's rebuke stung Johnston and apparently became a topic of conversation at the army's headquarters. Chief of staff William Mackall wrote to his wife on June 3 that Davis would liken Johnston's methodical retreat from

24 Johnston, *Narrative of Military Operations*, 332; Castel, *Decision in the West*, 244–246; John S. Jackman, *Diary of a Confederate Soldier: John S. Jackman of the Orphan Brigade*, ed. William C. Davis (Columbia, SC, 1990), 133. William Hardee and perhaps Joseph E. Johnston seem to have understood that Bate's men distrusted him after the battle of Dallas. Bate no longer occupied positions on the flank of the army while Johnston served as commander. Instead, Bate was positioned toward the center of Hardee's defensive alignments.

25 Poe to Wife, May 30, 1864, LC.

26 *O.R.* vol. 38, pt. 4, 752–753, 755.

Dalton to Bragg's precipitous flight from middle Tennessee after the battle of Murfreesboro in January 1863. Mackall further commented that "it is unjust to put a man at the head of an army and then try to destroy his capacity for usefulness by expressing fears and distrust." Similarly, Johnston's aide and close confidant Lt. Richard Manning informed his mother on June 9 that "I understand that in consequence of the General not having provoked a General Engagement with Sherman that the enemy at Richmond (who I regard as the most dangerous that this army & its general have) are busy criticizing—blaming—abusing & undermining."[27] Clearly Johnston believed that Davis and his advisors were engaged in engineering his downfall. There is no indication, however, in either his own correspondence or in that of his aides that Johnston knew, or even suspected, that Hood might also have intended to undermine the commanding general when he sent Brewster to Richmond.

Though Johnston had not managed to inspire the confidence of the administration, his defense of the line between Dallas and Pickett's Mill restored the buoyancy of the troops under his command. A. J. Neal commented that "it is fun for our troops to stand in the trenches and mow down their lines as they advance." He hoped that the enemy would continue its attacks indefinitely but feared they might soon fall back. Lieutenant Colonel Columbus Sykes proclaimed "the army is ready and anxious to fight the enemy whenever 'Old Joe' gives the word." The conviction that the mounting Union casualties would eventually give the Confederates the advantage permeated Johnston's headquarters as well. William Mackall opined that the Northerners had sustained a casualty rate three or four times higher than the Confederates and that "if we can keep this up, we win." Sherman also considered the stalemate near Dallas too costly and shifted back toward the Western & Atlantic Railroad in another of his flanking marches. By this point Sherman's penchant for maneuver had become so frequent that captured Confederates complained that Sherman himself must have entered "into the world by a flank movement." In response, Johnston moved to Lost Mountain on June 4 and established a new defensive line.[28]

With a growing conviction that the administration intended his downfall, Johnston looked for new methods to stop Sherman and his seemingly ceaseless maneuvers. Considering that Sherman had penetrated nearly 100 miles from

27 W. W. Mackall to Wife, June 3, 1864, Mackall, *A Son's Recollections of His Father*, 212; Castel, *Decision in the West*, 268.

28 Neal to Ella, June 2, 1864, KNBL; Castel, *Decision in the West*, 261; W. W. Mackall to Family, May 29, 1864, Mackall, *A Son's Recollections of His Father*, 212; Poe, Family Correspondence, May 30, 1864, LC; Mackall Diary, June 4, 1864, JP WM.

his base of supplies in Chattanooga, Johnston hoped that cavalry could disrupt Sherman's ability to feed his army and compel a retreat. In fact, Bragg reported on June 2 that cavalry from S. D. Lee and Nathan Bedford Forrest were on their way to Johnston's army. Johnston welcomed the news, as he considered the strength of Wheeler's cavalry insufficient to keep him informed regarding Sherman's activities and at the same time conduct a substantial raid on the Union supply lines. Unfortunately, a Federal raid in the direction of Okolona, Mississippi forced the recall of both Lee and Forrest. Still, on June 11 Johnston wired S. D. Lee and urged the importance of a cavalry expedition against Sherman's communications. He emphatically stated that "your troops can do no other service so valuable to the country." Two days later, Johnston learned that Forrest had crushed the Union advance near Tishomingo and was now free to operate against Sherman's rear. Thereafter, Johnston immediately requested that Bragg order Forrest to accomplish the design. The administration, however, ignored Johnston's plea, and the general made a second request on June 16. Concerned that his poor relationship with the president was to blame for the administration's refusal to order Forrest into action against Sherman's supply lines, Johnston asked Polk and Hardee to make similar requests.[29] Johnston apparently did not request that Hood make the same appeal, an indication that he had lost trust in his lieutenant. Despite Davis's close friendship with Leonidas Polk, even Polk's requests went unanswered.

As historian Craig Symonds has noted, it is likely that personal allegiances and petty politics played a significant role in the administration's handling of Johnston's repeated pleas for Forrest's intervention. Joseph Wheeler and Braxton Bragg had become close associates during Bragg's tenure as commander of the Army of Tennessee. Wheeler continued to correspond with Bragg after his removal and complained that Johnston would not allow him to conduct a raid on Sherman's communications. Wheeler's correspondence with Bragg, like Hood's in March and April, circumvented military protocol requiring Wheeler to send all communications through Johnston. Yet, like Hood's activity, the administration accepted or even encouraged Wheeler's behavior. Bragg's relationship with Forrest, however, could not have been more different as the two men were avowed enemies. In essence, Johnston was asking Bragg to reward an adversary at the expense of an ally.[30]

Further, Wheeler's bad habit of overestimating his own strength gave the administration reason to believe that Johnston possessed a sufficient number of

29 *O.R.* vol. 38, pt. 4, 755, 769, 777, 774; Symonds, *Joseph E. Johnston*, 304; Mackall Diary, June 3, 13, 1864, JP WM.

30 Symonds, *Joseph E. Johnston*, 304.

cavalry forces to provide adequate scouting while at the same time launching a raid on Sherman's rear. Johnston too had played a role in the administration's assessment when he forwarded Wheeler's inflated troop returns to the War Department. According to the June 10 returns, there were 10,903 effective cavalry troopers. In reality, the mounts had suffered greatly during the relentless campaign from Dalton to Lost Mountain, and Wheeler later recalled that he could put only 5,700 "fighting men" in the field by early June. But Johnston failed to identify the limited number of available mounts in his June returns as he had done in April.[31]

Consequently, with the administration's dwindling confidence in the army's commander, ensuing from a series of disputes predating the campaign, the army's retrograde movements from Dalton to Pine Mountain, Brewster's recent report, and Wheeler's claims that he could conduct a raid, Bragg declined the appeals to order Forrest to attack Sherman's supply line. The decision was unfortunate, as Forrest could have impeded Sherman's progress. Sherman's chief engineer, Orlando Poe, certainly thought so when he wrote to his wife that Forrest had "whipped Sturgis" and "doubtless he will at once strike for our communications." At the very least, Forrest's threat to the Union supply lines would have required Sherman to order troops from his own army to confront the Confederate cavalier and thereby lessen his ability to flank Johnston repeatedly. Further, Forrest could be counted on to damage portions of the rail line even if pursued by a sizable force from Sherman's army. After the war, Sherman claimed that his success in the Atlanta campaign would not have been possible without the use of the railroads from Louisville to Atlanta. He commented that "every mile of the single track was so delicate, that one man could in a minute have broken or moved the rail."[32] If Forrest's record on the battlefield is any indication, he might have done a great deal of damage to Sherman's railroads in addition to forcing the redeployment of Sherman's available force to meet Forrest's troopers.

In fact, Forrest could have done much greater damage than the destruction of rail, which was always reparable; he might have been able to shut down the railroad altogether had he targeted either of two vital tunnels. The easiest target might have been, as Joseph Parks has suggested, at Cowan, Tennessee. Sherman's engineers did not possess the machinery to mend the tunnel quickly enough to enable the Federal army to continue operating so deep in enemy territory. If not Cowan, the

31 Symonds, *Joseph E. Johnston*, 304, 311; *O.R.* vol. 38, pt. 3, 676–677; Connelly, *Autumn of Glory*, 385. In a report to the Atlanta newspaper, *Southern Confederacy*, on June 16, for example, a trooper in William Martin's division claimed that since May 10 they had been in the saddle for all but three days. See *Southern Confederacy*, June 16, 1864; *O.R.* vol. 32, pt. 3, 801.

32 Poe, Family Correspondence, June 15, 1864, LC; Sherman, *Memoirs of General W. T. Sherman*, 889.

passage through Chetoogeta Mountain at Tunnel Hill, Georgia also presented the Confederates with an opportunity to disable the railroad. Indeed, when Hood sent Wheeler on a raid in August, Northerners feared that he intended the destruction of the tunnel at Tunnel Hill.[33] The concept, then, was not particularly far-fetched and under the guidance of an officer of Forrest's skill might well have been accomplished.

Mark Elam has suggested that the Confederates should have demolished the tunnel while it was still in their possession and obvious that Sherman intended to advance in that direction.[34] To have blown up the tunnel in June would have been far more devastating to Sherman's chances of success. Without the ability to supply his army, Sherman would have been compelled to retreat to Chattanooga with Johnston on his heels the entire way. Even if Sherman had managed to return to Chattanooga with his army intact, he would have been right back at his starting point with little hope of advancing upon Atlanta soon thereafter. As a result, Atlanta would almost assuredly have remained in Confederate hands when Northerners went to the polls in November to select their president.

Nevertheless, conflict between members of the Confederate high command deprived Johnston of Forrest's services and meant that he needed to resist Sherman's advance on his own. While still at Lost Mountain, Johnston again devised a plan to strike Sherman on the move. On June 12, Johnston determined to withdraw Hood's Corps from the entrenchments and mass his troops on the army's right flank for the purpose of establishing a "strong mobile force" to assail Sherman while in motion. Severe weather, however caused a delay in the proposed movement. The following day Johnston inquired if Polk could spare some men for the purpose of augmenting Hood's column. Polk replied that 5,000 men could hold the present line, thereby allowing Hood to operate with nearly two corps. Consequently, Johnston ordered that the transfer commence at daybreak on June 14.[35]

Johnston's decision to assign the "mobile force" to Hood proves that Johnston was not aware of Brewster's mission to Richmond. If he had been, it is inconceivable that he would allocate such an important task to a general committed to undermining his credibility. Further, it demonstrates that while Johnston's faith in Hardee had significantly grown since the opening of the campaign, he still considered Hood's offensive prowess an asset. Hood, after all, had produced the only successful assault since the abandonment of Dalton when he attacked the Federal left at Resaca. Hardee, meanwhile, had performed admirably while acting on the defensive—first

33 Parks, *General Leonidas Polk C.S.A.*, 364; *Richmond Daily Dispatch*, Aug. 20, 1864, "News from the North."

34 Elam, "The Road to Atlanta," 73.

35 *O.R.* vol. 38, pt. 4, 770–773; Mackall Diary, June 12, 1864, JP WM.

at Resaca and especially at Cassville where he held against the advance of half the Union army on May 19. Considering that the plan required a greatly diminished force inside the Confederate entrenchments, it probably seemed wise to assign a defensive specialist like Hardee to hold them. Unfortunately, Johnston's plan, like most of his other offensive schemes, never materialized. The following day, while Johnston, Hardee, and Polk were inspecting the Confederate defensive position on Pine Mountain, a Union artillery shell struck Polk, killing him instantly, and postponing the attack once again.[36]

Federal cannonading on June 17 exposed the fact that a significant portion of Johnston's army was vulnerable to a devastating enfilade fire. As a result, Johnston ordered his chief engineer to map out a new defensive line to the rear. Providentially for the Confederates, poor weather precluded the Union gunners from taking advantage of the exposed Confederate alignment the following day, and on the night of June 18 the Rebels retreated to more formidable lines upon Kennesaw Mountain. The defensive alignment was the same as it had been through most of the campaign, Hood on the right flank, Polk's Corps temporarily commanded by William Loring in the center, and Hardee on the left flank.[37]

On June 21, Sherman moved against the Confederate left and Johnston transferred Hood's Corps to meet the threat with orders to prevent any progress of the Federal right toward the railroad. The next afternoon, Hood interpreted his commander's instructions liberally and launched an assault against the Federals under Joseph Hooker and John Schofield at Kolb's Farm. The Union commanders learned of Hood's presence in their front prior to his advance and ordered the construction of defensive works in case of assault. Exactly what Hood was thinking is unclear and he left no explanation for his actions in his postwar memoir. He failed to notify his commanding general of his intentions and launched the attack of his own accord. The assault ended badly for the Confederates, who suffered approximately 1,500 casualties compared to the Federal loss of a mere 250. Perhaps the rumors circulating in Richmond that Davis was considering Johnston's removal from command of the army had reached Hood and he hoped to impress the administration with a successful attack. His report of the affair certainly embellished the facts when he claimed victory. He asserted that he had driven the enemy from one line of works before retiring in the face of withering fire from fixed batteries.[38]

36 *Southern Confederacy*, June 16, 1864.

37 Johnston, *Narrative of Military Operations*, 338.

38 *O.R.* vol. 38, pt. 4, 784; Johnston, *Narrative of Military Operations*, 339; McMurry, *John Bell Hood and the War for Southern Independence*, 112; Castel, *Decision in the West*, 295; *O.R.* vol. 38, pt. 4, 788.

After the battle of Kolb's Farm, the two armies settled into their defensive lines near Kennesaw Mountain. During the stalemate, Senator Wigfall visited Johnston on his way home to Texas. Wigfall took the opportunity to inform Johnston that Davis was contemplating his removal.[39] Considering Johnston's relative success in checking Sherman's advance, the threat of removal makes little sense unless viewed in the context of Hood's communication to the administration via Brewster. Indeed, when compared to Davis's tolerance of Bragg's two years of ineptitude at the helm of the Army of Tennessee, the Brewster mission offers the most plausible explanation. While the pre-existing enmity between Davis and his commander had been enhanced by Johnston's failure to take the offensive at the start of the campaign, he had not yet suffered a genuine defeat during the present campaign. Removal under the circumstances would have been unwise and dangerous while in such proximity to the enemy. Hood's communication must be considered the primary cause of Davis's impending decision.

With the knowledge that Davis was considering his removal, Johnston discussed his strategy with his staunchest political ally. Johnston hoped Wigfall might influence the administration to order Forrest or S. D. Lee to move against Sherman's communications, but failing that, he would continue his strategy since Dalton. He would strike at Sherman if given an opportunity, but otherwise he planned to stay on the defensive. When Wigfall pressed him as to whether he intended to hold at the Chattahoochee River, Johnston asserted that it would be best to strike Sherman after he crossed Peachtree Creek south of the Chattahoochee. If the attack was successful, the Federals would have a river at their back; if the attack failed, the Confederates could retreat to the defenses of Atlanta.[40]

Johnston's conversation with Wigfall provides a great deal of insight into Johnston's state of mind. First, he clearly felt that the administration's refusal to send cavalry against Sherman's rear was inspired by animus rather than strategic considerations. Believing that political concerns motivated the administration's actions, Johnston determined to enlist politicians to argue in favor of his cause: a disruption of Sherman's communications.[41] Additionally, Johnston still hoped he might be able to deliver an offensive blow, though not until Sherman's army advanced to within a few miles of Atlanta. Finally, it seems that Sherman's repeated flank marches throughout the campaign had resigned Johnston to the

39 Symonds, *Joseph E. Johnston*, 310.

40 Louis Wigfall to Johnston, undated memorandum, LC.

41 In addition to Wigfall, Johnston secured assistance from Joseph E. Brown and Senator Benjamin Hill of Georgia, both of whom petitioned the president on Johnston's behalf. See *O.R.* vol. 52, pt. 2, 704–705.

fact that he would eventually be forced to abandon the impressive defensive line at Kennesaw Mountain.

While Johnston held his position at Kennesaw, the Georgia militia finally made its way to the front, though at numbers well below the 10,000 that Governor Brown later claimed that he had mustered. Instead, Gen. Gustavus Smith reached Johnston's army with only 3,000 militia under his command. Though these forces provided admirable service on Johnston's left flank, as previously discussed, their meager numbers limited their usefulness at Kennesaw. If Brown had raised even half of the available men between the ages of seventeen and forty-five, Smith could have fielded at least 8,000, a number sufficient to hold the defenses of the mountain itself and free the current defenders to strike an enemy flanking column. An additional 4,000 could be added to the total if 50 percent of the militia proper between forty-five and fifty answered the call to duty. But Brown was still shielding a significant portion of his eligible male population from military service. On June 25, rather than insisting that some of these state officers take up arms against Sherman's invading army, he issued a proclamation sustaining their exemptions. Brown called upon "Judges of the supreme, superior, and inferior courts, ordinaries, solicitors general, sheriffs, clerks of the superior and inferior courts, tax collectors and receivers," among others to assist in the apprehension of nonexempt male citizens that failed to report for militia duty. The group included approximately 3,000 men engaged in the administration of a court system that had been, for the most part, suspended.[42] Without a sufficient militia force, Johnston was compelled to keep his veterans entrenched on the mountain and hope that Sherman might advance against his strong defensive lines.

On June 27 Sherman complied with Johnston's wishes and assailed the Confederate lines. The attack commenced against Samuel French's division, posted on Pigeon Hill on the Confederate right. The affair was brief and cost the Union 850 casualties and claimed only 200 Rebels. Sherman's primary target, however, was the Confederate left where David Stanley's and John Newton's divisions of Howard's Corps along with Jefferson C. Davis's division of John Palmer's Corps advanced on Benjamin Cheatham and Patrick Cleburne. There too the Confederates easily repulsed the Union troops, who lost over 2,000 men, while the Confederates counted only 700 casualties, approximately half of whom were captured while on picket duty in the first moments of the attack.[43]

42 *O.R.* vol. 52, pt. 2, 782; Smith, "The Georgia Militia About Atlanta," 331; Scaife and Bragg, *Joe Brown's Pets*, 5; *Southern Confederacy*, June 25, 1864; *C.R. Ga.*, III, 506.

43 Symonds, *Joseph E. Johnston*, 312; Castel, *Decision in the West*, 319–320.

Under the circumstances it seemed unlikely that Sherman would attack the nearly impregnable defensive line a second time, and while Johnston waited for Sherman's inevitable flanking march, he received a visit from Senator Benjamin Hill of Georgia. On the evening of July 1 Johnston held a conference with Hill, a close friend of the president, in hopes of securing a cavalry raid on Sherman's communications. Johnston insisted that a raid made in considerable force might compel Sherman to make an immediate and rash attack on the Army of Tennessee, like he had four days earlier, in hopes of gaining Atlanta and the city's supplies. Otherwise, Sherman would have to retreat from his position in front of Kennesaw and repair the damage caused by the marauding cavalry. According to Johnston, if Sherman retreated, it would delay his advance at least a month. Hill asked if such a tactic could still prove useful so late in the campaign, and Johnston replied in the affirmative. Hood, who was also present at the meeting, was less enthusiastic. He suggested that unless a foray was made against Sherman's rear immediately it was unlikely that it could work, and that even then it might be too late.[44]

Hood's assertion that any attempt at breaking up Federal communications required immediate action was absurd and possibly calculated to discredit Johnston in the presence of Davis's close friend. Whether Confederate cavalry disrupted Sherman's supply lines with his army north or south of the Chattahoochee made little difference. So long as Lee or Forrest badly damaged the rails or destroyed one of the tunnels, Sherman would probably be forced to retreat or launch an impetuous assault against Johnston's defensive line in hopes of ending the campaign before he ran out of provisions. Moreover, if Hood really believed that Johnston's proposal could only achieve success if launched immediately, then he had no reason to order a similar foray a month later, which he did at the beginning of August when he instructed Wheeler to break up the railroad feeding Sherman's army.[45] Hood's comments, therefore, were probably intended to support Brewster's thesis that Johnston had no plan and that he could not arrest Sherman's advance with the army at his disposal.

Hood's claims were not the only damaging comments to Johnston's future as the army's commander. Johnston himself made a great mistake when he assured Hill that the Confederate army could hold its position north of the Chattahoochee for a month or more.[46] The assertion largely depended upon an immediate cavalry sortie against Sherman's communications. Johnston knew that his elongated

44 *O.R.* vol. 52, pt. 2, 704–706.

45 *O.R.* vol. 38, pt. 5, 940.

46 *O.R.* vol. 52, pt. 2, 704–706.

lines along his current position on Kennesaw could not be stretched much further. He also knew that only one or two locations between Kennesaw and the Chattahoochee afforded adequate topography for a defensive stand. Therefore, unless the Confederate cavalry could imperil Sherman's supply line, Johnston's claim was unrealistic, particularly in light of events the following day.

By the beginning of July, Johnston's defensive lines extended as far as he deemed acceptable. He worried that Sherman's men were already closer to the Chattahoochee River than his own army and imperiled his rear. Fearing that he would soon need to abandon Kennesaw, Johnston ordered his engineer, Colonel Presstman, to prepare defenses at Smyrna Church ten miles south of their present position. In the middle of June he had dispatched Brig. Gen. Francis Shoup to construct a line of redoubts on the north side of the Chattahoochee covering the railroad crossing. Shoup, however, had not yet finished the project, probably because Johnston had insisted that he expand the project to extend all the way to Turner's Ferry (See map of Operations on the Chattahoochee.)[47] The lines at Smyrna were likely intended to delay Sherman long enough to finish Shoup's scheme on the banks of the Chattahoochee.

On the morning of July 2, two divisions of the Army of the Ohio moved close to Nickajack Creek near the Chattahoochee. The force consisted of approximately 13,000 men, a rather small detachment, and like Wood and Johnson at Pickett's Mill, fairly isolated from the rest of Sherman's host. A sufficient militia force would have enabled Johnston to attack Schofield's men with his veteran troops and perhaps score a decisive victory. If he had been willing to strip his defenses near Lost Mountain to establish a "strong mobile force" during the second week in June, the same strategy could be used at Kennesaw.[48]

This time, however, the Confederate defensive lines extended much further than they had at Lost Mountain. The two-week stalemate at Kennesaw allowed Sherman to lengthen his trenches a little more every day, a process that forced Johnston to make a corresponding elongation of his own works. As a result, the Confederate lines covered a greater distance and required more troops for their defense. In fact, Wheeler's cavalry already occupied the trenches Hood had vacated when he marched to Kolb's Farm on June 21.[49] Without sufficient militia, then, Johnston could not strike Schofield without weakening his defenses to such an extent that it could not repel an advance by Thomas and McPherson.

47 Johnston, *Narrative of Military Operations*, 345; Shoup, "Dalton Campaign," 263.

48 Castel, *Decision in the West*, 327–329; Mackall Diary, July 1, 2, 1864, JP WM; See *O.R.* vol. 38, pt. 4, 770, 772.

49 *O.R.* vol. 38, pt. 4, 551–552, 783–784.

Schofield's advance so close to Nickajack Creek on July 2 resulted in Johnston's abandonment of his Kennesaw lines. The latest retrograde movement did not bode well for his pledge to Hill that he would hold north of the Chattahoochee for at least a month. Johnston's retreat took him to within three miles of the river, where he halted at Smyrna Church. The Confederates did not remain long in their new position. On July 4 a Federal corps under the command of Maj. Gen. Francis Blair endangered Hood's rear near Nickajack Creek. Soon thereafter, Johnston received a report from Gustavus Smith, whose militia was on Turner's Ferry Road, that he would "be compelled to withdraw at daylight." The threat to his left flank and news that the Federals would soon be near the Chattahoochee led Johnston to redeploy the army to the redoubts that Shoup had prepared north of the river. That same day, Orlando Poe scaled Kennesaw Mountain, looked through his telescope, and saw for the first time the streets of Atlanta.[50]

The works that Shoup had constructed were unusual and the soldiers did not know what to make of them. Shoup, with the help of impressed slaves, had built a series of "detached log redoubts packed in with earth." Each required only eighty men for its defense. The redoubts were placed between 60 and 175 yards apart with interlocking fields of fire and connected with a stockade of eight-foot high logs that ran between them in order to allow the transfer of men in case one of the redoubts required reinforcement. Perplexed by their purpose, a number of men immediately destroyed sections of the stockade and erected traditional trenches. William Norrel, for example, commented that the works "looked more like a pen for stock to be driven in," and that the engineer responsible for them "should be publicly branded as incompetent." Though Hardee and Cleburne appreciated Shoup's scheme, other members of the high command, chief among them Joseph E. Johnston, failed to understand the design. The goal, according to Shoup, was to defend the one bridge that allowed for a rapid crossing of the Chattahoochee with a single division. The Federals would then be forced to cross either at one of the ferries, fords, or by pontoon bridge, all of which would require a significant amount of time to complete, thereby allowing the bulk of the Confederate army time to concentrate on that point. Shoup complained that Johnston's insistence on extending the fortifications all the way to Turner's Ferry proved that he did not fully comprehend his design.[51]

50 Johnston, *Narrative of Military Operations*, 345; *O.R.* vol. 38, pt. 5, 860; Mackall Diary, July 2, 4, 1864, JP WM; Johnston, *Narrative of Military Operations*, 346; Poe to Wife, July 4, 1864, LC.

51 Shoup, "Dalton Campaign," 263; National Park Service American Battlefield Protection Program Grant No. 2255-09-013, *Archaeology Inventory and GIS Analysis for the Chattahoochee River Line Battlefield (July 5-10, 1864)*, by Scott Butler and Keith Bohannon, 9. One witness estimated that there was an average of one redoubt every 150 feet. See Butler and Bohannon, *Archaeology Inventory*

According to one observer, the new defensive line stretched from just north of the railroad bridge "over a series of rugged hills and hollows through dense timber and underbrush to the river." An archaeological survey of the Confederate

and GIS Analysis for the Chattahoochee River Line Battlefield, 10; Norrel, Diary, July 5, 1864, KNBL; Shoup, "Dalton Campaign," 263–264. See C6-Map 04.

defenses later revealed that the lines ran approximately six miles. As a result, the works required a larger portion of the army to defend than Shoup had originally intended and correspondingly weakened the mobile reserve force that could strike any Union attempt to cross the Chattahoochee upriver or downriver from the fortifications. Still, according to William Palfrey on Shoup's staff, the line of redoubts enabled a brigade to defend the same amount of territory that otherwise required a division.[52]

Almost immediately upon arrival, Hood declared that the new line was indefensible and that the army should retire to the south side of the river. His assertion prompted Johnston to call a meeting of the army's high command. During the gathering Hood argued for the abandonment of the works and seemed to Shoup as though he too did not understand the purpose of the redoubts. Shoup was granted an opportunity to discuss the design, but he could not develop a consensus in favor of his scheme and the meeting ended with no resolution. Captain Palfrey lamented that "the tone favoring holding on to the side of the river next to the enemy was not such as I could have wished."[53]

Whether Hood understood the purpose of Shoup's defensive line or not, his characterization that it could not be held conflicted with the observations of officers in his own corps. After the war J. C. Thompson of A. P. Stewart's division observed that "our position on the Chattahoochee (meaning that of our division) was impregnable to assault," and that the "extreme left was very strong." Gustavus Smith, whose militia defended the same section of Shoup's line as Stewart's men, also commented favorably on the strength of the defensive works north of the Chattahoochee. Federal officers were extremely impressed with Shoup's design as well. Sherman asserted that the works were "one of the strongest pieces of field fortification I ever saw." Orlando Poe wrote: "[T]his line, owing to the care bestowed upon its construction and the nature of its approaches was by far the strongest we had yet encountered." His description included Hood's section of the line where he noted the presence of a seven-gun redoubt.[54]

Considering the testimony of Confederates and Federals alike, Hood's allegation that his section of the line was indefensible seems strange. Perhaps he intended to discredit Johnston who had promised Senator Hill that the army could

52 W. L. Trask, Diary, July 6, 1864, Kennesaw Mountain National Battlefield Library; Butler and Bohannon, *Archaeology Inventory and GIS Analysis for the Chattahoochee River Line Battlefield*, 9–10, 17.

53 Shoup, "Dalton Campaign," 264; Butler and Bohannon, *Archaeology Inventory and GIS Analysis for the Chattahoochee River Line Battlefield*, 22.

54 J. C. Thompson to A. P. Stewart, Box 1, Folder 5, JP WM; Smith, "The Georgia Militia About Atlanta," 333; Sherman, *Memoirs of General W. T. Sherman*, 536; *O.R.* vol. 38, pt. 1, 129–130.

hold north of the Chattahoochee for a month. There can be little doubt that in the first week of July Hood distrusted Johnston's handling of the army, and their relationship had cooled dramatically since the opening of the campaign. Further, he must have known by then that Davis was considering Johnston's removal. Hood had apparently recently written to his fiancée, "Buck" Preston, that he expected Johnston's removal and his own promotion to command of the army.[55] If Hood believed that Johnston would not prevent Sherman's seizure of Atlanta, a likelihood given Brewster's mission to Richmond, his insistence that the army retire from the Chattahoochee seems designed to effectuate a change in the army's leadership. Consequently, his criticism of Shoup's works was probably an effort to undermine his commander.

While the army's high command debated the merits of the defensive line north of the Chattahoochee, Jefferson Davis and Braxton Bragg finalized the restructuring of the officer corps in the wake of Leonidas Polk's death. Two features of their selections stood out; none of them were Johnston's recommendations and each was on friendly terms with Braxton Bragg. The administration appointed A. P. Stewart to take over Polk's Corps, thereby restoring Loring to divisional command. Johnston had requested Richard Ewell, apparently unaware that the general suffered from physical and psychological problems so severe that he was no longer able to command troops in the field. The administration assigned Henry Clayton to Stewart's divisional post. Clayton, a politician from Alabama, had no prewar military experience, but was "one of Bragg's favorites." Bragg labeled Johnston's recommendation for the position, Mansfield Lovell, "incompetent" as a result of his losing New Orleans, a charge from which he was later exonerated by military tribunal. Hindman also had to be replaced after receiving a wound on June 27, and the administration appointed John C. Brown in his stead. Brown, like Clayton, had no military training prior to the commencement of hostilities in 1861. Two of Hood's divisions, therefore, were now commanded by men with limited military experience and unimpressive wartime records.[56] Their best performance had been during the battle of Chickamauga, one of Bragg's few victories, however pyrrhic. The administration had once again deprived Johnston of at least one general whom he trusted, Lovell, in favor of Bragg's close associates.

55 Louis Wigfall had visited Johnston with news of the rumors two weeks earlier. It is also likely that Brewster had returned to Hood's staff by that time. He was certainly present on July 11 when Halsey Wigfall made mention of him in a letter to his mother. See Halsey Wigfall to Louis T. Wigfall, July 11, 1864, Louis T. Wigfall Papers, Library of Congress; Connelly, *Autumn of Glory*, 417.

56 Halsey Wigfall to Louis Wigfall, July 15, 1864, LC; Woodworth, *Jefferson Davis and his Generals*, 112; Castel, *Decision in the West*, 338; McMurry, *John Bell Hood and the War for Southern Independence*, 115; *The Papers of Jefferson Davis*, X:506; *O.R.* vol. 38, pt. 5, 868.

Thus, Johnston was faced with a lack of cooperation from his superiors in Richmond, and at the same time with a disagreement among his subordinates concerning the question of retaining the army in its present position on the north bank of the Chattahoochee. Johnston seems to have been impressed by the strength of the works as he later inquired whether Shoup could reproduce them around Atlanta. Nevertheless, he had clearly misunderstood the scheme with respect to holding the Chattahoochee when he directed the construction of redoubts all the way to Turner's Ferry. Further, Johnston positioned most of the army inside Shoup's works on the north side of the river and retained only two infantry divisions on the south side, hardly the mobile force that Shoup had envisioned.[57]

The extant crossings of the Chattahoochee River exacerbated Johnston's misunderstanding of Shoup's design. The Confederate works covered three ferries and the railroad bridge, but that left several points north of the works uncovered, including Pace's, Power's, and Phillip's Ferries and Isham's Ford. Southwest of the Confederate line, there were sufficient crossing opportunities and Johnston believed Sherman likely intended to head in that direction.[58] Consequently, even a large mobile force would have had difficulty defending against the possibility of Union passage of the river at so many points. If necessary, Sherman could march a diversionary column in one direction, thereby drawing the attention of the Confederate main body, and subsequently pass a large force across the river in the opposite direction. Once the crossing column had entrenched, Johnston would be compelled to withdraw his army.

As a consequence, the Chattahoochee, unlike so many rivers in the Eastern theater, did not offer defenders a particularly strong point at which to halt the advance of opposing forces. Jefferson Davis failed to understand the distinct differences in the topography between the two theaters of operation. When explaining his decision to remove Johnston from command of the army, he asserted that Johnston had been unable to hold "positions of great strength like those at Dalton, Resaca, Etowah, Kennesaw, and on the Chattahoochee."[59] Though Dalton and Kennesaw provided excellent terrain for defensive lines, the other three were positions with meandering rivers, slow currents, and numerous crossings.

As it happened, Union troops crossed the Chattahoochee at two locations north of the Confederate line at Phillip's Ferry and Roswell Factory on July 9. Orlando Poe witnessed the crossing at Philip's Ferry and recorded that Colonel

57 Shoup, "Dalton Campaign," 265; Butler and Bohannon, *Archaeology Inventory and GIS Analysis for the Chattahoochee River Line Battlefield*, 22.

58 See Poe to Wife, July 10, 1864, LC; Castel, *Decision in the West*, 341.

59 Davis, *Rise and Fall of the Confederate Government*, II, 557.

Brownlow took a squad of his regiment, the 1st Tennessee Cavalry, and all stripped of their clothing until they were stark naked, and holding their carbines above their heads they swam that river and in the condition they were, charged the rebel rifle pits intended to command the ferry and took them, capturing some prisoners. They could not pursue because the briars tore their flesh.[60] Poe's testimony also provides evidence that rivers in the Western theater offered little defensive value as compared to rivers in Virginia. The fact that Brownlow's troopers could swim the river with their weapons held above their heads indicates that the Chattahoochee, like many waterways in northern Georgia, lacked a sufficient current to impede would-be attackers.

Toward Atlanta and Johnston's Removal

Soon after discovering that Sherman's army had made a lodgment across the Chattahoochee, Johnston ordered a retreat. He believed that Shoup's fortifications could not be held by a small enough force to allow a concentration of troops that would enable an assault against Sherman's latest flanking endeavor. Apparently Johnston failed to realize that his own modification of Shoup's design had caused the shortage in manpower. Further, his estimation that Shoup's works required a large number of soldiers lacks credibility. Assuming that Shoup built an average of one redoubt every 150 feet, as one witness observed, the line included as many as seventy-two forts.[61] A single corps could probably have held Shoup's line and certainly two corps would have been sufficient. That left at least one corps to act as a mobile force against Federal river crossings. Instead, it is likely that upon observing the works himself and realizing the multiple points at which the Chattahoochee could be crossed both north and south of the Confederate position, Johnston decided against long-term defense of the Chattahoochee. That at least one of his corps commanders objected to remaining north of the Chattahoochee probably also influenced Johnston's decision. Finally, if Johnston had planned an attack against Sherman after the Federals crossed the Chattahoochee, as he informed Wigfall, and the evidence supports, he had little reason to remain north of the river after the crossings at Philip's Ferry and Roswell Factory.

Other than his comments to Wigfall, the evidence that Johnston intended to attack the Federals while crossing Peachtree Creek is circumstantial, but compelling. First and perhaps most convincing is the postwar statement of Gen.

60 Poe, Family Correspondence, July 10, 1864, LC.

61 Mackall Diary, July 9, 1864, JP WM; Butler and Bohannon, *Archaeology Inventory and GIS Analysis for the Chattahoochee River Line Battlefield*, 10.

A. P. Stewart, who claimed that on July 17 Johnston had ordered him to place his corps "in position to attack Sherman's force at daylight the next morning." Additionally, after crossing the Chattahoochee and moving his army to Proctor's Creek, south of Peachtree Creek, Johnston did not entrench, the expected practice if he intended to remain on the defensive. In fact, on July 17, his last day as commander, Johnston published an address to the army announcing that he would attack Sherman once he crossed the Chattahoochee, which was received with enthusiasm among the troops. Moreover, in an article disparaging Johnston's conduct along the Chattahoochee, Francis Shoup noted, "On the 17th of July, Sherman advanced on Atlanta, and Johnston disposed his forces to meet him on Peachtree Creek." Finally, a newspaper correspondent described the scene he witnessed when he rode to army headquarters after having learned of Johnston's dismissal and noted that he had witnessed Johnston discussing his plans with Hood.[62] The episode suggests that Johnston was explaining his plans for an attack against Sherman. Hood undoubtedly intended to engage in offensive action and unless Johnston was describing such a movement, it seems unlikely that the new commander would have been so interested. The evidence, therefore, suggests that Johnston hoped to strike the enemy once Sherman crossed Peachtree Creek, a plan that likely influenced his withdrawal from the Chattahoochee.

Johnston's plans for defending Atlanta should his attack fail, however, were haphazard and influenced by his feud with the president, particularly concerning matters of departmental design. On July 10 he met with Shoup to discuss the construction of defensive works around Atlanta similar to those north of the Chattahoochee. Shoup said that it could be done, but that he would need a large number of impressed slaves from south of Atlanta as the Confederates did not control the region north of the city. Johnston informed Shoup that his department terminated at Atlanta and he did not have authority over the territory to the south. When Shoup suggested that he apply for an extension of his department, Johnston said that "he would not apply to the authorities at Richmond for anything." Shoup then suggested that Johnston apply to Governor Brown, which Johnston also refused, though he did authorize Shoup to make the request on his own. Shoup met with Brown that evening, and the governor eschewed responsibility for demanding that local planters provide slaves for the enterprise.[63]

62 T. G. Dabney, "When Hood Superseded Johnston," *Confederate Veteran* XXII (1914): 406; Halsey Wigfall to Louis Wigfall, July 15, 1864, LC; Bell Wiley, "The Confederate Letters of John W. Hagan: Part II," *Georgia Historical Quarterly* 38, no. 3 (Sept. 1954): 285; *O.R.* vol. 38, pt. 3, 717; Dabney, "When Hood Superseded Johnston," 406; Shoup, "Dalton Campaign," 265; *Richmond Daily Dispatch*, Aug. 1, 1864.

63 Shoup, "Dalton Campaign," 265.

Johnston's unwillingness to apply for an extension of his department was the product of a long and bitter struggle with the administration over the course of the war. The awkward departmental design had frustrated Johnston during the defense of the Virginia peninsula against McClellan's advance upon Richmond. The problem surfaced again immediately after Johnston's appointment to departmental command in the Western theater when Davis had given him authority over Pemberton's and Bragg's armies in late 1862. In that instance Johnston could not convince Davis to transfer men from the Trans-Mississippi, thereby creating a force large enough to take the offensive against Grant. Davis allowed the provincialism inherent in his departmental system to go unchecked when Holmes insisted that threats to his own theater of operations required that his troops remain in their present position. Holmes's claim was later proven false when Richard Taylor, serving in the Trans-Mississippi, informed the administration that he had sufficient forces to help lift the sieges of Vicksburg and Port Hudson.[64] Johnston's latest conflict with the president over departmental cooperation was his ongoing effort to convince the administration to order a cavalry strike against Sherman's communications from S. D. Lee's Department of Alabama, Mississippi, and East Louisiana. Clearly, Johnston's frustration with Davis's departmental design and the president's reluctance to overrule the localism that the system produced influenced his decision against requesting an extension of his own department.

Meanwhile, the process that led to Johnston's removal from command began in earnest on July 10. Senator Hill met with the president and presented him with Johnston's request for a cavalry strike against Sherman's line of supplies. Davis responded that Forrest could not be spared from the defense of Mobile. When Davis asked Hill how long Johnston had claimed that he would hold north of the Chattahoochee, Hill told him that he had said that he could hold there a month or more. Davis then read him a telegram that Johnston had sent that day that announced his withdrawal to the south side of the river.[65] Johnston had fallen shy of his boast by at least three weeks.

The following day Johnston recommended the relocation of prisoners at Andersonville, more than 100 miles south of Atlanta, a communication that implied the general might retreat indefinitely. After receiving the telegram, Davis wired Robert E. Lee and asked if Hood was qualified to assume command of the army. Lee advised against the measure and considered Hardee preferable to Hood if removal were absolutely necessary. Davis was not the only member of the

64 *O.R.* vol. 11, pt. 3, 499; *O.R.* vol. 17, pt. 2, 783–784; *O.R.* vol. 24, pt. 2, 461.

65 Davis, *The Rise and Fall of the Confederate Government*, II:560.

administration alarmed by recent events in Georgia. James Seddon, who had played a significant role in Johnston's appointment to the position the previous December, now clamored for his removal and requested on July 10 that Hill prepare a summary of his interview with Johnston for the purpose of persuading Davis that Johnston no longer deserved his position. The rest of the cabinet apparently needed little convincing that the administration should replace him. Davis worried, however, that a change in command with the army so close to Atlanta could be dangerous. Even so, Johnston's communication regarding Andersonville, in combination with his interview with Hill, induced the president to seriously consider the possibility. After all, he had contemplated relieving Johnston in May when Brewster visited him, and the safety of Atlanta was in far greater jeopardy in July with Sherman at the city gates.[66]

Davis had sent Bragg on a fact-finding mission to Atlanta on July 9 for the purpose of determining whether to retain Johnston as commander of the Army of Tennessee. On July 13 Bragg reached Atlanta, and before conferring with Johnston, informed Davis that all indications were that Atlanta would soon be evacuated. That afternoon Bragg wired Davis that "the army is sadly depleted, and now reports 10,000 less than the return of 10th June. I find but little encouraging." Clearly Bragg had begun a campaign to ensure Johnston's removal from command. What was not clear, however, was who Bragg had in mind as a replacement. There is no doubt that Bragg disliked Hardee, who had been a prominent member of the anti-Bragg faction of the army during his tenure as commander. Most historians have asserted that Bragg helped manufacture Hood's appointment and have assumed that was his preference all along. In reality, as Judith Hallock argues, Bragg might have hoped that Davis would reinstate him to command of the army. During his time as the president's chief military advisor Bragg had received communications from officers in the Army of Tennessee proclaiming that he "possessed the confidence and affection" of the army.[67] He traveled to Atlanta under the impression that many in the army would support his return.

Davis, however, did not consider Bragg for the position and, in fact, intended to follow Lee's advice if Bragg's investigation revealed a need to replace Johnston. Undoubtedly, Davis and Bragg had discussed the possibility of a change in command prior to Bragg's journey, and the president clearly favored Hardee as the

66 *O.R.* vol. 38, pt. 5, 876; Lee, *Lee's Dispatches*, 283–284; Davis, *The Rise and Fall of the Confederate Government*, II:560–561; Woodward, *Mary Chesnut's Civil War*, 635.

67 *O.R.* vol. 38, pt. 5, 878; McMurry, *John Bell Hood and the War for Southern Independence*, 118–120; Castel, *Decision in the West*, 355–357; Connelly, *Autumn of Glory*, 418–420; Woodworth, *Jefferson Davis and his Generals*, 283–285; Symonds, *Joseph E. Johnston*, 325–326; Hallock, *Braxton Bragg and Confederate Defeat*, II:199–200.

proper choice. After receipt of Bragg's initial communications, Davis replied that "if C. is thus indicated adopt advice and execute as proposed." The C. probably denoted "change," and the telegram plainly suggests that the two had discussed the matter and Davis had instructed Bragg to promote a specific candidate. Bragg's response indicated that the candidate could have been none other than Hardee. Bragg insisted that adopting that course "would perpetuate the past and present policy which he has advised and now sustains. Any change will be attended with some objections. This one could produce no good." In effect, Bragg claimed that to replace Johnston with Hardee would generate the same results as if Johnston retained command. Bragg emphasized his point in a dispatch later that day that concluded that Hood and Wheeler considered offensive action necessary while "on the contrary, General Hardee generally favored the retiring policy."[68]

It was folly for Davis to have sent Bragg to Atlanta to conduct the investigation in the first place. Bragg's history with the Army of Tennessee and the grudges he retained against several of its officers meant that he was incapable of providing a fair assessment of the situation. His communications immediately upon his arrival demonstrated that he wanted Johnston relieved without conducting a proper investigation. Further, he most certainly never intended to carry out Davis's wishes and appoint his bitter rival, William Hardee. Davis should have known that Bragg would undermine any effort to elevate Hardee. His penchant for cronyism, a trait that inspired his appointment of Bragg as chief military advisor, however, blinded him to the inevitable revival of the deep-seated political rancor that had been so prominent during Bragg's time with the army.

When Davis failed to offer him the job, Bragg immediately helped to manufacture Hood's appointment as army commander. At some point on July 13, Bragg met with Johnston who, according to William Mackall, looked uneasy. Mackall opined that Bragg's mission was intended to "make a display" of the president's "distrust of Johnston and if he finds he can infuse it into the army, to relieve him." If Mackall understood the gravity of the visit, Johnston undoubtedly knew that his tenure was in peril. The threat to Johnston increased the following day when Bragg met with Hood. Hood, in a final act of treachery against his commander, produced a memorandum detailing his objections to Johnston's conduct throughout the campaign. Hood's memo lamented Johnston's failure to pursue an aggressive course of action. Hood bemoaned that his efforts to persuade Johnston to fight had gone unheeded, and he asked that Davis be notified that he "would continue to do his duty cheerfully and faithfully, and strive to do what I think is best for our country, as my constant prayer is for our success." Historians of the campaign have

68 *O.R.* vol. 52, pt. 2, 704, 707; *O.R.* vol. 39, pt. 2, 712–714.

universally recognized that Hood's memorandum was rife with falsehoods and a blatant machination to replace Johnston as the army's commander.[69]

The meeting between Bragg and Hood was a microcosm of Davis's failures as a political and military leader since December of the previous year. He had appointed Bragg as his military advisor for no other reason than their friendship; Bragg's disastrous record on the battlefield did not warrant the new assignment. Nor did Bragg's abrasive personality, which had alienated many of his subordinates while acting as the commander of the Army of Tennessee, suit him for the role. Yet, Davis's complete confidence in Lee meant that Bragg's input would necessarily focus on his old command. Considering his record, Bragg's appointment was a recipe for disaster. Indeed, Bragg had begun undermining his replacement almost immediately when he demanded that Johnston take actions that he had never attempted while serving with the army.[70]

Davis's appointment of John Bell Hood to command a corps in Johnston's army also proved ruinous for the Confederate hopes in the Western theater. Hood's accomplishments merited the promotion, but Davis's instructions that he keep the administration informed about the army's condition and Johnston's capacity as commander inherently promoted disloyalty. Rather than suppressing Hood's repeated communications with the administration in March and April, Davis encouraged the improper conduct. Once Johnston suggested that Hood had acted inappropriately at Cassville, the temptation to undermine his superior became too enticing. Hood thereafter engaged in a series of dubious schemes designed to secure command of the army for himself. It is no wonder, then, that the meeting between the two men sealed Johnston's fate.

After his summit with Hood, Bragg wrote two reports. The first noted that Johnston had not asked for his advice, though Bragg neglected to mention that he did not volunteer any. In addition, the report concluded that Johnston had no specific plan for saving Atlanta. Bragg's second report advocated Johnston's removal and suggested that Hood be placed in his stead. Bragg's communications confirmed Davis's inclination to remove Johnston from command. Even so, Davis did not act rashly; rather he sent Johnston a demand for information concerning his intentions for the defense of Atlanta. The general responded that the size of Sherman's army meant that his own actions depended upon the

69 Mackall to Wife, July 13, 1864, UNC; Richard McMurry suggests that the memorandum might have been Bragg's idea. See McMurry, *John Bell Hood and the War for Southern Independence*, 118; *O.R.* vol. 38, pt. 5, 880; McMurry, *John Bell Hood and the War for Southern Independence*, 118; Castel, *Decision in the West*, 356; Symonds, *Joseph E. Johnston*, 324; Connelly, *Autumn of Glory*, 417.

70 Hallock, *Braxton Bragg and Confederate Defeat*, II:189.

enemy's movements and that he hoped for an "opportunity to fight to advantage." He further suggested that "We are trying to put Atlanta in condition to be held for a day or two by the Georgia militia, that army movements may be freer and wider."[71] Like his responses to similar queries during the Peninsula campaign and the siege of Vicksburg, Johnston provided little detail to the president. He had not trusted Davis since the first year of the war when the president ranked him fourth among full generals. Nevertheless, in this instance he was playing with fire. Bragg's presence meant that removal was a distinct possibility, and Johnston's ambiguous response to the president's pointed question gave Davis few alternatives.

Davis considered his general's plan unworkable. After all, even if the Georgia militia had been composed of veterans from past campaigns, it mustered less than 3,000 effectives when Davis relieved Johnston of command. Davis's lengthy struggle with Joseph E. Brown regarding the establishment of the Reserve Force meant that he was keenly aware that the militia lacked sufficient strength for Johnston's scheme to work. The Confederate president had good reason to be concerned that Johnston intended to hold Atlanta with such a diminutive force. Moreover, men he trusted, Bragg and Hood, insisted that Johnston intended to retreat once again without putting up a serious fight for the Gate City. Additionally, two Northerners, James Jaquess and James Gilmore, were then in Richmond waiting to visit Davis. They possessed a letter from Abraham Lincoln and claimed they hoped to find a way to end the war. Lincoln therefore seemed willing to negotiate, but the loss of Atlanta would damage Davis's position in any such discussions.[72] Under the circumstances Davis determined to replace Johnston with Hood.

The president's failures as commander-in-chief had played a decisive role in Johnston's inability to arrest Sherman's advance. Davis's lack of appreciation for the advantages of a centralized command system meant that Johnston had begun the campaign with an army significantly smaller than his adversary's. Further, the Confederate departmental design hampered Johnston's capacity to order S. D. Lee or Nathan Bedford Forrest to assail Sherman's supply lines. Davis's ineffective management of his subordinate's personalities exacerbated the situation. His long history with Johnston meant that he viewed the general's pleas for a cavalry raid with suspicion. Meanwhile, the president apparently ignored Braxton Bragg's open hostility toward Forrest when considering his chief of staff's advice on the matter.

71 *O.R.* vol. 38, pt. 5, 881; *O.R.* vol. 39, pt. 2, 712–714. The second report was delivered in person and might not have reached Richmond before Davis made the decision to relieve Johnston; *O.R.* vol. 38, pt. 5, 883.

72 Even if Davis had retained Johnston, the militia never exceeded 5,000 muskets. See Smith, "The Georgia Militia About Atlanta," 334; Castel, *Decision in the West*, 361.

His decision to send Bragg to Atlanta to determine whether to retain Johnston further demonstrated Davis's willingness to allow his personal friendship to cloud his judgment. Bragg, with his long and troublesome history with the Army of Tennessee, should not have been in a position to determine the army's leadership. In addition to allowing his distrust of Johnston and his misplaced confidence in his friend Bragg to influence his decisions, Davis also permitted his relationship with Joseph Brown to affect the outcome of the campaign. Without the presence of a substantial militia force, Johnston had been outflanked at Dalton and Resaca and had been unable to implement his mobile force strategy near Kennesaw Mountain. Finally, and most importantly, Davis had initiated a policy that resulted in John Bell Hood undermining his commander in hopes of securing the post for himself. After his dispute with Johnston at Cassville, Hood used the president's invitation to engage in back-channel communications with the administration to achieve his goal.

Even though Davis's failings as commander-in-chief had helped produce the army's withdrawal to the outskirts of Atlanta, the president had little choice but to relieve Johnston from his position. On the afternoon of July 17 Gen. Samuel Cooper informed Johnston that Hood had been assigned to replace him as commander of the army.[73] Considering the circumstances, Davis's decision was reasonable. Johnston's unwillingness to disclose any specific plans for the defense of Atlanta, while at the same time suggesting the removal of prisoners from Andersonville, understandably did not inspire the president's confidence. Johnston's secretive behavior, a characteristic he had displayed during the campaigns on the Virginia peninsula and again at Vicksburg, was particularly unwise under the circumstances he then faced. Bragg's presence with the army undoubtedly meant that the administration was considering relieving him from command, but Johnston maintained his enigmatic posture. Johnston's behavior was all the more perplexing because the evidence suggests that he intended to launch an assault once a portion of Sherman's army crossed the Chattahoochee River. Johnston certainly understood that the president desired him to attack the enemy as soon as an opportunity presented itself. Had he informed Davis of his plans to engage Sherman along Peachtree Creek, the president might well have retained him as commander. Johnston, however, refused to divulge his strategy and suffered the consequences. As a result, because Johnston remained noncommittal, and the retention of Atlanta gave Davis his best chance of success in any potential negotiations with the Lincoln administration, he replaced Johnston with a man he knew would act aggressively: John Bell Hood.

73 *O.R.* vol. 38, pt. 5, 885.

Chapter 7

With Drawn Sabers Flashing in the Light

The decision to promote John Bell Hood rather than William Hardee proved yet again that Jefferson Davis had not learned how to manage the contentious personalities associated with his chief western army. Sending Braxton Bragg to Atlanta to play a pivotal role in personnel decisions for an army whose officer corps had split into factions under his leadership was imprudent. Not only should the president have known that Bragg would attempt to elevate someone other than Hardee, but he also should have anticipated that Hardee might react negatively if he were passed over in favor of Hood. Davis risked resurrecting the internal strife that had plagued the army's officer corps during Bragg's tenure as commander. Indeed, Hardee had been at the epicenter of the anti-Bragg cabal, demonstrating his capacity for obstruction.[1] Davis seems not to have recognized that he might be replacing one dysfunctional relationship, between Johnston and Hood, and exchanging it for another.

Hood assumed command of the Army of Tennessee on the evening of July 17 with a clear mandate from the administration that he launch an offensive. He obliged, and within five days of his appointment Hood ordered two separate general assaults against Sherman's armies. Both attacks demonstrated Hood's tactical ability and provide evidence that he was not incompetent as an army commander nor was he suffering from any addictions as some historians have surmised. Though the attacks at Peachtree Creek on July 20 and at Bald Hill on July 22 were well planned and stood a reasonable chance of success, neither

1 Connelly, *Autumn of Glory*, 21–22.

achieved the desired goal thanks to William Hardee's lethargy. Then, on the night of July 27, Hood developed a plan intended to thwart Sherman's flanking movement on the Confederate left only to have his newest corps commander, S. D. Lee, botch the affair. Hood's greatest error in his defense of Atlanta was his decision to send the inept Wheeler on a raid against Sherman's communications. Wheeler failed miserably in his mission and in the process deprived Hood of a sufficient number of cavalry troops to keep him informed of the enemy's activities. Sherman took advantage of Wheeler's absence and by the end of August threatened Jonesboro and Hood's last rail line into Atlanta. On September 1 Sherman broke the Confederate line at Jonesboro and forced Hood's evacuation of Atlanta, thus ending the campaign and with it any reasonable chance that the Confederacy might win the war. After the conclusion of the war, Hood offered two explanations for his inability to defeat Sherman in the battles around Atlanta. First, that Hardee had performed poorly during the engagements at Peachtree Creek and Bald Hill. Hood's second observation was that Johnston's policy of retreating in the face of the repeated enemy flanking maneuvers had demoralized the army and resulted in a high rate of desertion and unwillingness to engage in offensive tactics. While Hardee deserved Hood's castigation, the troops likely did not.

State of the Army

Hood claimed that Johnston's slow retreat from Dalton to the Chattahoochee cost the army 25,000 men, many of whom had deserted. Further, he charged that those who did remain in the ranks after the Confederates crossed the Chattahoochee had been so dispirited by the long retreat that they no longer resembled the army that had begun the campaign encamped around Dalton. Not surprisingly, Johnston countered Hood's assertions and argued that the soldiers understood that Sherman's superiority in manpower necessitated Johnston's strategy and that they would eventually defeat Sherman when the opportunity presented itself. Johnston also insisted that the troops crossed the Chattahoochee with an even higher level of confidence than they had exhibited at Dalton.[2]

Most scholars of the campaign have accepted Johnston's claims, an interpretation Richard McMurry argued is flawed. According to McMurry, the "Johnston school" had acquired much of its evidence from postwar accounts that were influenced by Hood's subsequent loss of Atlanta and his disastrous campaign

2 Hood, *Advance and Retreat*, 134–135. Hood made the same observations in his official report on the campaign in mid-Feb. 1865, though he estimated then that the casualties amounted to 22,750. *See O.R.* vol. 38, pt. 3, 629; Johnston, *Narrative of Military Operations*, 351.

into Tennessee. McMurry argued that the contemporary Confederate and Federal diaries, letters, and accounts corresponded more closely with Hood's explanation of Rebel morale than Johnston's. Further, McMurry asserted that the army's morale under Hood during his defense of Atlanta remained relatively high and that many of the troops believed that the battles fought late in July resulted in Confederate victory.[3] McMurry's claims about the army's morale under Hood while he defended Atlanta are accurate, but the historical record does not clearly reflect the charge that the army suffered severe demoralization during Johnston's retreat from Dalton to the Chattahoochee.

There can be little doubt that many soldiers expressed anxiety whenever Johnston ordered a retreat. The almost universal dissatisfaction among both officers and enlisted men, however, when the administration removed Johnston proves that the army did not suffer a significant loss of morale under his leadership. As McMurry acknowledged, a number of soldiers expressed regret when the president relieved Johnston. A Georgia soldier, for example, lamented "all moan the loss of our great leader and believe if the war department only knew what confidence the army has in their great leader he would have been retained." Lieutenant W. L. Trask commented that "General Johnston had the abounding confidence and esteem of almost every man in the army and he had inspired it with the utmost enthusiasm. . . . He was beloved far beyond any commander that ever controlled any fraction of the army, and the soldiers will part with him with much regret." Halsey Wigfall, on Hood's staff, noted "a universal gloom seemed cast over the army for they are entirely devoted to him [Johnston]." Lieutenant A. J. Neal, who often expressed disappointment during Johnston's retrograde movements, observed that "the change was very unexpected in the army and deeply regretted but I cannot regard it as calamity." Taylor Beatty, also on Hood's staff, commented: "I am afraid it may do harm at this moment because the army still has confidence in Johnston and does not know Hood."[4] Surely if Johnston's retreat from Dalton to the Chattahoochee had generated the despondency that Hood later claimed permeated the army when he took command, some contemporary accounts would reflect enthusiasm among at least a portion of the troops at Johnston's removal. Yet such accounts are not found in the historical record.

3 Richard McMurry, "Confederate Morale the Atlanta Campaign of 1864," *Georgia Historical Quarterly* 54, no. 2 (Summer 1970): 228–229, 235; Richard McMurry "The Atlanta Campaign of 1864: A New Look," *Civil War History* 22 (1976): 10.

4 Richard McMurry "The Atlanta Campaign of 1864: A New Look," *Civil War History* 22 (1976): 10; John Hagan, "The Civil War Letters of John W. Hagan," ed. Bell Wiley, *Georgia Historical Quarterly* 38 (1954): pt. II, 282; Trask Diary, July 19, 1864, KNBL; Halsey Wigfall to Mother, July 31, 1864, LC; Neal to Father, July 20, 1864, KNBL; Beatty Diary, July 18, 1864, UNC.

Instead, the most convincing evidence of rampant desertion among the Confederates can be found in Federal accounts of the campaign. McMurry produced several Union reports that testified to a high rate of Confederate desertion. In early July, one Northern general commented that "A good many Rebel stragglers and deserters have been taken on each abandonment of Rebel camps." Despite the impressions of individual Federal soldiers that Confederate morale had deteriorated during the campaign, the official Union records do not concur. Rather, the Federal army reported only 1,141 Confederate desertions from May through June. In July Union authorities reported an additional 732 Confederate deserters, but some of those desertions undoubtedly occurred after Davis relieved Johnston from command. Because the deserters were processed through Chattanooga, some of that number were certainly from other Confederate commands including S. D. Lee's department. Considering that the reinforcements from Polk's department in Mississippi increased the army to between 70,000 and 74,000 troops by May 19, the percentage of desertions seems negligible. Indeed, the Army of Northern Virginia might have suffered a higher proportion of desertions during that same period. While the Federal Army of the Potomac confronting them did not differentiate between Confederate deserters and prisoners captured during battle, they reported a total of 13,548 prisoners apprehended from May through July 31.[5] As a result, a comparison between the two primary Confederate armies suggests that Johnston maintained a well-disciplined and enthusiastic army from Dalton to the outskirts of Atlanta.

The most recent evidence of elevated rates of Confederate desertion can be found in Stephen Hood's *The Lost Papers of Confederate General John Bell Hood*. Regimental surgeon Walter Byrne, for example, estimated that the army had suffered between 17,000 and 20,000 desertions by the time it reached the outskirts of Atlanta. That estimate, given ten years after the conclusion of the campaign, does not comport with the Federal records in any way. Additionally, if the Confederates had suffered such astronomical desertion rates one would expect to find commentary about it in the letters, diaries and journal entries of a significant number of officers and enlisted men alike. Considering the absence of such commentary, the claim does not seem reliable. Affidavits from John Smith and E. B. Wade claim a loss of 25,000 from all causes (casualties, illness, desertion) between May 7 and July 18.[6] Bearing in mind that there had been relatively little

5 McMurry, "Confederate Morale in the Atlanta Campaign of 1864," 230, 240. See footnote 6; *O.R.* vol. 38, pt. 1, 147, 153, 159; Castel, *Decision in the West*, 198; McMurry, "The Atlanta Campaign of 1864: A New Look," 12; *O.R.* vol. 36, pt. 1, 196.

6 Hood, *The Lost Papers of Confederate General John Bell Hood*, 128–129.

combat during that time, the bulk of such losses would have had to have come through desertion. Again, such large-scale defection would almost certainly have been documented by a fair number of soldiers. It seems reasonable to accept the proposition, therefore, that the Army of Tennessee was in good shape and still in good spirits when John Bell Hood took over as its commander.

Federal accounts of Hood's first battle as commander of the army also suggest that the Confederate soldiers retained their fighting spirit even after crossing the Chattahoochee. General John Geary, in command of a Union division, reported that the "officers were in plain view, with drawn sabers flashing in the light. . . . The rebel troops also seemed to rush forward with more than customary nerve and heartiness in the attack." Colonel Horace Boughton of the 143rd New York commented that the "attacks were made with great desperation" and that the enemy approached "to within twenty yards of my line." Another Northern officer, Gen. Nathan Kimball, reported that the Confederates charged "with great confidence with a rapidity and an absence of confusion I have never seen equaled. . . . He was repulsed with terrible loss of my front." Hood's claim, therefore, that he inherited a dejected army, is not borne out by contemporary accounts. Even if Hood is given credit for having inspired confidence in his army, there can be little doubt that they fought hard when he called upon them to assault the enemy along Peachtree Creek. Georgia soldier John Hagan's letter on July 4 likely reflected the mood of the army when he noted "some of our troops grow despondent but it is only those who are always despondent all good soldiers will fight harder the harder he is pressed."[7]

Nor did Hood's aggression in the battles of late July result in a loss of confidence among the soldiers of the Army of Tennessee. As McMurry demonstrated, most of the contemporary accounts indicate that the soldiers believed that Hood's assaults had successfully prevented Sherman's various flanking maneuvers. The pragmatic A. J. Neal informed his mother on July 23 that the Confederates had gained a great victory on the previous day and that his corps had "captured 3,500 prisoners and 22 pieces of artillery" and that the "enemies killed and wounded amounted to more than twice our own." On August 4, Neal wrote that the army had "been strengthened by the militia and reinforcements from Forrest," which allowed the Confederates to "hold our long lines and have force enough to operate on the flanks." He concluded that "General Hood watches his flanks closely and has twice whipped the flanking columns out." The Confederate soldiers did not realize at the time that the battles fought between July 20 and July 28 had been Union victories and, as a result, maintained a fairly high level of morale until the fall of Atlanta.

7 *O.R.* vol. 38, pt. 2, 140, 107, 306; Wiley, "The Civil War Letters of John W. Hagan," 282.

Only after the war with the hindsight of the abandonment of Atlanta and the disastrous Franklin and Nashville campaign did Southerners conclude that Hood's promotion had been an unmitigated disaster and that they had always suspected his deficiencies.[8]

A Reassessment of John Bell Hood as a Commander

In addition to the fabricated memory that Confederate morale suffered during Hood's defense of Atlanta, the subsequent campaign in Tennessee also produced the fiction that Hood had performed poorly during the Federal investment of the Gate City. To the contrary, Hood developed bold plans that failed primarily because of the performance of his subordinates. While it seems fairly certain that Johnston had developed the initial plan to strike Sherman's army when it was divided by Peachtree Creek and that he probably informed Hood, it was Hood who had to finalize the details and put the plan into motion. Hood wisely determined to make the attack with his most seasoned commanders after the Federals crossed the creek. He therefore placed Stewart on the army's left, Hardee in the center, and Cheatham, in temporary command of Hood's former corps, on the Confederate right. Cheatham, the least experienced, was to defend Atlanta from any advance from the northeast. Hood ordered that Hardee, with significantly more experience as a corps commander than either Cheatham or Stewart, lead the assault. According to the plan, Stewart would advance after Hardee had struck the enemy flank. If all went well, the attack would drive Sherman's right wing into the convex of Peachtree Creek and the Chattahoochee River. If the Confederates succeeded they could destroy half of the Union army, as both waterways were passable only by bridges. As at Resaca, Hood instructed Wheeler to send his best scouts to Peachtree Creek to keep him informed when the enemy's left crossed toward Decatur to the east, thereby isolating the Federal right. Hood also ordered Hardee to "thoroughly examine" the ground over which he would advance when the assault commenced.[9]

Hood had performed as well as any newly appointed commander could have performed under the same circumstances. His handicap, however, was precisely that he was new and therefore unfamiliar with the capabilities of the divisional commanders designated to make the assault. His former corps, now under Cheatham, was properly assigned a defensive role. Of the seven divisions charged

8 McMurry, "Confederate Morale in the Atlanta Campaign of 1864," 236; Neal to Mother, July 23, 1864, KNBL; Neal to Ella, Aug. 4, 1864, KNBL; McMurry, "Confederate Morale in the Atlanta Campaign of 1864," 228.

9 *O.R.* vol. 38, pt. 5, 892–893. Hood, *Advance and Retreat,* 166; *O.R.* vol. 38, pt. 2, 389.

with advancing upon the Union right wing, five—Bate's, Cleburne's, Cheatham's, Loring's, and Walthall's—had developed good reputations during their wartime service. Unfortunately, serious challenges faced two of those divisions on July 20, 1864. Bate's division, in the aftermath of the battle of Dallas, no longer trusted their commander and blamed him for the senseless slaughter they had endured on May 28. Whether they could be depended upon during the coming attack remained to be seen. Cheatham's division also posed a problem, not because his men had performed poorly in any engagement thus far, but because they were under a new commander with no experience at the divisional level.[10] Without knowledge of the strengths and weaknesses of the various brigades and divisions in his army, Hood could not direct the alignment of the assaulting force to ensure that the most battle-tested units were assigned the most difficult duties.

By contrast, over the course of the campaign, Johnston had learned which divisions were the most trustworthy and had personally directed their placement when he felt it necessary. While at Dalton, for example, Johnston had ordered Patrick Cleburne's division to Dug Gap when he realized the Federal threat to his left. Soldiers in both armies considered Cleburne's men to be the best division in the army. On May 26, when Johnston feared that Sherman was moving toward his right flank, he had detached Cleburne from Hardee's Corps on the left and sent him to Pickett's Mill to strengthen the right of Hood's position. The following day, after discovering the Union menace to his right flank more serious than he had previously realized, Johnston had ordered Stewart's division to Cleburne's support.[11] Clearly, experience with the army had given Johnston a better feeling for the capabilities of his divisional commanders and he had acted accordingly. Hood could not draw upon the same knowledge when organizing the planned assault along Peachtree Creek.

William Hardee's indignation that Davis had passed him over and given command of the army to Hood posed an even graver danger to operations than Hood's unfamiliarity with his new army. Hardee was so incensed that when Bragg returned to the army on July 27 after having visited S. D. Lee on the 19th, he requested a transfer. From Hardee's point of view, he had seniority since he had

10 Not only was Cheatham inexperienced as a corps commander, but his divisional commanders, John Brown, Henry Clayton, and Carter Stevenson possessed limited or unimpressive records in their respective posts. Jackman, *Diary of a Confederate Soldier*, 133; Castel, *Decision in the West*, 373.

11 *O.R.* vol. 38, pt. 3, 678. They were so celebrated that they were the only division in the Confederacy that was permitted their own distinctive battle flag, a blue field with a white circle in the center. See Castel, *Decision in the West*, 36; Buck, *Cleburne and his Command*, 218; Castel, *Decision in the West*, 231. As previously discussed, Stewart's defense of New Hope Church on May 25 had impressed Johnston.

been a lieutenant general since October 1862, while Hood had only achieved that rank the previous winter. It seems likely that Hardee understood that Bragg—his old nemesis—and Hood had engineered Johnston's removal and replacement with Hood. After all, between his arrival in Atlanta on July 13 and Hood's assumption of command five days later, Bragg had spent most of his time conversing with Hood.[12] Hardee was understandably angry and disinclined to assist his new superior any more than was absolutely necessary. Davis's decision to replace Johnston with Hood rekindled the factionalism within the officer corps that had been a prominent feature of Bragg's time with the army.

On July 20 the renewed schism within the high command of the Army of Tennessee manifested itself for the first time. On the night of July 19, Hood informed his subordinates that he wished to commence the attack against the Federals south of Peachtree Creek at 1:00 p.m. the following day. He instructed Hardee and Stewart to advance *en echelon* from Hardee's right. Hood acknowledged that the troops would likely encounter some breastworks, but he concluded that the Federals would not have time to construct strong defenses and that most would be caught without any at all. Consequently, the Northerners would be susceptible to "a bold and persistent attack," and if necessary the Confederates should charge the enemy defenses at "the point of the bayonet." Having delivered his orders, Hood expected that his corps commanders would make prudent decisions regarding the placement of their divisions during the advance. Hood had little choice but to rely upon his subordinates, as he had limited knowledge of the abilities of individual commanders in either Hardee's or Stewart's corps. It is likely true that Hood modeled his command style after Robert E. Lee. In Lee's system, the army commander produced the grand design and allowed his subordinates to work out the details. Still, if Hood had known that William Bate's division considered their commander a butcher, he would have assuredly intervened when Hardee assigned Bate the most vital role in the attack. Hardee positioned Bate on the extreme right of his corps, thereby giving him the crucial task of striking the enemy first, preferably on the flank and rear.[13]

If Bate failed in his assignment the entire assault stood limited chance of success. An *en echelon* attack rested on the principle that the success of the initial blow would force Gen. George Thomas, in command of the Union troops on the south side of the creek, to redeploy his troops to the threatened sector of his line,

12 *O.R.* vol. 52, pt. 2, 712–713; Connelly, *Autumn of Glory*, 423; Symonds, *Joseph E. Johnston*, 324; Castel, *Decision in the West*, 355–357.

13 *O.R.* vol. 38, pt. 3, 871; McMurry, *John Bell Hood and the War for Southern Independence*, 129–130; Castel, *Decision in the West*, 373.

thereby weakening the rest of his defenses. The weakness could then be exposed when the remaining attacking columns advanced sequentially from right to left according to Hood's design. If the initial strike failed in its mission, however, the subsequent assaults would likely dissolve into a series of frontal attacks that rarely proved successful in Civil War combat. The success of the attack largely hinged on the performance of Bate's division, an odd choice for the assignment considering Cleburne's availability. It is doubtful that Hardee's positioning of Bate was a purposeful attempt to undermine the attack. Rather, it is more likely that in his resentment over Hood's appointment, Hardee failed to give the matter serious thought.

Union activity on the morning of July 20 delayed the planned attack, which exacerbated Hardee's agitation. At approximately 10:00 a.m., McPherson advanced on the Confederate right more rapidly than Hood had anticipated and threatened Atlanta from the railroad east of the city. To confront McPherson, Hood was forced to deploy Cheatham's Corps further to the right, which created a significant gap between Cheatham's left and Hardee's right. Hood ordered that Cheatham extend by one division front to the right to cover the railroad, and correspondingly he directed Hardee and Stewart to extend half a division front to the right. Anticipating possible confusion, Hood directed Hardee to send a staff officer to the new location for his left flank to make sure that the troops did not march beyond that point. Cheatham, however, marched much further than he had been instructed. Hardee, without consulting Hood, ordered his troops to follow suit and maintain a half division front between themselves and Cheatham's Corps. Cheatham made several movements eastward and in each instance Hardee's column halted and formed a line of battle, whereupon Cheatham marched further to the right.[14]

Rather than requesting additional guidance from Hood, Hardee kept pace with Cheatham. After the battle Hardee justified his failure to inform Hood about the repeated eastward movements by claiming that Hood was too far away in Atlanta. Hood was in reality nearby, having moved to Stewart's headquarters at noon. Hardee was aware that Hood had moved and he informed his commander at approximately 3:30 p.m. that he feared the numerous lateral movements had caused "some disorder." His refusal to consult his chief prior to the mid-afternoon communication was the product of his simmering anger at having been placed

14 T. B. Roy, "General Hardee and the Military Operations around Atlanta," *Southern Historical Society Papers* 8 (1880): 348; Sherman, *Memoirs of General W. T. Sherman*, 544; Castel, *Decision in the West*, 372; McMurry, *John Bell Hood and the War for Southern Independence*, 128.

under Hood's command. As the afternoon wore on, Hardee's resentment grew, and he complained to his staff about the repeated delays in the planned assault.[15]

Hardee's irritation over the postponement of the attack was based on the belief that the delay enabled the Federal column that had crossed Peachtree Creek to construct serviceable breastworks. Stewart also feared that the opportunity might be lost and, unlike Hardee, sought guidance from the commanding general. Stewart hoped that Hood would instruct Hardee to cease moving to his right and advance upon the enemy. Hood, however, did not intervene, a decision likely modeled on Lee's *modus operandi* that allowed corps commanders freedom to make tactical decisions based upon the situation before them. Perhaps Hood remembered a similar situation the previous July when he had requested permission to move farther to the right to commence his attack against Little Round Top at Gettysburg.[16]

As it turned out, both Stewart's and Hardee's apprehensions that the Federals might construct adequate entrenchments before the assault proved inaccurate. Furthermore, the new Confederate dispositions meant that the right of Hardee's Corps extended beyond the left of the Federal position. Rather than hitting the Union troops head-on, as they would have if they had made the advance from their original position, the Confederate right now had an opportunity to strike the enemy flank and rear. Unfortunately for the Rebels, a miscommunication nullified Hood's *en echelon* design. At approximately 2:30, Hardee informed Stewart that he was ready to attack. Stewart then ordered his troops to prepare for action. Apparently, William Loring mistook the communication as an indication that Hardee had already commenced his advance, and he moved forward well before any of Hardee's troops. Loring achieved initial success, capturing the enemy's position, but the fact that Maney on his right had not yet begun his advance meant that the Federals could concentrate on Loring. Soon, the Union enfilade fire into his right flank compelled Loring to withdraw.[17]

Meanwhile, Hardee's advance began around 3:00 p.m. with Bate's division moving forward first followed by Walker and Maney in intervals thereafter. Historians have excused the behavior of Bate's division that afternoon. They have apparently accepted Hardee's claim that after Bate encountered no opposition

15 *O.R.* vol. 38, pt. 3, 698; Mackall Diary, July 20, 1864, JP WM; Hughes, *General William J. Hardee*, 221; Roy, "General Hardee and the Military Operations around Atlanta," 348.

16 Hughes, *General William J. Hardee*, 221; *O.R.* vol. 38, pt. 3, 871.See Hood, *Advance and Retreat*, 57.

17 *O.R.* vol. 38, pt. 1, 71; *O.R.* vol. 38, pt. 2, 34, 442-43; Castel, *Decision in the West*, 375; *O.R.* vol. 38, pt. 3, 871, 876–877: Hughes, *William J. Hardee*, 221–222.

to his front, he attempted to follow Hardee's instructions and turn the enemy flank, but the impenetrable thickets impeded his progress.[18] In reality, Bate's men behaved badly when they encountered meager resistance. It is doubtful that they could not locate the enemy position. While most of the after-action reports describe the terrain as inhospitable, covered with heavy undergrowth and scarred by ravines, John Newton, in command of the Union left flank, observed Bate's approach. If Newton could see Bate, it seems logical that Bate could also see Newton. Nevertheless, Bate continued moving in a northerly direction toward the confluence of Peachtree Creek and Clear Creek. Bate's advance concerned Newton, who believed Bate intended to seize the only bridge across Peachtree Creek in the vicinity. Newton, therefore, decided to obstruct Bate's progress. He directed a detachment of two cannons to concentrate on Bate and ordered "a few of the pickets who had been driven in" to position themselves alongside the two-gun section. With this feeble force Bate's column "was checked and driven back into the woods."

From there, Bate managed to organize his troops and advance toward the Union flank at approximately 4 o'clock but was again repulsed by Federal artillery. Bate spent the rest of the afternoon stumbling through the underbrush on the Union left flank. Only after 6:00 p.m. was he able to reorganize his division and advance against Newton again. By that juncture the battle, for all intents and purposes, had ended.[19] Bate's performance was disgraceful; the division had inexplicably failed to advance on Newton's flank and had fled when confronted with bombardment from a two-gun battery. Its second advance was also checked by Federal artillery, though the two-gun section had been reinforced with four additional pieces. Clearly, the men remained skittish after the affair at Dallas. Hardee made a dreadful decision when he placed them in such a pivotal position, knowing that Bate's troops distrusted him.

Hardee compounded his error in the positioning of Bate's division when he failed to press Walker and Maney to attack Newton's line of defense. Newton deployed his troops along a ridge that dominated the ground in its front. Newton later observed that "had the enemy obtained this position the right wing of the army would probably have been rolled back into the angle between Peachtree Creek and the Chattahoochee and entirely separated from the left and center." Further, he had only enough men to form a single line, which proved insufficient to "cover the space enveloped by the enemy," forcing Newton to move regiments from one point

18 *O.R.* vol. 38, pt. 3, 698. See Castel, *Decision in the West*, 376; Connelly, *Autumn of Glory*, 443; Hughes, *General William J. Hardee*, 222.

19 *O.R.* vol. 38, pt. 1, 297, 298; Hughes, *General William J. Hardee*, 222–223.

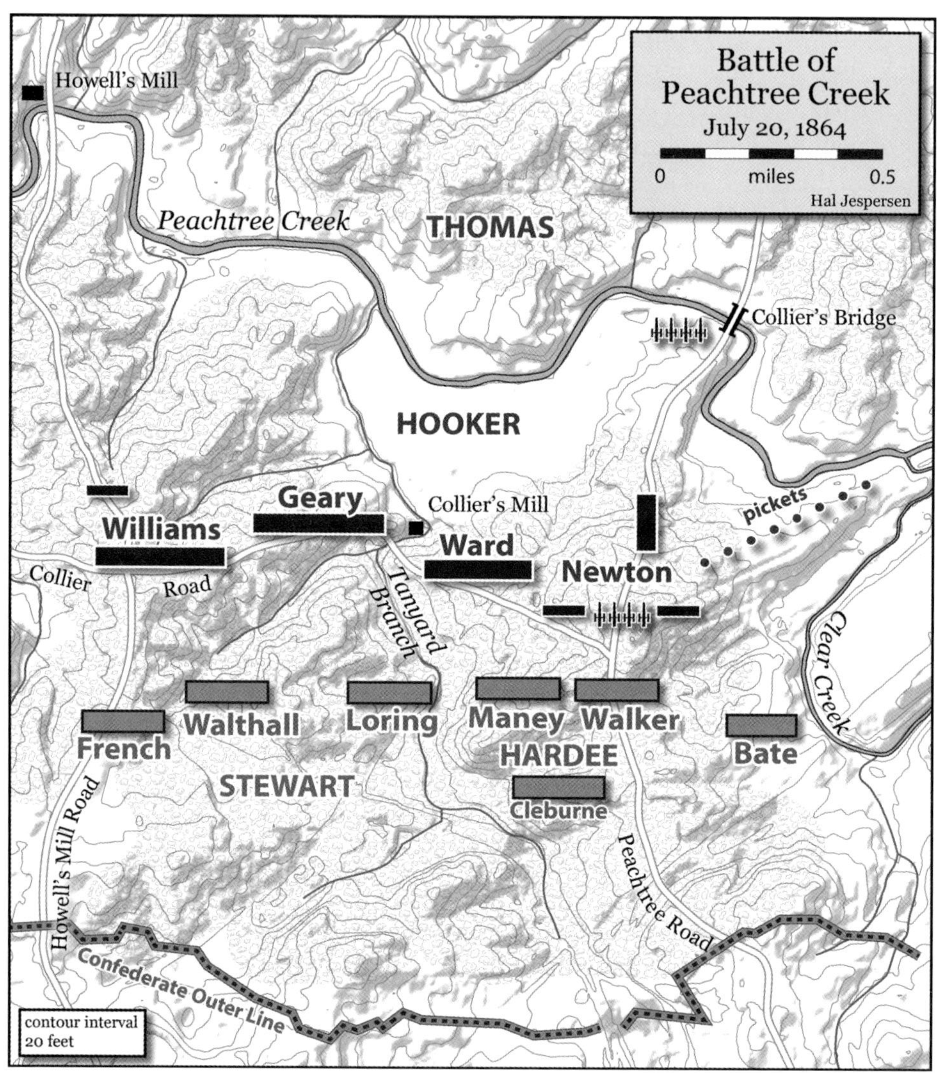

to another "to meet some exigency." Despite overlapping the enemy line, Hardee failed to take advantage of the situation. He kept Cleburne in reserve throughout the entire assault and did nothing about Maney's and Walker's reluctant advances. Both Maney and Walker engaged with only half of their divisions. Moreover, according to Newton, Walker's initial advance posed the only significant threat to his fragile line.[20]

20 *O.R.* vol. 38, pt. 1, 298–299; Castel, *Decision in the West*, 376, 381.

Both Newton's and Hardee's losses demonstrate that Hardee's attack was poorly managed and mounted with little energy. Newton suffered only 102 casualties during the engagement. In comparison, Federal losses against Stewart's assault amounted to about 1,600, indicating a significantly more aggressive advance. Hardee's casualties are more difficult to calculate, as only Maney provided official returns, reporting a loss of 277 men. Assuming that Walker suffered a similar rate of loss and accounting for some losses to Bate's division as a result of artillery fire, Hardee's Corps could not have sustained more than 1,000 casualties, and quite possibly much less. That figure represented less than ten percent of Hardee's force, an uncommonly low number for an assaulting column. Not until 6:00 p.m. did Hardee instruct Cleburne to prepare for an advance against Newton's position. Cleburne's attack, however, was called off when McPherson advanced from the direction of Decatur, and Wheeler appealed for reinforcements. Hardee sent Cleburne, and the assault on the Union position along Peachtree Creek ended in Confederate failure.[21]

Hardee had been granted a great opportunity when the realignment of his corps meant that his line extended beyond the enemy's left flank. Instead of taking advantage of the circumstances, Hardee had complained vociferously about the delays and worried that the enemy was in the process of building imposing breastworks. According to Hood, Hardee became so concerned with the prospect of attacking fortifications that while riding along his lines in the company of Patrick Cleburne, he proclaimed that the column should "be on the lookout for breastworks." Hood claimed that Cleburne had informed him of Hardee's statement several days after the assault. Unfortunately, Cleburne was killed at the battle of Franklin and left no written account of his meeting with Hood, so it is not possible to verify Hood's assertion. Still, considering the ferocity of Stewart's attack, Hardee's lethargic performance comports with the proposition that he told his subordinates to advance with caution and avoid strongly constructed defensive works.[22]

Some of Hardee's men also believed that their commander had acted too cautiously. Lieutenant W. L. Trask, serving as a courier for Hardee, dryly observed that "Stewart captured some 200 prisoners, Hardee not more than 20." A. J. Neal was dumbfounded by Hardee's lack of aggression and complained that "our troops advanced within 15 paces of the Yankee works and could have taken them

21 *O.R.* vol. 38, pt. 1, 299; Castel, *Decision in the West*, 380–381, 378; Hughes, *General William J. Hardee*, 222–223.

22 Hughes, *General William J. Hardee*, 221; Hood, *Advance and Retreat*, 185–186. Loring's division lost over 1,000 men in the attack. See Castel, *Decision in the West*, 381.

but the order was countermanded and we remained for three hours." News of Hardee's passivity during the attack reached headquarters that night, and Thomas Mackall recorded that "Hardee does not think [it] proper to attack [the] enemies strong works."[23]

William Hardee's disgust at Hood's elevation to army command clearly influenced his behavior during the battle of Peachtree Creek and cost the Confederates a chance at a substantial victory. John Newton admitted that the initial assault menaced the entire right wing of Sherman's army. If he had advanced with zeal and delivered "a bold and persistent attack" as Hood had instructed, Newton's position could easily have been turned and exposed the entire Federal force south of Peachtree Creek.[24] Hardee enjoyed the advantage of position and numbers as he faced only one Union division. Yet he let pride overcome him and displayed little energy in carrying out Hood's plan. Hardee's actions at Peachtree Creek conflicted with the past performances that had earned him the sobriquet "Old Reliable." The most reasonable explanation for the transformation in Hardee's demeanor was that he resented Davis for Hood's appointment and believed that Bragg had engineered the change in command at his expense.

Some historians, including Richard McMurry and Thomas Connelly, have found fault with Hood's handling of the affair. Connelly suggested that Hood was absent from the field, having returned to Atlanta, and was therefore unable to coordinate matters on the front. In support of this contention, Connelly cites communications from army headquarters, located in Atlanta, as proof that Hood had returned to the city. The communications from headquarters were signed by William Mackall, still serving as the army's chief of staff after Johnston's removal. While that does not exclude Hood's presence at army headquarters on the afternoon of July 20, the diary of Thomas Mackall does. The younger Mackall noted at the beginning of the battle that Hood was at Stewart's headquarters on Pace Ferry Road and, consequently, near the battlefield.[25]

Richard McMurry asserted that, while Hood had developed a good plan, his failure to maintain a tight control of the army by properly supervising troop deployments influenced the outcome of the battle. McMurry suggested that Hood

23 Trask Diary, July 21, 1864, KNBL; Neal to Father, July 20, 1864, KNBL; Mackall Diary, July 20, 1864, JP WM.

24 *O.R.* vol. 38, pt. 1, 298. Most historians agree that Hardee's poor management of his sector was the primary reason for the Confederate defeat at Peachtree Creek. See Castel, *Decision in the West*, 382–383; Connelly, *Autumn of Glory*, 443; McMurry, *John Bell Hood and the War for Southern Independence*, 128–130.

25 Connelly, *Autumn of Glory*, 443, 441; *O.R.* vol. 38, pt. 5, 895–897; Mackall Diary, July 20, 1864, JP WM.

should have personally overseen Cheatham's deployment toward the railroad because Cheatham was new to command. Yet Cheatham had not been charged with making an assault, as was the case with his other two corps. Stewart had assumed his new responsibilities less than two weeks before and if any of the three corps commanders needed guidance, he was the obvious candidate. Accordingly, Hood traveled to Stewart's headquarters in anticipation of the attack. Presumably Hood could have gone into Atlanta to oversee Cheatham's maneuver, but there was no reason to suspect that conducting a march would be overly complicated. In fact, the irregular progress of Cheatham's corps that afternoon was likely the product of McPherson's activities, which required Cheatham to move further right whenever McPherson moved in that direction.[26]

McMurry also argued that Hood should have supervised Hardee more closely.[27] Hood was undoubtedly aware that Hardee harbored resentment for having been passed over for command of the army. Yet for Hood to have spent time at Hardee's headquarters rather than Stewart's could only have incensed Hardee further. After all, he was the army's senior corps commander and Hood's presence would have added insult to injury. Thus, Hood had developed a plan that should have worked; Hardee's refusal to follow explicit orders was not something that Hood could control.

During July 21 McPherson advanced along the railroad between Decatur and Atlanta, pushing Cleburne's division and Wheeler's cavalry. Cleburne characterized his defense against McPherson as "the bitterest" of his career. Throughout the day working parties from Stewart's and Cheatham's corps constructed a new defensive line closer to the city. By the close of the day McPherson had captured and held Bald Hill and positioned a battery of artillery on its crest capable of shelling the streets of Atlanta.[28] Federal possession of Bald Hill made a Confederate defense of the city more difficult. Hood, therefore, developed a new plan designed to evict McPherson from his position.

Hood summoned his corps commanders to headquarters, including Wheeler and militia commander Gustavus Smith, and explained his plan. He ordered Stewart, Cheatham, and Smith to occupy the newly constructed line of entrenchments and to improve them to the best of their ability. Hood instructed

26 McMurry, *John Bell Hood and the War for Southern Independence*, 129; Mackall Diary, July 20, 1864, JP WM; Roy, "General Hardee and the Military Operations around Atlanta," 348, 353.

27 McMurry, *John Bell Hood and the War for Southern Independence*, 129–130.

28 Buck, *Cleburne and his Command*, 233; Hood, *Advance and Retreat*, 176; *O.R.* vol. 38, pt. 3, 544; Connelly, *Autumn of Glory*, 444; McMurry, *John Bell Hood and the War for Southern Independence*, 130.

Francis Shoup, in charge of the artillery, to mass his guns on the Confederate right. He directed Hardee to withdraw his corps from its present position after dusk. Hardee would then march "south on the McDonough Road, across Entrenchment Creek at Cobb's Mill and completely turn the left of McPherson's army, and attack at daylight, or as soon thereafter as possible." Hood suggested that Hardee might have to march as far as Decatur to maneuver beyond McPherson's flank. Lastly, he instructed Wheeler to guide Hardee's march and then to advance on the right of Hardee's Corps once the assault commenced. Cheatham would then continue the attack when Hardee succeeded in driving in the Federal flank, thereby throwing the enemy into confusion.[29]

The strategy was bold, and if conducted with energy, offered an opportunity to crush McPherson's entire force. Thomas, with the largest army under Sherman's command, remained separated from McPherson and Schofield, making it difficult for him to assist against any Confederate attack on the Union left. Whether Hardee was the proper man for the job is open to debate. Hood later reasoned that Cheatham was too unseasoned as a corps commander to trust with the maneuver and that Stewart was too far away and had not yet had time to recover from his attack at Peachtree Creek. Hardee, much to Hood's chagrin, had not been heavily engaged on July 20 and Cleburne was already in the vicinity of the starting point for the intended march. Hood's rationale makes sense, although Cleburne's division had fought throughout the day and was worn out.[30]

In addition to the plan's reliance on the truculent Hardee, Hood's strategy suffered from two other potential flaws. First, he was apparently unaware of the extremely difficult terrain over which the assault would progress. In the open fields of the Eastern theater of operations, similar tactics had produced magnificent results, including Hood's own assault at the battle of Second Manassas. According to the men who advanced on McPherson's position on July 22, they encountered "one vast densely set thicket," and "impassable undergrowth," that prevented visibility over fifty yards. At Cobb's Mill a local farmer also informed Hardee that a millpond a half mile long and ten feet deep was to his front.[31] Even so, Stonewall Jackson's charge through the dense underbrush near Chancellorsville had resulted in one of the most spectacular victories of the war. The rough terrain, while difficult to traverse, also meant that the enemy would not be able to fire upon the advancing Confederates until they were within a short distance of the Union lines.

29 Hood, *Advance and Retreat*, 177.

30 Hood, *Advance and Retreat*, 176,174; *O.R.* vol. 38, pt. 3, 737, 747

31 *O.R.* vol. 38, pt. 3, 731, 737; Buck, *Cleburne and his Command*, 235.

A second potential problem was the distance the line of march would cover before Hardee reached McPherson's rear. Estimates ranged from six miles to as many as eighteen. Participants in the affair were equally divergent in their assessment. W. L. Trask claimed that at dawn the troops were only six miles outside Atlanta, while Irving Buck asserted that the march had been at least fifteen miles. The widely differing calculations are further proof that the Confederate high command operated with a disparate set of maps, which had the potential to generate confusion and, ultimately, distrust. The actual distance of the march as it was initially planned, according to a local resident familiar with the roads, was fourteen or fifteen miles.[32] Consequently, the movement required that Hardee begin soon after dark if he hoped to reach the designated location by dawn.

The movement did not start until midnight. As Hardee's Corps began marching south through the city the citizens panicked, believing that the army was in the process of abandoning the city. Wheeler's cavalry exacerbated the chaos when they raided the principal storehouses and "gutted them completely," taking "rations, cigars and whiskey." Troops from Hardee's Corps participated in the mayhem, gulping down large quantities of whiskey as they ransacked the town. The citizenry responded with the "greatest alarm" and fled south, obstructing the roads in that direction. Hardee apparently made little effort to contain the bedlam, and the following morning his corps was bedecked with "fancy ornaments" of all sorts including "brass and porcelain doorknobs."[33]

Though Hardee did nothing to prevent his troop's disorderly behavior, he seems to have recognized that the plan as originally designed could not succeed; it was impossible to march to Decatur by the route indicated within the allotted time frame. He therefore met with Hood and Cheatham to revise the plan. Hardee argued that his men were much fatigued, having had little rest for thirty-six hours, and that he should be permitted to shorten his route and strike the enemy in the flank, rather than marching all the way to Decatur. After the war Hood claimed that he refused the alteration. At least two accounts of the meeting, however, contend that Hood granted Hardee's request. William Mackall asserted that owing to the "lateness of the hour, the distance to be traveled and the condition of the troops,

32 Hood, *Advance and Retreat*, 178; McMurry, *John Bell Hood and the War for Southern Independence*, 131. A direct march between Atlanta and Decatur along the railroad comprised a distance of approximately six miles. See Buck, *Cleburne and his Command*, 235; Trask Diary, July 24, 1864, KNBL; Buck, *Cleburne and his Command*, 235; Stephen Davis suggests that the Confederate knowledge of the topography around Atlanta was limited and that Hood possessed neither "adequate cavalry reconnaissance [nor] expert maps on hand." See Davis, *Atlanta Will Fall*, 140–141; Roy, "General Hardee and the Military Operations around Atlanta," 356.

33 Trask Diary, July 24, 1864, KNBL.

it was finally determined that General Hardee should make the assault on the flank and the rear of McPherson." Cheatham also recalled that Hood consented to allow Hardee to "make the assault on the flank and rear of McPherson," without requiring that the column reach Decatur prior to its attack.[34]

With the modification to the plan agreed upon, Hardee embarked on his mission. The revision meant that he would need to travel a shorter distance, perhaps twelve or thirteen miles, but under the time constraints the march needed to be conducted with alacrity. Considering the fatigue of most of his men, it is not surprising that Bate's division, the first in line, did not arrive at its destination until well after daylight. Further, Wheeler's cavalry troopers continued their disruptive behavior, cutting in and out of Hardee's column and impeding their progress. Soon after dawn Hardee halted his column. While the troops rested and drew additional ammunition, Hardee met with Wheeler and his divisional commanders. Wheeler informed Hardee that his scouts reported no enemy forces between his present position at Cobb's Mill and Decatur. Local civilians confirmed Wheeler's claim and Hardee issued instructions to prepare for battle.[35] He then sent a messenger to Hood alerting him that the attack would begin shortly.

Hardee, however, did not advance with his corps for several hours. Instead, his men rested and cooked breakfast while Cleburne's division brought up the rear of the column. As he waited for the arrival of Cleburne's weary men, Hardee positioned Bate's division on the east side of Sugar Creek. To Bate's left and on the west side of the creek, Hardee placed Walker's division. Cleburne's division, then moving along Flat Shoals Road, would fall in next to Walker on the east side of the road with Maney's division formed to the west.[36]

Hardee's alignment, as at Peachtree Creek, deserves criticism. This time Bate's position made sense. With Bate further east than any of the other divisions, it was unlikely that he would encounter a strongly posted enemy, and if all went well he would strike McPherson's rear. The decision to place all four divisions abreast, however, meant that Hardee would have no reserve available. Thomas Connelly suggested that Hardee elected to employ his troops in one line because he was unaware of the precise location of the enemy and wanted to be sure that his force extended beyond the Federal flank. While it is true that Hardee remained ignorant of McPherson's exact position, the intelligence he received during his conference with Wheeler at daybreak meant that he was fairly certain that he had

34 Davis, *Atlanta Will Fall*, 140; T. B. Roy to Mackall, Oct. 15, 1881, UNC.

35 Castel, *Decision in the West*, 389; Roy, "General Hardee and the Military Operations around Atlanta," 365, 359; Castel, *Decision in the West*, 391.

36 Davis, *Atlanta Will Fall*, 143; Castel, *Decision in the West*, 391.

reached the Union rear. Consequently, there was no need to expend valuable time on the extension of his lines. Moreover, the alignment required that he wait for Cleburne's arrival and his subsequent deployment into line of battle. Whether he was purposely dragging his feet or permitting his anger to overcome his strategic sense is unknown. Hardee should have started forward with the three divisions available to him during the mid-morning hours and used Cleburne as a reserve force. Instead, he lingered until after 11:00 a.m. waiting for Cleburne's deployment before moving forward. The tangled terrain to his front further delayed the advance and the assault did not begin until sometime between 12:30 and 1:30 p.m.[37] By the time Hardee finally made contact with the Federal left, Sherman's dispositions had changed dramatically.

When the sun rose on July 22, Sherman realized that the Confederates had withdrawn to their new defensive works closer to Atlanta. He therefore ordered his own troops to advance, a maneuver that allowed him to concentrate his lines as well. The advance meant that Grenville Dodge's Corps was no longer needed in its present location and Sherman decided to send it to Decatur to break up the railroad there. Later that morning Sherman encountered McPherson and the two discussed their expectations of Hood. Both agreed that he would be aggressive and McPherson requested that Dodge move to the rear of his own corps and form facing east to protect his flank and rear. McPherson suggested that the pioneers could be sent in Dodge's stead to Decatur to dismantle the railroad. Sherman agreed and ordered Dodge's Corps to redeploy on McPherson's flank.[38]

Just as Hardee's Corps burst through the underbrush, marshes, and briar patches southeast of McPherson's line of entrenchments, Thomas Sweeney's and John Fuller's divisions of Dodge's Corps deployed in their path. As a result, an assault that was designed to strike the enemy's flank and rear collided head-on with two Union divisions and a battery of artillery. Bate's division engaged the foe for a few minutes until canister from the Federal guns swept the Confederate lines and his men once again fled the scene, ending their participation in the assault. With Bate's departure, the strength of both sides was fairly even. The Confederates, of course, had endured a long night march and nearly impenetrable terrain before the opening shots. Nevertheless, Hardee's men fought gallantly but were unable to gain ground on the enemy. Though they relentlessly battered the Federal position, the Confederate advance was piecemeal. Further, the thickets impaired alignment, which meant that the Rebel brigades moved forward unevenly and the attacks

37 Connelly, *Autumn of Glory*, 448; Buck, *Cleburne and his Command*, 235; Mackall Diary, July 22, 1864, JP WM.

38 Sherman, *Memoirs of General W. T. Sherman*, 548–549.

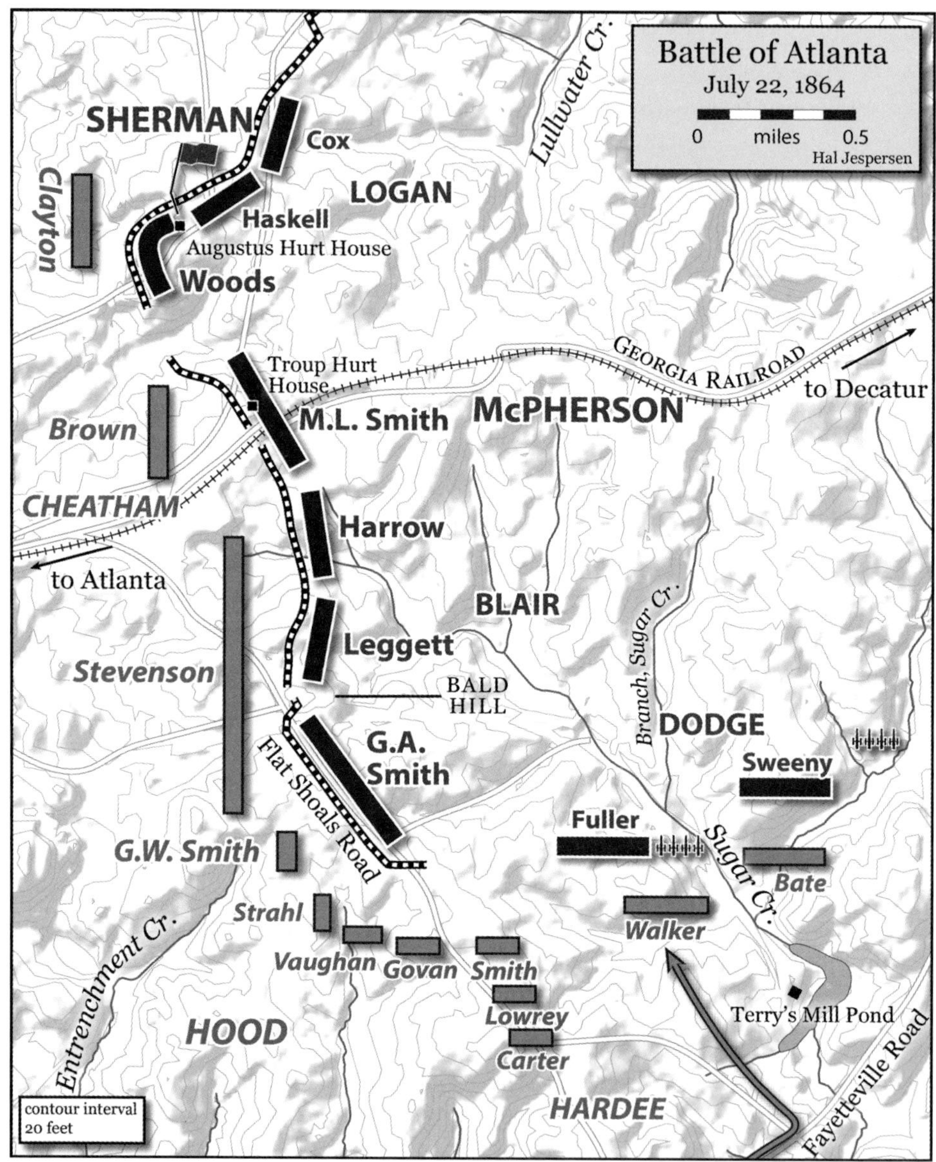

were consequently disjointed. Even brigade commanders lost contact with much of their command, making the attack more difficult.[39]

At two o'clock Hood rode from army headquarters to Cheatham's line in expectation of Hardee's success, which would give him the opportunity to order

39 Roy, "General Hardee and the Military Operations around Atlanta," 363; Castel, *Decision in the West*, 396–397; *O.R.* vol. 38, pt. 3, 731.

Cheatham's advance. One hour later a staff officer dispatched by Hood returned with news that Hardee had been checked. Fearing Hardee's destruction, Hood ordered Shoup's 64-gun battery to open fire and directed Cheatham to prepare for advance after the barrage. Hood apparently hoped that Cheatham's Corps could save Hardee from annihilation. He then returned to headquarters in Atlanta, believing that the assault had failed. Soon thereafter, however, Hood received a dispatch that Hardee was "driving the enemy capturing guns and prisoners." Hood immediately ordered Cheatham to advance and exploit the breakthrough.[40]

Hardee's troops had finally managed to exploit the gap between Fuller's right flank and McPherson's left flank. Unfortunately for the Confederates, Cheatham's attack was as uncoordinated as Hardee's had been. John C. Brown, whom Braxton Bragg had elevated to divisional command earlier in the month, spoiled any chance for Confederate success. Brown issued contradictory and confusing orders to brigade commanders in his own division as well as Clayton's. Two of Brown's brigades, under Arthur Manigault and Jacob Sharp, managed to break through the Union defenses about three quarters of a mile north of Bald Hill, but Brown ordered them to retreat. Thereafter, Brown changed his mind and instructed them to retake the position, which they accomplished. Facing a counterattack from the Northerners, Manigault sent repeated requests for reinforcements. Brown commandeered two brigades from Clayton's division and directed them to Manigault's aid. In doing so, he diverted two brigades that were en route to strike Bald Hill in support of Hardee's attack. Consequently, with no Confederate pressure from the west of Bald Hill, McPherson's men were able to direct their attention solely on Hardee. The two forces engaged in a savage confrontation until nightfall that often degenerated into hand-to-hand combat. By nightfall the Confederates were forced to call off the attack and return to their lines.[41]

The Federals later recognized that they had been fortunate in their repulse of the Confederate assault. They had been completely unaware of Hardee's flanking maneuver and the Confederates were able to approach "quite near" the Union line before they were discovered. General Blair, in command of McPherson's left flank, observed that only when a division of Dodge's Corps engaged with Hardee's men did he realize that "my whole position had been turned." He further commented that "the position taken up accidentally by the Sixteenth Corps [Dodge] prevented the full force of the blow from falling where it was intended to fall." According to

40 Mackall Diary, July 22, 1864, JP WM; Castel, *Decision in the West*, 404.

41 Castel, *Decision in the West*, 406–410; Arthur Manigault, *A Carolinian Goes to War: The Civil War Narrative of Arthur Middleton Manigault, Brigadier General, C.S.A.*, ed. R. Lockwood Tower (Columbia, SC, 1983), 225–229; Mackall Diary, July 22, 1864, JP WM.

Orlando Poe, "the enemy succeeded in passing around our left flank and attacked the 17th AC [Army Corps] in rear. The movement was handsomely made and was very nearly successful." Only Dodge's arrival, noted Poe, secured the safety of McPherson's flank.[42]

The Confederate failure at the battle of Bald Hill was the product of Hardee's sluggishness and, to a lesser extent, Brown's incompetence. Both, it should be noted, were the result of Bragg's meddling in the affairs of his former army. Hardee, still simmering from the administration's appointment of Hood, performed his assignment with minimal conviction. He began his march much later than Hood's initial instructions required. Afterwards, he made only desultory efforts to end the mayhem wrought in Atlanta by plundering troops. Even so, he arrived with most of his corps at a point beyond McPherson's flank soon after dawn. Understandably, the troops needed time to deploy into line of battle and perhaps a brief rest after their arduous march. Assuming a three- or four-hour respite, the troops should have been in motion toward McPherson's flank and rear by 9 or 10 o'clock in the morning. Allowing for the difficulty of the terrain, the assault ought to have emerged on McPherson's rear by 11:30 a.m., well in advance of Dodge's arrival on the Union flank. Brown mismanaged the deployment of his own troops as well as those of Clayton's division, a calamity that prevented the exploitation of Hardee's success in finding the gap between Dodge and McPherson. Thus, despite a plan worthy of Jackson and Lee at Chancellorsville, Hood had failed for a second time to crush a divided wing of Sherman's army. The battle cost the Confederates approximately 5,500 casualties, 3,300 of them to Hardee's Corps. Union losses, meanwhile, amounted to 3,722, increasing the disparity in numbers between the two armies.[43]

Less than a week later the disparity in troop strength became more profound when S. D. Lee mishandled affairs near Ezra Church. The administration had decided to appoint Lee to command Hood's former corps, thereby replacing Cheatham who returned to his division. On July 27 Hood learned that Sherman was disengaging from the right of the Confederate line and threatening the left. As a result, he decided to send Lee to Lick Skillet Road west of Ezra Church to prevent Federal seizure of the railroad at East Point. (See South of the Chattahoochee map.) He instructed Lee to halt and entrench at Ezra Church, facing north. Stewart's Corps was then to move behind Lee and establish a position to his left. Hood hoped that Lee could hold his position against the Federal advance on

42 Sherman, *Memoirs of W. T. Sherman*, 553; Roy, "General Hardee and the Military Operations around Atlanta," 363; Poe Diary, July 22, 1864, LC.

43 Hood, *Advance and Retreat*, 177; Beatty Diary, July 23, 1864, UNC; Roy, "General Hardee and the Military Operations around Atlanta," 367; Castel, *Decision in the West*, 412; *O.R.* vol. 38, pt. 3, 28.

July 28 and that Stewart could then strike the union column in the flank the next morning when the Northerners resumed their attack.[44] The plan resembled Lee's masterpiece at the battle of Second Manassas, when Jackson defended against a Union frontal assault until Longstreet, with Hood in the lead, assailed the Federal left flank and drove the northerners from the field in disarray.

On the following day, S. D. Lee approached the junction of Lick Skillet Road and Marietta Pike near Ezra Church only to find McPherson's army already in control of the crossroads. (See Battle of Ezra Church map.) Lee, inexperienced as a corps commander, did not seek Hood's guidance. Rather he launched a frontal attack against the entrenched enemy. Howard, in command of the Federal force, had faced Wheeler's cavalry all morning and believed that their strong presence in the area meant that the Confederates intended to attack him with infantry. Lee's piecemeal assault compounded his rash decision to advance without orders from Hood. John C. Brown's division, the first in the line of march, was repulsed twice and cut to pieces before Lee's second division under Henry Clayton arrived. To make matters worse, when Clayton did appear on the battlefield, his brigades were sent into the fray without any coordination. Lee then convinced Stewart, who had followed him on Lick Skillet Road, to deploy Edward Walthall's division and strike the Union position. Walthall advanced on his own and met the same fate. Lee's uncoordinated and unwise assaults cost the Confederates nearly 3,000 men while Howard's Corps suffered only 632 casualties.[45] Though Hood had crafted yet another admirable plan, his subordinates failed him again.

Some historians have faulted Hood for sending the inexperienced Lee, at the head of two thirds of his army, to thwart Sherman's latest flanking effort while remaining in Atlanta with Hardee's Corps.[46] In reality, Hood had few other options. Hardee had sustained significant casualties at Bald Hill and his performance during the first two battles of Hood's tenure as commander had not been particularly auspicious. Hood's plan had been for Lee to act on the defensive during the 28th, a task suitable for his general new to command. The difficult operation was given to the more seasoned Stewart, who was to deliver the flank attack the next morning. Hood's assignments, in other words, were reasonable. Furthermore, because the

44 *O.R.* vol. 38, pt. 5, 912–913; *O.R.* vol. 38, pt. 3, 632, 762, 872; Castel, *Decision in the West*, 426; Davis, *Atlanta Will Fall*, 150–151; McMurry, *John Bell Hood and the War for Southern Independence*; Connelly, *Autumn of Glory*, 453.

45 Davis, *Atlanta Will Fall*, 151; *O.R.* vol. 38, pt. 3, 723–724, 767–768, 776, 781–782, 785–786, 789–790, 799-800, 821; Castel, *Decision in the West*, 434.

46 McMurry, *John Bell Hood and the War for Southern Independence*, 134; Davis, *Atlanta Will Fall*, 153; Connelly, *Autumn of Glory*, 454.

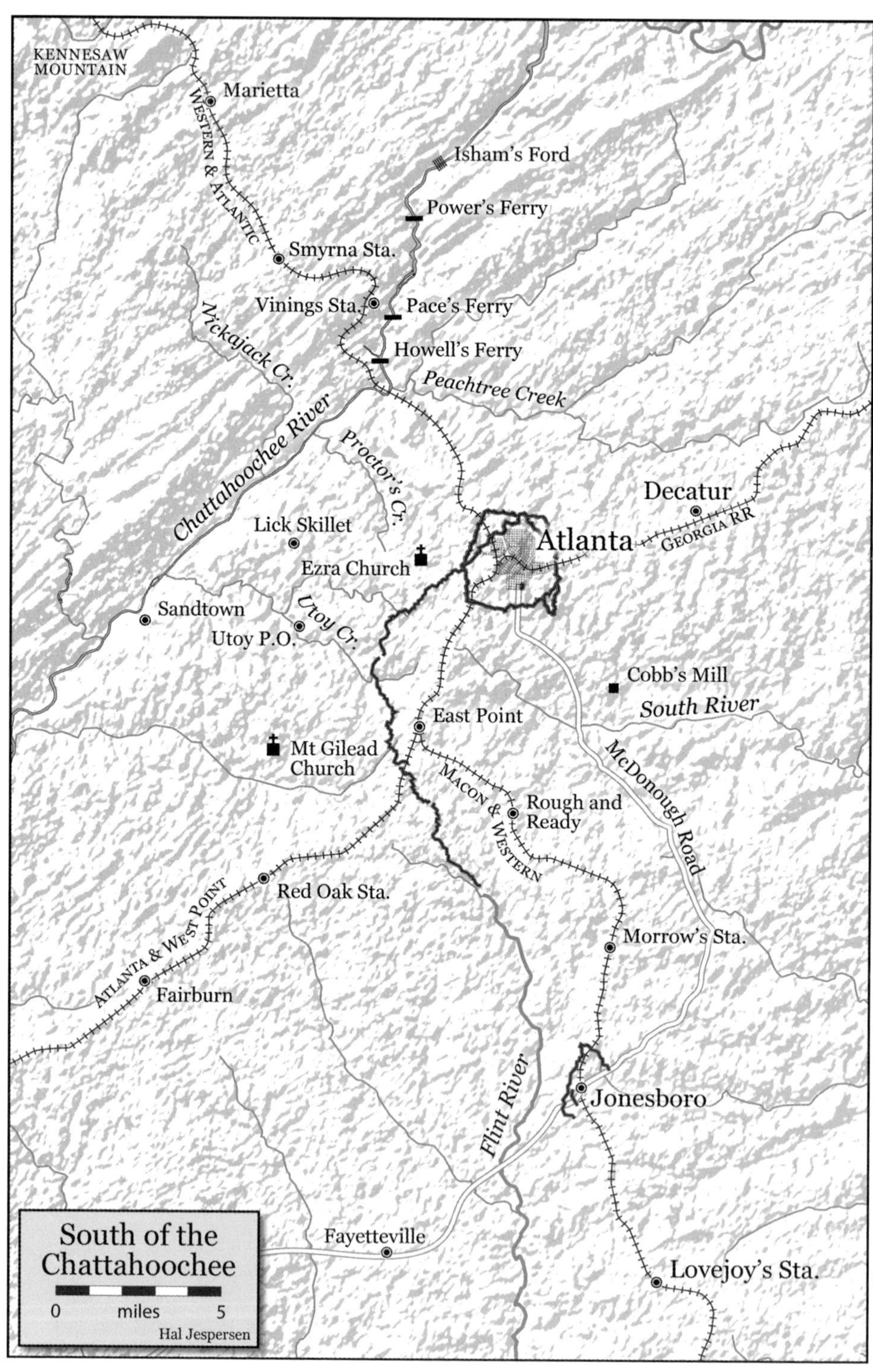
KENNESAW MOUNTAIN
Marietta
WESTERN & ATLANTIC
Isham's Ford
Power's Ferry
Smyrna Sta.
Vinings Sta.
Pace's Ferry
Howell's Ferry
Nickajack Cr.
Peachtree Creek
Chattahoochee River
Proctor's Cr.
Decatur
Lick Skillet
Atlanta
GEORGIA RR
Ezra Church
Sandtown
Utoy Cr.
Utoy P.O.
Cobb's Mill
South River
East Point
Mt Gilead Church
McDonough Road
MACON & WESTERN
Rough and Ready
Red Oak Sta.
Morrow's Sta.
ATLANTA & WEST POINT
Fairburn
Flint River
Jonesboro
Fayetteville
Lovejoy's Sta.
South of the Chattahoochee
0 miles 5
Hal Jespersen

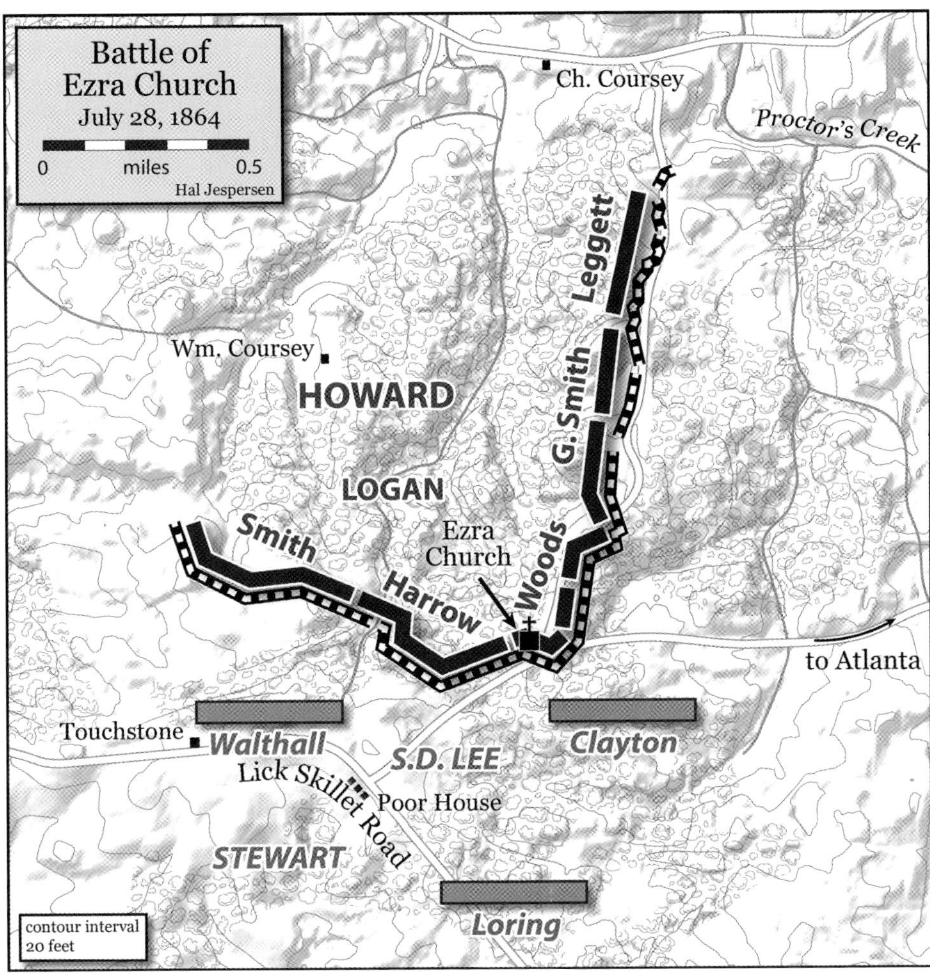

crucial element of his plan was not set to occur until the morning of July 29, Hood's presence at Ezra Church on the 28th was not necessary.

Despite his loss at Ezra Church, Hood succeeded in resisting Sherman's attempt to gain East Point and destroy the last rail line supplying Atlanta. Thereafter, the armies settled into a siege that lasted a little over a month. Both sides slowly extended their trenches, Sherman aiming toward East Point. Though in hindsight historians have recognized that Hood had been defeated in each of the engagements at the end of July, many in the army believed otherwise and their spirits remained high.[47]

47 McMurry, *John Bell Hood and the War for Southern Independence*, 135; McMurry, "Confederate Morale in the Atlanta Campaign of 1864," 235–239.

While the armies remained mostly static, Hood and Hardee attempted to convince Davis to permit Hardee's transfer. Bragg had wired the president on July 27 that Hood and Hardee were not compatible and that perhaps Hardee could be exchanged with Richard Taylor serving in the Trans-Mississippi. Hardee renewed the request on August 3, pleading "I rely upon your kindness to relieve me from an unpleasant position." The following day, the president responded: "I regret that your position is felt to be so unpleasant, you need no assurance that no wound was intended." Undeterred, on August 6 Hardee again requested that Davis relieve him from the "personally humiliating" assignment, an appeal that was "due an old soldier who has faithfully endeavored to perform his duty." Davis refused and Hardee stayed with the Army of Tennessee. Clearly, Hardee remained incensed at being passed over for command. In fairness to Davis, the president had few options available to him. As he observed in his August 5 communication with Hood, Hardee was a native Georgian and had excellent knowledge of the country in which the army was then operating.[48] Furthermore, the Confederates were running out of experienced officers and Hardee had served with the army for most of the war.

With Sherman slowly entrenching toward East Point, Hood decided that it was time for Wheeler to make a raid against Sherman's supply line. He ordered Wheeler to take half of the army's cavalry, about 5,000 troopers, and destroy the railroad to Sherman's rear. He hoped that Wheeler would do as much damage as he could in a few days and then return to the army. Considering Wheeler's abysmal performance since Sherman advanced against the Confederate position at Dalton, the decision was imprudent. Indeed, Wheeler behaved as he had throughout most of the campaign and accomplished virtually nothing. He set off on August 10 and did minimal damage to the railroad between Atlanta and Chattanooga. Afterwards, he inexplicably took his column north of Knoxville and then rode into middle Tennessee. He did not return to the army for more than a month, and his absence deprived Hood of sufficient cavalry to stay informed about Sherman's activity.[49]

Wheeler's absence allowed Sherman to embark on another flanking maneuver west of Atlanta and to strike Jonesboro, a town through which Hood's sole rail line ran. Confederate scouts discovered that Sherman had evacuated his trenches north and east of Atlanta on August 26. At first Hood believed that Wheeler had accomplished his task and forced Sherman to retreat. Soon, however, the Confederates learned that Wheeler had failed and had "gone into middle Tennessee

48 *The Papers of Jefferson Davis*, X:566, 584; *O.R.* vol. 38, pt. 5, 988; *The Papers of Jefferson Davis*, X:586.

49 McMurry, *John Bell Hood and the War for Southern Independence* 144–145.

without doing Sherman's rear much harm." Hood was entirely uncertain as to what had become of Sherman's forces that had been entrenched north and east of Atlanta. By August 27, Hood discovered the Federals in force on his left and concluded that Sherman had determined to strike the Macon & Western Railroad. The following day he strengthened his defenses at East Point accordingly. Also on the 28th, Hood instructed Brown's division to depart for Rough and Ready. Still unsure of Sherman's intentions on August 30, Hood ordered Hardee to "take whatever measures you may think necessary to prevent the enemy from reaching Jonesboro or Rough and Ready."[50] Considering the distances between East Point, Rough and Ready, and Jonesboro, it is apparent that Hood remained completely in the dark as to Sherman's intentions. Without adequate cavalry he could only guess at the enemy's destination.

On August 31 at three o'clock in the morning, Hood wired Hardee that he "must not fail to attack the enemy as soon as you can get your troops up." That afternoon, Hardee assailed John Logan's Corps that had crossed the Flint River and had established a line about a mile northwest of Jonesboro with his own corps as well as Lee's whom he had taken with him. The attack did not go well, but Hardee was not responsible for its failure. Some of Cleburne's usually stout division became concerned with Union cavalry on their left flank. They diverted from their attack and drove westward against meager opposition. As a result, the Confederate assault on the Union right lost steam and petered out. Soon after, the attack on the Federal center and left also suffered repulse. In the end, the battle proved the most lopsided of the entire campaign with a Confederate loss of 2,200 men compared to only 172 Northern casualties.[51]

That night Hood ordered Lee to return to East Point, believing that Sherman intended to strike the city the next day. If Hood had known the location of Sherman's entire force he would not have instructed Lee to march back to East Point. On the night of August 31, Sherman had six army corps between Jonesboro and East Point. The following day, with Hood's men widely dispersed, Sherman concentrated on Hardee at Jonesboro. Hardee defended his position all afternoon against repeated assaults. By nightfall, however, Hardee was compelled to retreat to Lovejoy's Station to the south. With his only supply route into Atlanta broken and Hardee South of Jonesboro, Hood was compelled to withdraw from Atlanta and reunite the army at Lovejoy's Station. On September 2, Sherman attempted

50 McMurry, *John Bell Hood and the War for Southern Independence* 146–147; Trask Diary, July 26, 1864, KNBL; Hood, *Advance and Retreat*, 203; *O.R.* vol. 38, pt. 5, 997–998, 1000.

51 *O.R.* vol. 38, pt. 5, 1005; Castel, *Decision in the West*, 502–503; Davis, *Atlanta Will Fall*, 184–185.

to destroy Hardee's Corps once again, but "Old Reliable" lived up to his nickname and fended off the Union attack. Finally, on the morning of September 3, Hood reached Lovejoy's Station with Stewart and Lee. Sherman, satisfied that he had compelled the Confederates to abandon Atlanta, withdrew from Hood's front and occupied the city, thereby ending the campaign.[52]

Jefferson Davis had allowed his friendship with Braxton Bragg to cloud his decision when he relieved Joseph E. Johnston from command of the Army of Tennessee. The president had intended that if Johnston must be removed, Hardee should be his replacement. He should have realized that Bragg's long-standing feud with Hardee made him the wrong candidate for the mission. Nevertheless, Davis permitted Bragg to steer him toward the promotion of John Bell Hood without considering the ramifications of the decision. As a result, William Hardee's resentment over the president's decision influenced the outcome of Hood's defense of Atlanta. Despite relatively high morale among the troops and Hood's well-designed plans, Hardee's bitterness cost the Confederates victories on July 20 and July 22. Then on July 28, S. D. Lee demonstrated his inexperience when he attacked Oliver Howard at Ezra Church without seeking Hood's direction. Hood erred when he sent the incompetent Joseph Wheeler on a raid against Sherman's supply route. Without adequate cavalry Hood lost track of Sherman's army, which ultimately resulted in Hardee's defeat at Jonesboro. Overall, Hood performed well after assuming command of the army, but his subordinates' behaviors, particularly Hardee's, undermined his ability to defend the Gate City. Hardee's conduct must have been a particularly bitter pill for Hood to swallow, considering the manner in which he had achieved command of the army.

52 *O.R.* vol. 38, pt. 5, 1007–1008; McMurry, *John Bell Hood and the War for Southern Independence*, 148, 148–149; Davis, *Atlanta Will Fall*, 191.

Conclusion

Despite the Southern deficit in manpower and industrial capacity, the Confederacy assembled substantial armies in both Virginia and Georgia in 1864. Moreover, the Confederate armies were adequately armed and supplied as the campaign season commenced. In January 1864 the Confederacy had good reason to believe that a successful conclusion to the war might still be achieved, but the loss of Atlanta in September all but sealed its fate. Consequently, the Atlanta campaign proved to be the final turning point of the conflict and demonstrated Jefferson Davis's primary weaknesses as a commander-in-chief. Davis's willingness to allow his personal feelings for other members of the Confederate high command to affect his judgment played a key role in the outcome of Sherman's advance against the Gate City. In fact, the president's poor relationship with Joseph E. Johnston inspired his appointment of John Bell Hood to command a corps in Johnston's army with the additional assignment of keeping the administration informed regarding Johnston's handling of the army. In so doing, Davis undermined military protocol and, when the relationship between Hood and Johnston deteriorated in the aftermath of Cassville, resulted in Hood's campaign to secure command of the army for himself. Davis's reliance upon a departmental system rather than a unified command structure exacerbated the fissures within the Confederate hierarchy. The president's departmental design, in combination with his distrust of Johnston, ensured that reinforcements did not reach his general until the Federals had begun their advance, and that Sherman's supply lines remained intact. Though many factors contributed to Southern defeat, Davis's failings as commander-in-chief stood in stark contrast to his counterpart Abraham Lincoln and deserve a prominent role in understanding the Confederate loss of Atlanta and, ultimately, the war.

Davis's penchant for permitting enmity between himself and other members of the high command played a key part in the Army of Tennessee's poor performance at the outset of the campaign. In particular, the president had developed acrimonious relationships with the governor of Georgia, Joseph Brown, and his new commander in the West, Joseph E. Johnston. In both cases the hostility developed over the course of the war, and all the parties—Davis, Johnston, and Brown—bore responsibility for fanning the flames of discontent. By contrast, Lincoln, proved adept at handling difficult personalities while Davis did not. Lincoln's dealings with George McClellan, for example, differed dramatically from Davis's treatment of Johnston and Brown. McClellan's impertinence toward his commander-in-chief became a matter of public record. The general even went so far as to avoid meeting with the president when Lincoln visited headquarters on one occasion. Having been informed of the president's presence upon his return from a social outing, McClellan went to bed. Rather than criticizing his commander, Lincoln simply ignored the affront. Even after McClellan's failure on the Virginia peninsula, Lincoln determined that his talent for organization and his defensive acumen made him the best candidate for the defense of the capital in the aftermath of the Confederate victory at the second battle of Manassas.[1]

Davis, however, lacked Lincoln's ability to move beyond personal grievances. Though Joseph Brown was primarily responsible for the discord between himself and the president, Davis's management of the relationship in the months prior to Sherman's advance proved injudicious. During the first three years of the war, Brown's rigid states' rights ideology led him into conflict with the administration on numerous occasions. At the outset of hostilities, Brown challenged the central government's approach to the recruitment of troops and the appointment of officers. The governor also considered the security of his state paramount to the security of the Confederacy when he competed with the Davis administration for the acquisition of arms and munitions. Brown even demanded the return of state-purchased muskets when an 1861 law permitted the tender of troops directly into Confederate service, thereby bypassing state authorities. The passage of the Conscription Act in 1862 ensured a deeply dysfunctional relationship between the Confederate president and the Georgia governor. Brown responded by exempting all state officers from conscription, which included offices such as constable,

1 Joseph T. Glatthaar, *Partners in Command: The Relationships Between Leaders in the Civil War* (New York, 1994), 63–64; Goodwin, *Team of Rivals*, 479.

public notary, and justices of the peace even though the state had suspended most court activities.

While Davis made a reasonable effort to assuage the governor's anger over the Conscription Act, he amplified the Georgian's hostility when he failed to release the State Guard from duty after the Confederate victory at Chickamauga in September 1863. Brown warned the administration that Georgia's citizens would be unlikely to heed future calls for enlistment into the state militia unless the administration allowed the guardsmen to return to their homes. Brown's pleas underscored his own reticence to assist the central government in any subsequent activation of state militia unless Davis acquiesced to his demands. The president, undoubtedly fatigued by Brown's unrelenting agitation, refused the governor's petition. Instead, Secretary of War James Seddon insisted that the exigent circumstances required the continued service of the State Guard. In reality, the Union retreat after the defeat at Chickamauga meant that Georgia was free from Federal menace. Davis then exacerbated the governor's discontent when he appointed Brown's adversary, Howell Cobb, commander of the newly-established Georgia Reserve Force in 1864. The foreseeable result was that Brown refused the administration's militia calls in the early months of 1864. The lack of militia severely hampered Johnston's defense against Sherman's flanking marches, particularly at Snake Creek Gap, Resaca, and Kennesaw Mountain. The Georgia militia arrived at the front more than a month after the commencement of the campaign and mustered only a fraction of the available manpower. The president's maladroit handling of Brown played a significant role in the Union capture of Atlanta.

Davis's rapport with Joseph E. Johnston was equally unstable. Johnston's antagonism had originated in the dispute over rank that predated the war and intensified when the president ranked him third among the Confederacy's generals. On the Virginia peninsula in 1862, Johnston's distrust of Davis escalated when the administration interfered with the management of forces ostensibly in his department. Nor was Johnston able to secure significant reinforcements from the other Confederate departments, even though he advocated an advance on the Union capital. The episode illustrates Davis's lack of appreciation for a centralized command system. It also shows that Johnston was willing to engage in offensive operations when he deemed the size of his force sufficient for the task. The Vicksburg Campaign and the consequent fallout over blame for the loss of the Mississippi bastion cemented Johnston's negative opinion of Davis. Johnston had proposed a concentration of forces for an offensive against Grant, but the president rejected the plan in deference to Theophilius Holmes, commander of the Trans-Mississippi Department.

Though Davis's hostility toward Johnston emerged only after the commencement of the war, it was no less palpable. The initial signs that the president felt resentment toward his general surfaced after the first battle of Manassas when Johnston complained that Robert E. Lee lacked the authority to give him orders. Davis responded by listing Johnston third among the Confederacy's full generals. The ranking did not comport with the legislation that granted him the power to appoint generals. Johnston's intermittent and incomplete communications during his retreat up the peninsula in 1862 deepened the president's misgivings about his commander. Ultimately, Johnston's unwillingness to assault Grant at Vicksburg embittered the president, who blamed Johnston for the loss of the city. When the disaster at Missionary Ridge forced Davis to seek a replacement for Braxton Bragg, only political pressure from a coalition of pro-Johnston and anti-Davis politicians and soldiers paved the way for Johnston's appointment.

The president continued to allow his personal feelings toward his subordinates to influence his decisions after Johnston took command of the army at Dalton in December 1863. Johnston hoped to reorganize his army in a way that diminished the effects of the political squabbling prevalent during Bragg's tenure as commander. In particular, he sought new corps commanders who had not been involved in the infighting. Davis denied Johnston's recommendations and instead appointed John Bell Hood in February. The appointment of Hood meant that the president ignored talented officers already serving in the Army of Tennessee, including Benjamin Cheatham and Patrick Cleburne. Cheatham and Cleburne were likely the victims of political machinations. Despite Bragg's dreadful record as a commander, Davis's personal affinity for him garnered the general a position as the president's new military advisor. Both Cheatham and Cleburne had been part of the army's anti-Bragg faction, which undoubtedly affected their candidacies.

In selecting Hood, Davis chose a general with an impeccable record as a field commander. Hood's wounds, though severe, resulted neither in psychological handicap nor addiction. Hood's reputation for aggressive action on the battlefield appealed to the president, particularly after he and Johnston could not agree upon a strategy for the spring campaign. The impasse between Davis and Johnston gave the president an additional reason to appoint Hood to corps command. Davis instructed Hood to report on the condition and capability of the army. In so doing he encouraged the disloyalty that Abraham Lincoln correctly identified as subversive to morale and productive of animosity among the army's officers. Thus, even prior to the commencement of the campaign, Davis had sown the seeds of political tumult that had been a staple of Bragg's leadership.

The upcoming spring campaign provided additional evidence of Davis's principal weaknesses as commander-in-chief. The president's delicate relationship with his western commander grew more tenuous over the course of the winter of 1863–64. While Davis allowed his acrimony with Johnston to color his assessment of the general's activities, he permitted his friendship with Bragg to influence his calculations concerning the condition of the army and its readiness for offensive operations. Having received conflicting reports on the army's condition, the president accepted Bragg's advice and insisted that Johnston move into eastern Tennessee, a plan that had little chance for success. In addition to illustrating Davis's meager management skills, the stalemate revealed the president's poor appreciation for the advantages of centralized command. As a consequence, the Confederate leadership could not produce a unified vision for the upcoming campaign season. Instead, a number of plans surfaced, but a fractious high command failed to adopt any of them. Perhaps most importantly, Davis's distaste for P. G. T. Beauregard caused him to reject a proposal that offered the Confederacy the most reasonable prospect for victory.

As the spring approached, Georgia faced several threats. First, Sherman's army outnumbered Johnston by more than two to one. Still, Davis refused to send reinforcements to Dalton when Johnston rebuffed the administration's proposed advance into eastern Tennessee. Davis's distrust of Johnston therefore affected the time-table for Leonidas Polk's arrival in Georgia. By the time Polk reached Johnston with the bulk of his forces, Johnston had already retreated from Rocky Face Ridge. Had Polk arrived earlier, Johnston could have held his position at Rocky Face for an extended period, if not indefinitely.

Inadequate mapmaking posed a second impediment to Confederate operations in the West. While Sherman possessed well developed and technologically advanced topographical capabilities, Johnston did not. Sherman's Army Corps of Engineers produced accurate and uniform maps for the entire army. Johnston's officers manufactured their own maps, which resulted in discrepancies from one map to another. Indeed, some Confederate maps failed to identify critical topographical features, an oversight that likely impaired their ability to hold their position at Dalton.

A third obstacle facing Johnston was the condition of the cavalry's horses and the incompetence of their commander, Joseph Wheeler. The limited number of serviceable mounts made effective observation of Sherman's movements more difficult. Wheeler failed to follow Johnston's instructions that he keep headquarters informed of Federal activity in the direction of Taylor's Ridge to the west of Confederate defensive lines at Dalton. Johnston exacerbated Wheeler's feeble performance when he misapprehended Sherman's strategic plans. Johnston became convinced that his adversary intended an assault against the Confederate right near Mill Creek and therefore neglected his left flank at Snake Creek Gap. Though several factors not of Johnston's making contributed to the Confederate retreat from Rocky Face Ridge, the commander's loss of the army's lines near Dalton was one of his worst performances of the war. At Resaca, however, Johnston redeemed himself and demonstrated a willingness to adopt the tactical offensive. On May 14 Johnston ordered an attack against the Union left, to cut Sherman off from his only line of retreat through Sugar Valley. He intended to make a similar attempt the following day, but a Federal flanking party threatened his communications and compelled his withdrawal southward. Even the presence of the Georgia militia would not have allowed Johnston to maintain his position at Resaca for very long. The shallow and winding Oostanaula and Connasauga rivers and plentiful ferries near Resaca made a prolonged defense against Sherman's flanking maneuvers almost impossible. Flawed maps forced the army's continued retrograde movement from Calhoun to Cassville.

At Cassville, Johnston again determined to attack Sherman. He devised a plan that envisioned a concentration of Confederate forces against Sherman's widely divided columns. Hood was to deliver the decisive blow against the Union advance from the direction of Adairsville. Hood, however, encountered Federal cavalry moving along the Spring Place Road and inexplicably abandoned his assault. He mistakenly informed Johnston that Federals on the Canton Road, threatened his flank. That evening Hood compounded his error when he insisted that the army could not hold its lines south of the town. The day had begun with great promise for Confederate victory and with Johnston and Hood as confidants; it ended with retreat and animosity. Johnston suspected that Hood had fabricated the report of a Union column operating on the Canton Road. Meanwhile, Hood knew that a Federal force had appeared on his flank. In fact, Sherman's ability to approach the Confederates without warning, something that Hood's staff member Taylor Beatty had indicated was a reoccurring phenomenon, might have raised doubts about Johnston's fitness. The dispute between the two men caused a rupture that eventually culminated in Hood's campaign to replace Johnston as commander of the army.

After Johnston's withdrawal from Cassville, Davis's failures as commander-in-chief continued to affect Johnston's ability to command. Davis's encouragement of improper communications with Hood inspired Hood's effort to secure Johnston's position. He sent his aide, Henry Brewster, to Richmond as soon as the army took position near Allatoona. Brewster undoubtedly gave Davis an inaccurate picture of Johnston's performance to that date. Thereafter, Hood behaved erratically in his duties as corps commander. At Pickett's Mill, he marched to the Federal left flank with only a third of his troops and failed to deliver the anticipated assault. Later, during Johnston's consultation with Senator Hill, Hood suggested that a cavalry raid would be unsuccessful unless launched immediately. His assertion was patently absurd, particularly since he had ordered Wheeler to conduct a similar raid a month later. Hood insisted that his position within Francis Shoup's works along the Chattahoochee River was impossible to defend. Hood's contention lacked merit, as both Confederate and Federal observers commented on the strength of the line.

In addition to Hood's back-channel communications with the administration, Davis's commitment to parochialism inhibited the defense of Georgia. The president's departmental design precluded Johnston from ordering S. D. Lee or Nathan Bedford Forrest to damage Sherman's communications. Davis's handling of his subordinates' personalities aggravated the problem. His distrust of Johnston made him skeptical of the general's pleas for a cavalry raid. His decision to send Bragg to Atlanta to ascertain whether Johnston should remain in command of the army further demonstrated Davis's willingness to allow his personal relationships to dictate his actions. Bragg's turbulent history with the Army of Tennessee meant that he could not render an impartial judgment and should not have been assigned the task.

Despite his own role in producing the army's retreat to the outskirts of Atlanta, the president had few options but to relieve Johnston from his position. Johnston's secrecy about the defense of Atlanta rightfully gave the president cause for concern. Johnston's suggestion that the government remove prisoners from Andersonville further eroded Davis's confidence in his commander. Considering that Davis had made it abundantly clear that he desired offensive operations, Johnston's refusal to share any specific plans was puzzling. The evidence suggests that he intended to attack Sherman's divided army once a portion of it crossed the Chattahoochee River. Yet Johnston remained silent and suffered the consequences when Davis replaced him with Hood.

The president's friendship with Bragg clouded his judgment in determining Johnston's successor. Davis had instructed Bragg to replace Johnston with Hardee if removal was necessary. Bragg's feud with Hardee, however, ensured that he would do everything in his power to avoid that result. Bragg suggested that Hood offered the best hope for Confederate victory, and Davis quickly accepted the recommendation. In doing so, he failed to account for Hardee's foreseeable resentment in having been passed over for the promotion. Hardee's reticence influenced the outcome of Hood's defense of Atlanta. Hood inherited an army with relatively high morale. Moreover, he designed admirable plans for the Confederate attacks at Peachtree Creek and Bald Hill. Hardee's lethargy in carrying out his orders, however, led to defeat. At Ezra Church, Hood was the victim of S. D. Lee's inexperience as a corps commander when he attacked Oliver Howard's entrenching troops without seeking Hood's direction. Hood's primary miscalculation in his defense of Atlanta was his decision to send the incompetent Joseph Wheeler on a raid against Sherman's supply route. With the bulk of the Confederate cavalry on a joy ride, Sherman took advantage and marched on Jonesboro almost undetected. Hardee's outnumbered troops could not repel the Federal capture of Hood's last supply line into Atlanta, and Hood was forced to yield the city. Generally, Hood's performance as commander was commendable. But in this case, his subordinates did not rise to the occasion.

With the fall of Atlanta, the re-election of Abraham Lincoln in November was a foregone conclusion and the Confederacy's defeat all but certain. Scholars have long recognized that a multitude of factors contributed to Union victory in the campaign. Even so, the dysfunctional nature of the Confederate high command stands out as having been pivotal in the loss of Atlanta. Though each of the key figures in the high command warrants some measure of blame for Confederate defeat, Jefferson Davis stands out. Davis's inability to manage difficult personalities, his promotion of inappropriate communications, and his dismissal of a unified command system proved most consequential. Davis's leadership style fueled conflict and controversy among members of the Confederate high command and, as a consequence, substantially determined the outcome of the war.

Appendix 1

Polk's and Longstreet's Plans for a Spring Offensive

In addition to the spring plans outlined in the third chapter, there were two other plans proposed by members of the Confederate high command, one by Leonidas Polk and the other by James Longstreet.

Polk, charged with the defense of Mississippi, Alabama, and East Louisiana, suggested a spring offensive to the president on February 28, 1864. Polk assumed that Sherman's raid on Meridian from Vicksburg earlier that month was a precursor to a Federal advance from Chattanooga. Polk believed Johnston's force at Dalton inadequate to resist the Union invasion. He observed that when the Federal army, then in Chattanooga, made a forward movement, its already extended supply lines from Nashville could prove advantageous for a Confederate counter-stroke. Any advance on Atlanta meant that the Federals would need to supply themselves through Polk's department. He hoped to convince Davis to reinforce him with enough men to allow him to ravage the Federal supply route.

Polk sought the reinforcement of his old division, now with the Army of Tennessee, under the command of Benjamin Cheatham. He thought that the division could return to its home in western Tennessee and recruit and believed he could double the division's strength from 4,000 to 8,000 men. Once Polk completed recruitment, he intended to advance upon the Federal supply line with 15,000 infantry and an additional 15,000 cavalry. To help ensure success, Polk advocated for Kirby Smith to pressure Union forces in the Trans-Mississippi, preventing them from sending reinforcements to harass Polk's own endeavor.

Meanwhile, Longstreet was to act in a similar fashion on the eastern flank of the Federal column advancing toward Atlanta.[1]

Polk's plan, while better than the Davis-Bragg plan, was unlikely to achieve success. Sherman commenced his advance with approximately 100,000 men. To confront Sherman, Johnston mustered only 40,000 effective infantry and approximately 2,500 effective cavalry in Dalton. Without the addition of Polk's army to Johnston's force, as the administration eventually ordered, Johnston faced overwhelming odds. If the campaign had progressed according to Polk's strategy, Sherman would have had little difficulty in sending an adequate force to confront Polk. Indeed, once the campaign commenced and the Army of the Tennessee under Gen. James McPherson recalled those on detached duty, it mustered approximately 35,000 soldiers.[2] If Polk had remained in Mississippi rather than joining Johnston and then attempted to advance on Sherman's communication lines, Sherman could easily detach McPherson's army to deal with the threat. Even if he did so, Sherman would still have outnumbered Johnston's army by nearly 25,000 men and McPherson would have enjoyed a significant advantage over Polk's column. Polk would have been outnumbered and forced to deploy cavalry against McPherson's infantry. Further, all of McPherson's soldiers were veterans, while Polk's proposed force would have included approximately 4,000 newly recruited troops.

Polk was not alone in offering alternatives to the Davis-Bragg plan. James Longstreet proposed an advance through eastern Tennessee that would include his own forces in combination with Johnston. Longstreet's plan mirrored the Davis-Bragg plan in advocating an advance through eastern Tennessee, but Longstreet demonstrated a greater understanding of the difficulty of such an approach. Longstreet recommended that he and Johnston unite at Madisonville in eastern Tennessee, and suggested two routes that could be used, the first "passing some fifteen miles south of Knoxville, the other by passing down north of Knoxville." Both, as Longstreet noted, faced a "serious difficulty" with respect to the "scarcity of supplies."

Upon hearing Longstreet's plan, Johnston lodged his objections. Johnston observed that Longstreet's southern route required the fording of at least six rivers, five of which lacked bridges. Johnston said that he could make the movement, but only if he was met at Madisonville with "subsistence stores and forage for my army." Johnston also laid a condition on the northern approach to Madisonville. He commented that it would require him to cross the Holston and Tennessee

1 *O.R.* vol. 32, pt. 2, 813–814.

2 Sherman, *Memoirs of General W. T. Sherman*, 473; *O.R.* vol. 32, pt. 3, 866.

rivers, the latter of which "would require a bridge, which I cannot haul; but if you [Longstreet] can meet me there, so as to prevent forces from Chattanooga molesting my march, I can make a bridge and unite my forces with yours."[3]

Johnston undoubtedly understood that his conditional acceptance of Longstreet's design meant that the plan could not go forward. The experiences of Burnside, Schofield, and Buckner all attested to the impossibility of providing adequate forage by way of the roads in the eastern part of the state. The notion that Longstreet might converge on Madisonville with sufficient supplies for both his own command and Johnston's strains credibility. After all, Longstreet's initial proposal suggested that his own column could not supply itself properly. Longstreet marshaled approximately 15,000 men, a force significantly less than Johnston commanded at Dalton.[4] If his primary concern was to secure supplies for his own men, Longstreet could not hope to combine with Johnston at Madisonville with supplies for both columns. Nor could Longstreet meet Johnston along the Tennessee River to defend the river against interference from the Union forces in Chattanooga with sufficient forage for his own and Johnston's troops.

In attaching conditions to Longstreet's plans, Johnston was in reality arguing against the venture, something he did more forcefully in a later communication. On March 13 Johnston raised two specific objections with Longstreet. First, the Federal forces might interpose themselves between Longstreet and his own force before either could reach Madisonville. If so, the Union army would enjoy a great numerical advantage over either of the separated Confederate armies. Second, he again questioned the quartermaster's ability to supply a large Confederate column marching through eastern Tennessee.[5] Johnston was right to reject Longstreet's proposal. The only real difference between Longstreet's plan and the strategy the administration advocated was that Longstreet acknowledged the difficulty to supply forces operating in eastern Tennessee. Like the Davis-Bragg plan, Longstreet's proposal offered the Confederacy little hope of success in the spring campaign.

3 *O.R.* vol. 32, pt. 3, 587, 618.

4 James Longstreet, *From Manassas to Appomattox: Memoirs of the Civil War in America* (1896; repr., New York, 1992), 482.

5 *O.R.* vol. 32, pt. 3, 618.

Appendix 2

The Mackall Journal Reconsidered

To understand what transpired in and around the town of Cassville on May 19, 1864, it is necessary to evaluate the veracity of a key piece of evidence, the diary of Thomas Mackall. Thomas Mackall was the cousin of Johnston's chief of staff, William Mackall, and served on Johnston's staff throughout the campaign. Thomas Mackall's diary has caused controversy among historians of the campaign and was most famously investigated by Richard McMurry, who identified five separate versions of the document. The most controversial of these is the version that appears in the *Official Records of the War of the Rebellion* (hereafter the *Official Records*). McMurry concludes that it was a postwar attempt to enhance Joseph E. Johnston's reputation at the expense of John Bell Hood and contains misleading information in Mackall's effort to achieve that goal. In challenging Mackall's veracity, McMurry removed Mackall's observations of events at Cassville from historical analysis.[1] Accordingly, scholars have dismissed Mackall's assertion that no Federal column appeared on the Canton-Cassville road. Instead, each has endeavored to discover the identity of the supposed force. The present study accepts Thomas Mackall's observations—that no Federal column threatened Hood

1 See *O.R.* vol. 38, pt. 3, 978–991; McMurry, "The Mackall Journal and its Antecedents," 325–327. He also suggests that Johnston likely participated in Mackall's deception while engaged in his postwar writing campaign against Hood. See McMurry, "The Mackall Journal and its Antecedents," 326–328; Castel, *Decision in the West*, 589. In footnote 100 Castel cites McMurry's "The Mackall Journal and its Antecedents," and characterizes the official version of the diary as "spurious." See also Timothy Weiss, "I Lead You to Battle: Joseph E. Johnston and the Controversy at Cassville," *Georgia Historical Quarterly* 91, no. 4 (Winter 2007): 436; Davis, *Atlanta Will Fall*, 50.

from the Canton Road—and therefore rejects the argument that the *official* version of the journal is spurious. Consequently, McMurry's conclusion deserves analysis.

McMurry has identified five separate versions of the Thomas Mackall journal. The first is the small pocket diary housed at the College of William and Mary that McMurry suggests was the original version and served as the foundation for the other four adaptations of the diary. Two other versions bear the same handwriting as the original field diary. The more substantial of the two, also found at William and Mary and written on loose-leaf paper, is longer and provides more details than the field diary, though the dating of the document remains a mystery. The third version bearing Mackall's handwriting is a memorandum at the Huntington Library in California, which contains entries only for May 14 and 15, 1864. McMurry argues that the Huntington memorandum served as a guide to Johnston when he was preparing his official report on the campaign soon after his removal from command, and that Mackall produced it upon Johnston's request. Considering the similarity in language between the Huntington memorandum and Johnston's campaign report, McMurry's assertion should be accepted.[2] His characterization of the final two versions, however, deserves further review. If McMurry is correct, and the official version of the Mackall diary includes fabricated evidence, then it stands to reason that it must be dismissed insofar as it makes claims that are at the center of the controversy at Cassville. If, on the other hand, McMurry's interpretation of the official version of the Mackall diary is either partially or entirely incorrect, then the official account remains a viable option for interpreting the events that occurred on the morning and afternoon of May 19, 1864.

McMurry's contention that the Mackall journal as published in the *Official Records* should be characterized as a postwar polemic includes an analysis of its relationship with another version of the journal, located in the National Archives. The two contain virtually identical narratives, and McMurry suggests that the manuscript in the National Archives predates the diary found in the *Official Records*. He then argues that the genesis of the version at the National Archives must have been some time after the preparation of the memorandum at the Huntington Library that Johnston received in October 1864, as it incorporated that document almost verbatim.[3] Assuming that McMurry's charge is accurate, he

2 McMurry, "The Mackall Journal and its Antecedents," 322, 319, 325. See footnote 25. Johnston's report is dated Oct. 20, 1864, which suggests that the Huntington memorandum dates to sometime before that.

3 McMurry, "The Mackall Journal and its Antecedents," 325–326. See footnote 25. According to McMurry, the copy available in the National Archives appears to be merely a handwritten edition that bears a few minor alterations from the journal published in the *Official Records*. A comparison of handwriting between the manuscript at the National Archives and the original field diary demonstrates

has only managed to date the Huntington and the National Archives versions of the diary to some time after the middle of October 1864, which does not necessarily mean that the latter falls into the category of postwar apologetics. It is equally possible, of course, that both the National Archives version and the Huntington memorandum based their narratives on the diary published in the *Official Records* and not the other way around. The fact that they incorporate similar language does not prove that Mackall produced the Huntington document first.

McMurry argues that the journal in the National Archives, and consequently the diary in the *Official Records*, must not have existed at the time Mackall produced the Huntington memorandum at Johnston's request because Mackall would have provided him with a copy.[4] There is, however, no evidence that Mackall provided Johnston with a copy of the original field diary or the slightly longer version written on loose-leaf paper at that time either. If he had, there would not have been any need to submit the Huntington draft, particularly since May 14 and 15 did not produce any controversy between Johnston and Hood. As a result, it is reasonable to suggest that all the documents attributable to Mackall found in Johnston's personal papers, other than the Huntington letter, made their way into Johnston's possession after the war when he was engaged in writing his memoir.

In concluding that the official diary was a postwar apologetic McMurry does not consider William Mackall's memorandum on Cassville written on September 22, 1864. McMurry most likely refrained from considering the memorandum because William Mackall rather than Thomas Mackall authored the document. Nevertheless, William Mackall's recollection of the events at Cassville supports the veracity of the official version of Thomas Mackall's journal. The memorandum, though not as detailed as the diary entry for May 19 found in the *Official Records*, is far more consistent with the official diary and the copy in the National Archives than with any other version of the journal.

In particular, the memorandum exhibits a healthy skepticism about Hood's claim of an enemy body on the Canton Road. According to the memorandum, William Mackall rode out to Hood's position to convey orders from headquarters when he encountered Hood's Corps moving to the rear. The document centers on a conversation between Mackall and Hood regarding the possible presence of Northern forces on Hood's flank and rear. Hood claimed that his own staff officers had discovered the enemy on both the Canton and Spring Place Roads and asked, "[D]id you not see them?" Mackall responded that he "had seen no enemy." After

that the former was undoubtedly prepared by a person or persons other than Thomas Mackall. Even so, as McMurry notes, Mackall may very well have dictated his account.

4 Ibid.

riding off, Mackall realized that he had not delivered the orders and returned to Hood's side. The memorandum indicates that he stayed with Hood until his corps established a new position. In all that time Mackall made no reference to having seen any enemy troops. The document therefore suggests that Hood's claim that enemy forces appeared on the Canton Road had generated a skepticism at army headquarters and remained a point of dispute soon after the conclusion of the campaign. The fact that William Mackall felt compelled to write the memorandum so soon after the fall of Atlanta implies that he considered Cassville a turning point of some significance.[5]

A report in the *Richmond Daily Dispatch* on July 16, 1864, lends further credence to the proposition that the events at Cassville caused consternation at headquarters during the campaign. The article offered a general defense of Johnston's conduct of the campaign and specifically of his actions at Cassville. The article's detailed defense of Johnston indicates that the correspondent had access either to the general himself or a knowledgeable member of his staff while preparing his account. The reporter noted that "the Lieutenant General [Hood], fearing to move, failed to comply with the orders of his commanding general."[6] The article, published just prior to Johnston's dismissal from the army, indicates that Hood's failure to attack at Cassville had generated a level of hostility, or at least anxiety, at general headquarters prior to Johnston's removal from command. When considered in tandem with William Mackall's memorandum, there seems little doubt that the events at Cassville caused significant controversy prior to the close of the war. For the reasons above, dating the official diary to the campaign itself, or soon thereafter, rather than a part of some postwar deception intended to enhance Johnston's prestige (and diminish Hood's) seems reasonable.

Still, there are features of the official diary that remain problematic. McMurry makes several additional arguments against the acceptance of an early provenance for the official version of the diary. He contends that the dates covered in the official journal—May 14 to June 4—should raise questions about the document. He suggests that these dates cover, a little too coincidentally, the most notorious postwar controversies between Hood and Johnston, particularly Hood's failure to launch assaults at Cassville on May 19 and at Little Pumpkin Vine Creek on May 28.[7] The argument appears sound but must be considered within the context of McMurry's overarching thesis, that the official diary developed as part of a postwar

5 W. W. Mackall, "Memoranda of the Operations at Cassville on May 19, 1864," *O.R.* vol. 38, pt. 3, 622. Mackall produced no other memoranda concerning events during the campaign.

6 *Richmond Daily Dispatch*, July 16, 1864.

7 McMurry, "The Mackall Journal and its Antecedents," 316.

effort to rehabilitate Johnston. If the thesis is accurate, there can be little doubt that the official version of the diary ought to conclude only after Johnston's dismissal.

Almost immediately after his removal, Johnston's plans for the defense of Atlanta generated significant controversy. Indeed, Johnston's official report, written October 20, 1864, demonstrates his desire to appear resolute in his effort to defend the Gate City. He specifically claimed credit for planning the operations along Peachtree Creek and insisted that he intended to defend Atlanta with the Georgia militia while he assailed the flanks of the Federal army with the remainder of his own forces. In fact, Jefferson Davis decided to relieve Johnston from command of the army primarily because he did not believe Johnston intended to adequately defend the city.[8] Consequently, any fraudulent postwar attempt to cast Johnston in a favorable light should include entries for the final days of Johnston's tenure. Journal entries supporting Johnston's claim that he had planned to assault the Federal army once it crossed Peachtree Creek and had imparted those plans to his successor, as well as his intentions to hold Atlanta indefinitely, seem almost necessary in any postwar forgery. Therefore, the entry dates in the official journal should not be considered evidence of compromised veracity.

Nor should the journal's length. In addition to his many other arguments against the authenticity of the official version of the Mackall diary, McMurry contends that the length of daily entries provides evidence of postwar polemics. McMurry argues that the entries are too long and much too detailed to be the product of a busy staff member during an active campaign. A fair comparison to other journals and letters produced during the campaign, however, sheds more light on this contention. Colonel Joseph Fullerton, Assistant Adjutant General of the Union's IV Army Corps, kept a journal that contained entries far greater in length and detail than the entries found in the official Mackall diary. Fullerton produced his account while on campaign from early May through the end of August. His diary was sealed after the battle of Nashville and remained unopened until sent to the War Department. The account, therefore, survives in its original state.[9]

The corpus of material found in the Orlando Poe papers at the Library of Congress also provides evidence for accepting the Mackall journal's authenticity. Poe served as General Sherman's chief of engineers throughout the campaign. Poe's field diary, like Mackall's, generally included fairly short entries. His letters home

8 *O.R.* vol. 38, pt. 3, 618; Davis, *The Rise and Fall of the Confederate Government*, II, 557.

9 McMurry, "The Mackall Journal and its Antecedents," 315; Fullerton's journal includes numerous entries that approach or exceed 1,000 words. His entry for May 27 exceeds 1,500 words. See "Journal of Lieut. Col. Joseph Fullerton," *O.R.* vol. 38, pt. 1, 839–931. By contrast, Mackall's journal entry for May 19, deemed too long and too detailed by McMurry, contains approximately 770 words. See Mackall Journal, May 19, 1864, *O.R.* vol. 38, pt. 3, 983–984; *O.R.* vol. 38, pt. 1, 839.

to his wife, however, often provided a significant number of details left out of the pocket diary. He clearly found opportunities during his busy days to reflect upon his activities and record them in both his diary and in his letters home. Poe therefore left at least two separate accounts of his daily activities: one short and lacking specifics, and a second that provided a significant number of details. It is not unreasonable to conclude that Thomas Mackall followed a similar pattern and produced more than one account of his daily activities during the campaign itself and that the official version of the diary resulted from that practice.

As a consequence of the foregoing analysis, McMurry's assertion that the official version of the Mackall journal was the product of a postwar campaign intended to support Johnston in his contest against John Bell Hood and Jefferson Davis deserves reconsideration. McMurry's thesis has influenced scholars in their interpretation of the events at Cassville since the publication of "The Mackall Journal and its Antecedents" in 1974.[10] Given this reassessment, historians should reconsider the possibility that no enemy force ever appeared on the Canton Road.

10 Castel, *Decision in the West*, 589. See footnote 100; Weiss, "I Lead You to Battle: Joseph E. Johnston and the Controversy at Cassville," 436; Davis, *Atlanta Will Fall*, 50.

Bibliography

Primary Sources

Manuscripts

Alabama Department of Archives and History, Montgomery, AL.

Hardee, William. Letters.

Kennesaw National Battlefield Library, Kennesaw, GA.

Cox, Jacob D. Diary.

Doss, Ambrose. Letters.

Neal, A. J. Letters.

Norrell, William O. Diary.

Trask, W. L. Diary.

Library of Congress, Washington, D.C..

Burton, Norvel Harrison. Papers.

Gorgas, Josiah. Diary.

Johnston, Joseph E. Papers.

Lovell, Mansfield. Papers.

Poe, Orlando M. Papers.

Polk, Leonidas. Papers.

Schofield, John M. Papers.

Wigfall, Louis T. Papers.

Southern Historical Collection, University of North Carolina, Chapel Hill, NC.

Beatty, Taylor. Diary.

Harrison, James Thomas. Papers.

Mackall, William W. Papers.

Swem Library, The College of William & Mary, Williamsburg, VA.

Johnston, Joseph E. Papers.

Government Collections

A Compilation of the Messages and Papers of the Confederacy: Including the Diplomatic Correspondence, 1861–1865. Edited by James D. Richardson. 2 vols. Nashville, TN: United States Publishing Company, 1906.

The Confederate Records of the State of Georgia. Edited by Allen D. Candler. 6 vols. Atlanta, GA: C. P. Byrd, State Printer, 1909–1911.

The War of the Rebellion: A Compilation of the Official Records of the Union and Confederate Armies. 128 vols. Washington, D.C.: Government Printing Office, 1880–1901.

Published Books & Papers

Buck, Irving A. *Cleburne and His Command.* Jackson, TN: McCowat-Mercer Press, Inc., 1959.

Bull, Rice. *Soldiering: The Civil War Diary of Rice Bull.* Edited by Jack Bauer. Nevada, CA: The Presidio Press, 1977.

Chesnut, Mary. *Mary Chesnut's Civil War.* Edited by C. Vann Woodward. New Haven, CT: Yale University Press, 1981.

Cox, Jacob. *Atlanta.* New York, NY: C. Scribner's Sons, 1882.

Davis, Jefferson, *Jefferson Davis, Constitutionalist, His Letters, Papers, and Speeches.* Edited by Dunbar Rowland. 10 vols. Jackson, MS: Mississippi Department of Archives and History, 1923.

_____. The Papers of Jefferson Davis. Edited by Lynda Lasswell Crist, Kenneth H. Williams, Peggy L. Dillard, and Mary Seaton Dix. 13 vols. Baton Rouge, LA: Louisiana State University Press, 1971–2012.

_____. The Rise and Fall of the Confederate Government. 2 vols. 1881. Reprint. New York, NY: Thomas Yoseloff, 1958.

Foster, Samuel T. *One of Cleburne's Command: The Civil War Reminiscences and Diary of Capt. Samuel T. Foster, Granbury's Texas Brigade, C.S.A.* Edited by Norman D. Brown. Austin, TX: University of Texas Press, 1980.

French, Samuel G. *Two Wars: An Autobiography.* Nashville, TN: Confederate Veteran, 1901.

Hood, John Bell. *Advance and Retreat: Personal Experiences in the United States and Confederate Armies.* 1880. Reprint. New York, NY: Da Capo Press, 1993.

Jackman, John S. *Diary of a Confederate Soldier: John S. Jackman of the Orphan Brigade.* Edited by William C. Davis. Columbia, SC: University of South Carolina Press, 1990.

Johnston, Joseph E. *Narrative of Military Operations: During the Late War Between the States.* New York, NY: D. Appleton & Co., 1881.

Jones, John. *A Rebel War Clerk's Diary at the Confederate States Capital.* Edited by Earl Miers. 1866. Reprint. Baton Rouge, LA: Louisiana State University Press, 1993.

Kean, Robert Garlick Hill. *Inside the Confederate Government: The Diary of Robert Garlick Hill Kean, Head of the Bureau of War.* Edited by Edward Younger. New York, NY: Oxford University Press, 1957.

Kurtz, Wilbur Sr. "Why Was Snake Creek Gap Left Un-Guarded? An Episode of the Retreat of the Confederate Army of Tennessee from Dalton, Georgia, May, 1864." Wilbur G. Kurtz Papers, Atlanta Historical Society.

Lee, Robert E. *Lee's Dispatches: Unpublished Letters of General Robert E. Lee, C. S. A., to Jefferson Davis and The War Department of the Confederate States of America 1862–65*. Edited by Douglas Southall Freeman. 1957. Reprint. Baton Rouge, LA: Louisiana State University Press, 1994.

Lincoln, Abraham. *The Collected Works of Abraham Lincoln*. Edited by Roy P. Basler. 8 vols. New Brunswick, NJ: Rutgers University Press, 1953.

Longstreet, James. *From Manassas to Appomattox: Memoirs of the Civil War in America*. 1896 Reprint. New York, NY: Da Capo Press, 1992.

Mackall, William W. *A Son's Recollections of His Father*. New York, NY: E. P. Dutton & Company Inc., 1930.

Manigault, Arthur M. *A Carolinian Goes to War: The Civil War Narrative of Arthur Middleton Manigault, Brigadier General, C.S.A.* Edited by R. Lockwood Tower. Columbia, SC: University of South Carolina Press, 1983.

Schofield, John M. *Forty-Six Years in the Army*. New York, NY: The Century Co., 1897.

Sherman, William Tecumseh. *Memoirs of General W. T. Sherman*. Edited by Charles Royster. 1875. Reprint. New York, NY: Library of America, 1990.

Taylor, Richard. *Destruction and Reconstruction: Personal Experiences of the Late War*. 1879.

Reprint. New York, NY: Longmans Green and Co., 1955.

Van Horne, Thomas. *History of the Army of the Cumberland*. 2 vols. Cincinnati, OH: Robert Clarke & Co., 1875.

Welch, Spencer Glascow. *A Confederate Surgeon's Letters to his Wife*. 1911. Reprint. Marietta: GA., Continental Book Co., 1954.

Periodicals

Breckinridge, W. C. P. "The Opening of the Atlanta Campaign." In *Battles and Leaders of the Civil War* 4: 326–331. New York, NY: Castle Books by arrangement with A. S. Barnes and Co., Inc., 1956.

Campbell, Albert H. "The Lost War Maps of the Confederates." *The Century Magazine* 35, no. 3 (Jan. 1888): 479–481.

Chamberlin, William H. "Hood's Second Sortie at Atlanta." In *Battles and Leaders of the Civil War* 4: 277–281. New York, NY: Castle Books by arrangement with A. S. Barnes and Co., Inc., 1956.

Cox, Rowland. "Snake Creek Gap and Atlanta." In *The Atlanta Papers*, comp. Sydney Kerksis, 329–351. Dayton, OH: Press of Morningside Bookshop, 1980.

Dabney, T. G. "Campaigning in North Georgia." *Confederate Veteran* 14 (1906): 75–76.

_____. "When Hood Superseded Johnston." *Confederate Veteran* 22 (1914): 406–407.

Dawes, E. C. "Confederate Strength in the Atlanta Campaign." In *Battles and Leaders of the Civil War* 4: 281–283. New York, NY: Castle Books by arrangement with A. S. Barnes and Co., Inc., 1956.

Dodge, Grenville M. "The Battle of Atlanta." In *The Atlanta Papers*, comp. Sydney Kerksis, 489–503. Dayton, OH: Press of Morningside Bookshop, 1980.

Foster, Wilbur. "Battle Field Maps in Georgia." *Confederate Veteran* 20 (1912): 369–370.

French, Samuel G. "Joseph E. Johnston's Campaign in Georgia, Criticisms of Gen. S. G. French." *Southern Historical Society Papers* 22 (1894): 1–9.

Grant, Ulysses S. "The Vicksburg Campaign." In *Battles and Leaders of the Civil War* 3: 493–539. New York, NY: Castle Books by arrangement with A. S. Barnes and Co., Inc., 1956.

Guthrey, D. M. "Wheeler's Cavalry Around Atlanta." *Confederate Veteran* 13 (1905): 267.

Hagan, John W. "The Confederate Letters of John W. Hagan: Part II." Ed. Bell Wiley. *Georgia Historical Quarterly* 38, no. 3 (Sept. 1954): 268–290.

Harvie, E. J. "Gen. Joseph E. Johnston." *Confederate Veteran* 18 (1910): 521–523.

Howard, Oliver O. "The Struggle for Atlanta." In *Battles and Leaders of the Civil War* 4: 298–325. New York, NY: Castle Books by arrangement with A. S. Barnes and Co., Inc., 1956.

Johnston, Joseph E. "Jefferson Davis and the Mississippi Campaign." In *Battles and Leaders of the Civil War* 3: 472–482. New York, NY: Castle Books by arrangement with A. S. Barnes and Co., Inc., 1956.

_____. "Manassas to Seven Pines." In *Battles and Leaders of the Civil War* 2: 202–218. New York, NY: Castle Books by arrangement with A. S. Barnes and Co., Inc., 1956.

_____. "Opposing Sherman's Advance to Atlanta." In *Battles and Leaders of the Civil War* 4: 260–277. New York, NY: Castle Books by arrangement with A. S. Barnes and Co., Inc., 1956.

Newberry, Thomas Jefferson. "The Civil War Letters of Thomas Jefferson Newberry." Ed. Enoch C. Mitchell. *Journal of Mississippi History* 10 (1948): 44–80.

Owen, Urban G. "Letters of a Confederate Surgeon in the Army of Tennessee to his Wife." Ed. Enoch C. Mitchell. *Tennessee Historical Quarterly* 5 (1946): 142–181.

Roy, T. B. "General Hardee and the Military Operations around Atlanta." *Southern Historical Society Papers* 8 (1880): 337–387.

Shoup, Francis. "Dalton Campaign—Works at Chattahoochee River—Interesting History." *Confederate Veteran* 3 (1895): 262–265.

Smith, Gustavas W. "The Georgia Militia About Atlanta." In *Battles and Leaders of the Civil War* 4: 331–335. New York, NY: Castle Books by arrangement with A. S. Barnes and Co., Inc., 1956.

Stone, Henry. "Part I: Opening of the Campaign;" "Part II: From the Oostanaula to the Chattahoochee;" "Part III: The Siege and Capture of Atlanta;" "Part IV: Strategy of the Campaign." In *The Atlanta Papers*, comp. Sydney Kerksis, 11–162. Dayton, OH: Press of Morningside Bookshop, 1980.

Newspapers

Atlanta Appeal, 1864

Atlanta Intelligencer, 1864

Atlanta Southern Confederacy, 1864

Macon (GA) *Telegraph,* 1864

*Richmond Daily Dispatch,*1864

Richmond Enquirer, 1864

Southern Watchman (Athens), 1864

Secondary Sources

Books & Dissertations

Allen, Felicity. *Jefferson Davis: Unconquerable Heart*. Columbia, MO: University of Missouri Press, 1999.

Bailey, Ronald. *Battles for Atlanta: Sherman Moves East*. Alexandria, VA: Time-Life Books, 1989.

Ballard, Michael. *Vicksburg: The Campaign That Opened the Mississippi*. Chapel Hill, NC: University of North Carolina Press, 2004.

Beringer, Richard E., Herman Hattaway, Archer Jones, and William N. Still Jr. *Why the South Lost the Civil War*. Athens, GA: University of Georgia Press, 1986.

Bragg, William Harris. *Joe Brown's Army: The Georgia State Line, 1862–1865*. Macon, GA: Mercer University Press, 1987.

Brown, Russell K. *To the Manner Born: The Life of General William H. T. Walker*. Macon, GA: Mercer University Press, 2005.

Buell, Thomas. *The Warrior Generals: Combat Leadership in the Civil War*. New York, NY: Crown Publishers, Inc., 1997.

Carter III, Samuel. *The Final Fortress: The Campaign for Vicksburg, 1862–1863*. New York: St. Martin's, 1980.

Castel, Albert. *Decision in the West: The Atlanta Campaign of 1864*. Lawrence, KS: University Press of Kansas, 1992.

Connelly, Thomas, and Archer Jones. *The Politics of Command: Factions and Ideas in Confederate Strategy*. Baton Rouge: Louisiana State University Press, 1973.

Connelly, Thomas Lawrence. *The Army of the Heartland: The Army of Tennessee, 1861–1862*. Baton Rouge, LA: Louisiana State University Press, 1967.

_____. *Autumn of Glory: The Army of Tennessee, 1862–1865*. Baton Rouge, LA: Louisiana State University Press, 1971.

Cooper, William Jr. *Jefferson Davis, American*. New York, NY: Alfred A. Knopf, 2000.

Daniel, Larry J. *Soldiering in the Army of Tennessee: A Portrait of Life in a Confederate Army*. Chapel Hill, NC: University of North Carolina Press, 1991.

Davis, Stephen. *Atlanta Will Fall: Sherman, Joe Johnston, and the Yankee Heavy Battalions*. Wilmington, NC: Scholarly Resources Inc., 2001.

Davis, William C. *The Commanders of the Civil War*. New York, NY: Gallery Books, 1990.

_____. *Jefferson Davis: The Man and His Hour*. New York, NY: Harper Collins, 1991.

_____. *Lincoln's Men: How President Lincoln Became Father to an Army and a Nation*. New York, NY: The Free Press, 1999.

Dean, Eric. *Shook Over Hell: Post-Traumatic Stress, Vietnam, and the Civil War*. Cambridge, MA: Harvard University Press, 1997.

Dodson, W. C., ed. *Campaigns of Wheeler and His Cavalry, 1862–1865*. Atlanta, GA: Hudgins Publishing Co., 1899.

Donald, David Herbert. *Lincoln*. New York, NY: Simon & Schuster, 1995.

Durden, Robert. *The Gray and the Black: The Confederate Debate on Emancipation*. Baton Rouge, LA: Louisiana State University Press 1972.

Dyer, John. *The Gallant Hood.* New York, NY: The Bobbs-Merrill Company, Inc., 1950.

Eaton, Clement. *Jefferson Davis.* New York, NY: Macmillan, 1977.

Eckenrode, H. J., and Bryan Conrad. *James Longstreet: Lee's War Horse.* Chapel Hill, NC: University of North Carolina Press, 1936.

Elam, Mark. "The Road to Atlanta: The Role of Geography in Command and Decision Making During the Atlanta Campaign." PhD diss., Florida State University, 1996.

Fox, William F. *Regimental Losses in the American Civil War.* 1898. Reprint. Dayton, OH: Morningside Bookshop, 1985.

Glathar, Joseph T. *Partners in Command: The Relationships Between Leaders in the Civil War.* New York, NY: The Free Press, 1994.

Goodwin, Doris Kearns. *Team of Rivals: The Political Genius of Abraham Lincoln.* New York, NY: Simon & Schuster, 2005.

Govan, Gilbert E., and James W. Livingood. *A Different Valor: The Story of General Joseph E. Johnston, C.S.A.* New York, NY: The Bobbs-Merrill Company, Inc., 1956.

Griffith, Paddy. *Battle Tactics of the Civil War.* New Haven, CT: Yale University Press, 1989.

Hallock, Judith Lee. *Braxton Bragg and Confederate Defeat.* Vol. 2. Tuscaloosa, AL: University of Alabama Press, 1991.

Hennessy, John. *Return to Bull Run: The Campaign and Battle of Second Manassas.* New York, NY: Simon & Schuster, 1993.

Hill, Louise Biles. *Joseph E. Brown and the Confederacy.* 1891. Reprint. Westport, CT: Greenwood Press, 1939.

Hood, Stephen. *The Lost Papers of Confederate General John Bell Hood.* El Dorado Hills, CA: Savas Beatie, 2015.

Horn, Stanley F. *The Army of Tennessee: A Military History.* New York, NY: The Bobbs-Merrill Company, 1941.

Hughes, Nathaniel C. *General William J. Hardee: Old Reliable.* Baton Rouge, LA: Louisiana State University Press, 1965.

Jenkins, Robert. *The Cassville Affairs: Johnston, Hood and the Failed Confederate Strategy in the Atlanta Campaign, 19 May 1864.* Macon, GA: Mercer University Press, 2024.

Jones, Archer. *Civil War Command and Strategy: The Process of Victory and Defeat.* New York, NY: The Free Press, 1992.

_____. *Confederate Strategy from Shiloh to Vicksburg.* Baton Rouge, LA: Louisiana State University Press, 1961.

King, Alvy. *Louis T. Wigfall: Southern Fire-eater.* Baton Rouge, LA: Louisiana State University Press, 1970.

McElfresh, Earl B. *Maps and Mapmakers of the Civil War.* New York, NY: Harry N. Abrams, Inc., 1999.

McMurry, Richard. *Atlanta 1864: Last Chance for the Confederacy.* Lincoln, NE: University of Nebraska Press 2000.

_____. *John Bell Hood and the War for Southern Independence.* Lincoln, NE: University of Nebraska Press, 1982.

Miller, Brian Craig. *John Bell Hood and the Fight for Civil War Memory.* Knoxville, TN: University of Tennessee Press, 2010.

Neal, Diane, and Thomas Kremm. *Lion of the South: General Thomas Hindman.* Atlanta, GA: Mercer University Press, 1993.

Newton, Steven. *Joseph E. Johnston and the Defense of Richmond.* Lawrence, KS: University of Kansas Press, 1998.

Nichols, James L. *Confederate Engineers.* Tuscaloosa, AL: Confederate Publishing Company, Inc., 1957.

O'Connor, Richard. *Hood: Cavalier General.* New York, NY: Prentice-Hall, Inc., 1949.

Parks, Joseph H. *General Leonidas Polk C.S.A.: The Fighting Bishop.* Baton Rouge, LA: Louisiana State University Press, 1962.

_____. *Joseph E. Brown of Georgia.* Baton Rouge, LA: Louisiana State University Press, 1977.

Perret, Geoffrey. *Lincoln's War: The Untold Story of America's Greatest President as Commander in Chief.* New York, NY: Random House, 2004.

Polk, William. *Leonidas Polk: Bishop and General.* 2 vols. 1893. Reprint. New York, NY: Longmans, Green, and Co., 1915.

Scaife, William Robert, and William Harris Bragg. *Joe Brown's Pets: The Georgia Militia, 1861–1865.* Macon, GA: Mercer University Press, 2004.

Sears, Stephen. *Controversies & Commanders: Dispatches From the Army of the Potomac.* Boston, MA: Houghton Mifflin Company, 1999.

_____. *The Gates of Richmond: The Peninsula Campaign.* New York, NY: Houghton Mifflin Company, 1992.

_____. *Landscape Turned Red: The Battle of Antietam.* Boston, MA: Houghton Mifflin Company, 1983.

Strode, Hudson. *Jefferson Davis: Confederate President.* 2 vols. New York, NY: Harcourt Brace and Company, 1959.

Symonds, Craig. *Joseph E. Johnston: A Civil War Biography.* New York, NY: W. W. Norton & Company, 1992.

_____. *Stonewall of the West: Patrick Cleburne and the Civil War.* Lawrence, KS: University Press of Kansas, 1997.

Wilkerson, Warren. *Mother May You Never See the Sights I Have Seen: The Fifty-Seventh Massachusetts Veteran Volunteers in the Army of the Potomac, 1864–1865.* New York, NY: Harper & Row, 1990.

Williams, Harry. T. *Lincoln and his Generals.* New York, NY: Alfred A. Knopf, 1952.

_____. *P. G. T. Beauregard: Napoleon in Gray.* Baton Rouge, LA: Louisiana State University Press, 1955.

Woodworth, Steven. *Jefferson Davis and his Generals: The Failure of Confederate Command in the West.* Lawrence, KS: University Press of Kansas, 1990.

Articles

Butler, Scott, and Keith Bohannon. "Archaeology Inventory and GIS Analysis for the Chattahoochee River Line Battlefield (July 5–10, 1864)." National Park Service. American Battlefield Protection Program Grant No. 2255-09-013.

Coggins, Jack. "The Engineers Played a Key Role in Both Armies." *Civil War Times Illustrated* 3 (Jan. 1965): 41–46.

Davis, Robert Jr. "Every Crossroads and Farm: Confederate General Henry DeLamar Clayton's Civil War Maps of Northwestern Georgia." *Georgia Historical Quarterly* 82, no. 1 (Spring 1998): 151–167.

Davis, Stephen. "The Battles of Atlanta: Events From July 10 to September 2, 1864." *Blue and Gray Magazine* (Aug. 1989): 9–62.

_____. "John Bell Hood's 'Addictions' In Civil War Literature." *Blue and Gray Magazine* (Oct. 1998): 28–31.

Hay, Thomas R. "The Davis-Hood-Johnston Controversy of 1864." *Mississippi Valley Historical Review* 11 (June 1924): 54–84.

James, Alfred. "General Joseph Eggleston Johnston: Storm Center of the Confederate Army." *Mississippi Valley Historical Review* 14 (1924): 342–359.

McMurry, Richard. "The Affair at Kolb's Farm." *Civil War Times Illustrated* (Dec. 1968): 20–27.

_____. "The Atlanta Campaign of 1864: A New Look." *Civil War History* 22 (1976): 5–15.

_____. "Confederate Morale in the Atlanta Campaign of 1864." *Georgia Historical Quarterly* 54, no. 2 (Summer 1970): 226–243.

_____. "The Enemy at Richmond: Joseph E. Johnston and the Confederate Government." *Civil War History* 27 (1981): 5–31.

_____. "The Mackall Journal and its Antecedents." *Civil War History* 20 (1974): 311–28.

_____. "The Opening Phase of the 1864 Campaign in the West." *Atlanta Historical Journal* 27 (Summer 1983): 5–24.

_____. "Rocky Face to the Dallas Line: The Battles of May 1864," *The Blue & Gray Magazine* 6 (1989): 11–23, 46–62.

McPherson, James. "Was that Best Defense a Good Offense? Jefferson Davis and Confederate Strategies." In *Jefferson Davis's Generals*, edited by Gabor Boritt, 156–175. New York, NY: Oxford University Press, 1999.

McNeill, William J. "A Survey of Confederate Soldier Morale during Sherman's Campaign through Georgia and the Carolinas." *Georgia Historical Quarterly* 45 (1971): 1–25.

McWhiney, Grady. "Jefferson Davis and the Art of War." *Civil War History* 21 (1975): 101–112.

Muntz, Philip. "Union Mapping in the American Civil War." *Imago Mundi: A Review of Early Cartography* 17 (1963): 90–94.

Stevenson, Richard. "Mapping the Civil War." *Civil War Times Illustrated* (November–December 1992): 60–67.

Symonds, Craig. "A Fatal Relationship: Davis and Johnston at War." In *Jefferson Davis's Generals*, edited by Gabor Boritt, 3–26. New York, NY: Oxford University Press, 1999.

Weiss, Timothy. "I Lead You to Battle: Joseph E. Johnston and the Controversy at Cassville." *Georgia Historical Quarterly* 91, no. 4 (Winter 2007): 424–452.

Internet Sites

American Battlefield Trust https://www.battlefields.org/learn/maps/picketts-mill?ms=googlepaid gclid=EAIaIQobChMI7J7eu9Sz8QIVD5fICh2fzweyEAAYASAAEgIYnfD_BwE (accessed June 25, 2021).

Index

The Atlanta Campaign

VOLUME 1:

Dalton to Cassville, May 1–19, 1864

David A. Powell

Exclusive Excerpt

Savas Beatie
California

Chapter 1

February 1864

According to *The Official Records of the War of the Rebellion* the campaign for Atlanta formally commenced on May 1, 1864. It's opening however, was heavily foreshadowed (and in some ways shaped) nearly three months earlier, in February.

At that time Ulysses S. Grant, still headquartered at Nashville, ordered Maj. Gen. George H. Thomas, at Chattanooga, to move against the Confederate Army of Tennessee, which then was wintering in Dalton Georgia. Though unsuccessful, the Federals learned many important lessons about how best to assail the Rebels in Dalton, which would become the basis for William T. Sherman's strategy that Spring. This, it can be argued that the long drive to Atlanta really began on February 22nd, 1864.

Nashville, February 12, 1864.

Major General Thomas:

Should you not be required to go into East Tennessee, could you not make a formidable reconnaissance toward Dalton, and, if successful in driving the enemy out, occupy that place and complete the railroad up to it this winter?

GRANT,

Major-General[1]

Major General Ulysses S. Grant was a man of action. He hated to see troops sitting idle, even in winter, his recent victory at Chattanooga the previous November

1 U.S. War Department. *The War of the Rebellion: A Compilation of the Official Records of the Union and Confederate Armies*, 128 vols. (Washington D.C.: 1880-1901), Series I, Volume 32, pt. 2, 373. Hereafter cited as *OR*.

notwithstanding. Grant's elevation to command of the recently created Military Division of the Mississippi gave him purview over a vast swath of territory, from the mountains of East Tennessee to the bayous of Louisiana. In Mississippi, troops were already moving: 20,000 men under Maj. Gen. William T. Sherman from Vicksburg, and 7,000 more under Brig. Gen. William Sooy Smith from Memphis, all converging on Meridian.

Grant also desired action in East Tennessee, where Lt. Gen. James Longstreet's 20,000 Confederates still nominally threatened Knoxville. Grant wanted Longstreet driven entirely from the region, securing Knoxville once and for all. This objective proved too ambitious; correspondence with Maj. Gens. John G. Foster and John M. Schofield convinced Grant that the difficult terrain and poor weather limited any chance of success against Longstreet.

Thwarted, Grant turned his attention to the railroad town of Dalton in northern Georgia, 33 miles south of Chattanooga along the Western & Atlantic Railroad leading to Atlanta. Confederate General Joseph E. Johnston's 47,000 troops of the Army of Tennessee occupied Dalton, recovering from Grant's drubbing of them back in November. Opposing Johnston, Federal Maj. Gen. George H. Thomas's Army of the Cumberland occupied Chattanooga and environs. Though there were 80,000 troops in Thomas's department, only about 40,000 were available for a move against Dalton. The remainder guarded his supply line stretching back to Nashville. Nevertheless, when queried, Thomas's answer was hopeful: "I think an advance on Dalton would be successful," he wired, assuming he could be reinforced by a division from John A. Logan's XV Corps currently occupying northern Alabama.[2]

Dalton would be no easy nut to crack. Several steep mountain ridges separated the two armies, the most rugged being Rocky Face Ridge, which began three miles north of Dalton, rose to 1,500 feet, and extended 15 miles south. The Federal Road (the old treaty route through Cherokee territory) from Chattanooga ran east from Ringgold to skirt Rocky Face's northern end to Spring Place, east of Dalton; while a second road pierced Rocky Face at Mill Creek Gap (Buzzard's Roost Gap). Farther south Snake Creek Gap divided Rocky Face from John's Mountain, providing another water-level passage to the town of Resaca. Two lesser passages, Boyd's Gap (also sometimes called Mill Gap, not to be confused with Mill Creek Gap) and Dug Gap, pierced Rocky Face south of Mill Creek, but each of these

2 Ibid., 282-283, 373, 586, 776, 820. Thomas's force contained an aggregate of 91,253, of which 77,718 were listed as "present for duty." Logan's men in northern Alabama belonged to Sherman's Army of the Tennessee. Confederate returns for February show an army strength of 42,000, present for duty, but exclude Maj. Gen. Benjamin F. Cheatham's entire division of about 4,500, which had been temporarily transferred to Alabama.

offered limited access only through the sheer palisade at the mountain's crest. They required steep ascents and descents. Indeed, while Dug Gap was accessible to wagons, Boyd's Gap was little more than a footpath. Dalton was bounded on the east by ranges of lesser but still tactically formidable hills, and then the Conasauga River. Federal troops could approach Dalton from the north, via Crow Valley, thus bypassing Rocky Face, but would also run the risk of being isolated from the rest of the army.

Ever willing to gamble, Grant proposed a different strategy. On February 13 he suggested: "I would feel no hesitation in marching past all the force they have at Tunnel Hill and Dalton and come in on the railroad to their rear with a force from sixteen to twenty thousand effective fighting men."[3]

This very strategy would become the main Union plan of operations in May: a rapid move south from Ringgold to fall upon the Western & Atlantic near Resaca on the Oostanaula River. However, the risks of such a movement were high. At Dalton, Johnston's Confederates could use interior lines and (presumably) newly arriving reinforcements to fall on any expedition before it could be reinforced. But the rewards were equally high: If successful, the Rebel Army of Tennessee could be forced into a precipitate retreat across difficult country, or even trapped and destroyed outright.

Thomas considered Grant's proposal and demurred. "I have thought of the route you suggest," he wrote back on the 15th, "but find upon inquiry that the roads across the mountains are so difficult that they can hardly be considered practicable at this season of the year." Instead, Thomas planned to send a reinforced division from Maj. Gen. Gordon Granger's IV Corps through Crow Valley to threaten Dalton from the north, while Maj. Gen. John Palmer's XIV Corps advanced from Ringgold. Not all the forces for this movement were in place. Only half of Logan's men (seven regiments) had reached Chattanooga by the 15th, while Granger's IV Corps remained at Cleveland, Tennessee, ready to reinforce Knoxville if needed. Still, Thomas was equally impatient to set out. "Should the weather clear up, however, I will not wait."[4]

As it turned out, James Longstreet had a say in the matter. On February 10, Longstreet ordered Brig. Gen. Micah Jenkins, commanding John B. Hood's former division, to bridge the Holston River 20 miles northeast of Knoxville. General Schofield asked Thomas for reinforcements, a request that reached Chattanooga

3 John Y. Simon and John F. Marszalek, eds. *The Papers of Ulysses S. Grant*, 32 vols. to date (Carbondale, IL: 1967-present.), 10:119, hereafter cited as Simon, *PUSG*, followed by volume and page number.

4 *OR* 32, pt. 2, 395.

on the 16th—the day after Thomas informed Grant that he was nearly ready to move. Thomas immediately informed Grant that if he reinforced Schofield "it will also become necessary to give up any demonstration against Dalton."[5]

Longstreet's plans fizzled due to a lack of support. Confederate General Robert E. Lee proved reluctant to send Longstreet any more troops from his Army of Northern Virginia, while Johnston was dealing with a different crisis. On February 11 and again on the 16th, President Jefferson Davis in Richmond urged Johnston to hurry reinforcements to Lt. Gen. Leonidas Polk in Mississippi, who was facing an advancing Sherman. Johnston protested that he would have to send 24,000 men to accomplish anything in Mississippi, while "the small force left here could little impede the enemy's advance on Atlanta." Far from sending any reinforcements, Johnston's recall of Longstreet's cavalry force further derailed that general's plans.[6]

Dismissing Longstreet's activities as a feint, Grant's thoughts were also on Mississippi. He instructed Thomas to stick to the original plan and move directly against Dalton. As Thomas already indicated, however, February was not an ideal time to undertake active campaigning in the mountains of Georgia. A "heavy rain" on February 14 rendered Chickamauga Creek unfordable for most of the ensuing week, postponing the start date. Then Thomas fell ill: "I regret . . . that I do not think I shall be able to take the field, the cold and damp weather having brought on an attack of neuralgia, from which I suffer intensely." Instead, "I am getting troops prepared as rapidly as possible, and will send them out under General [John M.] Palmer if you think it best." Grant did think it best. "By all means send the expedition," he urged. "I think it should move as soon as possible, for the effect it will have in favor of Sherman and also . . . East Tennessee."[7]

Finally, on Monday the 22nd, Brig. Gen. Charles Cruft's two-brigade division of Palmer's IV Corps, reinforced by a brigade from Logan's XV Corps, departed Cleveland for Red Clay, the old Cherokee parley ground on the Georgia-Tennessee border. Cruft's 5,500 infantry were supported by a battalion drawn from the 4th Michigan and 4th Ohio cavalries—155 riders, which was everyone with a serviceable horse. Simultaneously, Palmer led the XIV Corps out of the Chattanooga at "early dawn." Brig. Gen. Richard W. Johnson's First Division led the corps, spearheaded by the 39th Indiana Mounted Infantry. Palmer reached Ringgold that afternoon, finding only "a small picket of the enemy, which fled."

5 James Longstreet, *From Manassas to Appomattox: Memoirs of the Civil War in America* (Philadelphia: 1896), 538; *OR* 32, pt. 2, 408.

6 *OR* 32, pt. 2, 752, 760-61.

7 Ibid., 414, 421.

Palmer halted there, forced to spend much of the day rebuilding a wagon bridge over the still-high East Chickamauga Creek.[8]

Cruft pushed one brigade forward to Varnell Station on the East Tennessee Railroad, three miles south of Red Clay, where it encountered another Rebel picket at the Wade house, who immediately retreated. Colonel William Grose, commanding the reconnaissance, ordered the accompanying cavalry to give chase, but no serious encounter resulted. One of Grose's regiments, the 84th Illinois, sported their new "very costly and beautiful flag—a present from the citizens of McDonough County" back home in Illinois. The 84th, recorded one Illini soldier, had just received this "splendid flag, bearing in gilt letters the names of our hard fought battles," the day before, borne by an officer returning from furlough.[9]

Guarding Cruft's left were 600 Union cavalrymen under Col. Eli Long moving down the Cleveland and Spring Place Road toward the Conasauga River. Long's force was also an amalgam of several commands: "350 men of the 98th Illinois Mounted Infantry and 250 cavalry [from] the 2nd Kentucky, 1st Ohio, 3rd Ohio, and 4th Ohio." Furloughs and broken-down horses left all those commands depleted. After an easy march the troopers camped at Waterhouse's Mill, southeast of Varnell's. Here, reported Long, "[We] have met or heard of nothing [of the enemy] as yet."[10]

The Federal activity caught Johnston in mid-move. Tired of cajoling, on February 17 President Davis simply ordered Johnston to send Lt. Gen. William J. Hardee and two of his three infantry divisions to reinforce Polk. Although this movement was not as large as the force Johnston thought would be required, it deprived Dalton of 15,000 men and reduced Johnston's available force to 27,000 of all arms. By February 20, Hardee and his headquarters staff were in the Alabama state capital of Montgomery. Two days later Benjamin F. Cheatham's Division began arriving in Selma (50 miles farther west). That same day, Maj. Gen. Patrick Cleburne's Division boarded the cars at the Dalton depot and reached West Point, Georgia, the next morning.[11]

This was not the first time Davis embarked on such a course, having drained the Army of Tennessee of sizeable forces at least twice, both at the expense of Gen.

8 Ibid., pt. 1, 423, 451-452.

9 *OR* 32, pt. 1, 432; L. A. Simmons, *The History of the 84th Reg't Ill. Vols.* (Macomb, IL: 1866), 136.

10 Nancy Pape-Findley, *The Invincibles: The Story of the Fourth Ohio Veteran Volunteer Cavalry, 1861-1865* (Tecumseh, MI: 2002), 193; *OR* 32, pt. 1, 469.

11 *OR* 52, pt. 2, 621; M. Todd Cathey, *Captain A. T. Fielder's Civil War Diary, Company B 12th Tennessee Infantry C.S.A. July 1861-June 1865* (Knoxville, TN: 2012), 310; Irving A. Buck, *Cleburne and his Command* (New York: 1908), 225.

Braxton Bragg. In December 1862, he ordered Bragg to send 10,000 men to bolster the Vicksburg garrison on the eve of the Battle of Stones River at precisely the time they were needed in Middle Tennessee. The next June, he ordered Bragg to send an infantry and a cavalry division west in an unsuccessful effort to relieve Vicksburg. Each time Johnston had vehemently objected, knowing that the lack of direct rail lines and the increasingly decrepit condition of the existing track made such transfers arduous affairs. In each case the move deprived one command of needed strength at a crucial moment while failing to make a difference at the destination.[12]

When Confederate cavalry commander Maj. Gen. Joseph Wheeler reported this new Federal movement, Johnston reacted. After seeing his wife off to Atlanta on the morning of February 23, Johnston ordered Wheeler that, if driven back by the enemy, he was to "destroy all bridges and make the road as impracticable as possible. Offer him every obstruction and difficulty in your power." That same morning Johnston informed Davis: "I have therefore suspended the movement [to Mississippi.] . . . Was I right?"[13]

Davis's frustration was evident in his reply. "The re-enforcement you were called on to send General Polk was for immediate service. Promptitude, I have to repeat, is essential," he scolded. "To hesitate is to fail. . . . To destroy Sherman will be the most immediate and important method of relieving you and best secures the future supply of your army. Speedy success in Mississippi restores the forces you detached, and adds others to enable you to follow up the advantage." That telegraphic tantrum, however, was soon followed by a more realistic acknowledgement of Johnston's situation, which led to Davis reversing course. "Information just received from General Polk indicates that the re-enforcements . . . are too late. Recall those troops which have not passed Montgomery."[14]

Though Davis's acquiescence probably further infused Joseph Johnston with a sense of vindication, it was at best cold comfort because a Federal army was still advancing on Dalton. "About 10:00 the night of the 22nd," penned Lt. L. C. Apperson of the 22nd Alabama, "we received orders to hold ourselves in readiness

12 Even when Johnston was on the receiving end of those reinforcements, as he had been for the two major transfers in 1863, he viewed Davis's policy as folly. In September 1863, Johnston was called upon to return those troops sent from Tennessee because Chattanooga was being threatened by Union Maj. Gen. William S. Rosecrans. Fearing that he could not hold what was left of Mississippi if Grant's army attacked him, he objected anew. Fortunately for Johnston, in this case, Rosecrans was defeated at Chickamauga, and the Federal Government responded by detaching 20,000 men from Grant to reinforce Chattanooga. This fundamental rift in Confederate strategy would never be resolved.

13 "My Darling," W. W. Mackall to wife, February 24, 1864, Joseph E. Johnston Papers, Swem Library, College of William and Mary, Williamsburg, VA; *OR* 32, pt. 2, 798.

14 Ibid., 52, pt. 2, 627. Davis consistently failed to grasp that such transfers could not be made as quickly as he supposed.

for immediate action. Three days rations were very hurriedly cooked, every feller was doing something [and] many were the conjectures of what was going to take place. Some thought a skedaddle was on hand, but . . . the more thoughtful saw something different from a run . . . it was 'be ready for action,' which meant prepare yourselves for a fight." As if to confirm the idea of retreat, "early on the morning of the 23rd," Apperson continued, "the Quartermaster (you never see a Quartermaster when there is danger) and the trains of wagons began to move to the rear, they were well after noon passing." Believing that "Johnston, as a prudent man, prepared for any emergency," Apperson still thought there might be a fight.[15]

Captain C. Irvine Walker of the 10th South Carolina wrote that as he "was quietly sitting down waging a war of 'Chess,' I was considerably astonished by an order coming down from Div. Hd. Qrs. to hold ourselves in readiness for action. Chess was at once abandoned for real war, and in a few minutes the hitherto quiet camp was one scene of indescribable bustle. . . . [A] great many of the men had their wives in camp, and all such were in a most piteous condition." As brigade adjutant, Walker was privy to more of the army's details, noting that "all our wagons were sent to the rear across the Oostanaula River. . . . Dalton was being rapidly cleared of all government stores. . . . [E]verybody expected to retreat . . . that night." As Walker noted, Johnston's wagons headed south toward Resaca and the Oostanaula, triggering a panic as civilians also flooded the trains headed south on Tuesday.[16]

That same morning, reinforced by Col. W. A. Dickerman's brigade from the XV Corps, Cruft continued to press south. At 2:00 p.m. Palmer ordered Cruft to shift west and join the XIV Corps near Ringgold. Departing within the hour, his column moved southwestward from Red Clay, reaching the Stone Church (very near Catoosa Platform, roughly two miles east of Ringgold) by 10:00 p.m. after a 12-mile march. Dickerman's troops, having come from Cleveland, had the hardest day's tramp with 25 miles.[17]

Colonel Long was not idle during this time. The cavalry officer pushed his troopers south along the Conasauga River toward Dalton and, at 11:30 a.m. six miles southeast of Varnell's, reported attacking a Confederate infantry regiment in "winter quarters (log huts). . . . They were completely surprised." The surprise

15 "Dear Grandpa," *The Troy Messenger*, March 18, 1864.

16 William Lee White and Charles Denny Runion, eds., *Great Things Are Expected of Us, the Letters of Colonel C. Irvine Walker, 10th South Carolina Infantry, C.S.A.* (Knoxville: 2009), 100-101.

17 *OR* 32, pt. 1, 423; Orendorff, H. H., et. al. *Reminiscences of the Civil War from Diaries from Members of the 103rd Illinois Volunteer Infantry 1904* (Chicago: 1904), 40. Catoosa platform was a temporary station on the Western & Atlantic, built by the Confederates the previous fall to unload supplies and troops when the destruction of several small bridges over East Chickamauga Creek rendered Ringgold depot unusable.

raid captured 12 Mississippians, but when the Confederates recovered from their discomfiture and formed for battle, Long prudently retired to Russell's Mill. Catching Confederate infantry in camp, within "3 ½ miles" of Dalton demonstrated that Rebel cavalry pickets were thin on the ground.[18]

Wheeler's headquarters were at Tunnel Hill. The cavalry corps was worn down by active service in East Tennessee and suffered from a severe shortage of forage for their animals. Wheeler reported only 4,600 officers and men present for duty. Worse, though they had just been recalled to Georgia, Brig. Gen. William T. Martin and four brigades were still in East Tennessee some 25 miles northeast of Knoxville, and would be some time arriving. Other regiments were as far away as Alabama and at Rome, Georgia.[19]

While Cruft joined Palmer and Long in the thrust toward Dalton, Richard Johnson's division, again led by the 39th Indiana, set out for Tunnel Hill. Brig. Gen. William P. Carlin's brigade followed Col. Thomas Harrison's Hoosiers. "About 2 miles beyond Catoosa Station I met Colonel Harrison falling back before superior numbers of rebel cavalry, under General Wheeler. Finding himself supported, Harrison immediately resumed his former line, where he had been skirmishing for some time." Deploying four infantry regiments, and with the 39th Indiana's mounted skirmishers in the van, Carlin "drove the enemy steadily for about 2 miles [to a] barricade of rails . . . from which a heavy volley was opened on my line." Shunning a frontal assault, Carlin dispatched the 88th Indiana to "seize a hill to the right and rear of the enemy," which forced Wheeler back to Tunnel Hill.[20]

A correspondent for the *Huntsville Daily Confederate* detailed the day's fight. "Our cavalry met and fought him at Stone Church, and kept him in check during the day," began the paper. "Early on [Tuesday] morning the enemy again began their advance and charged our cavalry, but it was handsomely repulsed, and such was the effect . . . that before attempting to advance further he deployed long infantry lines. We fought him successfully . . . frequently ambuscading him, but late in the evening permitting him to march into Tunnel Hill, we forming our cavalry lines on the ridge next to Dalton." Carlin described the capture of Tunnel Hill considerably differently: "Within 500 yards of the town, Colonel Harrison, with only 25 men, charged on the enemy and put him to a most disgraceful

18 *OR* 32, pt. 1, 470-472.

19 Ibid., pt. 2, 776.

20 Ibid., pt. 1, 453-454.

flight. . . . This was the most gallant and handsome exploit of cavalry I ever witnessed."[21]

Whether it was a disgraceful flight or planned withdrawal, Wheeler did not flee far. The Rebels soon rallied and engaged their pursuers with artillery. In addition to his own 39th Indiana, Colonel Harrison also commanded Col. William P. Boone's 28th Kentucky Mounted Infantry and elements of the 2nd Kentucky Cavalry. The Rebels "directed their fire principally at Colonel Boone's Kentuckians, who "advanced on Col. Harrison's right." Carlin's infantry did not escape unscathed. Sergeant James Jackson of the 19th Illinois was killed and three more—two from the 88th Indiana and one from the 10th Wisconsin—fell wounded. The strength of the Confederate fortifications, Wheeler's stiffening resistance, the Federal lack of artillery, and the distance from the main Union force were factored into Johnson's decision to fall back to Catoosa Platform.[22]

The Federals began a more serious advance on Wednesday, February 24. At 10:00 a.m., General Palmer ordered General Cruft to move three-and-a-half miles east to Doctor Lee's house, which sat near the intersection of the Tunnel Hill-Cleveland and the Ringgold-Varnell roads. This put Cruft at the north end of Chetoogeta Mountain (through which ran the railroad tunnel at Tunnel Hill) and Rocky Face Ridge, both of which begin rising sharply just south of that point. Cruft left Dickerman's borrowed brigade at Dr. Lee's while Col. Thomas Champion's brigade moved south along the west side of Rocky Face to connect with the XIV Corps. Colonel Grose's brigade marched southeast of the ridge into Crow Valley with orders "to feel the enemy sturdily."[23]

Meanwhile, all of the XIV Corps returned to Tunnel Hill. Johnson's men again led the movement, followed by Brig. Gen. Jefferson C. Davis's two-brigade division, then Brig. Gen. Absalom Baird three-brigade force. At Palmer's direction, Davis left his Second Brigade, currently under Lt. Col. Carter Van Vleck of the 78th Illinois, to hold Ringgold Gap in the corps' absence. This suited Van Vleck, who informed his wife that they caught up to the division "last night at midnight & were left here on account of our fatigue to garrison the town. [The rest of the corps] captured Tunnel Hill today and are pushing forward for Dalton. I think

21 W. C. Dodson, *Campaigns of Wheeler and His Cavalry 1862-1864 from Material Furnished by Gen. Joseph Wheeler, to which is added his Concise and Graphic Account of the Santiago Campaign of 1898* (Atlanta: 1899), 166; *OR* 32, pt. 1, 454.

22 "Important advance into Georgia," *Belmont Chronicle*, St. Clairsville, Ohio, March 3, 1864.

23 Ibid., 424.

there will be some hard fighting tomorrow, but the probabilities are that my Brigade will not participate."[24]

Richard Johnson made contact about 11:30 a.m., when Confederate artillery opened on the front of his command. "A number of shells were thrown with great accuracy into our ranks," wrote the *Cincinnati Gazette's* correspondent, and "several were killed or wounded." Thomas's chief of staff, Brig. Gen. William D. Whipple, observing the action in his commander's absence and "narrowly escaped death" from one of the bursts. Unlike yesterday's probe, the Federals now pressed the issue. Johnson deployed all three of his brigades in line opposite Wheeler's troopers, with Col. Henry Hambright's brigade on the right, and Carlin's and Brig. Gen. John H. King's commands filling in successively to the left. Davis's division deployed next, the available brigades deploying on King's left and connecting with Colonel Champion's men (Cruft's command) filing down from the north. The 2nd Minnesota and 19th Indiana batteries (each reduced to one section of two guns due to a lack of available horseflesh) returned the enemy gunfire. Despite a plague of faulty rounds, the Yankee gunners found the range and drove off Wheeler's horse artillery, whose retreat triggered a general Union advance. Facing six brigades of Federal infantry and overlapped on both flanks, Wheeler wisely ordered a retreat.[25]

To assist Wheeler, on the morning of the 23rd Joe Johnston ordered Maj. Gen. Thomas C. Hindman's corps to establish a line in Mill Creek Gap. Hindman sent two divisions. As he explained to Maj. Gen. Alexander P. Stewart, "it is expected that yours and [Maj. Gen. John C.] Breckinridge's shall hold the gap. Williams' battalion of artillery will be ordered to your support." Stewart formed three of his brigades in line north of the road and railroad, while Brig. Gen. Joseph H. Lewis, the temporary head of Breckinridge's division, deployed on Stewart's left. They spent a quiet night and morning improving their positions until, as Stewart reported, "the enemy appeared in our front."[26]

In his diary, the observant Pvt. John Jackman of Company B, the Confederate 9th Kentucky, observed how "at daylight [on February 23rd] all our baggage

24 Ibid., 455; Teresa K. Lehr and Philip L. Gerber, eds., *Emerging Leader, The Letters of Carter Van Vleck to his Wife, Patty, 1862-1864* (Bloomington, IN: 2012), 204.

25 "Important advance into Georgia," *Belmont Chronicle*, March 3, 1864. William Denison Whipple, West Point Class of 1847, arrived in December to assume the duties of the Army of the Cumberland's Chief of Staff, replacing James A. Garfield, who left in October to assume his seat in Congress. Thomas and Whipple's relationship must have been solid, for Whipple would continue to be associated with Thomas until the latter officer's death in 1870.

26 *OR* 32, pt. 1, 477-78. As senior major general and division commander, Hindman commanded a corps over the winter after returning from his Chickamauga wound. When John Bell Hood replaced him at the end of February 1864, Hindman reverted to division command. Breckinridge was assigned a new command in Virginia, and no new commander for the division had been appointed.

was loaded and the trains started for the rear." To Jackman "everything has the appearance of a retreat." He was dissuaded of that notion when "our brigade moved up to Mill Spring or Creek Gap . . . and formed lines on a ridge. . . . Seeing the troops clambering up the steep hills on either side of the Gap reminded me of pictures seen of Hannibal crossing the Alps. We are held in reserve. The day has been beautiful—springlike."

"This morning [February 24] is one of sunshine," continued Jackman in his diary. "We are quietly resting on arms—not having heard a hostile gun yet. The news from the front is, the enemy is advancing in strong force, slowly. . . . Things don't look so much like a retreat now—more like 'fight.'" At 4:00 p.m., "the skirmishers in front commenced a lively popping, our cavalry coming back to the rear, and one of our batteries opened on the gap." Sometime during this action, Jackman's brigade—the famed "Orphan Brigade" of Rebel Kentuckians—shifted to support "Steward [Stewart] who was having quite a lively skirmish."[27]

After outflanking Wheeler, Jefferson Davis's Federals gained the advance, and it fell to Brig. Gen. James D. Morgan's small brigade to lead the pursuit. Morgan had only the 10th Michigan and 60th Illinois with him. Both regiments had recently reenlisted as veteran volunteers, and the men were expecting to be sent home on furlough instead of leading a foray against the Rebel army. Near dusk, reported Morgan, "the enemy were found strongly posted, and opened a brisk fire of musketry and artillery."[28]

With almost no daylight left to launch an attack, and lacking a clear picture of the Confederate defenses, Davis halted. "I ordered the brigade commanders to put out strong pickets and to place the troops in bivouac for the night," explained the general. One of those pickets was Capt. Noah Hart of the 10th Michigan, who recorded "sharp skirmishing until sundown. [We were] shelled by the enemy in a manner not at all agreeable. After dark, went on picket. Posted sentinels within sixty rods of enemy pickets."[29]

End of Excerpt

27 William C. Davis, ed., *Diary of a Confederate Soldier: John S. Jackman of the Orphan Brigade* (Columbia, SC: 1996), 107.

28 *OR* 32, pt. 1, 459-60.

29 Ibid., 456; Noah H. Hart Diary, entry for February 24, Dominican University online collections, https://tinyurl.com/52jfun3n, accessed 7/27/2019.

About the Author

Dennis B. Conklin II earned a B.A. in political science from Blackburn College, a J.D. from Loyola University in New Orleans, and a Ph.D. in American history from the University of Southern Mississippi. He has taught at the University of Southern Mississippi, William Carey University, and Jackson Academy in Mississippi. He resides in Ridgeland, Mississippi, with his wife, Claudia, and their dogs, Attila, Gus, and Molly.